# Jaya Jagannātha!

# Jaya Jagannātha!

## The Culture and Worship of Lord Jagannātha East and West

Dhruva Mahārāja Dāsa

THE BHAKTIVEDANTA BOOK TRUST

Readers interested in the subjct matter of this book are invited by The Bhaktivedanta Book Trust to correspond with its secretary at the following address:

**The Bhaktivedanta Book Trust**
**Hare Krishna Land,**
**Juhu, Mumbai 400 049, India**
**E-mail:** bbtmumbai@pamho.net
**Web:** www.bbtindia.net

First Printing January 2007: 5,000 copies



ISBN: 978-81-89574-19-1



Published by Bhīma Dāsa for
The Bhaktivedanta Book Trust, Mumbai,
and printed at Replica Press, India.

---

COVER PHOTOS | Front background: Sunset at the main temple in Jagannātha Purī. Photo by Muralīvadana Dāsa. Front inset: Rathyātrā in New York City. Photo by Yamarāja Dāsa. Back: Lord Jagannāth on his cart surrounded by *dayitās* (servants). Photo by Bhārgava Dāsa.

This book is humbly dedicated to His Divine Grace A. C. Bhaktivedanta Swami Prabhupāda, who at great personal inconvenience traveled to the United States from India on a cargo ship at the age of sixty-nine, an age when most of us consider retiring from extensive physical endeavors. During the following twelve years, from 1965 until his departure from this mortal world on November 14, 1977, this saintly person traveled around the world fourteen times and established more than 100 temples of Kṛṣṇa worship. He wrote more than sixty authoritative books and brought the ancient culture of Jagannātha worship outside India for the first time in known history.

Western devotees of Lord Jagannātha are indebted to Jayānanda Dāsa, who worked tirelessly to establish Ratha-yātrā festivals in cities around the United States during the late 1960s and early '70s. I'd like to also dedicate this work to him, and I pray for his blessings. You will read more about him later in this book. (For more information about Jayānanda, visit www.jayananda.com)

# ACKNOWLEDGEMENTS

While I was compiling research and writing this book, so many people helped that it would be difficult to name everyone. I greatly appreciate even small favors performed by friends or duties carried out by paid experts; without their assistance it would not have been possible to put it all together. With my deepest gratitude I'd like to thank:

Advaitacandra Dāsa (from Italy)—research assistance
Anila Dāsa (USA)—computer consultant
Bhakta Charles (France)—photos
Bhaktivedanta Archives—photos
Caitanya-caraṇa Dāsa Bābāji—helped with some details in translating *Puruṣottama-kṣetra-māhātmya*
Daiviśakti Devī Dāsī—acquired a copy of *Skanda Purāṇa*
Dhaneśvara Dāsa—financial gift
Dibya Singha Deb (King of Purī)—was extremely hospitable, especially during Ratha-yātrā festivals, by allowing us to remain in and around the busy palace. He arranged Cordon Passes, which gave us facility to proceed close up to the *rathas* beyond the intense crowds, and he put me into contact with many others who offered valuable information
Gajendra Maharana (Suncrafts)—supplied arts and crafts for photographs
Kishore Ghosh—translated some of *Śrī Kṣetra,* by Sundarananda Vidya Vinode
Kaiśorī Devī Dāsī—edited my first manuscript
Krishna Candra Rajguru and his son, Ramesh Rajguru—the (late) *paḍichā* (superindendent) of the Jagannātha temple and his son both helped on numerous occasions with information about temple rituals and with matters involving the temple management
Kṛṣṇa Svarūpa Dāsa—Sanskrit editor
Kūrma Rūpa Dāsa—map drawings
Mahāmāyā Devī Dāsī—proofreader

Nāgarāja Dāsa—final editor

Odissi Research Center—permission to use drawings of Odissi dance postures

Pūrṇaprajña Dāsa—Sanskrit proofreader

Rādhāpāda Dāsa (India)—financial gift

Ramachandra Dash—a Purī resident and a friend who assisted in many ways throughout the years of our research in Purī

Ratnabāhu Dāsa (USA)—donated a copy of *Subjective Evolution*

Samapriyā Devī Dāsī—my wife and friend; anyone with a nice Vaiṣṇava wife knows how helpful and encouraging such a person can be

Sarvasatya Dāsa—donated computer products

Śeṣa Dāsa—brought a copy of *Skanda Purāṇa* back from India

Sudarsana Mahapatra (Goldie Studios)—supplied some photographs and gave valuable information during the Navakalevara ceremonies of 1996

Tāmraparṇī Dāsa (USA)—donated some computer products

Tattva Darśana Dāsa (USA)—research about *mūla* Sītā-Rāma Deities

Yamarāja Dāsa—layout and design

New York Public Library

Santa Monica Public Library

University of California at Berkeley Library

University of Hawaii Library

# CONTENTS

*"Subjects of philosophy and theology are like the peaks of large towering and inaccessible mountains standing in the midst of our planet inviting attention and investigation. Thinkers and men of deep speculation take their observations through the instruments of reason and consciousness, but they take different points when they carry on their work. These points are positions chalked out by the circumstances of their social and philosophical life, different as they are in the different parts of the world. Plato looked at the peak of the Spiritual Question from the West, and Vyāsa made the observation from the East. So Confucius did it from further East, and Schlegel, Spinoza, Kant, and Goethe from further West. These observations were made at different times and by different means, but the conclusion is all the same in as much as the object of observation was one and the same. They all hunted after the Great Spirit, the unconditioned soul of the universe. They could not but get an insight into it. Their words and expressions are different, but their import is the same. They tried to find out the absolute religion and their labors were crowned with success, for God gives all that He has to His children if they want to have it. It requires a candid, generous, pious, and holy heart to feel the beauties of their conclusions.*

*"Party spirit—that great enemy of truth—will always baffle the attempt of the inquirer who tries to gather truth from the religious works of his nation, and will make him believe that the Absolute Truth is nowhere except in his old religious book . . . But Truth is eternal and is never injured but for a while by ignorance."*

—Excerpt from a lecture by Kedaranath Datta (Śrīla Bhaktivinoda Ṭhākura), deputy magistrate in Jagannātha Purī 1871–1876

# INTRODUCTION

In the course of history, the world has known many cultures and civilizations, but few remain alive and flourishing for more than a few hundred years at a time. Consider the Vikings, Mayans, Aztecs, Incas, Greeks, Romans, the Pharaohs of Egypt, or even the land of Atlantis mentioned by Plato. Considering these cultures, one is compelled to question how the worship of Lord Jagannātha has continued to blossom despite centuries of wearing time and violent oppression from foreign invaders.

I began seriously researching this ancient religious culture sometime during the later part of 1988. One sunny winter day I stood atop the Raghunandana Library photographing the massive temple of Lord Jagannātha, when I heard a sarcastic voice declare, "You're a fool."

"Excuse me?" I asked, surprised by an Indian man who was also viewing the temple from the same rooftop.

"You worship a God who won't even let you into His temple," the man asserted in a British accent. In one sense he was right. Because of the cultural heritage in Purī, entrance into the temple is restricted only to those born in Hindu families.

"You see, chap," he continued more politely, "I've just arrived from England. I'm not even Hindu; I'm a Christian, but because my ancestors were Indian, they let me into the temple thinking I'm also a Hindu. What do you think? Is that wise? Here you are worshiping this God, and you can't even go into the temple, but because I look like a Hindu they let me in, even though I don't follow the Hindu religion."

This gentleman wasn't just idly conversing with a foreigner, the way many people in India do; I sensed a hint of interest on his part, and his thick British accent added an air of aristocracy that attracted my attention.

"The people of Orissa are steeped in ancient traditions," I replied, "and no doubt the temple management is a bit out of touch with today's world. But I've seen Lord Jagannātha in many places: Paris, London, Florence, Chicago, Los Angeles, Honolulu, Atlanta. I don't agree that it's foolish to worship Lord Jagannātha. The fools are those who are ignorant about God and His unlimited potencies."

Our conversation took place at the beginning of my research, when it wasn't really clear to me exactly why foreigners weren't allowed inside. It seemed odd that meat-eating drunkards were allowed into the temple if born in Hindu families (or with brown-skinned bodies that only looked Hindu), whereas those following more closely the Hindu religious codes were considered outcastes simply because of their birth.

Having to deal with Hindu orthodoxy in Purī and not being allowed into the temple, however, were only my first obstacles. One can hardly imagine the legends, theories, fantasies, folklore, myths, strange rituals, and speculations that have cropped up over the ages. Sifting through the labyrinth of informative resources gradually became an extremely tedious, arduous task—far more difficult than I had anticipated.

As my investigation slowly progressed over the course of several years, two paths of acquiring information surfaced. One source was scholars and historians; I found numerous publications filled with details and evidence supporting each writer's views of the culture, with many contradictions between them. Most scholars present historical information beginning from the seventh century A.D., with vague references to the spiritual writings of ancient sages. Of course, most of these thinkers consider religious texts mythology and their followers sectarian.

Next were the spiritual, religious texts. These writings, mostly compiled in a bygone age, declare that Lord Jagannātha appeared on earth millions of years ago in the age of Satya-yuga. Followers of these teachings consider materialistic historians and scholars to be groping in the dark, speculating and theorizing but never ascending to the transcendental region by such mental gymnastics.

I had to choose: scholars or spiritualists. Scholars and historians derided religionists as sentimental and sectarian, whereas spiritualists claimed that scholars and historians cheat the public with useless theories that constantly contradict one another. Who are we to believe?

I chose both—sometimes. From the scholars I learned of various kings and their exploits, many of whom were devoted to Lord Jagannātha. Naturally, the pious rulers in such kingdoms influenced the citizens to serve the Deity, and accounts of these rulers' lives enhanced my appreciation for the depth of this religious culture.

Spiritual writings were enlightening, but also mind-boggling. Many religious texts appear to contradict one another, and different religious sects view Lord Jagannātha according to their own orthodoxy. I came across numerous beliefs about who and what the unusual Jagannātha Deity really is.

The most practical way to put all this together was to synthesize relevant information, then condense it into a palatable presentation. I decided to tread the difficult middle path where scriptures and historical accounts corroborated one another, and in this way present a kind of bird's-eye view of the culture.

Lastly, I'd like to note that my desire to examine Jagannātha worship arose while writing the very last chapter of my first book, *Vṛndāvana Dhāma Kī Jaya!* That chapter discusses the exalted love of the *gopīs* for the Supreme Lord, Śrī Kṛṣṇa. The *gopīs'* love is considered to be the zenith of love of God, the very pinnacle of *rasa-tattva*. After enjoying amorous loving affairs with the young damsels in Vṛndāvana, however, Kṛṣṇa left His rural village and moved to the palatial cities of Mathurā and Dvārakā. This thrust the young *gopīs* into intense feelings of separation from the Lord. Indeed, they cried night and day for His return, thus elevating their loving emotions to an even higher plane.

Those same spiritual feelings of separation, called *vipralambha-bhāva*, were exhibited by Śrī Caitanya Mahāprabhu in Jagannātha Purī from 1510 until 1533. Reading about this uncommon and intense love of God in the *Caitanya-caritāmṛta* awakened my desire for further understanding. I wanted to go to Purī, where Caitanya Mahāprabhu spent His later years, and delve into the mysteries hidden there. I hoped to further realize why the Supreme Lord chose Jagannātha Purī, of all places in the entire universe, to exhibit His quintessential pastimes. After excavating numerous treasures from the unlimited mine of esoteric topics, I share in this book the essence of what I discovered.

# 1

# *The Lord of the Universe*

## Jagannātha Purī

Jagannātha Purī, one of the most popular pilgrimage sites in India, is located on the country's northeastern seashores about three hundred miles south of Kolkata.[1] Purī's main attraction is a hand-carved twelfth-century stone temple located on Badadanda, Grand Road. This massive shrine, which serves as a spiritual vortex for the entire town's activities, is dedicated to Lord Jagannātha, the Lord of the Universe.[2] (See plate 1)

Purī is not only a sacred *tīrtha*, or holy place, but also a pleasant seaside resort. Today this historic town's population comprises some 180,000 residents, with abundant hotels, guesthouses, and *dharma-śālās* throughout the district. Thousands of pilgrims and tourists can be seen on the beaches year round due to the agreeable, semi-tropical climate. The town is in the state of Orissa, a veritable museum of ancient stone-sculptured temples, 300 coastal miles of pristine beaches, the largest brackish lake in Asia, bird sanctuaries, and tribal folks living in remote villages of the hilly regions. (See plate 2)

To learn how the thriving worship of Lord Jagannātha began, we must look to the *Vedas*, ancient Sanskrit texts. There are no historical records prior to these writings. The *Vedas* are unique, especially when compared to our modern world of scientific theory and speculation, because they are not compilations of human knowledge. Vedic information is derived from another dimension—the spiritual world.

Within this universe one can find only material knowledge, but beyond this universe one can find transcendental knowledge. The *Vedas* give information of people and places beyond this material universe. Those who believe in experimental knowledge may doubt Vedic con-

---

[1] 19° 18' 17" latitude, 85° 51' 39" longitude

[2] *jagat* = world or universe; *nātha* = lord of, proprietor, controller, or maintainer

clusions, but they cannot even calculate how far this universe extends, nor can they reach far into the universe itself. If we can't even travel to the end of the universe, how can we possibly go beyond it? There is another nature beyond this material world, but how can we find out about that place where the planets and inhabitants are eternal? All this knowledge exists, but how can we conduct experiments to find it? That is not possible. It is not possible to obtain information of anything beyond this material nature by experimental means.

Another name for the *Vedas* is *śruti*, which refers to knowledge acquired by hearing. *Śruti* is considered to be like a mother. We take so much knowledge from our mother. For example, if we want to know who our father is, who can answer? Our mother. If the mother says, "Here is your father," we have to accept it. We cannot approach every man on earth and conduct experiments to find out which one is our father. We must take information from our mother. Similarly, if we want to know something beyond our experience, beyond our experimental knowledge, beyond the activities of our senses, then we have to accept knowledge from a transcendental source. There is no question of experimenting.

The *Vedas* are a vast collection of works including four primary books—the *Ṛg*, *Yajur*, *Sāma*, and *Atharva*—four subdivisions, including *Āyur-veda* (medicine), *Dhanur-veda* (economics, politics, and warfare), *Sthāpana-veda* (architecture and engineering), and *Gandharva-veda* (fine arts, music, dance, drama); eighteen *Purāṇas* (universal histories), *Itihāsas* (specific histories), 108 *Upaniṣads*, and supplementary works such as *Mahābhārata* and *Rāmāyaṇa*.

The most extensive Vedic information about the unique deity of Lord Jagannātha is contained in the *Puruṣottama-kṣetra-māhātmya*, a section of the *Skanda Purāṇa* (named after Lord Śiva's son). There are other sources of Purāṇic wisdom (*Matsya*, *Viṣṇu*, *Agni*, *Padma*, *Nārada*, and *Brahmā Purāṇas*), but the *Skanda* is the most detailed. The history of how, why, and when Jagannātha first appeared on earth according to this *Purāṇa* is summarized from the text as follows.[3]

[3] For a verse by verse English translation see Dr. G.V. Tagare's *The Skanda Purāṇa*, (*Volume 53*) *Vaiṣṇavakhaṇḍa*, *Puruṣottama-kṣetra-māhātmya*, or *The Land of Visnu* (a Ph.D. thesis by Dr. Gopinatha Mahapatra, head of the Sanskrit Department at Utkal University).

*Puruṣottama-kṣetra-māhātmya*

Long ago, in a forest gathering of venerable sages, everyone agreed Jaimini Ṛṣi would be the main speaker due to his vast scriptural knowledge and mature spiritual realizations.

During his discourse Jaimini explained that Puruṣottama-kṣetra is an abode of the Supreme Lord located in the middle planetary system on the planet Earth.[4] Jaimini declared that anyone simply desiring to visit that spiritual place would be relieved from past sinful reactions, what to speak of one who actually goes there. In the central part of that holy land near the sea stands a blue hill, Nīlācala, which appears like the bosom of Mother Earth when viewed from a distance.

After introducing Puruṣottama-kṣetra (Jagannātha Purī), the *ṛṣi* scientifically described how Brahmā was the first created being in this universe. Born on a lotus flower sprouted from Lord Viṣṇu's navel at the dawn of creation, Brahmā's initial duty was to arrange various facilities for the residence of all living beings. The Supreme Lord does the real creation by agitating His material energy with spirit. By His order, Brahmā then performs a secondary creation with ingredients supplied by the Supreme Lord.

While performing this *visarga* (secondary creation), Brahmā felt compassion for the fallen souls. He understood that this material world is a place of suffering due to birth, old age, disease, and death. Knowing that the conditioned souls would be afflicted by innumerable miseries, he prayed to Lord Kṛṣṇa for their deliverance from this terrible cycle of anguish.

*kṣut-tṛṭ-tridhātubhir imā muhur ardyamānāḥ*
*śitoṣṇa-vāta-varaṣair itaretarāc ca*
*kāmāgninācyuta-ruṣā ca sudurbhareṇa*
*sampaśyato mana urukrama sīdate me*

"O great actor, my Lord, all these poor creatures are constantly perplexed by hunger, thirst, severe cold, and secretion of bile, attacked

[4] Puruṣottama is another name for Lord Jagannātha; *puruṣa*=person or enjoyer, *uttama*=the best or topmost. Puruṣottama is the Supreme Person or the Supreme Enjoyer.

by coughing winter, blazing summer, rains, and many other disturbing elements, and overwhelmed by strong sex urges and indefatigable anger. I take pity on them, and am aggrieved for them."[5]

Pleased with Brahmā, Lord Viṣṇu appeared before him riding on the shoulders of His illustrious bird carrier, Garuḍa. In a pleasing voice the Lord explained how living beings remaining in the sacred tract of land north of the sea and south of the Mahānadī River may become purified and return home, back to the spiritual world. "The people who live there are pious," Lord Viṣṇu explained. "Those who are not devoted to Me, or those who have not performed pious acts, can never take birth in that land. Every step toward Śrī Kṣetra becomes more and more sacred. My Puruṣottama-kṣetra is never affected by creation or annihilation. O Brahmā, go there and witness its beauty."

Arriving in Nīlādri, Jagannātha Purī, Brahmā saw the beautiful four-armed form of Lord Nīla Mādhava (Viṣṇu) along with Lakṣmī, the goddess of fortune. While appreciating the serene atmosphere of the holy *dhāma*, Lord Brahmā also noticed a crow flying overhead. Suddenly the crow descended from flight into nearby Rohiṇī-kuṇḍa. Touching the pure waters of the *kuṇḍa*, the crow immediately transformed into a four-armed spiritual being and departed for the spiritual world!

At that time, Yamarāja, the lord of death, mystically appeared on the scene and began offering prayers to Lord Nīla Mādhava and Lakṣmī. Yamarāja submitted that his duty was to punish all sinful living beings at the time of death, according to their past misdeeds. Yamarāja was concerned about his duty after seeing a lowborn bird attain spiritual perfection simply by touching Rohiṇī-kuṇḍa.

"O Yama," Lakṣmī answered in a benevolent voice, "neither you nor any other demigod, including even Brahmā, have power or authority here. Living beings here are extremely dear to Lord Viṣṇu. Sinful seeds burn at this place, as cotton is burnt by fire. Your duty concerns

---

[5] *Śrīmad-Bhāgavatam* (3.9.8) I've interspersed verses from the *Śrīmad-Bhāgavatam* throughout this summarization, rather than quoting verses directly from *Skanda Purāṇa*, for three reasons: (1) most of my readers will be more familiar with them, (2) *Śrīmad-Bhāgavatam* is the ripened fruit of Vedic literature and was compiled by the same author, Śrīla Vyasadeva, in his spiritual maturity, (3) the translations by His Divine Grace A.C. Bhaktivedanta Swami Prabhupāda are clear and concise.

those living entities bound by the shackles of pious and impious activities. The people in this *dhāma* are freed from their sins simply by seeing the beautiful blue deity of Lord Nīla Mādhava. Therefore, O son of the sun-god, this is not the place for your duty."

Instructed in this way, Yamarāja replied, "O Mother Lakṣmī, please forgive any improper deed performed by me. How was I to know the glories of this holy place, which are unknown even to Brahmā? Please tell me about this blessed area. Reveal how many *tīrthas* are here and the result of staying in them. Please tell me if there are any other *kṣetras* like this so that I may leave those places and perform my duty without hesitation."

## Mārkaṇḍeya's Strange Experience

Lakṣmī-devī answered this inquiry by reciting before Yamarāja and Lord Brahmā the history of a sage named Mārkaṇḍeya. Due to many years of rigid practice in spiritual discipline, Mārkaṇḍeya was blessed with an incredibly long life of seven *kalpas*. A day in the life of Brahmā is called a *kalpa*. Lord Brahmā lives in the upper regions of this universe on the summit of Mount Sumeru, where the calculation of time is different from that on earth due to varying orbits of the planets. Vedic texts describe this universe as having fourteen planetary systems wherein hundreds of thousands of planets travel or rotate. Time is calculated according to each planet's location in relation to the sun. At the end of each of Brahmā's days there is a partial devastation in the cosmos.[6]

One day of Brahmā consists of a thousand cycles of four *yugas*, or universal ages: Satya, Tretā, Dvāpara, and Kali. Satya-yuga is characterized by virtue, wisdom, and religion and lasts 1,728,000 earth years. In Tretā-yuga vice is introduced. This *yuga* lasts 1,296,000 years. The Dvāpara-yuga lasts 864,000 years and virtue declines even further. Finally, in Kali-yuga (we have been in this age for the past 5,000 years) there is an abundance of strife, ignorance, irreligion, and vice, true virtue being practically nonexistent. Kali-yuga lasts 432,000 years.

---

[6] Even here on earth there are different "time zones" according to locality in relation to the sun.

These four *yugas* rotating a thousand times make up one day of Brahmā, and the same number make up his night. Brahmā lives for one hundred such "years." This "hundred years" by earth calculations total 311 trillion, 40 million earth years. By these calculations Brahmā's lifespan seems fantastic and interminable, but from the viewpoint of eternity it is as brief as a lightning flash. Brahmā and his creation are all part of the material universe, and therefore they are in constant flux.[7]

At the end of Brahmā's day terrible winds began to blow, whipping up hurricanes, cyclones, and typhoons. Torrential rains fell like sharpened darts from the sky; oceans and rivers overflowed their banks and inundated almost the entire universe. Mārkaṇḍeya Ṛṣi, protected by his promised long life, floated in the deluge, sometimes engulfed by great whirlpools, sometimes beaten by mighty waves, and at other times threatened by truculent aquatics. Sometimes he felt lamentation, bewilderment, misery, happiness, or fear, and at other times he experienced such terrible illness and pain that he felt himself dying.

While being tossed here and there in the water, the *brāhmaṇa* Mārkaṇḍeya discovered a small island with a young banyan tree bearing newly grown blossoms and fruits. On a branch of that tree he saw an infant boy lying upon a leaf. The child's effulgence was swallowing up the darkness. His dark-blue complexion was the color of a flawless sapphire, and His lotus face shone with a wealth of beauty. The exalted *brāhmaṇa* watched with amazement as the infant took hold of one of His lotus feet and with His graceful fingers, placed a toe within His mouth and began to suck.[8]

As Mārkaṇḍeya beheld that child, his weariness vanished. Indeed, so great was his pleasure that the lotus of his heart fully blossomed and the hairs on his body stood on end. Confused as to the child's identity, the sage approached Him. Just then the child inhaled, drawing Mārkaṇḍeya into His body as if inhaling a mosquito.

Making his way through the child's throat, the *ṛṣi* saw the entire fourteen planetary systems within the child's belly. He saw Lord Brahmā, Lord Indra, the Siddhas, Caraṇas, Gandharvas, masters of

[7] *Bhagavad-gītā* (8.17) purport

[8] See *Śrīmad-Bhāgavatam* (3.33.4 and 12.9.27)

the four directions, and all the other residents of various planets. He saw rivers, mountains, lakes, hills, and forests. Moving here and there within the child's belly, he could find no beginning or end. He saw the Himalayan Mountains, the Puṣpabhadra River, and his own hermitage, where he had previously had audience of the sages Nara-Nārāyaṇa. Then, as Mārkaṇḍeya beheld the entire universe, the infant exhaled, expelling the sage from His body and casting him back into the ocean of dissolution.

In the vast sea Mārkaṇḍeya again saw the banyan tree growing on the island and the infant boy lying on the leaf. The child glanced at him from the corner of His eye with a smile imbued with the nectar of love, and Mārkaṇḍeya took Him into his own heart through his eyes. Greatly shaken, the sage realized that the child was the Supreme Personality of Godhead and approached Him. Mārkaṇḍeya, completely bewildered by the mystic power of the Lord, bowed again and again as he glorified the Supreme Person. He then humbly requested, "My dear Lord, please reveal to me why this particular tract of land remains unaffected during the cosmic devastation."

"O *muni*," Śrī Bhagavān answered, "this is my transcendental abode known as Puruṣottama-kṣetra. This place is never influenced by material creation or destruction. Those who live here are blessed with eternal pleasure, and will never again suffer in a mother's womb."

Mārkaṇḍeya, his heart brimming with ecstasy, took shelter of the Lord's lotus feet and decided to remain at that holy place. As the violent waters of devastation gradually calmed, the universe again began to operate in its normal way. Mārkaṇḍeya then absorbed himself in yoga meditation.

## Blessings of Lord Śiva

Lord Śiva, an empowered cosmic administrator, along with his wife Umā, were intrigued after hearing of the austerities performed by Mārkaṇḍeya Ṛṣi. Therefore, they went to where the sage was performing *tapasya*. Because Mārkaṇḍeya's material mind had stopped functioning, the sage failed to notice that Lord Śiva and his wife had personally come to see him. Mārkaṇḍeya was so absorbed in meditation that he was unaware of either himself or the external world.

Understanding the situation, the powerful Lord Śiva employed his mystic power to enter the sky of Mārkaṇḍeya's heart, just as the wind passes through an opening. Sage Mārkaṇḍeya saw Lord Śiva suddenly appear within his heart. Lord Śiva's golden hair resembled lightning, and he had three eyes, ten arms, and a tall body that shone like the rising sun. He wore a tiger skin, carried a trident, bow and arrows, a sword, a shield, prayer beads, a *damaru* drum, a skull, and an ax.

Astonished, the sage came out of his trance and thought, "Who is this, and where has he come from?" Upon opening his eyes, the sage saw Lord Rudra, the spiritual master of the three worlds, together with Umā and his other followers. Mārkaṇḍeya offered his respectful obeisances by bowing his head and offering sublime prayers.

Pleased with Mārkaṇḍeya, Lord Śiva smilingly said, "Please ask from me some benediction, since among all givers of benedictions we three—Brahmā, Viṣṇu, and I—are the best. Seeing us never goes in vain, because simply by seeing us a mortal achieves immortality."

Mārkaṇḍeya, having been forced by Lord Viṣṇu's illusory energy to wander about for a long time in the water of dissolution, had become extremely exhausted, but Lord Śiva's nectarean words vanquished his suffering. Mārkaṇḍeya prayed, "I offer my obeisances to that Supreme Personality of Godhead, who has created this entire universe simply by His desire and then entered into it as the Supersoul. By making the modes of nature act, He seems to be the direct creator of this world, just as a dreamer seems to be acting within his dream. He is the owner and ultimate controller of the three modes of nature, yet He remains alone and pure, without any equal. He is the supreme spiritual master of all, the original form of the Absolute Truth.

"O all-pervading lord, since I have received the benediction of seeing you, what other benediction can I ask for? Simply by seeing you, a person fulfills all his desires and can achieve anything imaginable. But I do request one benediction from you, who are full of all perfection and able to shower down the fulfillment of all desires. I ask to have unfailing devotion for the Supreme Personality of Godhead and for His dedicated devotees, especially you."

Thus worshiped and glorified by Mārkaṇḍeya's eloquent statements, Lord Śiva replied, "O great sage, because you are devoted to Lord Adhokṣaja, all your desires will be fulfilled. Until the end of this creation cycle you will enjoy fame and freedom from old age and death. O *brāhmaṇa*, may you have perfect knowledge of past, present, and future, along with transcendental realization of the Supreme, enriched by renunciation. You have the brilliance of an ideal *brāhmaṇa*; may you achieve the post of spiritual master of the *Purāṇas*."

Having thus granted Mārkaṇḍeya Ṛṣi benedictions, Lord Śiva went on his way, continuing to describe to goddess Devī the sage's accomplishments and how he had viewed the Lord's illusory power while in the turbulent waters of devastation.

Mārkaṇḍeya remained in Puruṣottama-kṣetra and worshiped a Śiva-liṅga that is now known as Mārkaṇḍeśvara. The lake next to this Śiva temple is called Mārkaṇḍeya Tank.[9] (See plate 3)

To the southwest of Markandeśvara, near the Toṭa-gopīnātha temple, is a Śiva-liṅga worshiped by Yamarāja after he heard Lakṣmī-devī narrate this extraordinary pastime. That Śiva-liṅga is known as Yameśvara. It is mentioned in the *Skanda Purāṇa* that one receives the merit of worshiping thousands of Śiva-liṅgas by once worshiping Yameśvara. (Note: Non-Hindus are not allowed into either of these temples.)

## Śaṅkha-kṣetra

Lakṣmī-devī continued speaking to Yamarāja and Lord Brahmā: "Puruṣottama-kṣetra is formed like the silhouette of a *śaṅkha* (conchshell). The sea, having come into contact with that sacred land, is known as Tīrtharāja. Anyone who bathes in that sea is immediately freed from all kinds of past offenses. (See plate 4)

"Long ago, in a fit of rage and disgust, Rudra beheaded one of the heads of Lord Brahmā. Lord Brahmā's head stuck to the hand of Lord Śiva as he traveled throughout the universe. Finally, when Śiva appeared here, the head dropped from his hand. The *liṅga* known as Kapāla-mocana is situated where Lord Brahmā's head dropped to the earth. One who worships this *liṅga* is surely freed from the sin of killing a *brāhmaṇa*."[10]

---

[9] For more about Mārkaṇḍeya Ṛṣi, see *Śrīmad-Bhāgavatam* (12.8–10)

[10] Kapāla-mocana is located in a subterranean complex about thirty yards from the outer southwest corner of the Jagannātha temple compound (non-Hindus are not allowed inside).

Lakṣmī-devī continued, "To the northeast of Kapāla-mocana lies the *adyaśakti* named Bimalā. She is extremely powerful. One who worships her can get any desire fulfilled.[11]

"In the middle of Śaṅkha-kṣetra, Ardhāśani remains. She is the goddess who drinks half the water during universal destruction. Those who offer her respects and offerings are blessed with unending joy.[12]

"Surrounding the abode of Lord Jagannātha in eight directions are the *dik-pālas*, or protectors of the holy *dhāma*. In ancient times Rudra meditated upon me, so I expanded into the form of Gaurī (Pārvatī or Umā) to become his wife. She is the embodiment of exquisite beauty. Gaurī then expanded into eight forms to protect the *antarvedi* (navel area of the conch). These eight forms of Durgā are known as Aṣṭāchaṇḍi. They are: Batā Maṅgala, Bimalā, Sarvamaṅgalā, Ardhāśani, Alambā, Kālarātri, Marīcikā, and Candrarūpā.

"Seeing these expansions of Durgā, Lord Śiva also expanded himself to match each of her eight forms. The eight Śiva *dik-pālas* are: Kapāla-mocana, Yameśvara, Markaṇḍeśvara, Bilveśvara, Bateśvara, Nīlakaṇṭha, Īśāneśvara, and Kṣetrapāla.

"At the tip of the conch silhouette is the place of Lord Nṛsiṁhadeva. One who merely visits this *tīrtha* is freed from past sins. Lord Nṛsiṁhadeva ripped apart the powerful demon Hiraṇyakaśipu with His invincible nails. Who will doubt His power to kill the past sins of all who are devoted to Him? O Yamarāja, your duty to punish sinful, envious living beings has no place here."

Lakṣmī-devī then addressed Lord Brahmā, "O Pitāmaha, during Satya-yuga of Svārociṣa Manu, a king named Indradyumna will require your guidance. Please instruct him to perform one thousand *aśvamedha-yajñas* (horse sacrifices). At the completion of these *yajñas* the Supreme Personality of Godhead will appear before the eyes of the world. Viśvakarma will fashion the deity from wood. That form of Lord Jagannātha is non-different from the Supreme Lord Himself."

Hearing these glories of Puruṣottama-kṣetra and predictions of

---

[11] Bimalā Devī is established inside the Jagannātha temple complex—for more information see *Dasahera* in the *Festivals* chapter.

[12] The Goddess Ardhaśāni is now more popularly known as Mausi Maa. Her temple is located half way between the Jagannātha temple and Gundica temple on the eastern side of Grand Road (non-Hindus not are not allowed entrance).

future events from Mother Lakṣmī, both Lord Brahmā and Yamarāja were pleased. They offered respectful prayers to the goddess of fortune, then returned to their respective abodes.

The sages assembled in the forest were naturally eager to hear more about the king named Indradyumna. Understanding their interest, Jaimini Ṛṣi continued.

## In the Court of King Indradyumna

During Satya-yuga, King Indradyumna ruled the entire world from his capital city of Avantī. He was truthful, religious, and pious. This virtuous monarch ruled his subjects fairly, and his interest in spiritual wisdom exceeded his concern for military strategy. In other words, the king was a *rājarṣi*, a saintly king.

One day, King Indradyumna was seated among a group of poets, scholars, astrologers, and mendicants. He wanted someone in that learned assembly to tell him which holy place was the best of all places on earth. The emperor was eager to know where he could see the Supreme Personality of Godhead face to face.

Among the group was a traveling mendicant, gaunt from years of austerities, and wearing his hair in long matted locks. "O King," the mendicant declared, "I have been to many *tīrthas* throughout the land. During my childhood I heard of a sacred place on the northeastern shores of Bhārata-varṣa (India). In that place known as Puruṣottama-kṣetra, there are dense forests surrounding a hill known as Nīlagiri.

"In the center of that area grows a large *kalpa-vṛkṣa* tree which extends in all directions for two miles. Anyone who spends his days under that tree becomes free from the reactions to his past misdeeds. Close to the tree is Rohiṇī-kuṇḍa, whose pure waters are said to have liberated a simple crow. The bird had no special qualifications, but simply by touching the water of that sacred tank the crow attained salvation.

"O King, I lived in that blessed place for one year. Every night I saw demigods descending from heaven to worship the presiding deity, Lord Nīla Mādhava. They offered fragrant flowers and love-filled prayers. My dear Indradyumna, I assure you I have no uncommon qualifications, but by staying in Puruṣottama-kṣetra I developed an attraction of love for the Supreme Personality of Godhead.

"I do not ask for wealth or charity from you; I don't need any land. I simply pray that you, my dear king, always remember Lord Śrī Kṛṣṇa and continuously recite His holy name."

King Indradyumna was intrigued. He intensely desired to find the sacred place of which the mendicant had spoken. The king at once called his head minister and instructed that scouts should search for the place known as Puruṣottama-kṣetra. The minister's brother, Vidyāpati, a learned and intelligent *brāhmaṇa*, was eager to carry out the king's commands. Within a few days he began his journey toward the northeastern shores of Bhārata-varṣa in search of the Supreme Lord.

### Vidyāpati's Travels

Vidyāpati traveled for days. One evening, as a deep-orange sun globe sank below the western horizon, he came to the peaceful banks of the Mahānadhi River.[13] The *brāhmaṇa* stopped and rested after bathing in the refreshing waters. Continuing the next morning, Vidyāpati grew more and more eager to see the Supreme Personality of Godhead. He remembered the words of the traveling mendicant and became absorbed in meditation.

Proceeding through Bhuvaneśvara, Vidyāpati came across lush green tropical forests. Sparkling, radiant sunbeams passed through thick foliage, creating myriad colorful patterns, enchanting his mind. When he entered the sacred *tīrtha* of Śrī Kṣetra, Vidyāpati offered obeisances unto Lord Viṣṇu. The *brāhmaṇa* respectfully placed the dust of that holy land on his body and continued toward the bluish hill known as Nīlagiri. The forests gradually became thicker and the trekking more difficult. Vidyāpati was weary and exhausted, so he sat down to rest.

While sitting in the thickets of Nīlācala Hill, the lone traveler heard distant voices. Shuffling to the source of the sound, Vidyāpati found a group of Śabaras (tribal woodsmen) working in the forest. When they saw the *brāhmaṇa* who had obviously traveled a great distance, their elderly chief, Viśvavasu, welcomed him and invited him for food and refreshment.

---

[13] The Mahānadhi River runs along the northern side of the city of Cuttack.

"Dear sir," Vidyāpati replied wearily, "I have come all the way from the distant capital of Avantī for only one purpose: I must have *darśana* of Lord Nīla Mādhava. Please help me fulfill this desire. A traveling *brahmacārī* revealed the secret of Puruṣottama-kṣetra in the court of King Indradyumna. The king has sent me to find the Lord. I have taken a vow not to eat until I succeed in my mission. Please direct me to the lotus feet of the Supreme Personality of Godhead."

This news from an unknown *brāhmaṇa* initially disturbed Viśvavasu. It meant that a king and his retinue would soon come to Nīlācala. Until that time the Śabara tribe had been the only worshipers of the four-armed sapphire-blue deity of Lord Nīla Mādhava. Now, with the appearance of a wealthy king and his subjects, the simple, intimate exchange between the Lord and his servitors would be disturbed. Viśvavasu understood the situation clearly, but he did not want to lie to a *brāhmaṇa*.

"My dear friend, there is a legend amongst our tribe that someday a king will come to worship Lord Nīla Mādhava. I can understand by your arrival that this is not just the ambition of a mortal human being, but the desire of the Supreme Lord Himself. Come and I will show you the beautiful deity."

Leading Vidyāpati through the thickets, Viśvavasu took him to the banks of Rohiṇī-kuṇḍa. Vidyāpati placed the pure, clean water of the *kuṇḍa* on his head out of respect. Standing in the cool shade of a *kalpa-vṛkṣa* tree, Vidyāpati then saw Lord Nīla Mādhava in a nearby *kuñja* (grove).

Vidyāpati immediately bowed down to offer his respects and began to pray as follows: "O all-pervading Supreme Personality of Godhead, I offer my humble obeisances unto You. This entire universe is created, maintained, and annihilated by You. You are the light of the sun and the moon, and the sacred Ganges River emanates from Your lotus feet. I am afflicted by the disease of material existence, and pray to You to please save me from this constant suffering.

"You are the Supreme Personality of Godhead, who manifests His transcendental form in the uncontaminated mode of pure goodness. This transcendental eternal form can be understood only by Your mercy through unflinching devotional service. You are the reservoir of all pleasure, and Your auspicious presence is meant for everyone's benediction. Your affectionate smiling and glancing touch the core of the heart. Your beautiful bodily complexion is blackish, and Your broad chest is the resting place of the goddess of fortune. O Lord, please be merciful unto me."[14]

After offering many prayers for Lord Nīla Mādhava's satisfaction, Vidyāpati returned to the village of the Śabaras that evening and was received cordially and offered sumptuous food in the rustic forest dwelling of Viśvavasu. Puzzled by the dining opulence of mere aborigines, Vidyāpati inquired from Viśvavasu how he had obtained such rich and nice tasting food.

Viśvavasu answered, "Oh *vipra* [learned one], ordinarily I would not reveal the secret. However, because you are a guest in my home and a messenger from the king, I will tell you. Every day demigods such as Indra, Candra, and others descend from the heavenly planets to worship Lord Nīla Mādhava. They sing and dance before the Lord, then offer delicious food to please the Supreme Personality of Godhead. These things placed before you are His *prasāda*. This *nirmalya* can free us from worldly attachments and wipe out the results of past sinful activities."

Vidyāpati was awed. Tears of joy filled his eyes. He thought about the exalted nature of his host. *How rare to meet such a saint! Daily he sees the form of the Supreme Person and honors heavenly food. Perhaps there is no greater devotee in the world than this Śabara of Nīlaparvata. Why should I return to Avantī? Perhaps I should stay here to associate with this ocean of devotion.*

Although overwhelmed with admiration, Vidyāpati remained intent on his duty. He gradually informed Viśvavasu of his desire to return to King Indradyumna in Avantipura the following day with the good news. At sunrise, Vidyāpati and Viśvavasu bathed in the sea. Vidyāpati again took *darśana* of Lord Nīla Mādhava, and then headed back toward Avantī.[15]

## The Disappearance of Lord Nīla Mādhava

After Vidyāpati departed from the Śabara encampment, Viśvavasu began preparing the articles of worship for Lord Nīla Mādhava. As the elderly tribal chief was gathering ingredients, fierce winds began to howl, blowing sandy dust everywhere. Trees were suddenly ripped from their roots by gale winds, and frightened forest animals scattered for shelter. A violent tropical storm suddenly burst on the scene, blinding everyone with dust and then rain.

Hours later, when the winds eventually calmed and the sands settled, the deity of Lord Nīla Mādhava had disappeared! Viśvavasu and the others were overwhelmed with intense feelings of separation and were almost unconscious. Out of love for the Lord, they continued wandering here and there, searching everywhere for Lord Nīla Mādhava. Even the demigods were perplexed.

Unable to find Lord Nīla Mādhava anywhere, they began to pray, "O Mādhava, what terrible offense have we committed? How can we continue to live without Your benedictions? O Supreme Personality of Godhead, please be merciful to us."

While searching madly through the forests and offering numerous prayers and supplications, everyone suddenly heard a pleasing ethereal voice vibrating from the sky. "From this day forward, Lord Nīlamādhava will not be seen in this world. The Lord will appear in another form when King Indradyumna returns. Do not fear, and remain patient."

### "We Shall All Go to Puruṣottama-kṣetra"

Meanwhile, going west, Vidyāpati felt sublime pleasure after seeing Lord Nīla Mādhava. Exploring different areas around Śaṅkha-kṣetra, he saw a variety of terrain, trees, and blossoming flowers. Some places were so thick with greenery that the sun could barely creep

---

[14] See *Śrīmad-Bhāgavatam* (3.15.39,47)

[15] There are several popular variations of this story, but most originated through local oral traditions and thus are not included here. The most famous relates that Viśvavasu would not show the deity's location to Vidyāpati because he was secretly performing the worship. Vidyāpati stays for some time in Nīlācala and ultimately marries Viśvavasu's daughter, Lalitā. Gradually, Viśvavasu agrees to show his son-in-law the deity under one condition; he must go to the temple blindfolded. Vidyāpati agrees, but drops mustard seeds on the ground along the way. Thus, in the future he can retrace his path from the sprouted mustard plants and show King Indradyumna the whereabouts of Lord Nīla Mādhava. For further information, see the heading *Sarala Dasa* in part three, *Historical Influences Prior to the 15th Century*.

through the undergrowth. Streams and lakes were abundant with swans and lotus flowers. Hardly a place existed without the sweet fragrance of newly grown creepers.

When Vidyāpati finally arrived back at Avantī, he went to inform King Indradyumna at once of what he had seen. Seeing Vidyāpati enter the palace with a legion of common citizens, King Indradyumna arose from his royal throne and hurried to greet him.

"O Jagadīśa," he sighed, "please bless me." When the king saw the garland of flowers and the food Vidyāpati carried, he exclaimed, "This garland, having touched the body of Mādhava, removes the sins of even the most wicked. Lord Brahmā and other demigods always aspire to receive articles offered to the Supreme Personality of Godhead. I bow down to this *mālā*." Saying this, King Indradyumna fell prostrate before Vidyāpati, his hairs standing on end and horripilations all over his body caused by his spiritual emotions.

Gradually Vidyāpati narrated the story of his entire journey. He told everyone about Viśvavasu, Rohiṇī-kuṇḍa, the *kalpa-vāta,* and Lord Nīla Mādhava. "On the banks of Rohiṇī-kuṇḍa," he explained, "there is a crystal altar. Upon that sparkling clean area stands the sapphire-blue deity of Lord Nīla Mādhava, holding a club, a disk, a conch, and a lotus flower.

"The luster of His forehead is brighter than the moon, and the beauty of His eyes far excels that of a blue lotus. His shining face defeats the sun and can dispel the darkness of ignorance. The Lord's nose can be compared to a sesame flower, and His lips are curved into a perfect smile. A bejeweled necklace adorns His neck, and the celebrated Kaustubha-*maṇi* can be seen upon His chest. In one of His hands He carries a conchshell, which appears about to pour down pearls. The Lord's thighs resemble pillars, and He wears precious ankle bells just above His lotus feet.

"To His left stands the goddess of fortune, Lakṣmī-devī, beautifully adorned with costly ornaments. Only people who have performed numerous pious activities can see that most exquisite form of the Supreme Personality of Godhead."

King Indradyumna glanced affectionately at Vidyāpati. "I am pleased to come in contact with the Lord's *prasāda,*" he said. "I am fortunate to have been blessed by such a learned personality as your good self. All the sins of my past births now stand diminished, and I desire to see Lord Nīla Mādhava. I shall go with all my people to Puruṣottama-kṣetra, construct buildings, and live there permanently!"

### Nārada Muni Arrives

While King Indradyumna was speaking these words of inspiration before his subjects in Avantipura, Nārada Muni arrived at the palace. Nārada is an exalted saintly person, endowed with a spiritual body by the Lord's grace. He can travel in the outer space of both the material and spiritual worlds without restriction. As an eternal "spaceman," he can approach any planet in unlimited space within no time.[16]

Understanding Nārada Muni's exalted position, King Indradyumna washed the sage's feet with cool water, offered refreshments, and supplied a comfortable seat. The king then requested Nārada to enlighten everyone about the glories of the Supreme Personality of Godhead. Hundreds of citizens and palace attendants crowded around to listen.

"O King Indradyumna," Nārada began, "devotees of the Lord are pleased with your behavior. There is no higher form of worshiping the Supreme Lord than loving devotional service, *bhakti-yoga*. There are multifarious paths of devotional service according to the different qualities of the executor.

"Devotional service performed by a person who is envious, proud, violent, and angry is considered to be in the mode of darkness. One who approaches the Supreme Lord to render devotional service, but is proud of his personality, envious or vengeful of others, is in the mode of anger. He thinks that he is the best devotee. Devotional service executed in this way is not pure; it is mixed and is of the lowest grade. One may offer respects to such a devotee because he has accepted the Supreme Lord as the ultimate goal of life, but one should not keep company with a Vaiṣṇava in the mode of ignorance.

"Worship of deities in the temple by a separatist, with a motive

---

[16] See *Śrīmad-Bhāgavatam* (1.13.60) According to Vedic texts it is possible to travel through outer space by a *yoga-siddhi* called *laghimā-siddhi*, a subtle mystical perfection.

for material enjoyment, fame, and opulence, is devotion in the mode of passion. Mixed devotees—those in the mode of passion and ignorance—think that the interest of the Supreme Lord is in being the devotees' order-supplier. If a so-called devotee desires material enjoyment without considering the Lord's interest, or if he wants to become famous or wealthy by using the Lord's mercy or grace, he is in the mode of passion.

"When a person worships the Supreme Personality of Godhead and offers the results of his endeavors to the Lord in order to free himself from fruitive desires, his devotion is in the mode of goodness. Followers of the *varṇāśrama* system generally perform their duties with some self-interest. If there is any fault while performing their duties, they atone for it by offering the fruits of the activity to the Lord. Such activities are certainly better than activities performed in passion or ignorance, but they cannot be counted as pure devotion.[17]

"Pure devotional service is exhibited when one's mind is attracted spontaneously to hearing the transcendental name and qualities of the Supreme Lord. As the water of the Ganges flows naturally down toward the ocean, such devotional ecstasy, uninterrupted by any material condition, flows toward the Supreme Personality of Godhead. A pure devotee does not render loving service to the Lord for any cause or benefit, material or spiritual. This is the first symptom of unalloyed devotional service. The devotee has no interest but to fulfill the transcendental desire of the Supreme Lord. Such spontaneous service unto the Supreme Lord is never contaminated by the material modes of nature."[18]

Nārada Muni continued: "O King, taking shelter of insatiable lust and being absorbed in the conceit of pride and false prestige, those who do not care for the Supreme Lord are always sworn to unclean work and are attracted by temporary enjoyment. They believe that gratification of the senses is the prime necessity of human civilization. Thus, until the end of life their anxiety is immeasurable. Bound by

---

[17] The *varṇāśrama* system refers to a Vedic formula for social divisions in human society—See section entitled *Brahmanism* in *Historical Influences Prior to the 15th Century* for a brief explanation.

[18] See *Śrīmad-Bhāgavatam* (3.29.7–12)

a network of hundreds of thousands of desires and absorbed in lust and anger, they secure money by illegal means for sense gratification. Perplexed by various anxieties and bound by a network of illusions, they become too strongly attached to sense enjoyment and fall down into a hellish life.

"Self-complacent and always impudent, deluded by wealth and false prestige, they sometimes proudly perform sacrifices in name only, without following any rules or regulations. Bewildered by false ego, strength, pride, lust, and anger, they become envious of the Supreme Personality of Godhead, who is situated in their own bodies and in the bodies of others, and blaspheme against real religion. Such persons can never approach God. Gradually they sink down to the most abominable type of existence. There are three gates leading to this hell—lust, anger, and greed. Every sane man should give these up, for they lead to the degradation of the soul."[19]

Hearing these succinct descriptions of pure devotional service pleased the hearts of all who had gathered. "O *muni*," King Indradyumna humbly declared, "you are like the sun and can travel everywhere in the three worlds. Like the air, you can penetrate the internal region of everyone and know their innermost thoughts. Everything mysterious is known to you because you worship the original Supreme Personality of Godhead. Please be merciful unto us, and accompany us to the holy *tīrtha* known as Puruṣottama-kṣetra."

"Yes, I shall show you the power of that *kṣetra*," Nārada agreed, "and you will see for yourself how the Supreme Personality of Godhead reveals Himself to His devotees."

## Exodus

One can only imagine events that then transpired in Avantipura. The king issued orders to the entire kingdom. "Pack your belongings and accompany me to Nīlācala!" The citizens of Avantī loved King Indradyumna. They understood that he was a pure devotee of the Lord, so they agreed to leave their homes without lamenting. On an auspicious day chosen by the court astrologer, they all departed from

[19] See *Bhagavad-gītā* (16.10–21)

Avantī in a royal procession, east toward Puruṣottama-kṣetra.

The procession was indeed a fascinating sight. Thousands of women were carried in costly palanquins, protected by legions of armed soldiers dressed in colorful battle array. Townspeople brought their household belongings stacked high on bullock carts and wagons, while numerous cows, goats, horses, and buffaloes were herded by cowherds and shepherds. King Indradyumna was dressed in white silk, and a silk turban faceted with valuable gems adorned his head. He wore gem-studded earrings, golden necklaces, bracelets, rings, and extremely opulent shoes. The king rode on a well-protected chariot along with Nārada Muni. The clamor of elephants, horses, and armies combined with that of chariot wheels seemed to the people to be like the fierce roar of the ocean at the end of a *yuga*.

Days later, they arrived at the banks of the Mahānadhī River and set up camp. Everyone bathed in the purifying waters, performed ritualistic duties, and then assembled in an area set aside for meeting. Poets recited sublime compositions describing the king's character. Beautiful young girls danced before the king while expert musicians played various instruments. The king gave away wealth in charity, pleasing all who had gathered. Then King Indradyumna asked Nārada Muni to speak about the Supreme Lord's glories.

As Nārada prepared to speak, the King of Utkal (present-day Orissa) arrived. He and his small retinue were ushered forward by a servant and greeted by all. King Indradyumna welcomed the king cordially and asked about the welfare of his citizens.

"O King Indradyumna," the King of Utkal proclaimed, "I am fortunate to welcome you to our kingdom. How can darkness remain in the presence of the sun? The entire human society is satisfied by your virtues and good qualities. O King, it is our good fortune that you have come to this sacred land. As monarch of the entire world, you represent the Personality of Godhead. Our country is now in times of difficulty. During a recent storm our land was dreadfully disturbed, and now pestilence and famine are threatening the populace. The area of Nīlācala was covered by sand, and the deity of Lord Nīla Mādhava buried and lost!" Hearing this news, King Indradyumna felt faint, but he concealed his emotions.

A short time later, after the King of Utkal had been pacified and shown to his quarters, Indradyumna inquired from Nārada, "O *muni*, how has this happened? It seems all our endeavors are useless!"

Nārada eased the king's disturbed mind. "You are a faithful Vaiṣṇava. The Lord will certainly fulfill your desires. Only by devotional service can one please the Lord and know Him as He is. Although the Lord remains hidden within everyone's heart and is therefore known as Antaryāmī, He reveals Himself to those who worship Him with love and devotion. My dear King, it is getting late. Let us rest now, and then continue in the morning. Surely your heart's desire will be satisfied upon reaching Puruṣottama-kṣetra."

### Bhuvaneśvara

Traveling further the following morning, everyone heard distant sounds of ringing bells and the blowing of a conchshell. Thinking they had finally reached Puruṣottama-kṣetra and were hearing the sounds of Nila Mādhava's worship, King Indradyumna inquired, "Nārada, is this the divine abode of the Supreme Personality of Godhead?"

"No," Nārada answered. "Puruṣottama-kṣetra is still several *yojanas* from here.[20] We are now at the abode of Gaurī's husband, Lord Śiva. He sought refuge here during battle."

"Who does Lord Śiva fear?" the king inquired, astonished. "I thought Lord Śiva was an empowered personality."

"Long ago, Lord Śiva married a girl named Satī," Nārada answered, "the beautiful daughter of Prajāpati Dakṣa. Because Lord Śiva often remained in seclusion performing austerities, and didn't care for materialistic life, his in-laws slighted him by inferring that he was a pauper. To counteract this and to please Satī, who felt insulted by her parents, Lord Śiva built the famed city of Kāśī (known today as Benares or Varanasi) on the banks of the Ganges River. The city was filled with many palatial buildings and inhabited by those desiring liberation from material existence. Lord Śiva and Satī remained there for many years.

"Sometime later, during Dvāpara-yuga, there lived a king named Pauṇḍraka, who foolishly believed he was an incarnation of the Supreme Lord. This absurd king challenged Lord Kṛṣṇa to fight, but was

[20] One *yojana* is equal to eight miles.

ultimately killed. During that battle Lord Kṛṣṇa also killed the King of Kāśī, who had sided with Pauṇḍraka. Lord Kṛṣṇa threw the head of the King of Kāśī into the city of Kāśī specifically so that his relatives and family members could see it. The Lord did this just as a hurricane carries a lotus petal here and there. Lord Kṛṣṇa killed Pauṇḍraka and his friend Kāśīrāja on the battlefield, then returned to His capital city, Dvārakā.

"When the King of Kāśī's head rolled through the city gates, people gathered and were astonished to see it. At first they couldn't understand what it was, but when they saw the earrings they understood it was someone's head. They began to conjecture as to whose head it might be. Some thought it was Kṛṣṇa's head, because Kṛṣṇa was Kāśīrāja's enemy. They thought their king might have thrown Kṛṣṇa's head into the city so people would take pleasure in the death of an enemy. Finally, however, they realized that it wasn't Kṛṣṇa's head, but the head of their very own king. When they were certain, the king's wives approached and began to lament the death of their husband. 'Our dear lord,' they cried, 'upon your death, we have become just like dead bodies.'

"The King of Kasi had a son whose name was Sudakṣiṇa. After observing his father's funeral ceremonies, he vowed that since Kṛṣṇa was his father's enemy and had killed him, he would kill Kṛṣṇa. In this way he would fulfill his debt to his father. Therefore, accompanied by learned priests qualified to perform sacrifice, he began to worship Mahādeva Śiva because the worshipable deity of Kāśī is Viśvanātha (Lord Śiva).

"Lord Śiva was pleased with Sudakṣiṇa's worship and agreed to offer his devotee a benediction. Because Sudakṣiṇa wanted to kill Kṛṣṇa, he prayed for specific powers to do so. Lord Śiva advised that Sudakṣiṇa, assisted by the *brāhmaṇas*, execute a certain ritualistic ceremony for killing one's enemy. This ceremony is mentioned in the Tantras. Lord Śiva informed Sudakṣiṇa that if this black ritualistic ceremony were performed properly, then the evil spirit named Dakṣiṇāgni would appear to carry out any order given to him. He would not, however, kill a qualified *brāhmaṇa*. When Dakṣiṇāgni was dispatched, Lord Śiva's own ghostly companions would accompany him, and Sudakṣiṇa's enemy would be killed.

"With Lord Śiva's encouragement, Sudakṣiṇa was sure he could kill Kṛṣṇa. Assisted by the priests, he began to execute a black art of chanting mantras. Out of the fire arose a huge demoniac form, whose hair, beard, and mustache were the color of hot copper. The demon was massive and fierce. Hot cinders emanated from his eye sockets, and he appeared still more fierce as he began to move his eyebrows. He had long, sharp teeth and, sticking out his long tongue, licked both sides of his lips. He was naked and carried a trident that blazed like fire. As he stood weighing the trident in his hand, Sudakṣiṇa ordered him to go to Dvārakā with hundreds of Lord Śiva's ghostly companions and kill Kṛṣṇa. It seemed he would burn all outer space to ashes. The surface of the earth trembled at his steps. When he entered Dvārakā, the residents panicked, just like animals in a forest fire.

"At that time, Kṛṣṇa was playing chess in the royal assembly council hall. All the frightened citizens approached and addressed Him, 'Dear Lord of the three worlds, a great fiery demon is ready to burn the whole city of Dvārakā. Please save us!'

"When Lord Kṛṣṇa saw His citizens perturbed by the fiery demon's presence, He smiled and assured them, 'Don't worry. I shall give you protection.'

"The Supreme Personality of Godhead, Kṛṣṇa, is omniscient and all-pervading, so He understood the fiery demon was Lord Śiva's creation. To vanquish him, He took His Sudarśana *cakra* and ordered him to take the necessary steps. Sudarśana *cakra* then appeared with the effulgence of millions of suns. By his own effulgence, Sudarśana *cakra* illuminated the entire universe. Then the Sudarśana *cakra* began to freeze the fiery demon. In this way the fiery demon was checked.

"Having failed to set fire to Dvārakā, the fearful demon Dakṣiṇāgni went back to Varanasi. Because he returned without fulfilling his mission, all the priests along with their employer, Sudakṣiṇa, were burnt to ashes by the demon's glaring effulgence. According to the Tantras, if a mantra fails to kill the enemy, then, because it must kill someone, it will kill the original chanter. Sudakṣiṇa was the originator, and the priests had helped him; therefore, they were all burned to ashes. This is the way of the demons; the demons create something to kill God, but by the same weapon the demons themselves are killed.

"The Sudarśana *cakra* followed just behind the fiery demon and also entered Varanasi. Varanasi was at that time an especially opulent city. There were many big palaces, assembly houses, marketplaces, and gates. Lecturing platforms were found at every crossroad. There was a treasury house, and there were elephants, horses, chariots, granaries, and places for distribution of food. Although this city was so opulent, because the King of Kāśī and his son were against Lord Kṛṣṇa the Viṣṇu *cakra* devastated the entire city by burning down all these important places. Then, having finished his duty, Sudarśana *cakra* returned to Lord Śrī Kṛṣṇa at Dvārakā."[21]

Nārada concluded: "After this gastly incident, Lord Śiva humbly approached Lord Kṛṣṇa and offered reverent prayers for forgiveness. Lord Kṛṣṇa accepted Śiva's prayers and said, 'O Śambhu, I am pleased with your repentance and devotion. You showed extraordinary prowess during the battle. Now, if you desire to live somewhere with your consort, listen to My advice. Situated on the seashore is a sacred *tīrtha* named after Me, Puruṣottama-kṣetra. Within that area lies Nīlācala Hill. To the north of that place is the famous Ekamravana (Bhuvaneśvara). O Tripurāri, go to that beautiful place and remain there fearlessly with Pārvatī.' "

## Bindu-sarovara

Hearing this narration about Bhuvaneśvara increased everyone's desire to go there. It was noon when the procession arrived at the banks of a beautiful lake called Bindu-sarovara, where in a previous age Kardama Muni had performed austerities. It is also said that Lord Śiva collected water from all holy places in the universe to create Bindu-sarovara.

Hosts of eminent sages lived on the banks of Bindu-sarovara. Its holy water, flooded by the waters of the Sarasvatī River, was not only auspicious, but as sweet as nectar. The lake was called Bindu-sarovara because Lord Viṣṇu's teardrops fell into the lake when Kardama Muni sought His protection. By bathing in those sacred waters, one becomes healthy both in body and spirit.[22]

---

[21] See *Kṛṣṇa* (Chapter 31) and *Caitanya-caritāmṛta* (*Madhya-līlā* 5.140)

After performing ablutions in the sacred lake, King Indradyumna and others worshiped Lord Śiva. The king offered prayers while playing a stringed musical instrument called a *viṇā*.

Pleased with King Indradyumna, Lord Śiva appeared before him and said, "O great Vaiṣṇava, King Indradyumna, all good fortune unto you. Please continue with your conquest." Lord Śiva then disappeared from the sight of everyone except Nārada Muni.

Unseen and unheard by others, Lord Śiva spoke to Nārada Muni: "When you arrive at Puruṣottama-kṣetra, you will see me along with my consort, Durgā. The sapphire-blue deity, Lord Nīla Mādhava, has disappeared from the world's sight. Therefore, install a deity of Lord Nṛsiṁhadeva and offer sacrifices to Him. O *brāhmaṇa*, the king should perform one thousand horse sacrifices (*aśvamedha-yajñas*). After these rituals, Viśvakarma will arrive to help you. Your father Lord Brahmā will then personally come to install a deity carved from wood."[23]

After receiving these instructions from Lord Śiva, Nārada Muni offered his respectful obeisances. The entire caravan then proceeded south out of Bhuvaneśvara and headed toward Puruṣottama-kṣetra. Along the way, the king worshiped two more Śiva-liṅgas, named Kapoteśvara and Bilveśvara.

### Kapoteśvara and Bilveśvara

When the assembled sages heard this account from Jaimini Ṛṣi, one of them inquired about the two *liṅgas*. "Please tell us the history of those *liṅgas* and how they were established."

Jaimini explained that long before Mahārāja Indradyumna visited this area, the land just north of Śrī Kṣetra was overgrown with sharp-bladed *kuśa* grass. The place had neither trees or water. Indeed, it seemed to be inhabited by *piśacas* (ghosts). Lord Śiva stayed there,

---

[22] See *Śrīmad-Bhāgavatam* (3.21.38, 39) and *Caitanya-caritāmṛta* (*Madhya-līlā* 5.141)

[23] The Śiva *liṅga* on the banks of Bindu-sarovara is now known as Liṅgarāja. Non-Hindus are not allowed inside, but the temple of Ananta Vāsudeva is nearby, and non-Hindus may enter and observe many rituals commonly performed in Jagannātha Purī, especially the cooking in clay pots. This Ananta Vāsudeva temple was constructed by Candrikadevi, the daughter of Anangabhima III, out of love for her husband Paramardideva, who died in battle against Muslim invaders during the 13th century.

performing vigorous austerities, fasting, and meditating. Gradually, his body dwindled due to lack of food, and he became as thin as a pigeon or a dove.

Lord Kṛṣṇa was pleased with Śiva's penance, and He awarded him with a mystic *siddhi* called *aiśvarya*. Thus Lord Śiva could summon any opulence at will. Soon the area around him abounded with beautiful lakes, trees, birds, animals, and blossoming flowers. Because Lord Śiva had dwindled in size due to fasting, to the size of a *kapota* bird, the Śiva-liṅga at this place is known as Kapoteśvara. Those who worship and pray to Kapoteśvara are freed from past sinful deeds.[24]

Jaimini then explained about Bilveśvara and the famous Pāṇḍava brothers of the *Mahābhārata*. During their exile from Hastināpura, the five Pāṇḍavas traveled to Puruṣottama-kṣetra where Lord Kṛṣṇa came to visit them from Dvārakā. At that time there was a tunnel leading through the earth planet and down into the lower Pātāla planetary system. Numerous demons used to come up through that passage to cause havoc on earth. Lord Kṛṣṇa and the Pāṇḍavas subdued these demoniac forces, then blocked their route. After the battle, Lord Kṛṣṇa requested Lord Śiva to guard the blocked hole and since then Lord Śiva has been famous as Bilveśvara.[25]

## Arrival in Śrī-kṣetra

As the lead horsemen finally approached the holy land of Puruṣottama-kṣetra, King Indradyumna felt a strange quivering in his left eye and left arm. Considering this might be some kind of foreshadowing, he asked Nārada its meaning.

"Don't worry," Nārada explained. "Although there may be many

---

[24] To visit Kapoteśvara, one must go about nine kilometers north of Purī to the small town of Candanpura. From the Purī-Bhuvaneśvara Main Road, this temple is only half a kilometer to the east. *Caitanya-caritāmṛta* (*Madhya-līlā* 5.142–3) explains that this is the place where Lord Nityānanda broke the *sannyāsa* staff of Śrī Caitanya Mahāprabhu and threw the pieces into the river. For further information about this pastime, see section entitled *Śrī Caitanya Mahāprabhu Travels to Jagannātha Purī* in *Lord Caitanya's Purī Pastimes*.

[25] See *Mahābhārata, Vana-parva*—Bilveśvara is located about eighteen kilometers east of Purī. A street sign marks the turn off from Marine Drive between Purī and Konark. *Bila* means hole, and *īśvara* means controller.

impediments on the path of devotional service, remain steady in your determination. The day Vidyāpati left this place, it was inundated by a terrible storm. Lord Nīla Mādhava has disappeared from the vision of ordinary mortal beings. He will no longer be seen in this world."

Having traveled all the way from Avantī with his loyal subjects, this news stunned King Indradyumna; a breath gasped from his lungs, and he fainted. Immediately his ministers surrounded him and sprinkled cold water mixed with camphor on his face. To revive him, they massaged his body with cooling sandalwood pulp, *aguru*, and camphor, and they fanned him with palm leaves and a *cāmara*.

Slowly the king regained consciousness. Seated on his chariot, he felt humbled. "What sinful deeds have I performed in past lives to deserve this fate?" he asked. "I have never neglected my royal duties. I have always been careful not to offend the *brāhmaṇas* or anyone else. I have never insulted guests or been malicious toward anyone. What special merit could Vidyāpati have performed to be allowed to see Lord Nīla Mādhava? O Nārada, you knew all along that the Lord had disappeared. Why did you allow me to bring all my subjects to this desolate place?

"If I cannot see Lord Hari, this kingdom means nothing to me. I don't care to live a minute longer without the Lord's mercy. O *muni*, please arrange for my son's coronation. By his rule the people will remain happy. I am determined to remain here alone, fasting until death and meditating on the Supreme Personality of Godhead."

Nārada pacified the king, "Those who desire *śreyas*, long-lasting benefits, must develop patience. Why should you end your life? After countless births in this material world, a conditioned soul finally attains the human form of life. Human life is meant for understanding our relationship with the Supreme Personality of Godhead. We must remain equipoised if we are to be successful in self-realization.

"O King, Lord Brahmā instructed me to accompany you on this adventure. He explained that Lord Nīla Mādhava disappeared due to some anxiety in the mind of Lord Yamarāja. Lord Brahmā further explained that the Supreme Lord will soon appear again in a unique form especially to fulfill your earnest desire. Lord Brahmā himself is anxious to install the deity in a temple built by you and your subjects. Only with enthusiasm, confidence, and patience can you fulfill this task. Let us proceed. At this time we must worship Lord Nṛsiṁhadeva and propitiate Him with sacrifices."

### The Deity of Lord Nṛsiṁhadeva

Consoled and encouraged by these instructions, the king and his people gradually traveled on to Nīlakaṇṭha. There they worshiped Lord Śiva and Goddess Durgā. Leaving the chariots nearby, they then continued on foot through the thick forest surrounding Nīlagiri Hill, but their progress was slow due to thick underbrush and foliage. Guided by Nārada, they came to a clearing where they saw a ferocious deity of Lord Nṛsiṁhadeva. Lord Nṛsiṁhadeva's face was broad and He had four arms. His teeth were sharp, and His hands, with their long knife-like nails, were poised to kill demons. He held a conchshell and a *cakra* in two of His hands.

"O Nārada, I am grateful to you," King Indradyumna said, after bowing down before the deity. "You are truly a *mahā-bhāgavat!* This Nṛsiṁha deity is so ferocious that no one is worshiping Him. He can only be worshiped by someone spiritually elevated, like you. I offer you my heartfelt thanks for helping me come to this blessed place. Please show us where Lord Nīla Mādhava was previously situated."

Nārada led the group to the *kalpa-vṛkṣa* tree under which Lord Nīla Mādhava had stood. While they were offering prayers and appreciating the tranquil surroundings, everyone heard the beautiful divine voice of Goddess Sarasvatī from the sky: "O King Indradyumna, do not worry. Proceed as directed by Nārada, who has been instructed by Lord Brahmā."

Everyone was struck with wonder upon hearing this voice. The king turned and declared, "That you have been advised by Lord Brahmā has been confirmed by a heavenly voice! O sage, your words are as good as those of the Supreme Personality of Godhead. Please instruct us how to proceed and what to do."

"You should now return to Nīlakaṇṭha where we left the chariots," Nārada replied. "At that place build a temple facing west for Lord Nṛsiṁhadeva. After the temple is complete, you must perform one thousand *aśvamedha-yajñas* to please the Lord. I will remain here for a few days to worship this deity. I will also arrange for the son of the celestial architect Viśvakarma to come help you."[26]

The King Indradyumna and his subjects returned to Nīlakaṇṭha and found Viśvakarma's son waiting for them in a human form. Under his expert guidance, they gathered the materials and labored to build a temple for Lord Nṛsiṁhadeva's pleasure. The king offered proper hospitality and encouragement to all those who worked on the temple. Within four days, a small temple was erected.

As the king was finishing his morning ablutions on the fifth day, he suddenly heard the roaring of elephants and the sound of trumpets. The *brāhmaṇas*, *vipras*, and Vaiṣṇavas were perplexed—no one could tell where the sounds were coming from. Then breezes from the south increased, carrying the sound of bumblebees and the scent of heavenly flowers. Celestial Ganges appeared, flowing toward Nīlakaṇṭha.

Nārada Muni, who had gone to the heavens, now returned riding in a celestial airplane bedecked with fragrant flowers, carrying the deity of Lord Nṛsiṁhadeva. He was accompanied by residents of the heavenly planets. According to his instructions, the deity was placed on the altar while he, King Indradyumna, and others prayed to the Lord with selected verses from the scriptures.

"All glories to Nṛsiṁhadeva, the Lord of Prahlāda Mahāraja. Like the honeybee, He is always beholding the lotuslike face of the goddess of fortune. Lord Nṛsiṁhadeva is always assisted by Sarasvatī, the goddess of learning, and always embracing to His chest the goddess of fortune. The Lord is always complete in knowledge within Himself. Let us offer obeisances unto Nṛsiṁhadeva.

"Let us offer obeisances unto Lord Nṛsiṁhadeva. He is always enlightening Prahlāda Mahārāja within his heart, and He kills the nescience that attacks devotees. His mercy is distributed like moonshine, and His face is like that of a lion. Let us offer obeisances to Him again and again.

"Although very ferocious, the lioness is kind to her cubs. Similarly, although very ferocious to nondevotees like Hiraṇyakaśipu, Lord Nṛsiṁhadeva is very, very soft and kind to devotees like Prahlāda."[27]

---

[26] Nīlakaṇṭha is on the banks of Indradyumna Tank, about half a kilometer from the Nṛshiṁa temple in back of Guṇḍicā Mandir.

[27] *Caitanya-caritāmṛta* (*Madhya-līlā* 8.5, 6)—This Nṛsiṁha Temple is just in back of the Guṇḍicā Mandir at the north end of Grand Road.

## One Thousand Horse Sacrifices

After offering prayers, preparations began for the performance of one thousand *aśvamedha-yajñas*. A Vedic sacrifice is not an ordinary performance. In previous ages, the demigods participated in the sacrifices performed on earth. Animals were often sacrificed to test the efficiency of the mantras, but they came out of the fire reincarnated with new life. In this age of Kali, there are no *brāhmaṇas* powerful enough to invite the demigods or to regenerate animals in the sacrificial fire. In former ages, the *brāhmaṇas* well conversant in chanting Vedic mantras could prove the potency of the mantras by animal sacrifice, but because there are no such *brāhmaṇas* nowadays, such sacrifices are forbidden. The sacrifice in which horses were offered was called *aśvamedha*. Sometimes cows were sacrificed *(gavālambha)*. This was not for eating purposes, but to prove the potency of the mantras by giving them new life. In this age, therefore, the only practical *yajña* is *saṅkīrtana-yajña*, or to chant the Hare Kṛṣṇa mantra twenty-four hours a day.[28]

King Indradyumna invited thousands to attend the ceremonies. Kings from all over the world, the seven famous *ṛṣis*, prominent scholars learned in the *Vedas*, and many others arrived at Puruṣottama-kṣetra. The meeting place covered over two *krośas*.[29] Separate residential quarters were arranged according to the status of each guest, and the entire area was splendid. Colorful flags flew and festoons hung in the off-shore breezes, decorated canopies stood supported by pillars studded with gems, the lanes were sprinkled with scented water, and lilies and lotuses filled the ponds and lakes. Viśvakarma arrived with a host of heavenly associates and supervised the building of the sacrificial arena.

The king of heaven, Indra, was placed on a majestic throne in the center of all the demigods and sages, and Indradyumna pleased him by offering him flower garlands, valuable cloth, sandalwood pulp, and most significantly the presiding seat at the *yajña*. King Indradyumna bowed before Indra with such humility that Indra was pleased. Indradyumna then offered respects to all those who had

[28] See *Śrīmad-Bhāgavatam* (4.13.25) purport

[29] One *kroṣa* is equal to about two and a half miles.

assembled and, under the direction of a *brāhmaṇa* priest, began the *yajña*.

"O Yajñapuruṣa," King Indradyumna prayed, "You are the Supreme Personality of Godhead, Lord Viṣṇu. All those who live in the three worlds are subordinate to You. We are now engaged in offering one thousand horse sacrifices for Your pleasure.

"O Lord, You know the inner hearts of all men. Lord Nīla Mādhava has disappeared from the surface of the earth. This sacrifice is being performed just to please You and to invite You to reappear in Your deity form for everyone's benefit."

Elaborate Vedic rituals continued for days, and everyone was satisfied by the king's hospitality. He offered meals to the demigods on jewel-studded plates, and he presented food to the sages and *brāhmaṇas* on plates of gold, to the *kṣatriyas* and *vaiśyas* on plates of silver, and to the *śudras* on plates of bell metal. Each meal consisted of all six *rasas*, or tastes, and were served with expert efficiency. Even the demigods wondered how the king could arrange such good-tasting dishes. Each preparation surpassed the previous one in flavor. At night, everyone was offered comfortable quarters and entertained by song and dance. In this way the sacrifices continued.

## The Dream

Just before awakening at the end of the seventh night, King Indradyumna had a visionary dream. He saw the Lord of the universe in His abode at Śvetadvīpa, a white island in the ocean of milk. King Indradyumna saw Lord Anantadeva as a huge serpent with thousands of hoods, each decorated with dazzling jewels. Two terrible and fearful eyes looked out of each of Anantadeva's hoods. His body was white, His neck and tongues bluish. Lord Puruṣottama lay comfortably on Anantadeva's soft white body, and Lakṣmī-devī, the goddess of fortune, massaged the Lord's lotus feet.[30]

---

[30] See *Kṛṣṇa* (Chapter 20)—According to the *Vedas* there are millions of universes beyond this tiny one in which we live. All these universes come out from the bodily pores of Mahā-Viṣṇu, a portion of a plenary portion of Lord Kṛṣṇa. A further expansion of the Supreme Lord, known as Garbhodakaśāyī Viṣṇu, enters into each and every universe and is therefore known as the Lord of the universe. Also see *Bhagavad-gītā As It Is* (9.8) with purport, and *Śrīmad-Bhāgavatam* (1.3.2–5).

King Indradyumna was thrilled by this vision. Upon awakening he related the details of his dream to Nārada Muni, who said, "Now the sacrifices are almost completed, and the Lord of the universe has revealed Himself to you. You should not speak of this to others, but continue with the final *yajñas*."

Later that day, as the final *yajñas* were taking place, some citizens returned from bathing in the sea. They came before the king and announced, "O King, we have just seen a magnificent tree floating in the ocean's waves. This tree is no ordinary log. We could smell its sweet fragrance from a distance, and it glowed with uncommon luster. Looking closer, we found the symbols of Viṣṇu upon it!"[31] (See plate 5)

When the king heard this news, he asked Nārada Muni what it meant. "Last night," Nārada answered, "the Lord revealed Himself to you, but today He has been seen by many. For the benefit of all fallen conditioned souls, the Supreme Personality of Godhead will reveal Himself in a form carved from wood. There is no difference between the potencies of the *arca* and those of the personal forms of the Lord. The form of the deity is called *arca-vigraha*, or the form of the Lord that can be easily appreciated by the common man. The Lord is transcendental to our mundane senses. He cannot be seen with our present eyes, nor can He be heard with our present ears. We can only perceive the Lord to the degree that we have entered into His service or have become free from sin. Even though we are not free from sin, however, the Lord is kind enough to allow us to see Him in His *arca-mūrti* in the temple. The Lord is all-powerful. Therefore, He can accept our service through His *arca* form.

"You should all go to the seashore and bathe in the sea," Nārada continued. "Then arrange to have the tree brought here to the *mahāvedi*, the sacrificial altar."

### The Advent of Lord Jagannātha, Balarāma, Subhadrā, and Sudarśana *Cakra*

All the devotees who had gathered and taken part in the sacrifices were overjoyed to hear about the unusual tree, and they imme-

[31] The place where the sacred tree was discovered is known as *cakra-tīrtha*, located six kilometers east of the Jagannātha Temple on the seashore.

diately proceeded toward the sea to the accompaniment of musical instruments. King Indradyumna felt as if he was bathing in nectar as he took his bath in the sea. Following the advice of expert *brāhmaṇas*, the king worshiped the sacred tree according to Vedic rituals. Triumphant sounds filled the air and flowers fell from the sky. The king arranged to have the tree pulled out of the water and transferred to the *mahāvedi*, sacrificial platform.

Once the tree was in place, the king again performed many rituals. Then he became increasingly thoughtful. Who would know how to carve the Lord's transcendental form? What artist was qualified to perform the work? Again he heard a supernatural voice. "This sacred *dāru* (wood) should now be covered. A carpenter will soon appear with his tools to carve the Lord's proper form. He should be given complete privacy. While the carving is going on, play musical instruments so no one will hear the sounds of his tools on the wood. He who listens to the sound of the chipping and chiseling of the wood will undergo immense suffering. Even his children will be afflicted in future generations. No one should enter the *mahāvedi* to see the work. If these rules are broken, the state and the king will grieve."

After these instructions were followed, an old carpenter arrived and was offered facilities prescribed by the supernatural voice. As he prepared to work, the carpenter smiled and told King Indradyumna, "I will carve this *dāru* into the form you have seen in your dream."

Saying this, the carpenter entered the enclosed *mahāvedi* area. As each day passed, everyone's eagerness increased. Uncommon fragrances filled the air, and heavenly *parijata* flowers fell from the sky. Droplets of sweet Ganges water sprinkled down, cooling the atmosphere. The demigods and *brāhmaṇas* offered continuous showers of eloquent prayers.

Once again the king heard the divine voice of Goddess Sarasvatī: "Now you should have your men assist the old carpenter by covering the forms of Lord Jagannātha, Balarāma, and Subhadrā with nicely decorated cloth and have them painted correctly. Lord Jagannātha should be the color of a fresh monsoon cloud, Balarāma white like the full moon, Subhadrā saffron, and Sudarśana *cakra* red and white.

They should also be covered with bark-cloth (*balkala lepa*). O King, you should then construct a temple for the Lord of the universe, His brother, and sister. Make Viśvavasu and his descendants responsible for the deity's painting and restoration." After speaking these words, the goddess fell silent.[32]

A few more days passed while the carpenters and painters made final adjustments. Finally, the work period came to an end. The king ordered the doors opened, and everyone was pleased to see the Lord's form standing upon the altar. Lord Jagannātha was the color of a dark monsoon cloud about to burst. He was smiling and He had a broad chest. His eyes conquered the beauty of blossoming lotus flowers, and His neck was as lustrous as a mirror of sparkling sapphires. The Lord's chin, tinged with buff, conquered the beauty of the *bāndhulī* flower and increased the beauty of His mild smiling, which was like lustrous waves of nectar.

Lord Balarāma's white color defeated that of the full moon in autumn. His tall, strong, heroic stature made Him seem like Cupid himself. He had eyes like lotus petals and wore silk cloth on His body and a silk turban on His head. He wore golden earrings on His ears, and golden bangles on His arms. His body was anointed with sandalwood pulp, and He was nicely decorated with a garland of flowers around His neck.

Between the two brothers stood Their sister, Subhadrā, daughter of Vasudeva and his wife Devakī. Like the goddess of fortune, She supplies all opulences to the Supreme Personality of Godhead in the Vaikuṇṭha planets. She is supremely chaste because She never diverts Her attention from the Supreme Person. Her benevolent smile uproots the past sinful reactions of all who see Her.

To the left of Jagannātha stood the Sudarśana *cakra*, fashioned from a branch of the tree. Sudarśana means "auspicious vision," and the *cakra's* only concern is to annihilate the demons. Therefore, Sudarśana is described as *adharma-śilāsura-dhūma-ketave*. Those who are not devotees are called *adharma-śila*. The Sudarśana *cakra* is just like an inauspicious comet for all such demons.

---

[32] See "Anavasara" and "Navakalevara" in the *Festivals* section in part 2, *The Culture of Jagannātha Worship*, for more information about the restoration of the deities.

Nārada Muni said to King Indradyumna, "Your endeavors have now produced their fruit. O King, you are truly fortunate, for Lord Jagannātha has revealed Himself to the entire world due to your devotion. He is an ocean of kindness and bestows blessings upon all His devotees."

Under the direction of various *brāhmaṇas*, King Indradyumna offered prayers unto Lord Jagannātha. "O Lord, You are an ocean of kindness, the Supreme Personality of Godhead. For countless births I have been rotting in this material world without serving Your lotus feet. Attached to unlimited sense pleasures, to my family members, and to other worldly affairs, I received only temporary happiness that was like honey mixed with something bitter. I am most unfortunate.

"I now have a vast empire and abundant wealth, I am young and strong, my wives are pleasing, and no other king dares to invade us or cause us harm. Although possessing things desired by all men, I do not care for them. By Your causeless mercy, please save me from this ocean of short-lived pleasures mixed with despair.

"My only desire is that I may constantly remember Your lotus feet twenty-four hours a day. Your pure devotees have no material hankering. For them, even the pleasure of *brahmānanda* is considered insignificant. Your pure devotees, swimming in the nectar of devotion, certainly know ecstasies which immediately reduce the value of happiness from any other source. Such transcendental devotees regard any kind of happiness other than devotional service as no better than straw in the street. O Lord, please engage me in Your service."

Everyone present followed the king by offering prayers. The Vedic *brāhmaṇas* used the *Dvadaśākṣara* mantra to worship Lord Balarāma. They chanted the *Puruṣa-sūkta* to worship Lord Jagannātha, the *Devī-sūkta* for Subhadrā, and the *Sudarśana-sūkta* for Sudarśana.

King Indradyumna then offered charitable gifts to everyone assembled. To the *brāhmaṇas* he offered *tulapuruṣa*, gold and valuables equal to each man's weight. He gave away hundreds and thousands of cows nicely decorated with auspicious ornaments. The area where these thousands of cows were kept gradually created a large depression in the earth due to the animals' hooves. When filled with water, that place became a *tīrtha* known as Indradyumna Tank. According to *Puruṣottama-kṣetra-mahātmya*, bathing in this tank is equal to offering thousands of horse sacrifices. One can satisfy twenty-one generations of forefathers by offering *piṇḍa* at this place.[33]

## A Temple for the Lord of the Universe

After offering innumerable gifts in charity to the *brāhmaṇas*, King Indradyumna ordered architects to begin drawing plans for a temple. Meeting with his other subjects, King Indradyumna announced, "Whatever wealth remains in the treasury will be used to construct a temple. The labors we have undergone at home and abroad are meant to please the Supreme Personality of Godhead. What could be a superior fortune than offering the Lord of the universe all the wealth we've acquired? Even Śrī, the goddess of fortune, is attracted by the Lord's qualities.

"The Supreme Lord is actually the provider of all the wealth and riches we have earned, and He is always fully satisfied in Himself. Therefore, when something is offered to Him, the offering, by His mercy, benefits the devotees. The Lord does not need service from anyone. Therefore, according to our means, let us immediately prepare everything."

At that time, kings and various guests who had traveled from different lands left Purī, satisfied at having witnessed Lord Jagannātha's appearance. Court astrologers calculated an auspicious moment to begin the construction, and stone suppliers arranged for materials to be brought from various places.

As the months passed, construction slowly continued. Gradually a temple came to stand like a majestic masterpiece on Nīlācala Hill. King Indradyumna gave liberally from his treasury to please the Supreme Personality of Godhead. Even the demigods were enamored by the stunning architecture.

As the construction approached completion, Nārada spoke to King Indrayumna: "I came to help you at the request of my father, Lord Brahmā. Now I must go to inform him about Lord Jagannātha's

[33] Indradyumna Tank is about half a kilometer from the Guṇḍicā temple, just off the road to Konark by taking a left at the small fork in the road. If you decide to bathe, be careful because the steps are often slippery.

appearance and the construction of the temple."

"Prabhu," King Indradyumna appealed, "I wish to go with you to Brahmaloka. Because Pitāmaha (Brahmā) has been merciful to me, I want to invite him to inaugurate this temple. Please be tolerant of my shortcomings and allow me to accompany you." After saying this, King Indradyumna fell to the ground and offered his obeisances to Nārada Muni.

Nārada lifted Indradyumna to his feet and said, "O King, your fame is known throughout the three worlds. Your devotion is exemplary. You should continue worshiping Lord Jagannātha according to proper Vedic rituals and regulations, and you may now accompany me to Brahmaloka, where Lord Brahmā will further advise you about these *upacāras*."

### Easy Journey to Other Planets

Nārada Muni and King Indradyumna then offered obeisances to Lord Jagannātha and requested permission to go to Brahmaloka. They boarded a mystic celestial airplane and ascended toward the heavenly planets. While passing through space, they gradually saw all the upper planets of the solar system. Passing Maharloka, Janaloka, and Tapoloka, they saw gardens filled with fruits and flowers according to the season and beautifully decorated hermitages. The inhabitants of those lands are important leaders among the demigods. Always attended by their servants, they enjoy life in gardens alongside beautiful lakes. In this pleasing situation, the wives of the demigods smile playfully at their husbands and look upon them with lusty desires.[34]

Passing by all such places and arriving at the topmost planetary system, Brahmaloka, Nārada and the king were greeted by the gatekeeper. "O Nārada," the gatekeeper said, "you are always traveling throughout the three worlds for the benefit of all conditioned souls. Although many sages and demigods come to see your beloved father, this palace takes on special charm when you arrive. Lord Brahmā is now engaged in singing and asked not to be disturbed. Please wait a few moments until he has completed the *rāga* (musical composition)."

Brahmā was soon finished, and Nārada and King Indradyumna

---

[34] See *Śrīmad-Bhāgavatam* (5.17.13)—According to authoritative Vedic texts there is life on every planet in the universe.

entered his chamber. Seeing the four-headed creator of the universe and the two beautiful women standing on either side of him, King Indradyumna fell flat like a rod to offer his respectful obeisances and words of praise.

"My dear Lord Brahmā," Indradyumna said upon arising, "you are the first created being in this universe. Because you are surrendered to the Supreme Lord's will, you are empowered to perform acts of creation. By your mercy a temple has been built on the shores of the sea for Lord Jagannātha's pleasure. Everything was done according to the instructions of your son, Nārada Muni. After we completed one thousand *aśvamedha-yajñas*, the Lord appeared in a form carved from wood. It is by your grace that we have been able to perform this service. O Pitāmaha, I have come to request you to install the beautiful deity of Lord Jagannātha in the temple. Please shower your mercy upon us and come to Śrī Kṣetra for the inaugural ceremony."

As King Indradyumna was speaking, the well-known sage Durvāsā Muni entered Lord Brahmā's chamber and offered salutations. "O Brahmā," he said in a soft tone, "many exalted demigods and *siddhas* have been waiting to see you, but the gatekeeper is detaining them. Please permit them to have *darśana* of your lotus feet."

Lord Brahmā looked at Durvāsā and answered, "Those demigods and *siddhas* generally practice penances to attain fruitive gain and to enjoy life on the heavenly planets. This King Indradyumna is an unalloyed devotee of the Supreme Lord, Kṛṣṇa. Although I am engaged in speaking with him, you may allow the others to enter."

When Durvāsā Muni relayed Lord Brahmā's invitation, various demigods and *siddhas* ventured forth and offered their respects. Lord Brahmā blessed them with a benevolent smile, then continued speaking to Indradyumna. "O King, I am pleased to hear that you have built a temple for Lord Jagannātha at Śrī Kṣetra. Since you arrived here in Brahmaloka, however, a great deal of time has passed on the earth planet. One moment here is equal to an entire year on the middle planets. Seventy-one cycles of *yugas*, or one *manvantara*, has already passed since you departed. Hundreds of different kings and dynasties have come and gone on earth. Nevertheless, you should now return to Puruṣottama-kṣetra. I will be pleased to arrive there after proper arrangements have been made."

## "Half of My Life Is Now Over"

Lord Brahmā then turned and inquired from the demigods, "Why have you come?"

"Previously we worshiped the deity of Lord Nīla Mādhava in the forest of Nīlācala," one of the demigods said, "but now that same Lord Nīla Mādhava has appeared in a wooden form after the sacrifices of King Indradyumna. When we saw the king along with Nārada Muni approaching your abode, we came to inquire about this. What is the reason?"

Lord Brahmā, who is fully conversant with Vedic knowledge, answered: "This secret has never been revealed to anyone, but now I will disclose it. The *arcā-mūrti* forms of the Supreme Lord are manifest throughout the entire universe. The Lord has distributed Himself all over the universe to give pleasure to the devotees, to give the common man facility to eradicate his sins, and to establish religious principles in the world. It is enjoined in *śāstra, arcye viṣṇau śilā-dhīr guruṣu nara-matir*: 'No one should treat the deity in the temple as stone, metal, or wood. Nor should one think that the spiritual master is an ordinary human being.' One should strictly follow this śāstric injunction and worship the deity, the Supreme Personality of Godhead, without offense.

"For the first half of my life *(parārdha)* the Lord appeared as Nīlamādhava. The first fifty years of my life are now over. From this time on, the Lord will be worshiped in the wooden forms of Lord Jagannātha, Balarāma, Subhadrā, and Sudarśana *cakra*. They were carved from a tree marked with symbols of a conchshell and *cakra*. This tree is not ordinary—it is a transformed hair from the body of the Lord in Śvetadvīpa. Lord Puruṣottama has now appeared carved from that *dāru*. Those devotees who see the form of Lord Jagannātha become pure-hearted and devoted to Him.[35]

---

[35] "According to *Padma Purāṇa (Prabhasa-khanda)*, in thirty days of Brahmā many *kalpas* take place, such as the *Varāha-kalpa* and *Pitṛ-kalpa*. Thirty days make one month of Brahmā, beginning from the full moon to the disappearance of the moon. Twelve such months complete one year, and fifty years complete one *parārdha*, or one half the duration of the life of Brahmā."—*Śrīmad-Bhāgavatam* (3.11.35), Purport

"O demigods, King Indradyumna is now returning to Śrī Kṣetra to arrange for the *pratiṣṭhā* ceremony. Please go with him to assist in every way possible."

## The First Ratha-yātrā

King Indradyumna was pleased to see Lord Brahmā's luster and to receive these instructions. He bowed before Caturmukha Brahmā, and along with the demigods descended back to earth. King Indradyumna felt intense separation from Lord Jagannātha until he returned to Nīlācala. Upon seeing the cheerful forms of the deities, he offered heartfelt prayers.

*namo brahmaṇya devāya, go-brāhmaṇa-hitāya ca*
*jagad-dhitāya kṛṣṇāya, govindāya namo namaḥ*

"I offer my humble obeisances to Lord Jagannātha, the well-wisher of the cows and *brāhmaṇas*. My Lord, You are the well-wisher of the entire human society, the cause of maintenance and dissolution of the material universe, and the Lord of the universe."[36]

The demigods prayed, "Obeisances unto You who are the destroyer of all obstacles. The knowers of Vedānta describe You as the Supreme Brahman, while others describe You as the *pradhāna*, the totality of mundane elements. Some describe You as the supreme male person, the *puruṣa*. Others describe You as the Supreme Lord and the cause of the creation of the universe.

"Lord Jagannātha is the color of a new rain cloud. Therefore, He is compared to a transcendental cloud full of eternity, bliss, and knowledge. He is the original and supreme person. He is the origin of all activities and the one and only Lord of all. He is the worshipful Lord of the demigods, the controller of Brahmā, Viṣṇu, and Śiva. Kṛṣṇa is without any beginning. Whatever auspiciousness is found within or beyond this universe the devotee obtains from Lord Jagannātha alone."[37]

After taking *darśana* of Lord Jagannātha, Balarāma, and Su-

---

[36] *Viṣṇu Purāṇa* (1.19.65)

[37] *Kṛṣṇa Upaniṣad, Rg Veda*

bhadrā, King Indradyumna and the demigods proceeded toward Lord Nṛsiṁhadeva's temple nearby. Viewing the magnificent temple of Lord Jagannātha from a distance as they proceeded, the demigods were amazed and praised Indradyumna.

"Without divine guidance," the king answered humbly, "this could never have been done. A celestial voice directed me. The voice of a goddess instructed me to build a temple for the Lord of the universe, His brother, sister, and Sudarśana *cakra*. By the Lord's mercy, even though so much time has passed, the temple has been preserved. Soon Padmayoṇi (Brahmā) will arrive, so let us prepare for the *pratiṣṭhā* ceremony."

As they were speaking, Nārada Muni appeared. Overjoyed, the king offered obeisances and inquired from Nārada how to prepare for the installation ceremony. Nārada gave instructions to King Indradyumna, who in turn arranged for the ceremony. Palatial quarters were constructed for everyone according to their position. Viśvakarma built three enormous chariots to carry each of the deities from the *mahāvedi* to the temple. All three carts were decorated with gold and canopies of valuable silk.

Lord Jagannātha's chariot flew a flag with the symbol of Garuḍa; that of Subhadrā flew a flag decorated with a lotus flower; Lord Balarāma's cart was topped with a flag showing the insignia of a plough. Hundreds of strong white horses pulled the carts with gem-studded reins. [At this point in the narration, Jaimini Ṛṣi describes elaborate Vedic rituals, beginning with the inauguration of the chariots. We won't relate all these ritualistic details here. Readers interested in these intricate Vedic rituals are advised to see the *Puruṣottama-kṣetra-mahātmya* or the *Nīlādri-mahodaya*.]

Jaimini Ṛṣi continued, "O *brāhmaṇas*, I will now tell you how partial or complete damage to the chariots will cause havoc. If the steering mechanism of the chariot is broken, the *dvijas* (twice-born) will suffer; if the axle breaks, *kṣatriyas* (warriors) will suffer; if the balance beam breaks, *vaiśyas* (merchants) will suffer; and if the yoke pin breaks, the *śūdras* (laborers) will suffer. If the flag falls from the cart, surely the administration of the state will change hands, and if the chariot itself is damaged, the entire state will experience misfortune."

Fortunately, nothing was damaged during the first Ratha-yātrā.

The deities were ceremoniously placed upon the chariots and driven to the temple.

### King Gala

Ruling a nearby territory was a king named Gala. When he heard from messengers about someone performing elaborate ceremonies and planning to install deities in the temple, King Gala trembled with anger. He immediately gathered his army and headed toward Nīlaparvata to attack the opposing king who dared invade his territory.

As the army approached the Jagannātha temple, King Gala witnessed the regal arrangements for himself. The massive temple seemed to kiss the sky, and various chariots gleamed in the sun. King Gala was speechless. When he learned that King Indradyumna had returned from Brahmaloka and was preparing the *pratiṣṭhā* ceremony, he thought, *Let us stay here to witness the inaugural ceremony. How unfortunate I was not to understand the exalted form of Lord Jagannātha! Let me now surrender my life unto Him and to King Indradyumna. After establishing the deity, King Indradyumna will certainly return to Brahmaloka. Why would anyone who has gone there want to remain here?*

King Gala then approached King Indradyumna and offered his respects. "Ignorant of your power and influence, I came here prepared to attack," he confessed. "However, after seeing your activities, which excel those of Indra, I now surrender unto you. Please forgive me."

"O King," Indradyumna replied, "you are an emperor and a devotee of the Lord. By your rule, the citizens of the world remain peacefully engaged in pursuing the goal of human life. By worshiping the *arcā-mūrti* of Lord Jagannātha, Balarāma, and Subhadrā, all people can attain devotion and attraction for the Lord's lotus feet.

"It has been an entire *manvantara* since I was emperor of the world, and after Lord Brahmā inaugurates this temple, I will leave this place. At that time, you should continue worshiping the deities according to proper Vedic standards. Pitāmaha will instruct you about all these functions."

### Universal Cooperation

Soon everyone heard the sound of flutes, kettledrums, *vīṇās*, and *mṛdaṅgas*. Celestial music blended with the roar of elephants. Amid these unearthly sounds, fragrant flowers fell from the sky. Divine waters such as the Ganges, mixed with *mandara* flowers, sprayed down like mist. An uncommon luster filled the atmosphere.

All eyes looked up toward the heavens. Soon they sighted Lord Brahmā's white swan carrier, accompanied by thousands of heavenly beings. The masters of universal affairs surrounded the four-headed creator, fanning him with yak-tail wisks and peacock fans. The Ganges and Yamunā were to either side; the sun-god and moon-god held umbrellas. Gentle breezes blew colorful flags and festoons that flapped in the wind.

Perfected beings (*siddhas*) offered prayers. Beautiful *apsarās* danced to enchanting rhythms. Gandharvas, Vidyādharas, and other heavenly residents played various musical instruments, creating a soothing environment. Śāradā and Sāvitrī, ever radiant due to their chastity, accompanied Lord Brahmā.

Nārada, the Gandharvas, and the *siddhas* held gem-studded canes to form a path for Lord Brahmā. As this congregation of heavenly beings approached the earth, many demigods descended from their celestial airplanes. King Indradyumna and King Gala felt immense joy and offered respects to all who assembled.[38]

Someone fixed a golden ladder furbished with valuable jewels against Lord Brahmā's swan carrier, allowing him to alight. Lord Brahmā is the most exalted demigod in the universe because he is responsible for developing universal affairs. Born directly from the Supreme Personality of Godhead, he dedicates his activities to the welfare of the entire universe because he knows the purpose of creation. This supremely powerful Lord Brahmā, accompanied by his associates, left his own abode in the highest planet and descended to Lord Jagannātha's temple at Śrī Kṣetra.

As he climbed down the ladder, Lord Brahmā addressed King Indradyumna: "O Indradyumna, you are certainly fortunate, having pleased the residents of many planets. We are all assembled here due

---

[38] It is said that Lord Brahmā arrived near the seashore, south of the Jagannātha temple. The place is now known as *Svarga-dvara,* the doorway to heaven (*svarga*= heaven, *dvara*=door). Today *Svarga-dvara* is a cremation *ghat* where many believe that if their remains are burned here they will attain the heavenly regions or beyond in their next life.

to your unalloyed devotion to the Supreme Personality of Godhead."

Arriving moments later at the temple, Lord Brahmā saw the deities standing on their chariots. Turning to Lord Jagannātha's chariot, Lord Brahmā gave up all concerns for his own important position and prayed with a voice choked with emotion. "O my Lord, I do not see a form superior to Your present form of eternal bliss and knowledge. I surrender unto You because while I am proud of my material body and senses, Your Lordship remains completely untouched by matter.

"This present form, or any transcendental form expanded by the Supreme Personality of Godhead, is equally auspicious for all the universes. Since You have manifested this eternal personal form, upon whom Your devotees meditate, I offer my respectful obeisances unto You. Those who are on the path to hell neglect Your personal form because they speculate on material topics.

"O my Lord, Your devotees can see You through the ears by the process of hearing from bona fide sources. Thus their hearts become cleansed and You take Your seat there. You are so merciful to Your devotees that You appear in the particular eternal form of transcendence in which they always think of You.

"You are not satisfied by the worship of demigods who arrange to worship You with pomp but who are full of material hankerings. Out of Your causeless mercy You are situated in everyone's heart as the Supersoul. You are the eternal well-wisher, but You are unreachable by the nondevotees.

"Your Lordship, I offer my respectful obeisances unto You. You are indefatigable time and the enjoyer of all sacrifices. Although I am situated in an abode which will continue to exist for a time duration of two *parārdhas*, although I am the leader of all other planets in the universe, and although I have undergone many, many years of penances for self-realization, still I offer my respects unto You."[39]

After offering prayers to Lord Jagannātha, Brahmā then went before Lord Balarāma's chariot. He bowed his four heads to the earth, then again recited meaningful words:

"All glories to the Supreme Personality of Godhead, Lord Balarāma! Although Lord Śrī Kṛṣṇa is the original fountainhead of all

---

[39] *Śrīmad-Bhāgavatam* (3.9.3–20)

incarnations, Lord Baladeva is His second body. They are the same identity. They differ only in form. He is the first expansion of Kṛṣṇa, and He helps in Lord Kṛṣṇa's transcendental pastimes.

"Lord Balarāma is the original Saṅkarṣaṇa. He assumes five other forms to serve Lord Kṛṣṇa: (1) Mahā-Saṅkarṣaṇa, (2) Karaṇadakśāyī, (3) Garbhodakaśāyī, (4) Kṣīrodakaśāyī, and (5) Śeṣa. These five plenary portions are responsible for both the spiritual and material cosmic manifestations. In these five forms Lord Balarāma joins Lord Kṛṣṇa in all His activities. The first four of these forms are responsible for the cosmic manifestations, while Śeṣa is responsible for personal service to the Lord. Śeṣa is called Ananta, unlimited, because He assists the Personality of Godhead in His unlimited expansions by performing an unlimited variety of services. Śrī Baladeva is the servitor Godhead who serves Lord Kṛṣṇa in all affairs of existence and knowledge."[40]

Lord Brahmā then went before the beautifully decorated form of Subhadrā and prayed as follows: "O Parameśvarī, mother of the world, please be merciful unto me. You are known as Sarva-śakti, the source of all powers. O Goddess, you are the *māyā* of the Supreme Lord, known as Lakṣmī, Gaurī, Śacī, and Kātyāyanī all at the same time. While Nārāyaṇa is the father of all beings, you are the original mother. O auspicious Bhadra, all glories unto you!"

Brahmā finally offered prayers to Sudarśana *cakra*: "O Sudarśana, You are fire, You are the sun, and You are the moon. You are the master of luminaries, water, earth, and sky. You are the air, the five sense objects, and the senses also. O most favorite of Acyuta, the Supreme Personality of Godhead, You have thousands of spokes. O master of the material world, destroyer of all weapons, original vision of the Personality of Godhead, I offer my respectful obeisances unto You.

"You have a very auspicious hub. Therefore You are the upholder of all religion. You are just like an inauspicious comet for irreligious demons. Indeed, You are the maintainer of the three worlds. You are full of transcendental effulgence, You are as quick as the mind. You are able to work wonders. I can simply utter the word *namaḥ*, offering all obeisances unto You."[41]

---

[40] *Śrī Caitanya-caritāmṛta* (*Ādi-līlā* 5.4–10)

[41] *Śrīmad-Bhāgavatam* (9.5.3–6)

## The Inauguration

Lord Brahmā then went to the glorious temple on the peak of Nīlācala Hill. Accompanied by the other demigods, he inspected the *yajña-śala* (sacrificial arena). After all the guests were shown to their sitting places, Lord Brahmā sat on the *divya-simhāsana*, the presiding throne.

King Indradyumna requested the sage Bhāradvāja to perform complex Vedic rituals beginning with *śāntika* and *paustika*. The demigods who were to participate in the sacrifice began meditating on how the *homa* (fire) is compared to Lord Viṣṇu's mouth. All of them were then offered ornaments, flower garlands, and sandalwood paste.

While the fire crackled and devoured offerings of ghee, assembled *brāhmaṇas* chanted elaborate mantras. Bharadvaja then invited Lord Brahmā to inaugurate the temple. Brahmā rose from his seat and together with Nārada Muni, the *brahmarṣis*, and *brāhmaṇas*, performed rituals called *svastyayanā* to the angelic singing of the Gandharvas. The temple was now sanctified to become the abode of the Supreme Personality of Godhead.

Various musical instruments created a transcendental atmosphere as the demigods then proceeded to the deities' chariots. With love and devotion, Lord Jagannātha, Balarāma, Subhadrā, and Sudarśana-*cakra* were taken off the chariots and ceremoniously escorted to the temple on palanquins. Thousands of spectators chanted, "Jaya Jagannātha! Jaya Jagannātha! All glories to the Lord of the universe!" Nārada Muni played his transcendental *vīṇā*. Incense billowed. Many people stood in rows to fan Their Lordships and offer articles of worship and prayers.

They carried the deities with extreme care to the *maṇḍapa*, or altar for bathing. Lord Brahmā then performed the *abhiśeka* ceremony with water collected from holy *tīrthas* around the world. Others chanted the *Puruṣa-sūkta* and *Śrī-sūkta* mantras to the accompaniment of many musical instruments. Finally, Lord Brahmā placed Lord Jagannātha, Balarāma, Subhadrā, and Sudarśana-*cakra* on the *ratnavedi*, an altar inlaid with precious gems and dazzling jewels.

Lord Brahmā prayed, "O Supreme Personality of Godhead, Lord of the universe, please be satisfied to remain here in this temple. The inaugural ceremony is now complete by Your causeless mercy."

Jaimini Ṛṣi finally explained the auspiciousness and benefits of the installation. "It was the day of Bṛhaspati (Thursday), the eighth day of the waxing moon in the month of Vaiṣākha. The moon was in the eighth lunar mansion, Puṣya. Anyone who visits Lord Jagannātha, Balarāma, and Subhadrā with devotion at that time becomes free from unlimited sinful reactions accumulated in thousands of previous births."

### King Indradyumna's Desires Fulfilled

Following the ceremony, Lord Brahmā blessed King Indradyumna and instructed him in the chanting of a sacred mantra to Lord Nṛsiṁhadeva. Lord Nṛsiṁha's *mantrarāja* can dispel all evil. It is feared by all demoniac beings and can burn away sin.

Chanting the mantra, King Indradyumna entered deep into meditation. By Lord Brahmā's mercy, the king then had a divine vision of Lord Nṛsiṁhadeva. Lord Nṛsiṁhadeva was seated on a lotus flower and was embracing Lakṣmī, the goddess of fortune, to His chest. He had a pleasing smile and held the sacred symbols of Viṣṇu in His hands. Behind Nṛsiṁhadeva the king saw Anantadeva's hoods spreading like an umbrella over the Lord.

King Indradyumna became overwhelmed with ecstasy. He asked Lord Brahmā, "Oh Lokabhāvana, how can ordinary people like us possibly understand the unlimited Supreme Personality of Godhead? At the end of our *aśvemadha-yajñas*, the Lord appeared in the form of a tree floating in the sea. Divine voices from the heavens have spoken to guide me. Now I see the uncommon form of Lord Nṛsiṁhadeva before me! O Bhavabhāvana, please tell me if this is fact or illusion."

Understanding King Indradyumna's transcendental mood, Lord Brahmā answered: "O King, the Supreme Personality of Godhead has unlimited forms. All incarnations, such as Lord Nṛsiṁhadeva, are either plenary portions or portions of plenary portions of the Lord. Lord Śrī Kṛṣṇa is the original Personality of Godhead, the cause of all causes. Lord Jagannātha is that same Lord Kṛṣṇa. He is completely spiritual and full of transcendental bliss. You should never compare Him to a dull, destructible body composed of the inert, external energy. A devotee who knows the science of Kṛṣṇa consciousness makes no distinction between Lord Jagannātha and His body. He knows they are the same, as Lord Kṛṣṇa and His soul are the same. When the eyes are purified by devotional service performed on the spiritual platform, one can actually envision Lord Jagannātha and His body as being completely spiritual. The advanced devotee does not see the worshipable deity to have a soul with a body, like an ordinary human being. There is no distinction between the body and soul of Lord Jagannātha. Lord Jagannātha is *sac-cid-ānanda-vigraha*, as the body of Kṛṣṇa is *sac-cid-ānanda-vigraha*.[42]

"You should continue worshiping this form of Govinda carved from the sacred *dāru*," Lord Brahmā continued, "with the mantra I have given you. By doing so, the Supreme Personality of Godhead will be pleased with you. One who offers devotional service unto Lord Jagannātha is not required to perform sacrifices, offer charity, or undergo severe penances and austerities. Again I stress this: by worshiping this form of the Supreme Lord with devotion, anyone from any caste or creed can become completely free from all past reactions to sinful life."

Lord Brahmā then prayed to Lord Jagannātha: "O Prabhu Jagannātha, please accept my humble obeisances. All glories unto You! Please be merciful unto this devoted king, Indradyumna. For untold lifetimes he has been dedicated to serving Your lotus feet. Now he is engaged in the unalloyed process of *bhakti-yoga* simply to satisfy You. Please instruct him how to perform various *upacāras*, *yātrās*, and *vratas* for Your pleasure."

When Brahmā requested Lord Jagannātha in this way, the Lord smiled and spoke to the king. The Lord's speech was deep and extremely pleasing. He described in detail how each religious ceremony and ritualistic function was to be performed. [Again, I will not reproduce these details here. Those who are interested in the subject can find the information in the *Skanda Purāṇa*, *Nīlādri-mahodaya*, or *Hari-bhakti-vilāsa*.][43]

This conversation between Lord Śrī Jagannātha and the king is proof that the Lord in His form made of material elements is not ma-

---

[42] *Śrī Caitanya-caritāmṛta* (*Madhya-līlā* 5.91–158), Purport

[43] *Nīlādri-mahodaya* is a text about rituals and deity worship. The book is considered the authority on deity worship by the *sevaits* of the Jagannātha temple in Purī.

terial. Those elements, although separated from the Lord, are also part of the Lord's energy. This is stated in *Bhagavad-gītā*. Because the elements are the Lord's own energy, and because there is no difference between the energy and the energetic, the Lord can appear through any element. As the sun can act through the sunshine and thus distribute its heat and light, so Kṛṣṇa, by His inconceivable power, can appear in His original spiritual form in any material element. The *śāstras* warn, *arcye viṣṇau śilā-dhīḥ:* one should never think of the *arcā-mūrti*, the deity in the temple, as stone, wood, or any other material element.

The deity can act exactly as the Lord did in His original form as Kṛṣṇa. Lord Jagannātha was talking to the king. Those who have understood the science of Kṛṣṇa can also talk with the deity. To an ordinary person, however, the deity will appear to be made of stone, wood, or some other material. In a higher sense, since all material elements ultimately emanate from the supreme spiritual entity, nothing is really material. Being omnipotent, omnipresent, and omniscient, Kṛṣṇa can deal with His devotees in any form without difficulty. By the Lord's mercy, the devotee knows perfectly well about the Lord's dealings. Indeed he can talk face to face with the Lord.[44]

---

[44] *Śrī Caitanya-caritāmṛta* (*Madhya-līlā* 5.97), Purport

*1. 12th-century hand-carved temple of Lord Jagannātha*

2. *Fishermen at Purī*

3. *Mārkaṇḍeśvara, where Mārkaṇḍeya Ṛṣi stayed*

4. Śaṅka-kṣetra

6. *Sādhu in Purī*

7. *Snāna Yātrā—bathing the Deities*

9. *Carving wheels for Ratha carts*

10. *Carts under construction*

11. *Lord Jagannātha's Ratha, Nandighoṣa*

12. *Lord Balarāma's Ratha, Tāladvaja*

*13. Subhadrā's driver, Arjuna*

*14. Hundreds of gongs in unison*

15. *Getting a good seat*

*16. King Dibyasingh Deb at Purī Rathayātrā*

*17. Utsava deities going to Dola-yātrā*

18. *Narendra Sarovara, site of Candana-yātrā*

19. *Durgā Devī defeating Mahiśāsura in Harcana Sahi*

*20. Maṅgala Devī, the deity who reveals to* pūjārīs *in a dream where to find trees for construction of new deities*

*21. Worshiping the sacred Dāru before it is cut down*

*22. Preparing the Dāru tree for transport*

# 2

# *The Culture of Jagannātha Worship*

## Daily Pūjā

Many people consider Lord Jagannātha an idol and His worship idolatry. This misconception arises from not knowing the difference between idol worship and deity worship.

The word "idol" is derived from the Greek word *eidolon*, "image." An idol is a powerless *image* of a person or thing, such as a photograph, painting, or statue. An idol and the substance it represents are not the same thing. An idol is simply an *image* of the original, perhaps even something *imag*ined.

The word "deity," on the other hand, is derived from the Latin word *deus*, God. Unlike objects of this material world which are separate from their names and forms, the names and forms of God are transcendental and absolute. Because God is absolute, His name, form, and His person are not different from Him.

Here in this relative material world the name of something is not the same as the substance. For example, if we want some water, we cannot experience the taste or refreshment simply by calling "Water, water, water." That will not satisfy us. But spiritually, because God is absolute, you can chant God's name, see God's form, discuss God's activities, and you will experience direct union with God. The proof is in the experience itself. People from myriad religious traditions experience direct communion with God by glorifying Him, praying to Him, or seeing His form. That is the absolute nature of the Absolute Truth.

Although the Supreme Lord is transcendental and resides far away in His spiritual abode, the natural elements of earth, water, fire, and air are His creation. As the omnipresent Lord, He is simultaneously within these elements and aloof from them. What we call stone, wood, and metal are energies of the Supreme Lord, and energies are never separate from the energetic. Thus, the Lord can appear anywhere and everywhere because His diverse energies are distributed everywhere like sunshine.

In our present state it is not possible to see God in His spiritual form because our material eyes and senses cannot conceive of a spiritual form. We cannot even see the spiritual form of the individual soul. When a man dies we can't see how the spiritual form leaves the body. That is the defect of our material senses. Because conditioned souls are unable to see the Lord's spiritual form, He accepts forms made of material elements through which He accepts service. These forms are called *arcā-vigraha*.

In the *Śrīmad-Bhāgavatam* (11.27.12) there are eight types of *arcā-vigraha* forms listed:

*śailī dāru-mayī lauhī, lepyā lekhyā ca saikatī*
*mano-mayī maṇi-mayī, pratimāṣṭa-vidhā smṛtā*

"The deity form of the Lord is said to appear in eight varieties—stone, wood, metal, earth, paint, sand, the mind, or jewels."

The appearance of the Lord in so-called material ingredients can also be further explained as follows:

We find many mailboxes on the street. If we post our letters in these boxes, they will arrive at their destination without difficulty. But if we put our letters in any box not authorized by the post office, our letters will not arrive. Similarly, God has authorized the deity form, or *arcā-vigraha* mentioned in scripture, as the proper form for our worship. The *arcā-vigraha* is an incarnation of the Supreme Lord, and He will accept whatever service we render to Him in that form. When we fashion a form of the Lord as directed in *śāstra* from wood, stone, metal, jewels, paint, or even within the mind, it is a bona fide, spiritual, transcendental form. When the material energy is engaged in the service of Supreme Spirit, so-called material energy is transformed into spiritual energy, just as an iron rod becomes fire when held in fire and heated to red-hot. The Lord is omnipotent and all-powerful; therefore, by His incarnation as *arcā-vigraha*, He accepts the devotees' services and thus allows those of us with conditioned and imperfect senses to serve Him. Thus, according to proper etymological definition, worship of Lord Jagannātha is not idolatry.

In the temple of Lord Jagannātha at Purī, the worship is performed in an intimate mood of opulence and grandeur. As a king has thousands of servants seeing to his needs and comforts, so Lord Jagannātha engages His devotees. Officials estimate that more than 30,000 men, women, and children depend on their work with the temple for their livelihood. The following is a summary of a normal day's schedule:

A Day in the Life

*Dwāra-pīṭha*—The temple doors are opened at about 4:30 a.m.

*Bhītar-sodha*—The temple interior is cleansed and purified.

*Maṅgal-ārati*—Lamps are offered (21 camphor, 21 ghee—7 to each deity).

*Mailama*—Deities are dressed for bathing.

*Abhiśeka*—The deities are bathed by bathing their reflection in a silver mirror; just before bathing, the deities' teeth and tongue are also cleansed *(dantadhavana* and *jihva-lekhana)*.

*Mailama*—The deities are dressed in pure silk, fresh flowers, and ornaments.

*Homa* in the kitchen—As the deities are dressed on the altar, cooks begin their activities in the kitchen area.

*Sūrya-pūjā*—The sun-god is worshiped at about 8:30 a.m.

*Dwārapāl-pūjā*—The guardians of the various doorways are worshiped.

*Gopāl Vallabha Bhoga* (breakfast at 9 a.m.)—Offering of fused rice, coconut, butter, yogurt, banana, sweets, *papuri* (preparation made with skin of milk unique to Purī), and nutmeg all served in bell-metal bowls; betel nut is also offered at every meal.

*Sakala-dhūpa* (regular breakfast at about 10 a.m.)—Dahl cakes, gram cakes, *kitchuri* (rice and dahl cooked together), spinach with *hing, idli* (type of rice cake), and *payasam* (similar to sweet-rice boiled in milk).

*Sakala-ārati*—Lamps are offered.

*Mailama*—The deities' dresses and flower garlands are changed.

*Bhoga-maṇḍap bhoga* or *upala-boga* (anytime between 11 a.m. and 3 p.m.)—Offering of rice, dahl, and curries for sale to the public; this offering is not placed directly in front of the deities as are other offerings, but is placed in the area called *bhoga-maṇḍapa*.

*Madhyahna-dhupa* (lunch at about 12:30 p.m.)—Rice with ghee (clarified butter), dahl, sweet and sour vegetable, dahl cakes, rice-flour cakes, and sweets made of rice, rice flour, or wheat, with either sugar or gur.

*Madhyahna-ārati*—Lamps are offered.

*Madhyahna-pahuda*—Afternoon rest.

*Pahuda-phita*—The deities awaken around 6 p.m.

*Sandhyā-ārati*—Lamps are offered.

*Sandhyā-dhūpa* (dinner at about 7 p.m.)—Large varieties of rice, cakes, sweets, and cheesecake.

*Ārati*—Offering of lamps.

*Mailama*—The deities dress and flower garlands are changed.

*Candan-lagi*—Sandalwood paste mixed with camphor, saffron, and musk is offered.

*Bada-Siṁhara dhūpa* (evening snack around 11 p.m.)—Sweet cakes, sweet curd products, milk sweets, and banana cutlet.

*Khāṭa-sejā-lagi*—Beds are offered for the Lords' rest along with flowers, tender green coconuts filled with juice, and music from Jayadeva Gosvāmī's *Gīta-govinda*.

*Deva-dāsī dance*—Previously, specially trained girls would dance as the Lord relaxed before going to sleep late at night. However, this is no longer practiced.

## Dressing and Decorating the Lord

Maintaining this busy schedule day after day, month after month, year after year, generation to generation, requires an enormous temple staff and extremely efficient administration. The most popular of all activities is seeing the deities in the temple, called *darśana*, which means "to see face to face." Thousands of devotees visit the temple every single day of the year to see the Lord.

An attentive look at the *pūjā* schedule above reveals that the deities' clothing is changed several times each day. As we have the natural tendency to dress in a particular way for various occasions, our creator must also have this same inclination. Indeed, He's known to be a meticulous dresser and enjoys being decorated by His devotees. Those who dress the deities are known as *puṣpālaka*, and those who decorate them in special dresses on festival occasions are known as *śṛngārī*. Pure silk or cotton cloth and natural flowers are always used, never any polyester or plastic.

Other than the normal daily dress, on festival days the deities wear special outfits. Devotees in and around Purī are attentive to these special occasions, and it's quite common to hear someone ask, for example, "Did you see Lord Jagannātha in His *Nāgārjuna-veṣa*?"

The history of each individual *veṣa* is impossible to trace, but I offer a partial list below in order to note a few unique *veṣas* worn by Lord Jagannātha, along with the date on which they are worn:[1]

*Kāliya-damana-veṣa*—Bhādra Kṛṣṇa Ekādaśī
*Rāja-veṣa*—Aśvina Śukla Dasamī
*Rādhā-Dāmodara-veṣa*—from Aśvina Śukla Ekādaśī to Kārttika Śukla Daśamī
*Lakṣmī-Nṛsiṁha-veṣa*—Kārttika Śukla Cāturdaśī
*Nāgārjuna-veṣa* or *Paraśurāma-veṣa*—The last days of Kārttika when, according to astrology, there are six *tithis* rather than five between Ekādaśī and Pūrṇimā. (Note: on Nov. 26, 1993, Lord Jagannātha wore this *veṣa* for the first time in twenty-five years. An estimated 500,000 pilgrims took *darśana* on that day.)
*Padma-veṣa*—Māgha-śukla-dvitīya
*Hati-veṣa*—Jyeṣṭhā Pūrṇimā
*Suna-veṣa*—Āṣāḍha-śukla Ekādaśī, Kārttika Pūrṇimā

### Various Offerings to the Lord

Pilgrims visiting Purī are also anxious to honor the Lord's *prasādam*, foodstuffs offered to the deities. More than 5,000 cooks are engaged in preparing at least fifty-six different types of pure vegetarian dishes daily. These cooks work in daily rotations, preparing enough food each day to feed an average of 10,000 people. During festivals the number easily climbs to over 25,000.

---

[1] See *Appendixes* for an explanation of the calendar months and days.

Attraction for remnants of the Lord's food is not mundane. The *Bhagavad-gītā* (3.13) clearly asserts:

> *yajña-śiṣṭāśinaḥ santo, mucyante sarva-kilbiṣaiḥ*
> *bhuñjate te tv aghaṁ pāpā, ye pacanty ātma-kāraṇāt*

"The devotees of the Lord are released from all kinds of sins because they eat food which is offered first for sacrifice. Others, who prepare food for personal sense enjoyment, verily eat only sin."

The deities' offerings are prepared in a clean atmosphere. No dogs, cats, or animals are allowed near the cooking area. The kitchen compound, located several feet above and to the left of the *Siṁha-dvāra* (the eastern gateway or entrance) covers roughly one acre. The compound includes nine kitchens; two of them are more than 2,500 square feet each, and seven are slightly smaller. The cutting, chopping, grinding, and so on, are done just in front of the kitchens, in an open area called *agana*. Numerous small storage areas make up the rest of the kitchen compound.

These kitchens house an astounding 752 wood-burning stoves, called *chulas*, each about three feet square and four feet high. Small clay knobs, called *jhinkas*, are judiciously placed at intervals around the stove's surface to support and accommodate various sizes of pots. A circle of earthen pots rests directly on the stove's surface, kept in place by these *jhinkas*. Three more pots go in the open spaces above the pots to form a second layer, and one more pot goes in the center on top, forming a nine-pot pyramid. In this way, all nine pots receive heat and smoke from the wood fire below.

The new earthen cooking pots are called *kudias*. Most are jug-shaped, though some are shallow and wide, resembling Spanish paella pans or French saute pans without handles. As the food cooks in these unglazed pots, their thick walls become very hot and thus the pots provide amazing heat retention. Food stored in them remains piping hot for quite some time.

Approximately 1,000 men work in the kitchen daily. Five hundred attain the status of executive chefs, called *suaras*, and they are the only persons allowed to actually cook on the stoves. Three hundred "first string" assistants, called *jogunias*, are allowed to enter the kitchens to assist the *suaras*, but they mainly light fires, fetch water from temple wells, wash and clean the earthen cooking pots, and finally fill the pots with ingredients. The other two hundred assistants, the "second-string," are called *tunias*. They are not allowed to enter the kitchens, but work in front of them in the *agana*, engaged in such tasks as washing ingredients, cutting vegetables, grating fresh coconut, and stone-grinding herbs, ginger, and spice blends.

Once the preparations are complete, the *mahāsuara* knots the end of a damp jute rope and makes a noose around the neck of the pot. He places the pot in a basket and then deftly builds a stack of four or five pots. One basket is then hung at each end of a flexible five-foot bamboo pole. To carry the lot, the *mahāsuara* gingerly lifts the pole at its center and rests it on his shoulder. Now with a slightly awkward gait due to carrying the heavy load, hips shifting from side to side, he transports eight to ten pots at a time to the offering area through a tunnel connecting the kitchen to the inner sanctum. This tunnel path prevents anyone from viewing the Lord's meal before the offering. The carriers *(suaras and mahāsuaras)* are also careful to cover their mouths and noses with cloth tied around their heads so as not to breath or accidentally expectorate upon the offerings.

Meanwhile, a priest *(pūjā-panda)* at the altar cleanses the area in front of the deities with water. He then draws seven mystic *maṇḍalas* on the floor with rice flour, marking a spot for each deity's offering. When the offerings arrive from the kitchen, they are placed upon the appointed areas, then offered with sacred mantras. It should be noted that every pot that has been prepared is placed before the Lord, unlike many other temples of India, where only small portions of the entire meal are offered before the deities.

After the food is offered to the deities on the main altar, a portion is taken to the nearby Bimalā temple (still within the main compound) and offered to the goddess Bimalā. Residents of Purī believe that only after the foodstuff is offered to Bimalā-devī does it become *mahā-prasāda*, sanctified food in the form of mercy for the devotees.

## Unity in Diversity

As cooks and their assistants prepare food offerings according to precise practices and regulated schedules, thousands of other servants of Lord Jagannātha perform their numerous services according to strict Vedic rites and regulations. These numerous services and rituals are so complex and elaborate that it's nearly impossible to describe the details of each.

Most temple servants in this enormous administrative network are born into families that have performed a particular duty or service for generations. Only male members of the family are engaged directly in temple services, although the *deva-dāsīs* are (or were), naturally, female dancers. As the young boys mature, their fathers train them to perform the family's service to Lord Jagannātha. Ideally, thousands of people work for the Lord in one way or another throughout the district of Purī, and all of them perform their services according to the disciplines of Vedic culture. Some people cook, others clean, sew, work in the fields, make clay pots, collect flowers, supply milk, or engage in countless other occupations. Living in such a culture encourages all members of society to develop a mood of loving service toward the Supreme Personality of Godhead from the beginning of their lives. This culture was, of course, far more prominent in India's past. Since the Jagannātha Temple Act of 1952, the secular Orissan Government has taken control of many temple management positions and oversees a great deal of the temple administration.

## Services Rendered

It would be impossible to give a complete account of services offered to the deities, but here is a partial listing in order to give an idea of the diversity:

*Mudiratha*—Servant who, in the absence of the king, performs the king's rituals (*rāja-nīti*)

*Bhaṇḍāra Nekab*—Treasurer of the Lord's storage room where costly garments and ornaments are kept

*Bhitarachu Mahāpātra*—Opens the locked door of the temple each morning before anyone enters

*Talichu Mahāpātra*—Locks the temple doors each evening and accompanies Madana-mohana, the *vijaya-vigraha*, during travel

*Paricha*—An administrator who also holds a golden cane during festivals

*Deula Karana*—Secretary and keeper of *Madalapanji*, the daily temple records
*Cangada Mekapa*—Responsible for supplying and maintaining of clothing for the deities
*Dayita*—Servants of the deities, especially during the time of renovations known as *anavasara*
*Suarabadu*—Cleans the Lord's chamber
*Tulasīa*—Supplies *tulasī* leaves for *pūjā*
*Mahabhoi*—Supplies milk
*Pānīyapātra*—Supplies water
*Suara*—Cooks and carries *bhoga* (unoffered food)
*Pūjā Paṇḍā*—Performs ritualistic worship of the deities
*Mukhapakhala*—Supplies tooth-cleaning sticks
*Khuntia*—Calls out "Manima! Manima!" during various functions
*Vimāna Vadu*—Carries the palanquin
*Padhiari*—Security guard and receptionist
*Śaṅkhua*—Blows the conchshell
*Vīnākāra*—Plays music on the *vīṇā* as the deities retire
*Amunia Chatra*—Holds umbrella during processions
*Garuḍa* or *Ghunara Sevaka*—Places colorful flags atop the temple, and puts a lamp there on Ekadasi at sundown

## Festivals

The last eight chapters of *Puruṣottama-kṣetra-mahātmya* are devoted to rituals, *upacāras*, and methods of worship for Lord Jagannātha. There were only twelve annual religious festivals mentioned in the original text, but today more than sixty official festivals are performed each year. Devoted kings and supporters have added these extra celebrations in accordance with the Vedic calendar. Below is a listing and brief description of some of the more important festivals.[2]

### Snāna-yatra

Lord Jagannātha requested King Indradyumna to excavate a well near a banyan tree next to the temple, take water only from that

[2] See *Appendixes* for an explanation of the calendar months and days.

well, and bathe Him. Indradyumna built a large arena for the occasion, wherein he placed a variety of gates, flags, flowers, pearls, and jewels. Nearby, he set up flower *āsanas* for the demigods and sages. Moments before leaving the chariots, the Lord was offered red *kuṅkuma* powder, then carried by the demigods to the flower *āsanas*. Cool, clean, sandal-scented well water was then brought from that special well in golden water pots (*suvarna kumbhas*) and poured over the deities, who were dressed in linen outfits. Lord Brahmā bathed the deities, followed by the Lord's servants, who constantly chanted, "*Jaya, Jaya.*" Lord Jagannātha also instructed King Indradyumna that for fifteen days after this *snāna-yātrā*, no one should see the deities.[3]

Snāna-yātrā takes place on the full-moon day (Pūrṇimā) of Jyeṣṭhā, one of the hottest days of the year. It is said in *Skanda Purāṇa* that this is Lord Jagannātha's appearance day. Lord Jagannātha is Kṛṣṇa, but Kṛṣṇa's appearance day is the eighth day of the dark fortnight of the month of Bhādra. Therefore, when it is said that Jyeṣṭhā Pūrṇimā is Jagannātha's appearance day, it means that this is the day when Kṛṣṇa appeared in His form with large dilated eyes, a round face, and hands and legs withdrawn into His body. This feature is known as *mahābhāva-prakāśa*, Kṛṣṇa's manifestation of ecstasy while feeling separation from the residents of Vṛndāvana.

Just after sunrise, the deities are carried out of the temple. First Balarāma, then Sudarśana *cakra*, Subhadrā, and finally Jagannātha are carried in a procession called *pahandi*, which means "jumping" or "swaying step by step." Strong ropes are tied around the heavy *mūrtis*, and they are carried one at a time to the *snāna-vedi* located on the northeast corner of the outer boundary wall. Because the deities are so heavy, it requires many strong men to raise them to the platform.

Once in place, Lord Jagannātha, Balarāma, Subhadrā, and Sudarśana *cakra* stand before the public under a colorful canopy for the entire day. Following in the footsteps of King Indradyumna, servants bathe the deities with 108 golden water pots filled with cool sandal-scented water from a *suna-kua* (golden well). This ceremony, called

[3] The fever pastime is mentioned in *Nārada Purāṇa* (*Utkal Khanda* 59.29) and will be further described while discussing *anavasara*.

an *abhiśeka*, is meant to refresh their Lordships from the heat of the summer sun. (See plate 7)

As evening arrives, seeing the deities becomes a celestial delight. The summer sun sets in the west behind them as the full moon rises in the east, facing them. At that time, the deities appear in *Hati-veśa*, a regal outfit making them appear as if they had elephant trunks; the change into this *veśa* takes place during late afternoon. The *Dhar-dhayata-bhakti* tells of a devotee of Ganeśa (a demigod with an elephant's head) named Gaṇapati Bhaṭṭa who came to Purī one year to witness the *snāna-yatra*. When Gaṇapati Bhaṭṭa didn't see an elephant head on Lord Jagannātha, he went away, disappointed, planning to leave Purī. Lord Jagannātha, however, as the Paramātmā and knower of everyone's heart, understood this devotee's feelings. He secretly appeared as a *brāhmaṇa* on the streets of Purī and convinced Gaṇapati Bhaṭṭa to return in the evening for *darśana*. When Gaṇapati Bhaṭṭa arrived before the deities, he saw Lord Jagannātha with the head of an elephant, and all his desires were fulfilled. (See plate 8)

(Note: Because the deities come out of the temple for this festival, anyone from any caste, creed, or country may directly see them on this special day. Although Hindus approach the deities to embrace them, non-Hindus can witness the festivities from Grand Road, or climb the rooftops of many nearby buildings. We were amazed to see hundreds of pots filled with offerings of food placed before the deities as the full moon slowly rose in the eastern sky. If you plan to attend this festival, you might consider going to the temple in the morning for the bathing, then returning again in the late afternoon or early evening. In this way, you can see most of the ceremonies and still get a little rest in between.)

### Anavasara—Netrotsava and Nava-yauvana

Because the deities bathe in cool water during the high heat at *snāna-yātrā*, then stand outside in the cool evening air, they are said to catch a fever and become sick. To recuperate, they retire for a fortnight to comfortable private quarters where no one but their personal servants visit them. This fifteen-day period is known as *anavasara*. Special servants (*dayitās*) attend them in their seclusion. Lord Jagannātha instructed King Indradyumna that during this special time, the descendants of the Śabaras should renovate the deities. Thus, devotees born in these lower-caste families are privileged to perform services during the recuperation period.

During the fifteen days of *anavasara*, the deities are offered an infusion of drugs to cure the fever, represented by assorted fruit juices, herbs, and roots collected from Orissan jungles. They are also "renovated" by repainting them and making any necessary repairs. Śrīla Bhaktisiddhānta Sarasvatī explains that during this fifteen-day period, Lord Jagannātha, as an ideal husband, enjoys *svākīya-rasa* with His wife, the goddess of fortune, in a solitary place. Lord Jagannātha then asks her permission to leave and comes out for Ratha-yātrā. The Netrotsava festival, or reappearance of the Lord, is then performed in the early morning of the Nava-yauvana day, the day before Ratha-yātrā. Newly painted and looking youthful, Lord Jagannātha, Balarāma, Subhadrā, and Sudarśana *cakra* are placed on the altar in the main temple. This is known as their *navayauvana-veśa*, and this celebration is the life and soul of the devotees, because once again they can see the Lord on His temple altar.[4]

## Ratha-yātrā

Ratha-yātrā is celebrated on the second day of the waxing moon in Āṣāḍha. This Festival of the Chariots (*ratha* = chariot, *yātrā* = festival) is the most exuberant, colorful celebration of the entire year. As early as Vasanta Pañcamī, almost four months prior to the actual observance, wood for building the massive chariots is collected from the Ranapur forest in the district of Dasapalla, Orissa. Hundreds of carpenters, painters, and laborers are provided with materials necessary to build the carts. They begin work on *Akṣaya-tṛtīyā*, the first day of summer and *candana-yātrā*. Carpenters work in front of the Jagannātha temple office on Grand Road for two months preceding the festival, carefully constructing each cart in the same way year after year. The chariots are designed and decorated according to ancient traditions passed down from father to son, teacher to apprentice. (See plates 9 and 10)

Lord Jagannātha's chariot is called Nandighoṣa. It's about fifty

[4] See *Caitanya-caritāmṛta* (*Madhya-līlā* 1.122, 10.41, 12.204, 13.8,23,24).

feet high and has sixteen wheels. Each wheel has sixteen spokes. Many subsidiary deities, demigods, and other personalities are placed around the chariot in various places. Nandighoṣa flies the flag of Garuḍa holding a snake in his beak. The charioteer is Mātali, who controls four white horses. Garuḍa is the protector, Jaya and Vijaya the doorkeepers. Eight hundred thirty-two wooden parts are used, all fitting without nails, but occasionally iron clamps are inserted for reinforcment. The canopy's cloth is yellow and red. (See plate 11)

Lord Balarāma's chariot is named Taladvāja. It's 47 feet high and flies the emblem of a ploughshare on its flag. Taladvaja has fourteen wheels, each with fourteen spokes. Lord Śeṣa is the protector, the gatekeepers are Nandi and Sunandi, and the charioteer is Dāruka, who controls four black horses. 763 wooden pieces are used to construct this cart. The canopy is green and red. (See plate 12)

Subhadrā's chariot is called Padmadvāja, Devadalana, or Devīratha. It flies a flag with a lotus flower 43 feet above the ground. Padmadvaja has twelve wheels, each with twelve spokes. Jayadūrga is the protector, Gaṅgā and Yamunā are the gatekeepers, and the charioteer is Arjuna (see plate 13), who controls four chestnut-colored horses. 593 wooden pieces make up this chariot. Subhadrā and Sudarśana *cakra* ride on it, and are shielded by a red and black canopy.

The early morning calm of Ratha-yātrā day gradually fades, as thousands of eager spectators stretch, push, and shove to get a glimpse of the deities as they slowly emerge from the temple. In the morning, the first to emerge is Lord Balarāma. Then Sudarśana *cakra*, Subhadrā, and lastly Lord Jagannātha are carried in the procession known as Paṇḍu-vijaya or *pahandi*. The deities are ceremoniously placed upon their chariots, accompanied by the loud cheers of the spectators, many of whom have traveled from around the world to witness this sensational event. A short time later, the *utsava-mūrtis* are also placed on the chariots.

### *Chera-pahanra*

A regal procession led by an elephant then travels through the parting crowds to Śrī Nahar, the king's palace. After a formal invitation, the King of Purī advances slowly by palanquin toward the chariots to perform the *chera-pahanra* ceremony of sweeping for the Lord.

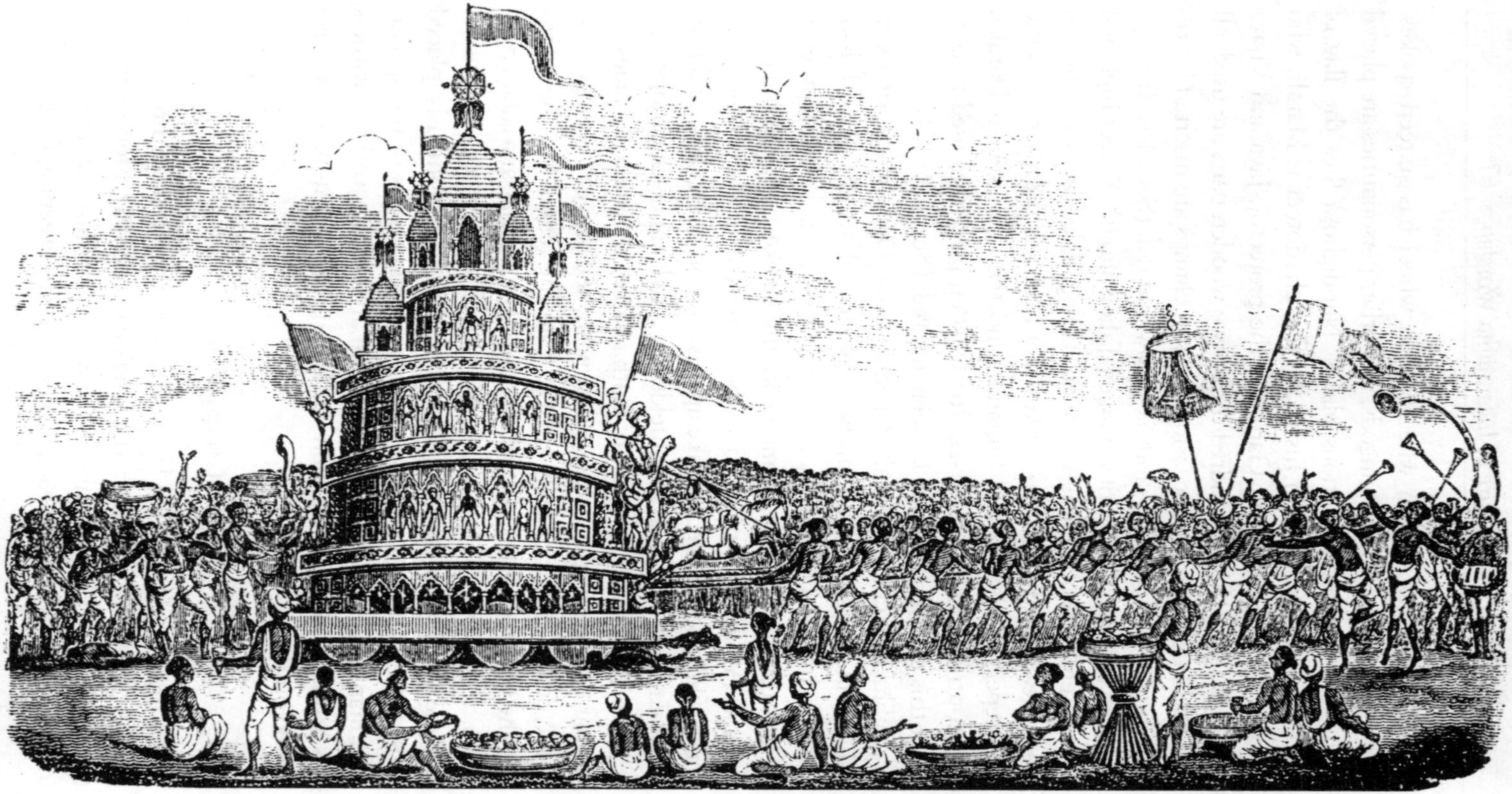

*An early version of the Ratha-yātrā festival.*

The king performs the menial service of sweeping the carts with a golden-handled broom. He then offers flowers with scented water on all three chariots, first Balarāma's, then Jagannātha's, and finally Subhadrā's. The meaning behind this function is that although the king is a leader among men, he humbles himself before the Supreme leader, Lord Jagannātha.

A unique street-sweeping festival of many years ago bears mention. King Puruṣottama (1467–1497) was to be married to the beautiful princess Padmavatī from a kingdom south of Kaliṅga. The father of the princess, King Saluva Narasimha, was invited to Ratha-yātrā, but he sent his minister Chinnūbhaṭṭa Godaraṇga in his place.

During the festival, Puruṣottama Dev performed the devotional tradition of sweeping the road in front of the carts. The visiting minister, however, rather than being impressed with the devotion of the king, did not approve of him sweeping the road. When he reported this to King Saluva Narasimha, the king objected to his daughter marrying the King of Purī because Puruṣottama Dev was merely a street sweeper.

Puruṣottama Dev was naturally offended, so he gathered his troops and went south to teach King Saluva a lesson. Unfortunately, during their first attempt King Puruṣottama Dev's army was badly defeated.

Returning toward Purī in a downcast mood, the army stopped at the simple cottage of Saikatācārya, a great ascetic householder devotee of Lord Jagannātha. Hearing what happened, Saikatacharya pointed out that the king had forgotten to ask permission from Lord Jagannātha before he went to attack. With this realization the king returned to Purī and visited the temple, crying over his defeat, asking why the Lord had allowed it. He spent the entire night in the temple. With doors closed, before the night came to an end, the king heard a voice asking why he was so distraught over such a simple thing. The voice instructed him to again gather his troops and that the two brothers, Jagannātha and Balarama, would go along to fight on the king's behalf. As this news spread, many people, both young and old, joined the king's forces to fight along with Their Lordships. However, as they went, the king was filled with doubts whether Their Lordships were really going with him.

While the king and his army went onward, far ahead were two soldiers that rode on one black horse and one white horse. They stopped to quench Their thirst at a small village near Chilika Lake by buying some yogurt from a devotee named Manika. She offered Them yogurt, but when she asked for payment, They said They had no money. Instead,They gave her a jeweled ring and told her to give it to King Puruṣottama Dev, who would then give her payment.

After some time, the king came upon the lady who flagged him down to give him the ring and ask for payment for the soldiers' drink. The king was shocked to see the *ratnamudrika* ring of Lord Jagannātha and then regained his confidence that, indeed, Their Lordships had certainly come with him. In payment for the ring, the king gave her the whole village, which is still named Manikapatna. After this, the king and his troops were victorious over King Saluva Narasimha, and subsequent to the battle King Puruṣottama angrily kidnapped the king's daughter, Padmavatī, and entrusted her to his chief minister with the instruction, "Give her to a street-sweeper!"

King Puruṣottama's intelligent minister kept Padmavatī carefully protected and hidden until Ratha-yātrā the following year. When King Puruṣottama came forward to perform *chera-pahanra*, the clever minister brought forth beautiful Padmavatī. "Your Majesty," he said, "you ordered me to deliver this girl to a street-sweeper, and now you are so engaged. Please take her and protect her."[5]

A famous painting depicting this pastime now adorns the Jagannātha temple complex.

Among other valuables collected during this invasion of Kañci was the deity of Sakṣi Gopāla. The deity was carried back to Purī and placed in the Jagannātha temple for some time.

After the king has completed his sweeping duties and returned to his palace, Lord Balarāma's cart is then pulled by thousands of eager men and women. Taladvāja moves forward in rhythm with the thun-

---

[5] See *Amṛta-pravāha-bhāṣya*, *Caitanya-caritāmṛta* (*Madhya-līlā* Chapter 5 summary), and in *Part Three, Historical Influences Prior to the 15th Century* chapter entitled *Puruṣottama (1467–1497)*. Note: some historians note that Padmavatī was also known as Rūpamvikā.

dering of the crowds and proceeds down *Badadanda* (Grand Road) toward the Guṇḍicā Temple.

Subhadrā's cart is second, and then Lord Jagannātha's cart follows last. The only scheduled stop along the way is at *Balagaṇḍi*, where the *rathas* stop to allow the *pūjārīs* to make delicious food offerings. It takes several hours to pull the massive carts the almost two kilometers to the Guṇḍicā temple. If for some reason the chariots do not arrive at the Guṇḍicā temple by sunset, the celebration continues the following day. The deities do not travel by night.[6]

## Herā-pañcamī

The Herā-pañcamī festival takes place on the sixth day of the bright fortnight in Āṣāḍha. Lakṣmī, the goddess of fortune and wife of Lord Jagannātha, becomes upset because her husband has gone away for such a long time during His vacation at the Guṇḍicā temple. Therefore, she dresses in regal attire and advances by palanquin to chastise Him. According to descriptions in the *Caitanya-caritāmṛta*, this festival took place during the morning hours five hundred years ago.[7] Today, the function takes place very late at night.[8]

## Bahudā-yātrā

Lord Jagannātha, Balarāma, Subhadrā, and Sudarśana *cakra* remain at the Guṇḍicā temple for eight or nine days, depending on how long it takes for the Ratha-yātrā to bring them to Guṇḍicā. On the tenth day of the bright fortnight in *Āṣāḍha*, they again board the chariots for their return trip, which is known as Bahudā-yātrā. The ceremonies and rituals are virtually the same as those already described for the Ratha-yātrā. However, while returning to His temple, Lord Jagannātha's chariot stops at the Ardhasani Temple, where the goddess offers Him a nice cheesecake.

---

[6] See *Lord Caitanya's Purī Pastimes*, chapter heading *Ratha-yātrā*, for further descriptions of Ratha-yātrā.

[7] *Caitanya-caritāmṛta* (*Madhya-līlā* 14.113, 233)

[8] See *Herā-pañcamī* in *Lord Caitanya's Purī Pastimes* for some beautiful descriptions and inner meanings of this festival.

Festival-goers may be advised that during Ratha-yātrā the massive crowds are zealous and full of anticipation. At times they become uncontrolled, even rowdy. Some people are uncomfortable in such an atmosphere, especially in India, while others enjoy the zesty spirit. If you don't like crowds, you can make arrangements a few days in advance to view the celebration from one of the many buildings along the route—get there early in the morning, or it will be difficult to fight the crowds.

During Bahudā-yātrā, however, the crowd is much more controlled. The Orissan police have plenty of men and women on duty during the entire ten days, but have their hands full controlling crowds of nearly one million people. If you plan to attend Ratha-yātrā or Bahudā-yātrā, consider bringing a small umbrella; during that time of year either you have to stand in the hot sun or it rains.

### Padma / Śayanā-ekādaśī And Suna-veṣa

The day after Bahudā-yātrā is Padma Ekādaśī, or Śayanā-ekādaśī. After returning from the Guṇḍicā Temple, Lord Jagannātha, Balarāma, Subhadrā, and Sudarśana *cakra* remain overnight on their chariots in front of the *Siṁha-dvāra* gate at the Jagannātha temple. On the Ekādaśī evening they are regally dressed in golden (*suna*) outfits. Visitors from all over Orissa and from neighboring states perform a special pilgrimage to take *darśana* on this mystical night. Local villagers place tarps over their bullock carts and line Grand Road with these simple dwellings. The police do an excellent job, always moving the rather mellow crowd so everyone has a chance to see the majestic deities dressed in sparkling gold armor.

Finally, on Dvādaśī, the deities return to the main temple. First Balarāma, Sudarśana *cakra*, and Subhadrā enter the temple. Then Lord Jagannātha begins His journey. As He approaches the temple, however, Lakṣmī-devi's servants close the door! A haughty dialogue then takes place between Lord Jagannātha's servants and Lakṣmī-devi's servants until finally Lord Jagannātha pacifies His wife with promises of precious gifts. He is then allowed back into the temple.

## Śayanotsava

*Cāturmāsya* begins during the bright fortnight of Āṣāḍha, from the day of Śayanā-ekādaśī. This period ends in Kārttika on Utthānā-ekādaśī, in the fortnight of the waxing moon. On Śayanā-ekādaśī, Lord Viṣṇu goes to sleep for the four months of the rainy season (*cātur* = four, *masya* = month). During these four months, all sections of society are recommended to follow strict vows and reduce their sense gratification.[9]

While the deities are on their chariots before the *Simha-dvāra* gate, they are offered special *bhoga*. Afterward, Ananta-Vāsudeva, Śrī Nārāyaṇa, and Bhuvaneṇśvarī come from the main temple onto the chariots. *Mahā-snāna* is then performed for them with sixteen articles of worship. The three *utsava* deities (ceremonial deities used in place for the larger ones) are later brought back to the main temple and placed in a special bed-chamber. They are then put to sleep by mantra.

## Jhulana-yātrā

From the tenth bright day of Śravana until the full moon, Madanamohana is brought daily to the *Mukti Maṇḍapa* and swung on a *jhulana*, or swing. This festival commemorates the Lord Kṛṣṇa's swinging pastimes in the forests of Vṛndāvana.

## Balarāma Janma

Lord Balarāma appeared on the full-moon day of Śravana. On this *tithi*, Sudarśana *cakra* is taken on a palanquin to Mārkaṇḍeya Tank. Temple servants known as *bisoi* and *sudusuara* work together to sculpt a figure of Balarāma on the banks of the lake. The *pūjā panda* installs the deity, then worships Lord Balarāma with five *upacāras*. After proper worship, the form of Balarāma is immersed in the sacred waters, and Sudarśana *cakra* returns to the temple.

---

[9] See *Caitanya-caritāmṛta* (*Madhya-līlā* 4.169). It should also be noted here that Lord Viṣṇu's sleep is not like our sleep. When the Lord sleeps it is called *yoga-nidra*, a mystic slumber.

## Kṛṣṇa Janmāṣṭamī

Throughout India this is one of the most widely celebrated festivals. On the eighth day of the dark fortnight in Bhādra, Śrī Kṛṣṇa appeared in the prison of His demoniac uncle, Kaṁsa. Born of Vasudeva and Devakī, Kṛṣṇa was then secretly transferred to the home of Nanda and Yaśodā in Gokula, where He and Balarāma were later brought up. Many childhood pastimes of Kṛṣṇa and Balarāma are reenacted by temple servants, lasting a little more than two weeks. Every day from the seventh day of the dark fortnight until the tenth day of the bright fortnight different plays are performed at various sites around the temple compound.

## Uttaravana-yātrā and Daksinayanotsava

Twice a year the sun crosses the equator, before its northern and southern journeys. On the day before Makara-saṅkrānti (when the sun begins moving north), Sali rice is prepared. At midnight the deities are worshiped with offerings of camphor, *ārati*, garlands, etc. The mobile *utsava* deities are then offered the Sali rice, *dūrvā* grass, mustard flowers, and new cloth. After receiving these items, they circumambulate the temple to the accompaniment of musical instruments. During this procession the Lord is worshiped as Trivikrama, the *brāhmaṇa*-dwarf who blessed Bali Mahārāja. The morning after, Makara-saṅkrānti, the Sali rice is mixed with ghee, yogurt, sugar, and camphor, and offered to Lord Jagannātha, Balarāma, and Subhadrā on silver plates.

Six months later, on the day before Karkata Sakranti (when the sun moves south), the deities are bathed with *pañcāmṛta* and smeared with sandalwood paste, *aguru*, and *kuṅkuma*. *Ārati* and *homa* are performed, then offerings of new cloth, flower garlands, etc., are presented to the deities and *brāhmaṇas*.

## Dasahera or Durgā Puja

From the first day of the dark fortnight in Aśvina to the Ekādaśī day, a grand festival is held for Bimalā-devī in the compound of the Jagannātha temple. Bimalā-devī is the prototype of Durgā-devī, the material energy personified. The appearance and activities of Durgā are narrated in the *Devī-māhātmya*, also known as *Durgā Saptasati* or *Caṇḍi*, a seven-hundred-verse section of the *Mārkaṇḍeya Purāṇa*.

According to the text, there have been many instances in universal history wherein the personification of material energy, Durgā, fought against demoniac influences. Her most famous battle was with a demon named Mahiṣāsura, who had acquired such mystic *siddhis* that he could change his form at will. This demon performed unbearable austerities and in turn received various benedictions from the powerful demigods. When asked what blessings he desired, Mahiṣāsura requested that he not be killed in heaven or on earth, and that he not to be killed by any man, demigod, or animal. Like Hiraṇyakaśipu, the rascal tried to outwit the laws of nature and become immortal. In his quest for immortality, however, he never asked for protection from women, considering them far inferior to himself.

After perfecting his various mystical powers, this *asura* terrorized the entire universe and usurped the position of all-powerful *devas* (universal administrators). These demigods then assembled and tried to find some way to stop the tyrant, but without success. Finally, they approached the Supreme Lord Viṣṇu and prayed for His protection.

After Lord Viṣṇu heard of the demigods' plight, a great light shone forth from His transcendental body, and a female form came into being. Material energy thus personified in the form of a beautiful woman riding a lion. She had ten arms, all carrying deadly weapons, and was endowed with extremely attractive feminine features. At that time, all the demigods bestowed blessings and mystic powers upon that woman, named Durgā.

When a battle finally took place between the *devas* and *asuras*, Durgā-devī exhibited her immense powers. Innumerable battalions of soldiers appeared from her breathing and began to devastate the demons. Infuriated at his army's defeat, Mahiṣāsura charged Durgā-devī as she rode on her lion.

Mahiṣāsura assumed the form of a gigantic buffalo. Crushed by the speed of his whirling here and there, the earth broke into tiny bits. When he lashed his huge tail, a tidal wave flooded the land. His swaying horns scattered clouds, and mountain ranges were reduced to dust by his blasting breath. Seeing the immense buffalo advancing, Durgā prepared for battle.

As the buffalo approached, Durgā flung a noose over its head and bound the animal. Suddenly, the buffalo became a lion. Durgā immediately cut off the lion's head with her sword. Mahiṣāsura then assumed the form of a man with a sword in hand, but Durgā chopped off his hands with her arrows. Then he became an elephant and attacked Devī's lion carrier, but as he was attempting to drag her lion away, Durgā cut off his trunk with a sharp sword.

The *asura* then again assumed the form of a buffalo and shook the entire outer space. The buffalo hurled mountains at Durgā-devī with his powerful horns. Enraged, Durgā-devī quickly drank a divine beverage provided by the other demigods. Her eyes now red with intoxication, Durgā pulverized the mountains with her arrows. She screamed in fury and pounced upon the buffalo, pressing its head to the ground with her foot. At that time, the defeated *asura* assumed his natural form as Mahiṣāsura.

The ten-day festival to commemorate Durgā's victory, known as Durgā-pūjā, is also an integral part of the tantric worship at the Jagannātha temple (see plate 19). During Mahāṣṭamī and Mahānaumi, three goats are offered in sacrifice before the Bimalā-devī deity.[10]

Curiously, this festival is extremely popular throughout Orissa. Although most people worship Jagannātha, Durgā holds such esteem that during this two week period government employees take leave, all public and private schools are closed, each neighborhood erects a Durgā deity, and numerous *pūjās* are held all over the state.

## Parsva-parivartana

On Ekādaśī during the bright moon in Bhādra, Lord Viṣṇu turns over while sleeping. The three *utsava* deities in the bed-chamber are bathed and offered sandalwood pulp in the morning. Later, the mobile *utsava* deity, Madana-mohana, is taken on procession around the temple. After evening *ārati*, the deities are offered flowers, and turned over in Their beds.

---

[10] See *Śrīmad-Bhāgavatam* (4.19.36) purport.

### Utthapanotsava or Prabodhana-yātrā

Utthānā-ekādaśī is the day Lord Viṣṇu awakens after four months of Caturmasya. In the evening, the three *uttsava* deities are awakened and placed on silver platters. *Mahā-snāna* is performed, then they go to the *ratna-siṁhāsana* to stand with Lord Jagannātha, Balarāma, and Subhadrā. Ananta-Vāsudeva, Śrī Nārāyaṇa, and Bhuvaneśvarī are then offered new clothes, flower garlands, ornaments, and *ārati* before retiring to a special room prepared for them.

### Kṛtika Dipavali

A fascinating lamp festival is performed on the fourth day of Margasira. This is a popular evening throughout India, and families everywhere place ghee lamps or candles at various places throughout their homes. On this evening thousands of years ago, Lord Rāma and His beloved consort Sitā finally returned to Their capital city, Ayodhya, after defeating the evil *rākṣasa* Rāvaṇa. As they traveled through the sky on a mystic airplane, the people below lit lights and torches to illuminate Their path.

### Oḍana-ṣaṣṭhī or Parvaranotsava

The sixth day of the bright fortnight in Mārgaśīrṣa is the first day of winter. New winter clothing is offered on this day to keep the deities warm. The purified cloth is carried in a procession around the temple three times, then presented to the deities during the morning dressing period. In the *Caitanya-caritāmṛta* (*Madhya-līlā* 16.76–81) it is described that one year one of Lord Caitanya's associates, Puṇḍarīka Vidyānidhi, saw that the cloth to be used during this festival was still full of starch because it hadn't been properly washed. Puṇḍarīka Vidyānidhi then began mentally offending the priest responsible for this oversight. That night as Puṇḍarīka slept, Lord Jagannātha and Lord Balarāma came to him and, smiling, began to slap his cheeks because of his mentally offending Their servant. Although his cheeks were swollen from the slapping, Puṇḍarīka Vidyānidhi was happy within.

### Puṣyābhiṣeka

Eighty-one pots are brought before the deities on the full-moon day in Pauṣa. Twenty-one pots are filled with ghee (clarified butter), the rest with clean, fresh water. All these pots are placed upon the *bhoga-maṇḍapa* under a colorful canopy. A large mirror is then placed before the deities. After morning rituals, *brāhmaṇas* perform a fire sacrifice and the deities put on new clothes. Water mixed with ghee is then poured before the mirror placed in front of Lord Jagannātha. Shortly after, Lakṣmī-devī is brought and bathed in a similar way. Temple servants also participate, representing Lakṣmaṇa and Hanumān. During this festival, also known as Rāmābhiṣeka, Lord Jagannātha is seen as Lord Rāmacandra, and Lakṣmī-devī as Sītā.

### Dola-yātrā

Dola-yātrā is celebrated in Purī on the full-moon day in Phalguna (also Lord Caitanya's appearance day). Dola-govinda is brought from the temple to the *dola-vedi* (swing platform). For five days prior to Dola-yātrā, various rituals are performed inside the main temple. Lakṣmī and Sarasvatī also travel by palanquin to the Jagannātha Vallabha Gardens during those days. On Cāturdaśī, *homa* is performed in the evening at the *dola-vedi*, while Holi is celebrated at the Lakṣmī temple inside the main temple compound.

During the afternoon of Pūrṇimā (at about 2 p.m. in 1990), the *utsava* deities circumambulate the main temple seven times (see plate 17). Then they go out in a simple procession through Lakṣmī Bazaar, stop at the Satya-Nārāyaṇa Temple for a few moments, and then proceed to circumambulate the *dola-mandapa* seven more times. According to the *Skanda Purāṇa*, the *dola-mandapa* should be constructed with sixteen pillars. The deities circumambulate these pillars seven times, then go around the swing another seven times. During the entire procession, musical instruments are played and red powder called *phagu* is tossed on the deities. Finally, their Lordships are placed upon the swing (*dola*). As Kṛṣṇa enjoyed swinging with His friends in the Vṛndāvana forests, so Dola-govinda enjoys swinging for the day with His consorts. In the evening, the deities return to the main temple.

Those who have visited India during this time of year know that it is customary to throw colored powder not only on the deities, but at each other. In Purī, the custom is to throw colors only on the deities the day of the full moon, and at each other the day after. Beware!

### Rāmanavamī

On the ninth day of the waxing moon in the month of Caitra, Lord Rāmacandra appeared in Ayodhya. For almost a week, temple servants reenact the pastimes of Rāma, Lakṣmaṇa, Sītā, and Hanumān throughout the temple complex and town of Puri. On Rāma-naumi, temple servants play the parts of Daśaratha and Kauśalya, while the Lord appears and *saṁskāras* are performed. On Daśami (the tenth day), *yajña-līlā* is performed, while the marriage between Sītā and Rāma is played on Ekādaśī. Rāma goes to the forest on the twelfth day, Sītā is abducted on the fourteenth, and Hanumān burns Laṅka on the full moon. On the first day of Vaiśākha, the army crosses the ocean, and on the second day of Vaiśākha, Lord Rāma kills the demon Rāvaṇa.

### Damana-bhanjika

The *Puruṣottama-kṣetra-mahātmya* tells us that in ancient times there was a demon named Damanāsura. Although Damanāsura lived in the sea, he enjoyed harassing *brāhmaṇas* and saintly people on the land. At Lord Brahmā's request, Lord Kṛṣṇa assumed the form of a fish and killed the demon. This pastime took place on the fourteenth day of the bright moon in Caitra. A unique type of grass, known as *damanaka* grass, grew on the shore where the Lord killed the demon. Nowadays the *utsava* deities of Rama-Kṛṣṇa (Kṛṣṇa-Balarāma) and a picture of Cupid are carried by palanquin to the Jagannātha Vallabha Gardens. There they are worshiped and offered two *damanaka* plants in commemoration of that battle. After Rama-Kṛṣṇa and Cupid are carried back to the main temple, Lord Jagannātha, Balarāma, and Subhadrā are also offered *damanaka* plants to hold.

### Aksaya-tṛtiya

*Aksaya-tṛitya* is the third day of the bright fortnight in the month of Vaisaka. The day before *tṛtiya*, fifteen seers of sandalwood paste are prepared and sanctified by ritual. On *tṛtiya* (third day of the moon) the deities are bathed with *mahā-snāna*, dressed in new garments, then smeared or painted with the sandalwood paste (*candana-yātā*). Sandalwood paste has a pleasant, cooling effect during this hot time of the year.

The *utsava* deities, Rāma-Kṛṣṇa and Madana-mohana, are then brought to the *ratna-siṁhāsana*. After worship, They leave the main temple along with Lakṣmī and Sarasvatī. The deities are then transported by palanquin to Narendra Sarovara for a boat ride.

As mentioned before, *Akṣaya-tṛtīyā* is the first day of summer and the day carpenters begin their work on the Ratha-yātrā chariots.

### Candan-yātrā

This charming festival continues for twenty-one days, starting on *Akṣaya-tṛtīyā* and ending on the eighth day in the dark half of Jyeṣṭhā. Grand Road is decorated with mango leaves, fruits, and various newly sprouted plants, which are hung overhead on simple wooden structures. Each evening at about 8 p.m., Rāma-Kṛṣṇa, Madana-mohana, Lakṣmī, Sarasvatī, and five Mahādevas (Śiva *utsava* deities) travel by palanquin to Narendra-sarovara. Upon arrival at the lake, they board two boats to the accompaniment of pleasing musical instruments. A boat with a white canopy is reserved for Madana-mohana, Lakṣmī, and Sarasvatī, whereas a boat with a red canopy is meant for Rāma-Kṛṣṇa and the five Mahādevas. (See plate 18)

While drums beat rhythmically, the two boats circle the *sarovara* four times, allowing the deities to enjoy a cooling boat ride during the humid summer evenings. In days gone by, a *deva-dāsī* would dance on the white boat, while a young boy would dance on the other, but this practice is no longer performed. On the last of the twenty-one days, the shores of the lake are specially decorated and the boats circumambulate twenty-one times rather than four.

### Rukmiṇīharaṇa

To celebrate the pastime of Kṛṣṇa kidnapping Princess Rukmiṇī to win her hand in marriage, one of the temple servants plays the part of foolish Śiśupāla. His *sikhā* is fastened to the back of Madana-mohana's palanquin, then the deity goes on procession around the temple, amusing all the devotees who join in the fun. This celebration takes place on the Ekādaśī day of Jyeṣṭhā.

### Ekādaśī

After *Sandhya-ārati* on the eleventh day of the waxing and waning moon of every month, a lamp (*mahā-dipa*) is placed on the top of the temple, just below the Nīla-*cakra*.

### Navakalevara

Navakalevara is not an annual festival. This unique ceremony was observed only five times during the twentieth century: in 1931, 1950, 1969, 1977, and 1996. Navakalevara (*nava* = new, *kalevara* = embodiment) is the process of replacing the four deities of Lord Jagannātha, Balarāma, Subhadrā, and Sudarśana *cakra*. The entire proceedings, filled with secret mystical rituals and uncommon Vedic rites, take more than three months.

The appropriate time for Navakalevara is determined when there are two full moons during the month of Āṣādha (June–July).[11] When this occurs, an additional month is added to the Vedic calendar. At least one year in advance, temple astrologers calculate the position of the planets, then temple authorities decide whether or not the ceremony is necessary. If the deities do not need to be replaced or the treasury can't handle the added expense, then there is no absolute rule saying this ceremony must be observed. An additional month in the Vedic calendar, known as *Adhimāsa*, *Malamāsa*, or *Puruṣottamamāsa*, is observed by Vaiṣṇavas throughout India by chanting names of God, reciting holy texts, and performing special *pūjās* to Viṣṇu.

The history of Navakalevara is obscure. No published manuscripts exist detailing the intricacies of the rituals because they have been passed down from father to son orally or on palm-leaf scrolls, which have then been kept by individual families. Navakalevara has probably been a semi-regular function of the temple since the fifteenth

---

[11] See *Appendixes* for explanation of calendar months. Note: the phenomena of having two full moons in the same month is commonly called a "Blue Moon." Thus the popular phrase "once in a blue moon" originates from this occurrence.

century, and was probably observed before that on an even less regulated basis. (There are records that Yayati Kesari renovated the deities during the ninth century.)[12]

There are five basic aspects to the proceedings, which will be described one after another:[13]

(1) Search for the *dāru* (sacred trees), study of their unique characteristics, and ceremonies to cut them.
(2) Procession back to Purī and carving the wood.
(3) Consecration of the new deities by transferring the *brahma-pādartha*.
(4) Burial of the old figures, the funeral, and purification of the *dayitās*.
(5) Addition of several layers of material over the wood and final painting.

## Search for the Dāru

*Dayitās* begin searching for sacred trees to be used to fashion the new deities on the tenth day of the bright fortnight in the month of Caitra, sixty-five days before Snāna-yātrā. Accompanied by *Pati Mahāpātra*, twenty-eight *dayitās* meet at the Jagannātha temple to perform some short *pujās*.[14] Each receives three *ājñāmālās*, flower garlands, to signify that they are authorized to search for the wood. The rite of accepting an *ājñāmālā* from the deities as a sign of their permission for a specific task is a common practice in rituals at the Jagannātha temple.

After receiving the *ājñāmālā*, three of the chief *dayitās* are presented a six-meter length of silk *sari* (unstitched garment), while the others receive a two-meter length. Another servant called the *mekapa*

[12] See heading *Śankarācārya* in *Part Three, Historical Influences Prior to the 15th Century*

[13] The bulk of this data comes from G.C. Tripathi's article in *The Cult of Jagannatha and the Regional Tradition of Orissa*, and another article, entitled *Lord Jagannātha's "Change of Body Pastimes,"* in *Śrī Kṛṣṇa-kathāmṛta*.

[14] In 1996 there were forty-seven members of the party, so this must not be a fixed number.

then applies sandalwood paste and red powder to the foreheads of all the *dayitās* to mark the auspicious beginning of the search.

The *Bitarachu Mahāpātra* then comes to the *Jaya-Vijaya* gate (doorway between the *Jagamohana* and *Nāṭmandir*) and wraps the silk garments onto the foreheads of the *Deula Karana* (secretary), *Tadhau Karana* (accountant), and *Beharana Khuntia*. The four *Visvakarmas* (carpenters) and the *Lenka* (carrier of the *cakra* during processions) are then presented a *silpi-sari* made of cotton.

The whole party then comes out of the temple to the accompaniment of trumpets, conchshells, drums, and gongs, and proceeds to the king's palace, located on Grand Road. The king greets the party and offers two metal plates filled with auspicious articles, including coconuts, gold pieces, and colored thread, to the *rājaguru*, who in turn offers these articles to the leader of the *dayitās*. *Dayitās*, as mentioned in connection with the *anavasara* ceremony, are descendents of the Śabara tribe and play an important role in the Navakalevara ceremony. Although twenty-eight *dayitās* are chosen for the traveling party, only twenty-one go on the search. The remaining six stay behind as reserves. After meeting with the King of Purī, the entire group moves further down Grand Road to the Jagannātha Vallabha Math, where they remain for a day or two, making final preparations.

Early on an auspicious morning, the entire party then travels barefoot (no motorized vehicles are used during the entire proceedings) more than fifty kilometers to the temple of Maṅgala-devī, located in the small village of Kakatpur on the banks of the Praci River, northeast of Purī. Messengers are sent ahead to announce the arrival of the *Vanayātrā* party, and the priests of Maṅgala-devī come forward to receive and welcome them with festive music. The *Vanayātrā* party in turn offers Maṅgala-devī a new garment and *mahā-prasādam* from Lord Jagannātha.

The priests of Maṅgalā-devī then perform an elaborate worship of the goddess, beginning with a ceremonial bath. While these *pūjās* are being performed, four *paṇḍitas* accompanying the *Vanayātrā* party and the *ācārya* recite the *Durgā-saptāsaū*. That evening, the *ācārya*, *brāhmaṇas*, and *Pati Mahāpātra* remain in the Maṅgala-devī temple. It is believed that while they are sleeping, the goddess Maṅgala-devī appears in a dream to one of these men and reveals the location of the sacred trees. In order to propitiate her, the *Svapnavatī* mantra is chanted 108 times immediately before the men go to sleep. As an alternative, Lord Nṛsiṁhadeva's *mantrarāja* is sometimes chanted an equal number of times.

If after three days Maṅgala-devī has not indicated the location of the trees, the priests again perform elaborate worship and the goddess is gorgeously bedecked with decorative flowers (see plate 20).

The first flower that falls down from the deity is then taken as a sign to indicate the direction where the first *dāru* is to be found, and subsequent falling flowers reveal directions for the three remaining trees. As we can easily imagine, trees used to fashion deities are not ordinary, mundane trees. Ancient texts and oral descriptions passed down from generation to generation describe the several unique characteristics that the tree must possess. Although each tree may not have all these characteristics, at least several noted features must be manifest. All four trees must be of *nīm* wood (*Melia Azadirachta*).

Dāru for Lord Jagannātha

(1) Color must be dark (*miśra*) or dark-red (*manjistha*).
(2) Trunk must be straight and pleasant to look at, and must be 7–12 cubits in height.
(3) Trunk should have four main branches.
(4) The tree should stand near a river or pond, near a crossing of three ways, or surrounded by three mountains.
(5) There should be a cremation ground near the tree.
(6) A Śiva temple should be near by.
(7) A hermitage should be close by.
(8) The tree must be free of parasite plants and creepers.
(9) There should not be nests of (carnivorous, according to some) birds on the tree.
(10) The tree should never have been struck by lightning, partially broken by storms, etc.
(11) There should be an anthill near by.
(12) There should be signs of snakes in the area.
(13) The trunk must contain sacred signs of Lord Viṣṇu, *śaṅkha* (conchshell), *cakra* (disc), *padma* (lotus flower), or *gada* (club).

(14) The tree should be surrounded by other trees, preferably *varuṇa*, *sahada*, or *bilva*, should be a distance from human settlements, and must not be situated in a marsh or swamp.

Dāru for Lord Baladeva

(1) Bark of the tree must be white or light brown.
(2) This tree should preferably have seven main branches.
(3) The upper branches should form a canopy, looking like the hood of a cobra.
(4) The tree should bear signs of a plough and club, the weapons of Lord Balarāma.

Dāru for Subhadrā

(1) Bark of this tree should have a yellowish tinge.
(2) The tree should have five main branches.
(3) It should have signs of a lotus flower with five petals.

Dāru for Sudarśana *Cakra*

(1) Bark should be reddish.
(2) The tree should have three main branches.
(3) It should bear the sign of a *cakra* (lines looking like spokes) with a small depression in the middle.

The order of selecting these *dārus*, transporting them back to Purī, and finally changing the *brahmapadartha* ("life-substance") remains the same for each function: first Sudarśana, then Balarāma, Subhadrā, and finally Lord Jagannātha.

The quest for the *dārus* sometimes lasts as long as three weeks. Members of the search party go out daily to search for the trees, then return each night to Kakatpur, where a camp is set up at the Deuli monastery, which is managed by the Rāmānuja-*sampradāya*. All of the participants walk barefoot, and all of them eat only one simple meal a day as they trek through the jungles and forests in search of the *dāru*.

When a sacred tree is finally located, members of the *Vana-*

*yātrā* party clear the surrounding area of brush and debris, place a Sudarśana *cakra* near its roots to ward off evil, and perform a small fire sacrifice. The tree is then circumambulated seven times to the accompaniment of musical instruments, sprinkled with water, smeared with sandalwood paste and vermilion, offered flowers, wrapped with a piece of new cloth, and finally offered the *ājñāmālā* of the deity it will become. After performing this small worship, a *yajña-śālā*, or sacrificial pavilion, is erected on the western side of the tree. The search party then remains by the tree rather than returning to Kakatpur. (See plate 21)

The next two or three days are filled with various rituals, fire sacrifices, and the chanting of mantras. A small campsite is established, and the remaining members of the *Vanayātrā* party set up tents nearby. The rituals are so elaborate that I cannot describe them all here. Readers who would like to read about these finer points may refer to Mr. Tripathi's article. When all the rites have been completed, the *ācārya* announces to Viṣṇu that he is now going to cut the tree. He chants the *mantrarāja* of Lord Nṛiṁhadeva and hands a small golden ax to the *Pati Mahāpātra*. The *Pati Mahāpātra* then moves around the tree clockwise while making a few symbolic strokes to the tree. All of the assembled *brāhmaṇas* chant Vedic hymns, especially the *Viṣṇu-sūkta*, while others play musical instruments.

After offering symbolic strokes with the golden ax, the *Pati Mahāpātra* then performs the same rituals again, this time with a small silver ax. (He is then allowed to keep both axes, which are each about the size of a dangling earring.) Finally, the *ācārya* surcharges a full-sized iron ax with a Sudarśana mantra and hands it to the carpenters (*viśvakarmas*). The *viśvakarmas* cut the tree while chanting the holy names of Lord Hari. Others chant Vedic hymns or play instruments. (See plate 22)

The tree should fall in the eastern, northern, or northeastern direction. Otherwise, it is considered inauspicious. Only the trunk of the tree is required, so after a large part of the trunk has been cut, the rest of the tree, along with its branches and leaves, is buried in a large hole that has been dug while the rites were being performed on previous days. The carpenters sometimes keep some of the larger branches, or even other parts of the trunk, to make the deities' arms. If these pieces are not used during the carving of the deities, they are kept in storage throughout the years in case the deities ever need repair.

### Procession Back to Purī and Carving the Wood

While the trunk of the tree is being prepared, other *viśvakarmas* in the *Vanayātrā* party cut nearby trees to construct a cart to transport the *dāru* back to Purī. There are specifications even for this: the cart's platform should be made from a *kendu* tree, the wheels from a *vata* tree, and the axle of tamarind wood. These are common trees in Orissa and are almost always readily available near the site where the sacred tree has been located.

The construction of the cart is simple. Two long pieces of *kendu* wood are joined together with cross bars or planks, and the wheels are three planks of wood joined together with iron clamps.

When all is ready, the *dāru* is lifted onto the cart while *brāhmaṇas* loudly chant various mantras. The *dāru* is then wrapped in colorful cloth and tied securely to the cart with ropes (see plate 23).

Party members who will be returning to Purī with that particular *dāru* then begin to pull the cart, starting in a direction considered auspicious for the day. (It is said in the *Vedas* that wood used to fashion a deity must be pulled by human hands rather than bullocks or other animals.) It is considered inauspicious to undertake a journey toward the east on Monday or Saturday, to the south on Thursday, toward the west on Sunday or Friday, on toward the north on Tuesday or Wednesday.

As the *Vanayātrā* party gradually proceeds toward Purī, villagers along the route, eager to take part in the function, assist by pulling the cart, offering flowers and prayers, and playing musical instruments. When the party finally reaches the outskirts of Purī, word is sent ahead to the temple priests. By the time the *dāru* arrives, a large crowd of people has gathered to greet it. As the procession continues along Grand Road toward the Jagannātha temple, onlookers play instruments, offer prayers, carry colorful festoons, or simply walk along with others until the *dāru* is transported to the inner compounds of the Jagannātha temple grounds, where a special pavilion has been erected. All the *darus* must reach the temple by the full-moon day in the month of Jyestha, for this is the day of Snāna Pūrṇimā.

On the Snāna Pūrṇimā day, the deities of Jagannātha, Balarāma, Subhadrā, and Sudarśana *cakra* are publicly bathed on a platform erected at the northeast corner of the temple. This ceremony has been described earlier under the "Festival" heading "Snāna-yātrā." Simultaneous to the public bathing, the newly procured *darus* are bathed privately in a shed constructed for them in the inner compounds of the temple. During a year with the double Āṣāḍha, the Jagannātha temple remains closed for the following six weeks after *Snāna-yātrā*, during which time the carving of the new deities takes place, along with the transference of the *brahmapadartha*.

The day after Snāna-yātrā, the *dārus* are transferred to a newly constructed area in the inner compound called *Nirmana-mandapa*. There the carpenters begin to carve the new deities. According to *Puruṣottama-kṣetra-mahātmya*, the only people allowed to take part in this work are the descendents of Viśvavasu and Vidyāpati. These carpenters receive silk turbans from the King of Purī on the first day of the dark half of Āṣāḍha as a symbolical authorization to begin. They start carving on the second day of the dark fortnight. It is also mentioned in *Puruṣottama-kṣetra-mahātmya* that no one should see or hear the carpenters' work. Thus devotees create tumultuous sounds just outside the *Nirmana-mandapa* by playing musical instruments.

Carving techniques used to fashion the deities are a closely guarded secret. Carpenters shape the *mūrtis* according to old palm-leaf manuscripts which they possess in their families, and some details are recorded in the *Madalapanji*. According to temple chronicles, the height of Lord Balarāma, Lord Jagannātha, and Sudarśana *cakra* amounts to eighty-four *yavas* each, while Subhadrā-devī is only fifty-two and a half *yavas* in height.[15]

The arms of both Lord Jagannātha and Lord Balarāma are added separately to the main body of the *mūrti*. Each arm is constructed of two pieces—one piece inserted into the shoulder area and protruding left or right from the main body, and one added to that, projecting forward. The length of Lord Jagannātha's arms, if added together, equals

[15] A *yava* (barley corn) equals the length of the middle part of the carpenter's middle finger, or approximately one inch.

His total height of eighty-four *yavas*. In this way, each arm is forty-two *yavas* long. The side arm protruding left or right has a length of twenty *yavas*, out of which twelve are invisible since they are inserted into the main body. The arms projecting forward are each twenty-two *yavas* in length. Thus each arm has a length of forty-two *yavas*, out of which twelve *yavas* are not visible.

Lord Balarāma's arms are thirty-six and three-quarter *yavas* each, or seventy-three and one half *yavas* when added together. They are similarly divided into two parts. The side arm is thirteen and three-quarter *yavas* long, out of which seven *yavas* remain inserted into the main body and are invisible. The rest of the six and three-quarter *yavas* protrude outward to the left or right. The length of the two front pieces amounts to twenty-three *yavas* each, one more *yava* than Lord Jagannātha's arms. However, the total length of Lord Baladeva's arms is still shorter than Lord Jagannātha's by almost ten *yavas*. Carpenters work for thirteen days carving all four forms, and in each *mūrti* they include a cavity where the mysterious substance known as *brahmapadartha* will be placed.

## Consecration of New Deities By Transferring Brahmapadartha

While the carpenters are fashioning the *mūrtis*, the *brāhmaṇa* priests and the *rājaguru* perform other ceremonies. The *pratiṣṭhā* consecration ceremonies they perform are unlike any other known *pratiṣṭhā* ceremonies in the world. Because the *mūrtis* have not yet been completed, the *pratiṣṭhā* rituals are performed on a separate piece of wood known as the *nyāsa dāru*, rather than with the entire deity. Elaborate rituals and ceremonies continue for two weeks, after which the *nyāsa dāru* is cut into four pieces of specified dimensions. Each piece will later be used to seal the cavity in the *mūrtis*.

On the first day (*dvitiya* of Āṣāḍha) the King of Purī nominates the *ācārya*, which signifies the beginning of the ceremonies. Several *maṇḍalas* are then drawn at various locations in the *pratiṣṭhā maṇḍapa*, located to the east of the shed where the carpenters are working. The *ācārya*, clad in white, performs a small *pūjā* to Lord Nṛsiṁha on the *cakrabjamaṇḍala* to invoke the Lord's blessings, then worships Ganeśa, the *dikpalas*, and the other *devatas*, who have been placed in water pitchers by mantra. He also offers *bali* (earth) to the *dikpālas* and *bhūtas* outside the *maṇḍapa*. This offering of *bali* continues each evening, and on the seventh lunar day (*saptami*), live *madgura* fish are brought into the temple, sacrificed to the *dikpalas* and *bhūtas*, then buried outside the *pratiṣṭhā maṇḍapa* in each of the ten directions. The offering of fish or any other animal is strictly forbidden in all other Vaiṣṇava temples around the world, and unfortunately the history and reason for this practice in the Jagannatha temple is now obscured by time.

On the sixth day, the *nyāsa dāru* is bathed in an *abhiśeka* ceremony. To begin, 108 offerings of clarified butter are offered in a fire sacrifice. Then the remaining ghee is sprinkled on each of ninety-eight pitchers containing water for the bathing ceremony (seventeen of these pitchers contain special ingredients in addition to sacred water). A talisman containing mustard seeds and *durva* grass is then tied around the *nyāsa dāru* to ward off evil, and finally the *nyāsa dāru* is placed upon a raised platform on the *Snāna-maṇḍapa*.

The *nyāsa dāru* is first bathed with the seventeen pitchers of water, each of which also contains flowers, fragrance, saffron, sand from the banks of the Ganges, fruits, ghee, and similar ingredients. The remaining eighty-one pitchers are kept on eighty-one squares drawn on a *Vastumaṇḍala*. Then water from them is poured into one large pitcher *(sashasradhara-kumbha)*, which is punched with innumerable holes. As the water cascades from the holes, it passes through an umbrella-like cloth erected above the *nyāsa dāru*, causing the water to sprinkle like rain onto the *nyāsa dāru*. During this bathing ceremony, *brāhmaṇas* recite the *Puruṣa-sūkta* prayers for Jagannātha, the *Radradhyaya* or *Nīlaśukta* for Balarāma, and the *Śrī-sūkta* for Subhadrā.

When the *abhiśeka* is over, the *dāru* is dried with a soft towel and offered flowers (as a substitute for clothes), *madhuparka* (refreshment), *snāniya* (a small amount of bathing water), *gorocana* (red powder), collyrium, incense, lamps, a mirror, and ornaments, all to the accompaniment of the *Nṛsiṁha Gāyatrī* or *Anustubha Nṛsiṁha Mantra*. Priests then offer *durva* grass and rice corns, and chant the *Saṅkalpa-sūkta* of the *Yajur-veda*. When everything is completed, the *dāru* is returned to the *pratiṣṭhā maṇḍapa* as *brāhmaṇas* chant the *Sakuna-sūkta* from the *Ṛg-veda*. Then it is placed upon cushions, and water and refreshments are offered. Finally, the *nyāsa dāru* is covered with cloth.

The following day, the *ācārya* performs preliminary rites to purify his body. He then meditates on Lord Nṛsiṁha in his heart, while worshiping the *nyāsa dāru* as the form of Lord Nṛsiṁhadeva. Rituals are performed throughout the day. Mantras are chanted to invoke auspiciousness. The *agni-hotra* (fire sacrifice) is performed from the sixth day of the dark fornight in Āṣāḍha, and once again Nṛsiṁhadeva presides. Ghee, twigs, and a mixture of half-cooked rice, sesame seeds, barley, coconut, and plant bulbs are offered into the sacred fire. 10,000 oblations are offered while chanting the *Anustubha Nṛsiṁha* mantra. Priests who perform this sacrifice cannot complete more than 2,000 oblations a day. Therefore the *agni-hotra* continues with these offerings for at least five days. On Ekādaśī, 1,008 *ahutis* are offered with the Vasudeva mantra, on Dvādaśī the same number are offered with the eighteen-syllable Gopāla mantra, and on Trayodaśī, 1,008 oblations are offered while chanting the Bhuvaneśvarī mantra along with the six syllable Sudarśana mantra. Cāturdaśī, and if necessary Amavasya, are reserved for offerings to Lakṣmī, Sarasvatī, Śiva, Kālī, Bimalā, Durgā, and other *devatas* until the stock of offerings is finished.

On the evening of Cāturdaśī, the *nyāsa dāru* is placed upon a simple wooden cart and taken around the main temple seven times. It is then taken outside the main temple and given to the *dayitās* or their carpenters, who cut it into the four pieces of the form and measurements mentioned in their palm-leaf texts.

The following day, Amāvasyā, the four newly-carved *mūrtis* are accompanied in procession around the main temple three times, then placed next to the old deities on the *anasara-ghara*, a verandah leading to the sanctum in the main temple. The old deities of Lord Jagannātha, Balarāma, Subhadrā, and Sudarśana *cakra* are covered with a thick layer of resin, strips of silk, sandalwood paste, and other substances. This thick layer is stripped off their forms by Dvādaśī, and they stand uncovered and unpainted next to the forms that will replace them.

When the newly constructed *mūrtis* are placed next to the old ones, all lights in the temple and the entire town of Purī are turned off. It is then that the *dayitās* entrusted with the service of changing the *brahmapadartha* perform this unusual ritual. The four *dayitās* are blindfolded, and their hands are wrapped to the elbow so that they can't see or feel the *brahmapadartha*. They go forward in the dead of night, on Amavasya, the dark moon night, and lift the mysterious substance out from the old *mūrtis* and place it into the cavity constructed for its placement in the new *mūrtis*. That cavity is then covered and sealed with one of the four pieces of the *nyāsa dāru*. Because the *dayitās* who perform this service are blindfolded and their hands and arms wrapped, the contents of the *brahmapadartha* remain unknown, although speculation abounds. If the men are indeed blindfolded and cannot see or feel what they have touched, then guess-work and speculation are the only evidence we will ever gather in our quest to find out what the mysterious substance is.

### Burial of the Old Figures, the Funeral, And Purification of the Dayitās

After the *brahmapadartha* has been transferred, the old *mūrtis* are placed on the same cart the new *mūrtis* were carried on and are transported toward the temple's western gate to a place known as *Koili Vaikuṇṭha*, the graveyard for discarded deities. In a pleasant garden area the old deities are sunk into a pit approximately four and a half meters deep, along with all the wooden images used during the Rathayātrā festival: the wooden horses from each chariot, the *parsvadevatas*, *apsarās*, etc.

When the "funeral ceremony" is completed, the *dayitās* weep in sorrow because their dear family member, Lord Jagannātha, has passed away. They remain in a state of ritual impurity for the next ten days, during which they do not shave, and they eat only frugal meals. On the tenth day, they cut their hair and nails, take a purificatory bath in the Mārkaṇḍeya Tank, and white-wash their homes. On the twelfth day, the *dayitās* hold a feast for Lord Jagannātha's servitors.

### Addition of Several Layers of Material Over the Wood and Final Painting

After the transference of the *brahmapadartha*, the newly carved deities remain standing in the *Anasara-ghara* during the bright half of the extra Āṣāḍha without rituals. They are hidden only by a bamboo curtain. During this time, the worship is offered to the *utsava* deities: Madana-mohana for Jagannātha, Dola-Govinda for Balarāma, Lakṣmī and Viśvadhatri for Subhadrā, and Nṛsiṁha for Sudarśana *cakra*.

After Pūrṇimā, during the dark fortnight, the new deities are entrusted to the temple servants known as *Datta Mahāpātra*. Their task is to infuse the *mūrtis* with "flesh" and "blood" by applying various substances and wrapping them with strips of cloth. According to the Āyur-veda, the human body consists of seven layers, or *dhātus:* skin (represented by a cloth covering), blood (red cloth), flesh (tree sap), marrow (perfumed oils), fat (sandalwood paste), semen (starch of rice or wheat flour), and bones (the wood itself).

When the *Datta Mahāpātras* are finished, the *mūrtis* are given over to the *Citrakāras*, who paint them with various substances: charcoal for black, mother-of-pearl for white, turmeric for yellow, etc. The most remarkable fact about the painting is that the painters are not allowed to color the pupils of the deities' eyes. This task is carried out by the temple priests on the first day of the bright half of the regular Āṣāḍha. This ritual, known as *Netrotsava*, has previously been described under its own heading in "Festivals."

After giving the last stroke of the brush to the deities' eyes, the priests bathe the deities reflections in bronze mirrors with *pañcāmṛta*, a mixture of milk, yogurt, ghee, honey, and sugar. They are then offered *acmaniya*, water to rinse the mouth, and once again bathed with scented water to the accompaniment of mantras from the *Ṛg-veda*. The bath following *Netrotsava* is a purificatory rite to free the *mūrtis* from any contamination they may have undergone at the hands of the carpenters, sculptors, and painters. With these final rituals, the Navakalevara ceremonies come to an end, and the following day (*Dvitīya* of the bright fortnight in the regular Āṣāḍha), the famous Ratha-yātrā takes place, and the new deities emerge from the temple to be greeted by millions of devotees.

## Art, Crafts, Music, Dance, and Architecture

Art forms of any civilization reveal people's attitudes and aspirations about life. From time immemorial these methods of expression have filled hearts young and old with awe, reverence, tragedy, humor, and joy. In the culture of Lord Jagannātha, the arts are created or performed as acts of worship. Paintings generally depict Lord Jagannātha's divine pastimes, music is most often played to express prayer and glorification (*bhajana*), dance relates the particular stories or philosophical ideas meant to awaken God consciousness, and sculpture and architecture are invariably used in temple construction.

## Music and Dance

Classical music in India is played on a variety of instruments, and the most popular in Orissa are the *mṛdaṅga* (clay, two-headed drum),

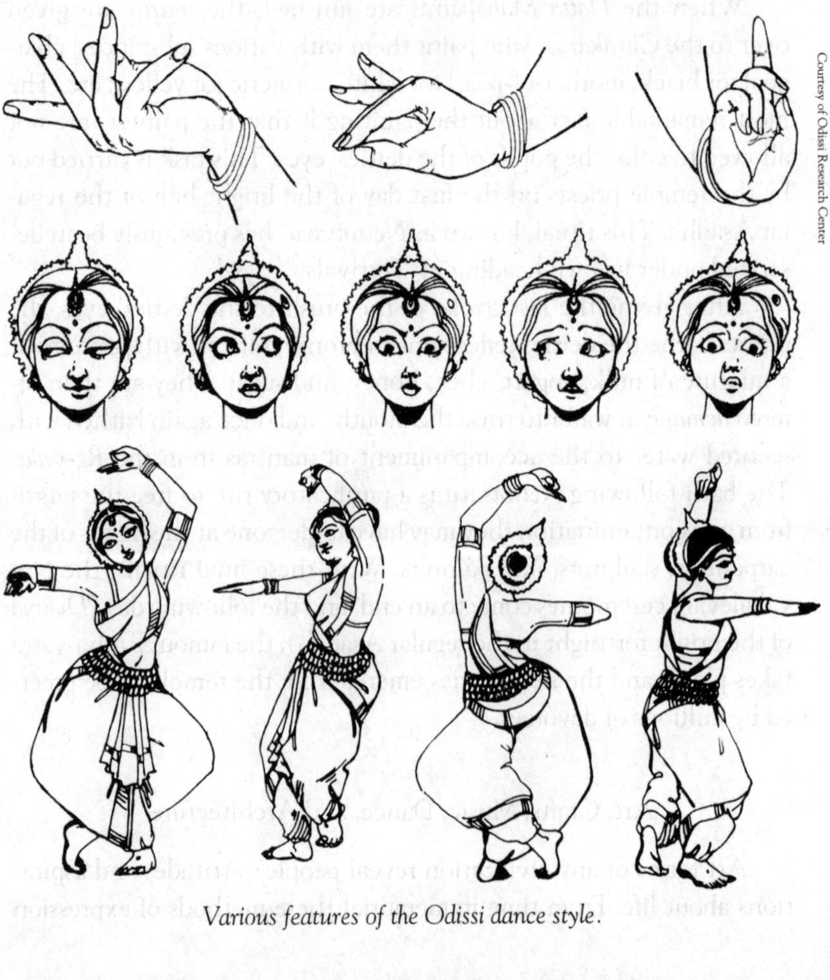

Courtesy of Odissi Research Center

*Various features of the Odissi dance style.*

*karatalas* (small hand cymbals), harmonium (small keyboard played by pumping a bellows), and *tablas* (two small drums—one high pitched, the other low).

Hearing the harmonious blend of sound from these instruments causes a natural rhythmic sensation, inspiring those who hear it to dance. Unlike popular dance in Western countries, a classical form of dance known as Odissi has evolved. In previous centuries, dance was performed by a class of servants living at the Jagannātha temple known as *deva-dāsīs*. These young girls dedicated their entire lives to Lord Jagannātha, and were even regarded as His wives because they would never marry a mortal man. At various times of the day, these dancing girls would perform plays or dramas in the form of dance for the deities' pleasure.

As one might imagine, this practice degenerated as Kali-yuga progressed. In fact, the *deva-dāsīs* became so degraded due to a lack of civility, and at times accusations of prostitution, that in some South Indian temples their services have been abolished by state law. This restriction on temple dance, however, has not restricted dance outside the temples. In Orissa today, many young girls, and even some boys, learn Odissi dance, and they regularly perform plays throughout the Purī district.

The Odissi form of dance is extremely fluid and graceful compared to the more popular Indian dance (Bhārata-nātyam), which is far more regimented and defined. Odissi dance originated from the *deva-dāsīs* performing erotic poses and postures included in the conjugal *rasa* for the pleasure of the Jagannātha deities, and therefore continues to portray the excitement of spiritual love and emotions.[16]

## Painting

Fragments of early cave paintings have been found in far western parts of Orissa, and today there remains a strong tradition in villages and tribal areas for wall painting, suggesting that artistic influence has been part of Orissan culture for a long time. Lovely intricate wall

[16] A unique example of how dance was taught and practiced is related in the chapter entitled *How Pradyumna Miśra Received Instructions from Rāmānanda Rāya* in *Lord Caitanya's Purī Pastimes*.

paintings on many village homes capture one's attention, whether painted in bright colors or with simple white rice powder.

Professional painters known as *citrakāras* are *śūdras* by caste, and most live in villages surrounding Purī. These artists create religious paintings known as *paṭa-citra.* Most works are still painted on traditionally treated cloth, and have a lacquered, hard surface and a bold primary color scheme. Dyes used to produce these indigenous paintings are made entirely from natural ingredients: black carbon from ash, white from powdered conchshell, and yellow, blue, and red from stones or minerals. These dyes are then mixed with the milky sap of the *bel* fruit to make paint. (See plate 24)

Classical painting and sculpture are primarily the province of a hereditary caste known by the names Mahāpātra, Mahārānā, Dās, and Datta-mahāpātra. Traditionally male members of the family do the actual artwork, while women generally prepare the canvases and paints. These painters also fulfill an important ritual role in Jagannātha worship. For example, artists are responsible for repainting the Jagannātha deities as well as painting the Ratha-yātrā chariots and the colorful subordinate deities that adorn each cart.

## Textiles

Even in a country famed throughout the world for its beautiful textiles, Orissa stands out. Thousands of weavers clustered in small villages throughout the state create unique silk and cotton *ikat* fabrics unrivaled the world over.

The term *ikat* comes from a Southeast Asian word, indicating that early trade between India and Indonesia resulted in considerable cultural and artistic exchange. This intricate and difficult technique is often referred to as "tie-dye" (and in Orissa as *bandha*). Bundles of yarn are dyed by wrapping (tying) different sections of the bundle and applying one color at a time. The dye penetrates the exposed sections, but doesn't touch the wrapped sections. A color scheme is predetermined with extraordinary precision, so when the dyed threads are finally woven together, a design appears in the finished textile. This technique results in a delicate haziness of design, with each element "feathered" into the next.

The genius of Orissan weavers, however, is most splendidly displayed in their weaving of *sārīs*. Deep scarlets and pleasing shades of rose, delicate mauves and intense purples, brilliant golds and oranges, elegant blacks and greys, blues ranging from robin's egg to velvety midnight—these are the colors of the Orissan weaver's palette, often combined with the natural creaminess of raw silk. Traditional Orissan motif, in addition to geometric designs, includes birds, elephants, peacocks, and flowers, all of which float through the background colors, often separated from each other by rich bands of jewel-like or brocaded detail.

## Applique

Orissa's colorful applique work (see plate 25) has long appealed to visitors, and the gay umbrellas, shoulder bags, and wall hangings are the most popular mementos. The center of this craft is the village of Pipli, fifteen kilometers south of Bhuvaneṣvara on the main road to Purī. The folk art of applique, as is true with other arts and crafts in Orissa, was originally related with the Jagannātha temple. Appliqued parasols, canopies, pillows, and *tarasa* (heart-shaped cloth shields) are still used during the Ratha-yātrā procession. The appliqued cloths on Lord Jagannātha's chariot are also traditionally made of bright red and yellow, while those on Lord Balarāma's chariot are bright red and green. Subhadrā moves through the streets in a chariot decorated with red and black.

Although the applique technique originated in Jagannātha worship, it has naturally broadened its horizons and become a popular source of decorations and souvenirs for millions of pilgrims who visit Purī.

## Metal Work

Orissan metal workers usually produce articles made of brass (an alloy of copper and zinc) or bell metal (an alloy of copper and tin). Household articles and religious utensils are the most common objects. The art of metal work originated in Jagannātha worship, where the *pūjā* items—incense holders, ghee lamps, bells, cups, spoons, and plates—are all made of metal.

## Stone Sculpture

Anyone who takes even a cursory look at an Orissan temple or monument will realize that this is a land of sculptural genius. Orissa is traditionally known as Utkal, or "the land of art," no doubt due to the brilliance of both her architectural and sculptural traditions.

A third-century B.C. carved elephant at Dhauli and the sculptured friezes and other decorations at the Khadagiri/Udayagiri caves of the first-century B.C. are the first indications of a strongly developed tradition. The major Buddhist sites at Lalitagiri, Ratnagiri, and Udayagiri until recently had yielded no stone sculptures that could be dated before the sixth century A.D. Recent excavation, however, has unearthed inscriptions that seem to take the history of the site back to still earlier centuries. (See plates 26–28)

Artisans from any background would also appreciate the intricate stone carvings in temples such as the Sun Temple at Konark. Although the saline climate has withered much of the thirteenth-century art to dust, remaining artifacts reveal an aesthetic sense of deep beauty and craftsmanship.

In Purī, the famous "Stone Carvers Lane," or Pathuria Sahi continues to practice the tradition handed down for generations. Most of the stone sculptures continue to be those of gods and goddesses, and are produced either for deity worship or for some other form of decoration in homes or public buildings.

## Architectural Design of the Jagannātha Temple

Churches, temples, and mosques adorn villages and city streets throughout the entire world. The architectural designs of these religious buildings and monuments indicate the nature of worship and beliefs of the society that built them. Each great cultural movement throughout history has made its own contribution to the art of building, so that the aspirations of the people, and even their way of life, stand revealed for all to see. In each of the major historical developments of architecture, there is one distinct feature by which it can be recognized: Greek architecture was based on refinement and perfection of the lines, Roman buildings are remarkable for their scientific construction, French Gothic reveals the passionate energy of the builders, and Italian Renaissance reflects the scholarship of its time. The foremost quality of Indian architecture is its spirituality.[17]

In the case of the Jagannātha temple, the building is so old and the architecture of the immense temple so detailed that archaeologists have spent decades examining it. The temple itself is an Indo-Aryan design from the middle period of Orissan-style temples (800–1250 A.D.). Historians believe the Mukteśvara Temple in Bhuvaneśvara, constructed in 975 A.D., to be the prototype of this particular design.[18]

Records show that the present Jagannātha temple was constructed as a pillar of victory by Chora Ganga (Chodaganga), the conqueror of Kalinga who reigned from A.D. 1078–1147, but that it wasn't consecrated as a temple until later. Most historians agree that construction began under the royal patronage of King Chodagangadeva, but was finished by his descendant, Anangabhima.[19]

The Jagannātha temple consists of four basic components. The tall, primary structure has a soaring, conical, convex spire, crowned with a lotus-shaped part at the top. This is called the *Deula* or *Śrī Mandir*. At the *Deula's* core is the inner sanctum where the temple deities reside. In front of the *Deula* is a rectangular building, the assembly hall known as the *Jagamohana* or *Mukhasālā*. Two buildings adjoining these are the *Nat Mandir* (Temple of Dance), and in front of this the *Bhoga Mandir* (Temple of Offerings). These buildings are all situated on the same axis, extending from east to west, but were not constructed at the same time. The original temple design consisted of only the *Deula* and *the Jagamohana*. The other two halls were added sometime in the fourteenth or fifteenth century.[20]

*Śrī Mandir* is eighty feet square on the ground, rising almost 215' above road level. The Sudarśana disc atop the *Duela* was installed by King Ramcandradeva in 1594. It is made of eight metals and has a circumference of about thirty-six feet and a diameter of almost twelve feet. Every afternoon the *Garuḍa Sevak* climbs to the top of *Śrī Man-*

---

[17] See *Indian Architecture* (p.1)

[18] *Indian Architecture* (p. 102)

[19] For dates see *Cult and Culture of Lord Jagannatha*.

[20] *Indian Architecture* (p. 105)

*dir* and fastens a number of flags to the mast fixed to Nīla-*cakra*. These flags are either bright red or bright yellow and have a crescent moon and sun in the middle, signifying that Lord Jagannātha's kingdom is anywhere in the universe where the sun and moon shine.

The temple complex covers more than 428,000 square feet and consists of many areas. Everything within the two rectangular walls resembles the inside of a fortress. The outer wall (665' x 640') is called *Meghanada Prachir*, the inner wall (420' x 315') is *Kūrma Prachir*.

Four entrance gates facing the cardinal directions serve as passageways for pilgrims. These gates are part of the twenty-foot-high outer wall. During the fourteenth or fifteenth century this wall was constructed all around the temple to ward off Muslim invaders. The four gates are *Siṁha-dvāra* (Lion-gate) facing east, *Aswa-dvāra* (Horse-gate) facing south, *Vyaghra-dvāra* (Tiger-gate) facing west, and *Hasti-dvāra* (Elephant-gate) facing north.

The *Siṁha-dvāra* gate is used as the main entrance to the temple, and it faces east toward Grand Road. Two crouching lions guard the gates, and before them stands a thirty-four-foot-high monolithic pillar, known as *Aruṇa-stambha*. This single-stone column supports a figure of Aruṇa, the Sun God's charioteer, and was transferred from the dilapidated Sun Temple in Konark during the eighteenth century.

Immediately to the right as one enters the *Siṁha-dvāra* gate one sees a deity of Lord Jagannātha known as Patita-pāvana. It is recorded that Rāmacandradeva (1732–1743) was forced by a political situation to marry a relative of a Muslim general. Because the king married a non-Hindu, he was outcast from Hindu society and was no longer allowed to enter the Jagannātha temple. Patita-pāvana Jagannātha was installed so King Rāmacandradeva and others who were not allowed entrance could still have the Lord's *darśana*. There is also a *Dasāvatāra* sculpture above the threshold, a row of small figures portraying the ten main incarnations of Lord Viṣṇu.

Proceeding through the *Siṁha-dvāra*, pilgrims climb twenty-two steps called *Baisi Pahaca*. The steps are considered sanctified because Lord Jagannātha, Balarāma, Subhadrā, and Sudarśana *cakra* travel over them as they go to and from the temple for Ratha-yātrā. After climbing the steps, devotees enter the inner compound.

Over 100 shrines of lesser importance surround *Śrī Mandir*. Each honors various expansions of Lord Jagannātha, or the demigods. Visitors to India are sometimes confused by the multitude of deities, and may think that Indian culture is polytheistic. According to Vedic philosophy, there are millions of powerful entities in the universe known as demigods, but there is only one Supreme God, whom everyone else serves. Although people may approach a highly placed minister for favor, this doesn't imply that the minister has become the king. Similarly, although people worship the Lord's highly placed universal administrators for favor, this doesn't mean they are worshiped as the Supreme God.

The Supreme Personality of Godhead is the cause of all causes and source of all energies. How that original person expands His energies and Himself throughout creation is too vast a subject to cover here, but it is obvious that in Purī Lord Jagannātha is accepted as that Supreme Personality. Other deities in the Jagannātha temple compound and surrounding area are expansions of Lord Jagannātha or demigods. These other deities are believed to be later additions to the Jagannātha worship, except perhaps for the deity of Bimalādevī.

The temple area also includes Rohiṇī-kuṇḍa, the *kalpa-vata*, Mukti Mandapa, probably the largest kitchen in the world, and Ananda Bazaar, where Lord Jagannātha's *mahā-prasāda* is sold.

Oriyan architecture is ornate on the outside, but simple within. While approaching the innermost sanctuary through various halls and past the many pillars and carved panels, a devotee is subtly influenced by the sacredness of the architecture. He finds himself enclosed with the Supreme Lord in a dim, soothing atmosphere. His eyes find rest after the fierce light of the day outside. Not only is the lighting dim, but the air is filled with the scent of flowers, burning oil lamps, and incense coming from the sanctuary. Gradually, his mood calms and his spiritual feelings are awakened as he approaches the deities.

Once inside the temple, devotees see in the distance seven forms standing on the *ratna-vedi* (altar): Lord Jagannātha, Balarāma, Subhadrā, Sudarśana *cakra*, Mādhava, Lakṣmī-devī, and Sarasvatī. As pilgrims pass through the various halls, they eventually enter the *Jagamohana*. Here Lord Caitanya would stand behind the *Garuḍa-*

*stambha*, a pillar in the hall with Viṣṇu's bird carrier on top. Most devotees, however, continue to the *garbha-gṛha* (sanctuary) through the passageways to circumambulate the *ratna-vedi*.

According to Vedic scriptures, the doors and the deities are closely related. The divinity to whom the temple is dedicated resides in the *garbha-gṛha*, the inner sanctum of the *Deula*. Stationed below, to the left and right of the door jambs, are the *dvāra-palas*, or gatekeepers. The door is the sacred entrance through which man enters into the presence of the Supreme Personality of Godhead. To enter such a divine atmosphere properly, a transformation of consciousness must take place. It is believed that only when the devotee has acquired a celestial body is he qualified to pass into the company of the Supreme Lord. This transformation or regeneration is promoted by the divinities carved on the door jambs.[21]

According to texts of sacred architecture known as *śilpa-śāstra*, each intricate aspect of a temple structure has some significance. I've included the above samples just to give the reader an idea of how detailed the ancient builders were.[22]

## The Jagannātha Temple Today

Due to the corrosive salt air in Purī, the massive stone temple has periodically required various repairs. Recently, the government's Archaeological Survey of India removed many old lime plaster coatings from the temple. These had been added in several layers by past kings to protect the building.

Engineers discovered that the lime was absorbing water during monsoons, and over the past few centuries tons of weight was being added to the super-structure. Archeologists removed the old plaster and reconditioned the entire outside of the *Deula*.

Prior to the 1991 Ratha-yātrā, a massive stone from atop the temple crashed to the ground. Apparently, water had seeped through the lime into the stone joints and iron frame, causing one stone to loosen.

---

[21] See chapter on *Daily-pūjā* in *Part Two* for times of worshiping gatekeepers.

[22] For further information about Vedic architecture see *The Hindu Temple* or *Indian Architecture*.

That one stone weighed an estimated five tons! Imagine the work involved to build such a temple eight hundred years ago, without the use of modern machinery.

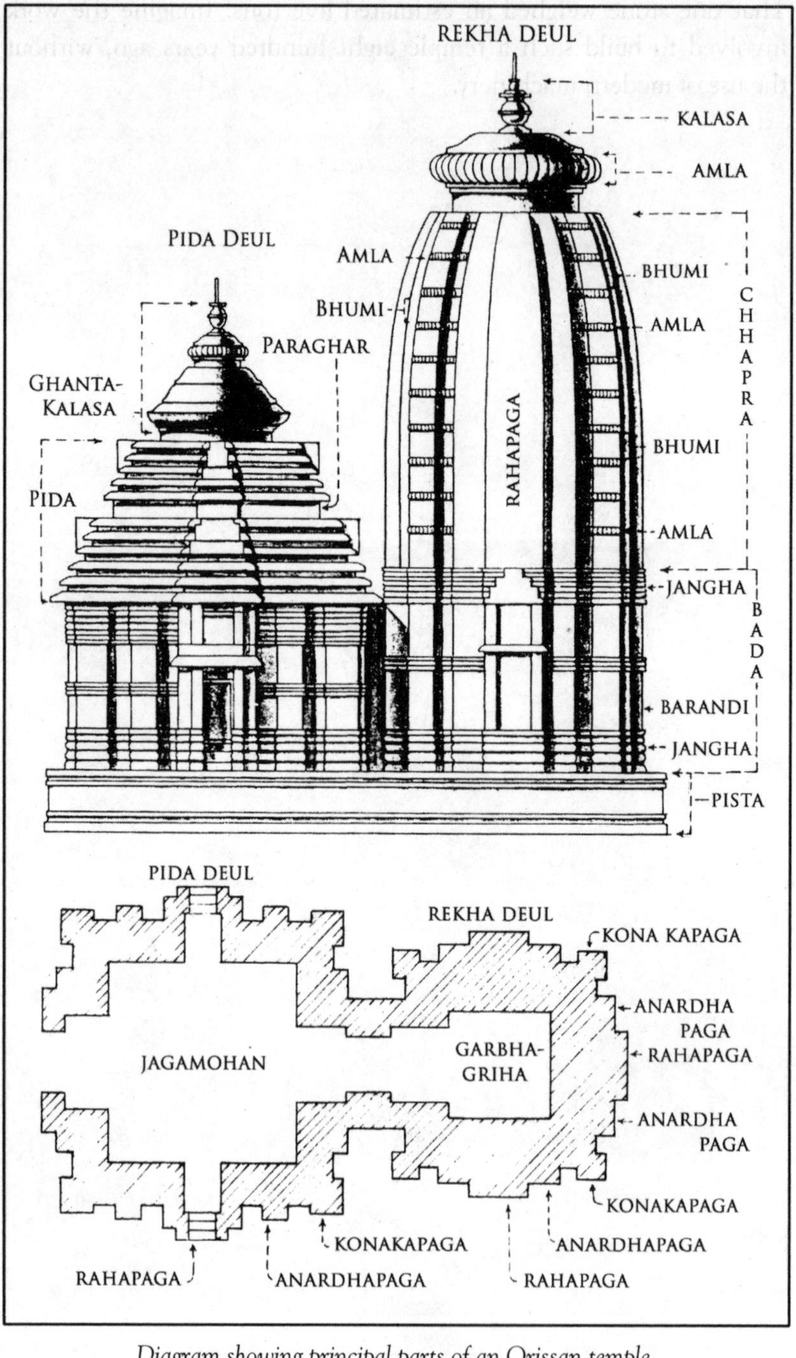


*Diagram showing principal parts of an Orissan temple.*

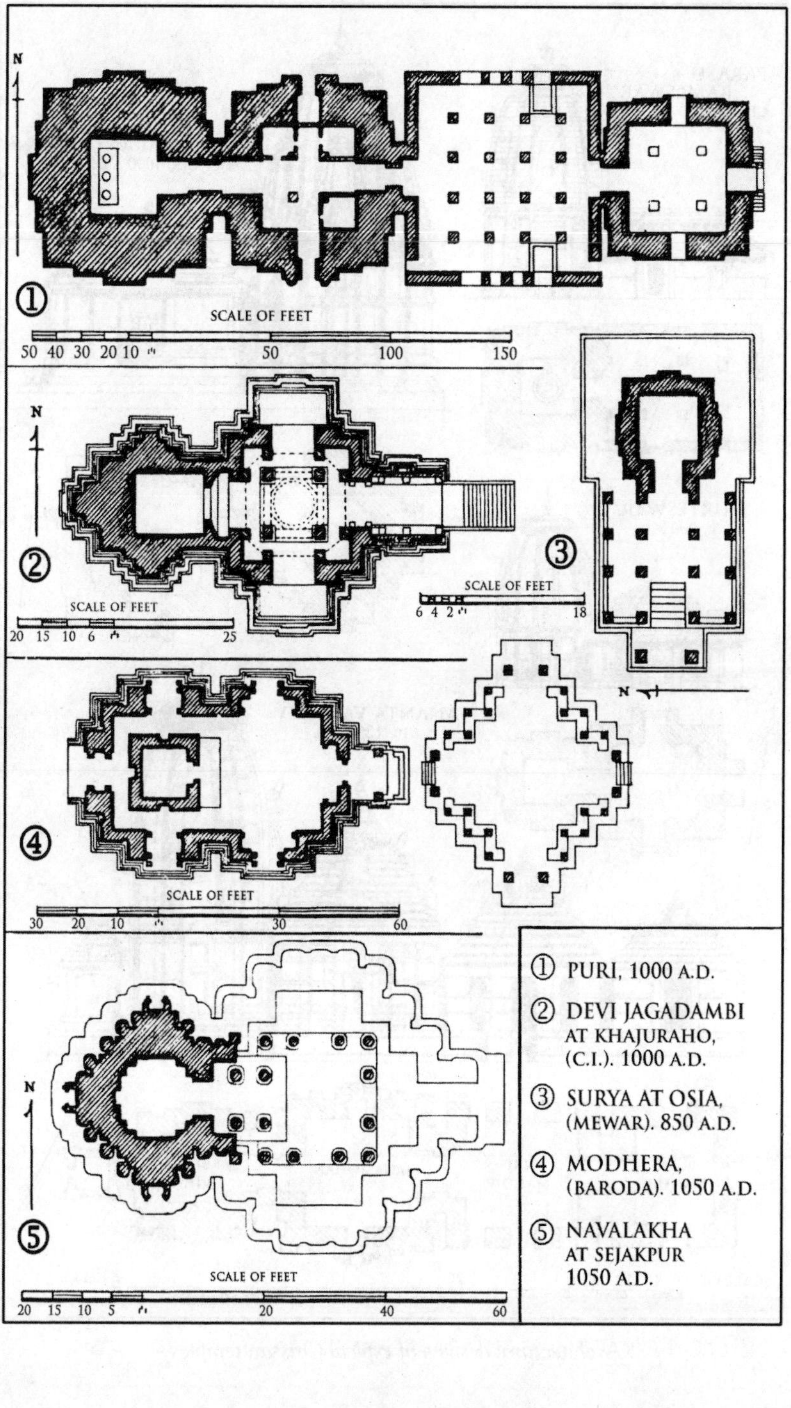
N
①
SCALE OF FEET
50 40 30 20 10 0 50 100 150
N
②
SCALE OF FEET
20 15 10 6 0 25
③
SCALE OF FEET
6 4 2 0 18
N
④
SCALE OF FEET
30 20 10 0 30 60
N
⑤
SCALE OF FEET
20 15 10 5 0 20 40 60
① PURI, 1000 A.D.
② DEVI JAGADAMBI AT KHAJURAHO, (C.I.). 1000 A.D.
③ SURYA AT OSIA, (MEWAR). 850 A.D.
④ MODHERA, (BARODA). 1050 A.D.
⑤ NAVALAKHA AT SEJAKPUR 1050 A.D.

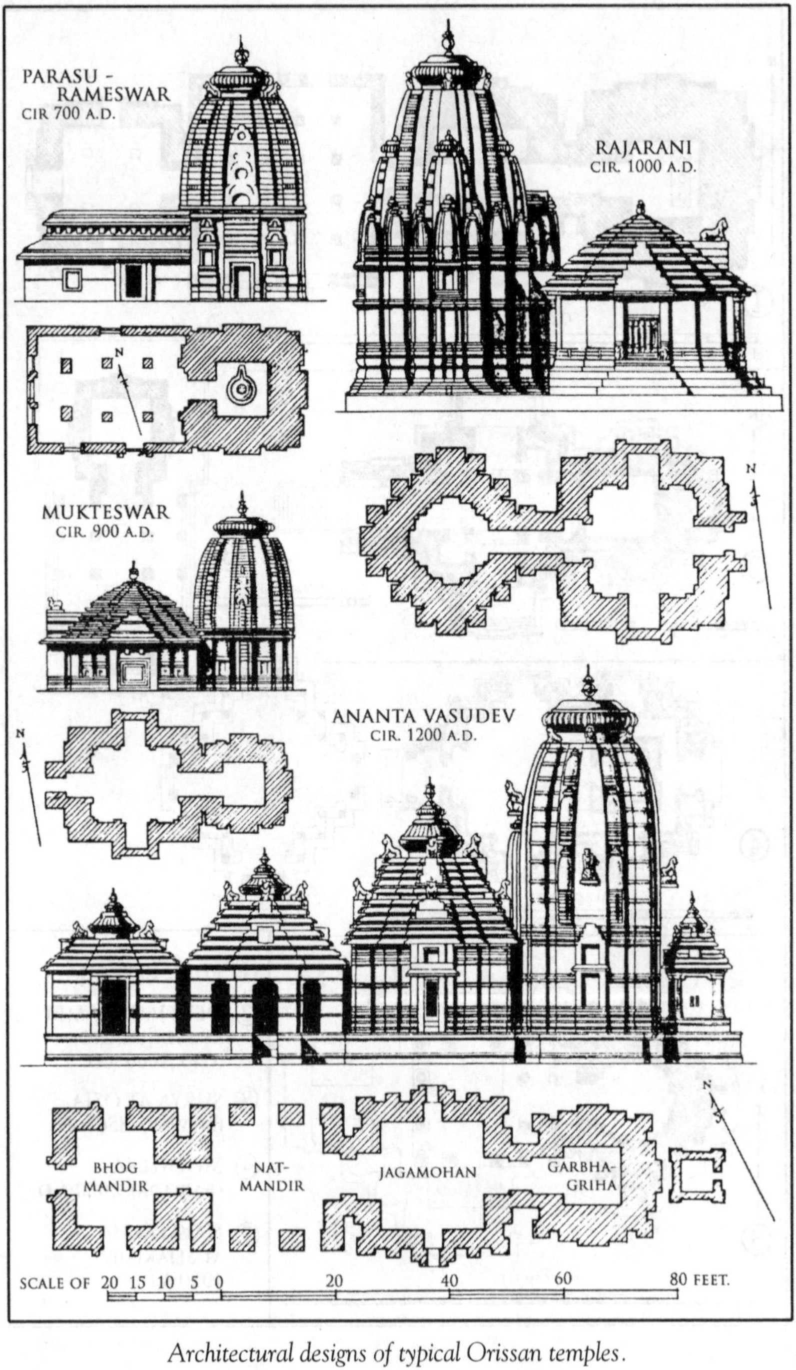


*Architectural designs of typical Orissan temples.*

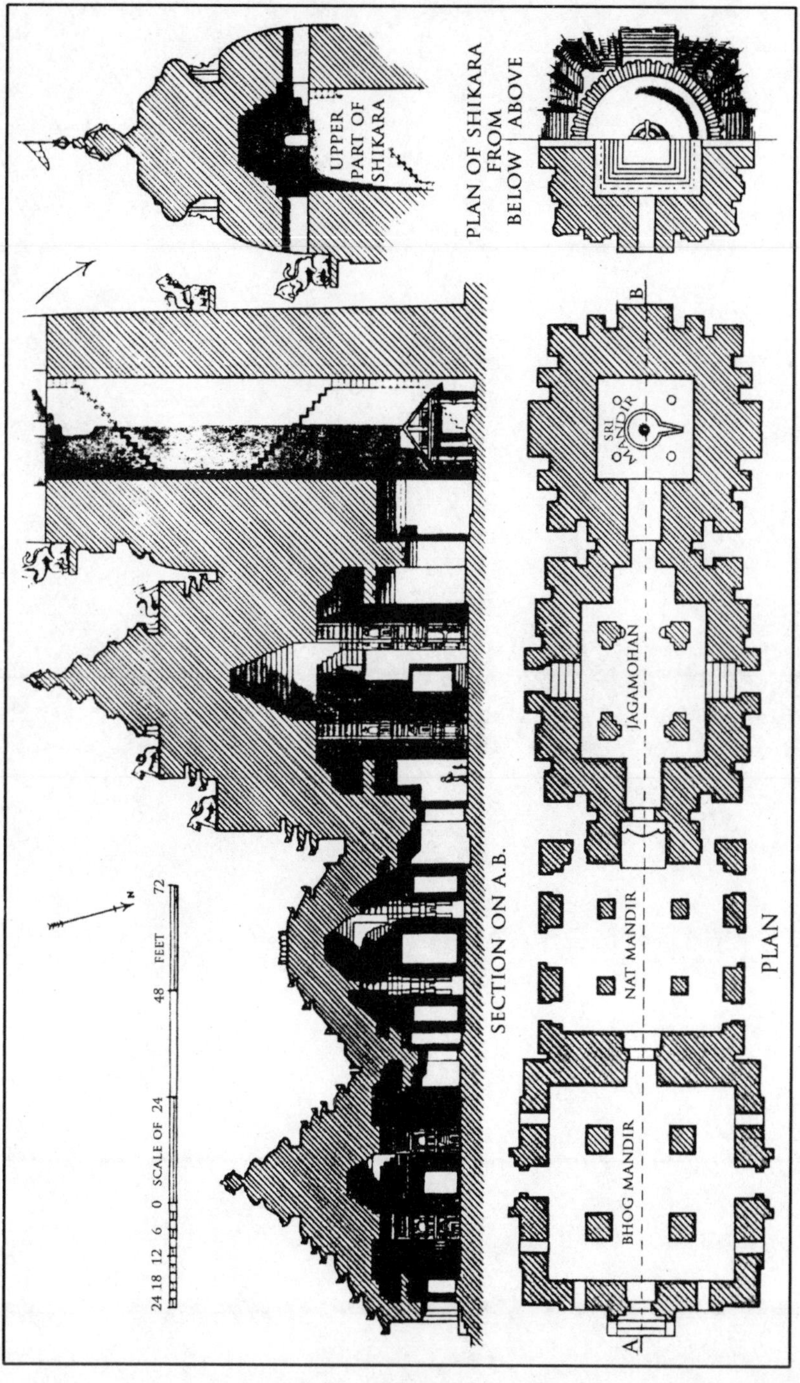


*Lingaraja Temple at Bhuvaneśvara, Orissa, circa 1000 A.D.*

# 3

# *Jagannātha Worship Prior to the 15th Century*

## A Brief Look At the History of India

To establish a well-rounded understanding of Jagannātha worship, it is necessary to look beyond the small town of Purī for historical information. Because the town is located on the seashore, excavation is difficult and the saline climate withers away remains more rapidly than at inland sites. A short sketch of India's history in general, therefore, will shed more light on how the worship has been influenced during the last several centuries and better help us to understand why some historians contradict each other and present Lord Jagannātha as a Jain, Hindu, Buddhist, or aboriginal deity.

Historians use various methods to determine how our ancestors lived. The study of ancient civilizations is based on historical literature, old buildings, monuments, works of art, numismatics (the study of coins), inscriptions on rocks, pillars, copper plates, stone tablets, and caves, and accounts written by foreign travelers.

Artifacts found at various sites around India reveal that some of the oldest civilizations known to man resided in fertile forested pockets along the banks of the Indus River.[1] Discovery of these ancient ruins came in the mid-nineteenth century, when it was commonly believed that India's history went back only to the time of Alexander the Great's invasion in the fourth century B.C. British engineers laying rail between the Punjab and Karachi observed that local laborers had an over-abundance of kiln-baked bricks with which to build the track's foundations. The time-worn bricks remained an enigma until the 1920s when archaeologists explored the region and changed

[1] There are no Vedic references for the common word "Hindus." This is actually a corruption of "Indus," a name for people who lived on the western banks of the Indus River during earlier times.

history books with the uncovering of Mohenjo-daro, an ancient city along the Indus. Nine layers of construction were unearthed with streets and lanes laid out in systematic designs, spacious houses, well-covered sewage drains both inside and outside the homes, hot and cold public baths, deep wells, public buildings, trading posts, and harbor ports along the rivers.

In *Part One*, we discussed the advent and appearance of Lord Jagannātha as described in the *Skanda Purāṇa*. According to ancient texts, Vedic culture flourished up to the end of Dvāpara-yuga, about five thousand years ago.[2] Now let us look at the development of Jagannātha worship from the beginning of the next universal age, Kali-yuga, which began around 3100 B.C.

## Brahmanism

The *Katakarajavamsavali*, a Sanskrit work compiled in the early part of the nineteenth century from older records available in the archives of the Jagannātha temple, vividly describes the political history of Orissa since the beginning of the Kali era, always keeping the temple of Puruṣottama-Jagannātha in the center. The text forms part of a body of literature broadly categorized as the *Madalapanji*, or the "Drum Chronicle," so called because the manuscripts are long palm leaves tugged together in a cylinder shape.

According to the *Katakarajavamsavali*, Mahārāja Yudhiṣṭhira began his rule as world emperor after the famous Battle of Kurukṣetra and remained in power until 3089 B.C. His successor, Mahārāja Parīkṣit, was succeeded by his son, Janemejaya, succeeded by his son, Samvara. Samvara's son Gautama became the next king, and his son in turn succeeded him. The *Katakarajavamsavali* gives a detailed list of all the subsequent rulers up until fairly modern times.

Gradually, a religion known today as Brahmanism became prominent throughout India. The *Vedas* describe how to divide the human race into four divisions according to quality and working capacity. This is a natural division. For example, whether or not one accepts the title *brāhmaṇa*, there is a class in society made up of intellectu-

---

[2] See *Part One*, *Markandeya's Strange Experience* for a review of the universal ages.

als. Such people tend to be interested in spiritual understanding and philosophy. Similarly, there is a class of men interested in administration and in ruling others. In the Vedic system, these martially spirited men are called *kṣatriyas*. Similarly, there is a class of men interested in business, industry, and agriculture. These are the *vaiśyas*. And there is a class of laborers, or *śūdras*. These divisions are meant to work cooperatively to create smooth social order. By 500 B.C., however, the selfish priestly class (*brāhmaṇas*) had artificially posed themselves as better than the weaker sections of society, although such social domination is against the true spirit of brahmanism.[3]

## Jainism

As time passed, the *brāhmaṇas* focused more on caste distinctions decided by birth, and not by the qualities of an individual. They focused society on expensive religious ceremonies and Vedic rituals that emphasized dependence on the priestly class. Around that time, a religious reformer named Vardhamana Mahāvīra preached the philosophy of Jainism, originally founded by King Arhat. He rejected the belief in a Supreme Creator, and instead taught that the universe is infinite and eternal. Mahāvīra taught that salvation is attained by complete renunciation of desire through nonviolence, difficult penance, and self-sacrifice. Jain monks became noted for their extreme asceticism. The Jain's cardinal doctrine of nonviolence to any living creature stems from their belief that all matter is eternal and that every object has a soul.

Because Mahāvīra encouraged equality among all beings, and thus did not honor the superiority of the *brāhmaṇas*, and because he rejected Vedic rules and rites as being misrepresented by the selfish brahminical class, thousands converted to Jainism.

## Buddhism

Shortly after Mahāvīra died, Lord Buddha, an incarnation of God, appeared sometime between 563 and 556 B.C. By the time of

[3] See *Śrīmad-Bhāgavatam* (1.2.13) and (7.11.35).

Lord Buddha's appearance, the people had become atheistic flesh-eaters. On the plea of Vedic sacrifice, animals were being slaughtered without restriction. Lord Buddha taught nonviolence out of pity for the poor animals. He claimed that he did not believe in the Vedic tenets and stressed the adverse psychological effects incurred by animal killing. Less intelligent men of the age of Kali, who had no faith in God, followed his principles and for the time being were trained in moral discipline and nonviolence, preliminary steps of God realization. Thus he deluded the atheists. Although the people tended toward atheism, they kept their absolute faith in him, but he was himself an incarnation of God. That was Lord Buddha's mercy: he made those who were faithless faithful to him.

Before Lord Buddha's advent, animals were killed in the name of Vedic sacrifice. When the *Vedas* are not accepted through the authoritative disciplic succession, casual readers are misled by their flowery language. The foolish scholars of Vedic literature who do not care to receive the transcendental message through the transcendental realized sources of disciplic succession are sure to be bewildered. To them, the ritualistic ceremonies are considered to be all in all. They have no depth of knowledge. According to the *Bhagavad-gītā* (15.15), *vedaiś ca sarvair aham eva vedyo:* the whole Vedic system is to lead one gradually to the path of the Supreme Lord. The theme of Vedic literature is simply to know the Supreme Lord, the individual soul, the cosmic situation, and the relation between all these. When we understand the relationship, relative functions begin, and as a result of such action, the ultimate goal of life, or going back to Godhead, takes place in the easiest manner. Unfortunately, unauthorized scholars of the *Vedas* become captivated only by the purificatory ceremonies, and their progress is thereby checked.

To such bewildered atheists, Lord Buddha is the emblem of theism. Therefore, he began by checking the habit of animal killing. It is nonsensical to say that animal killing has nothing to do with, or has no influence on, spiritual realization. By this dangerous theory many so-called *sannyāsis* have sprung up who preach animal killing under the umbrella of Vedic rites. The animal sacrifice described in the *Vedas* is different from unrestricted slaughter. Because the *asuras*, or so-called scholars of Vedic literature, put forward the evidence that animal killing is allowed in the *Vedas*, Lord Buddha superficially denied the Vedic authority in order to save people from the vice of committing such violence, as well as to save the poor animals from being slaughtered by their big brothers, who clamor for universal brotherhood, peace, justice, and equality. There is no justice where animals are being slaughtered. Lord Buddha wanted to stop animal slaughter, and therefore he preached *ahiṁsā* not only in India but outside the country as well.

### Alexander the Great

The first visitors from outside India were the Persians under Cyrus, followed by Darius (521–485 B.C.), who occupied the areas surrounding the Indus Valley region. The Persians later recruited soldiers from the north who fought with Darius's son Xerxes in the Persian invasion of Greece in 479 B.C. Fantastic tales of India had been circulating ever since the return of their first official envoy, Scylax, a decade earlier. Darius the Great, Emperor of Persia, had sent him to sail down the Indus River to its mouth and make his way home by the Red Sea. In so doing, Scylax followed the same route as the Phoenicians of the Levant, who traded with Western India as early as 975 B.C.

Spurred on by tales of exotic animals and birds—apes, crocodiles, and peacocks—as well as stories of ivory, cotton, and other fine fabrics, Alexander the Great invaded India in 326 B.C. An estimated army of 25,000 to 30,000 men first occupied Taxila, now in Pakistan, then usurped the Persians and headed further inland, defeating the Aryan King Porus and his vast army of elephants. Due to this crushing defeat, no Indian ruler seriously contested Alexander's advances, but the further inland he moved, the more mutinous his travel-weary army became. Leaving behind a few officers as petty princes in the Upper Indus Valley, the Greek army turned toward a homeland that Alexander never lived to see again. He died in 323 B.C. at the age of thirty-three, in Babylon. He had remained in India only nineteen months.

The influx of foreigners was influential. Alexander the Great's invasion caused political chaos within the country, and several small independent territories arose for a short time until the ascent of a powerful king named Candragupta Maurya.

## Mauryan Empire

Historians claim the real political genius behind the Mauryan throne was Candragupta's chief minister, Cāṇakya Paṇḍita (also known as Kautilya). Cāṇakya wrote a treatise on the art of government and taxation in 250 B.C. called *Arthaśāstra*, or *The Science of Material Gain*. (An interesting insight into Mauryan society was also compiled by a Greek traveler named Megasthenes, who lived in Candragupta's court for five years from 302–298 B.C. He wrote a book called *Indika* describing Candragupta's exploits.)

Mauryan society marked a unique transition from a rural monarchy to a strictly enforced civil administration. The Mauryan State controlled all major industries, with strict pay scales and taxes imposed on artisans and professionals alike. The Mauryan capital, Pataliputra (present-day Patna in Bihar), was administered by the traditional *panchayat* (five-member) council of elders, a structure that was repeated throughout the Mauryan Empire to govern India's cities, towns, and villages. Even today many Indian villages still use this system to govern themselves.

## Emperor Aśoka

Candragupta's son, Bindusara, reigned for twenty-five years, then was succeeded by his son, Aśoka. In 261 B.C., Aśoka invaded Kaliṅga (Orissa) in one of the bloodiest conquests recorded from that time. From Rock Edict XIII,[4] historians conclude that some 150,000 were captured, 150,000 slain, and thousands more unaccounted for. This Challenge War produced far-reaching ramifications; as a result of the massive slaughter and bloodshed, Emperor Aśoka repented. He ardently adhered to the nonviolent teachings of Buddhism and used

---

[4] Various inscriptions and carvings from Aśoka's time have been systematically numbered for clear identification. The particular inscriptions mentioned and a famous elephant carving can still be seen near the Buddhist Temple just south of Bhuvanesvara.

his government's vast treasury to propagate his faith.

Aśoka's grandfather had set up an excellent administration under the tutelage of Cāṇakya Paṇḍita, and the young monarch continued with this same framework. Although the administrative framework remained essentially the same, there was a significant change in attitude. Emperor Aśoka had the principal teachings of Buddhism inscribed on thirty pillars (of which only ten remain today) and eighteen rock faces across his domain, which included most of India. One inscription in stone reads, "All men are my children. As I desire for my children that they may enjoy prosperity and happiness both in this life and the next, so also I desire the same for all men."[5]

Although Aśoka was a Buddhist, he didn't persecute those who professed other faiths. On another stone inscription it is written: "There should not be honor only to one's own sect and condemnation to another's sect. On the contrary, another's sect should be honored on this and that occasion. By doing so, one promotes his own sect and benefits another sect."

Aśoka's death eventually led to the downfall of the Mauryan Empire. In 135 B.C. Pusyamitra Sunga assassinated the last ruler of the Mauryan dynasty, Brihadratha.

## Kharavela

In the Hathigumpha cave inscriptions, information is written about Pusyamitra Sunga's futile venture to invade Kaliṅga. During that period, a Jain king named Kharavela ruled the territory and managed to defend it against Pusyamitra's attacks. At Udayagiri (just outside Bhuvaneṣvara) rock inscriptions still remain above some caves the king had gutted out of a mountainside. Although these inscriptions have been damaged over time, historians and scholars have deciphered some of the lines.

The inscriptions open with salutations to various Jain saints, then give accounts of the life of Kharavela. It is said he was endowed with noble and auspicious bodily marks, was handsome, and possessed a

[5] Kaliṅga Edict II as translated in *History of India*.

powerful stature. By the age of fifteen he became proficient in sports and games and was then educated in royal correspondence, currency, finance, and administrative and religious law. A chronological list then informs us about thirteen years of his reign, sometime after 159 B.C., when he first began his rule. During the last year mentioned in these inscriptions, Kharavela excavated the caves for the benefit of various Jain ascetics. In this way historians deduce that Jain influences under Kharavela must have been prominent in and around Jagannātha Purī and surrounding districts.

After Kharavela's reign, Jainism dwindled in Kaliṅga, and the entire country of India once again fragmented into small independent provinces. For more than five centuries power shifted from one dynasty to another, ushering in half a millennium of unsettled, often barbaric, rule. Around that time (A.D. 120–160) Buddhism branched into two sects, Hīnāyāna and Mahāyāna. The Hīnāyānists believed Buddha to be a great saint; the Mahāyānists believed him to be an incarnation of God. Mahāyānists also introduced the worship of Buddhist images.

### Jesus Christ

Although most mainstream Christian sects may dismiss the idea that Jesus visited India, there is evidence that he did. During Jesus' time the legendary Silk Road, traveled by merchants from areas around the Mediterranean, passed just north of Jerusalem on its way to India. The Holy Bible gives information of Jesus' early life, until he was about twelve years old, then again narrates his later activities, when he was thirty. Where was he, and what were his activities during those precious missing years?

The first provocative book published on this subject was written in 1894 by a Russian journalist named Nicolai Notovitch, who stumbled onto some ancient Pali manuscripts at a Buddhist monastery in Leh, the capital of Ladakh in northern Kashmir. Notovitch's book, entitled *The Unknown Life of Jesus Christ*, was the outcome of the translated manuscripts. It informs us that at the age of thirteen, Jesus left the home of Mary and Joseph in Nazareth and traveled with a merchant caravan to the holy cities of India and even to the sacred

Ganges River. Later, he left for Egypt to penetrate the mysteries of the Great Pyramid. Finally, he explored the diverse philosophies of Athens and Persepolis. Jesus ultimately returned to Israel when he was twenty-nine—eighteen years later.

Levi H. Dowling's popular *Aquarian Gospel*, written in 1908, only fourteen years after *The Unknown Life*, is now known to be derived from Notovitch's work. Dowling originally claimed his book was a psychic document, given to him by revelation. Naturally the academic world was skeptical and maintained that it was simply plagiarism. With a few embellishments and Dowling's personal beliefs infiltrating the book, it largely tells the same story as Notovitch's authoritative work.

According to the ancient manuscripts found by Notovitch, Jesus spent six years learning and teaching the *Vedas* in Benares, Jagannātha Purī, and other cities in the state of Orissa. Later publications by Reverend C. R. Potter, Andreas Faber-Kaiser, Elizabeth Clare Prophet, and Dick and Janet Bock add further scholarly clarification. Unfortunately, this subject is far too complex to discuss in detail here. For further information, see *Jesus Lived in India*, by Holger Kersten (Element Books,1986). The bibliography in this book is extensive and can lead to further study.[6]

## Gupta Period

For almost a thousand years, from 600 B.C. to A.D. 300, Buddhism and Jainism flourished in India alongside a degenerating Vedic culture. The next two centuries, A.D. 320–540, are often called the Golden Age of Hinduism, or the Gupta Period. A Chinese pilgrim named Fahein traveled throughout India for six years, 405–411, and from Fahein's accounts historians learn that Buddhism was on the wane, although Fahein visited many Buddhist monasteries and was himself a Buddhist.

During the Gupta Period India grew in many ways. A large number of coins, sculptures, and architectural items of that time have

[6] For a short essay on the subject, see *Did Jesus Go India?* by Steven Rosen, in *Vedic Archeology*.

been excavated at various sites and are now in museums throughout the country. These items reveal something about the economic condition and personal accomplishments of the Gupta rulers. The Guptas established their base of imperial power in Magadha (present-day Bihar), where they controlled rich sources of iron ore. We also learn of their achievements in art, music, mathematics, astronomy, astrology, sculpture, architecture, and metallurgy. It was during the Gupta period that merchants increased trade with China, Ceylon, the East Indies, and the Roman Empire.

According to the inscriptions of Mādhava Raj II, Orissa also came under the influence of the Guptas as a result of an invasion by Samudra Gupta (A.D. 330–375).

### Political Chaos and Rise of Harsha Vardhana

Nomadic tribes such as the Huns began to invade India in A.D. 478. They gradually caused havoc throughout the Gupta Empire with their barbaric attacks on towns and villages. This led to the rise of many minor rulers, until Harsha Vardhana in 606.

During Vardhana's time, another Chinese traveler, Hieun-Tsang (Yuan Chwang), lived in India and wrote of his travels. Hieun-Tsang says that early in life, Harsa worshiped Lord Śiva and the sun-god as a Hindu, but due to the influence of his sister, Rajyasri, he took up Buddhism. Hieun-Tsang attended a Buddhist Sangha in A.D. 643 held by the emperor. Vardhana held such Sanghas every five years in Prayag to promote the Buddhist faith. It is also mentioned, however, that he gave liberally in charity to those of other faiths and often exhausted the treasury during such occasions.

Hieun-Tsang spent over fifteen years traveling throughout India, and upon returning to China he wrote a book entitled *Si-yu-ki*, *Records of the Western World*. Therein he mentions a famous Buddhist holy place of pilgrimage on the Orissan seashore. Many historians believe this place to be Purī, indicating that Buddhist influence must have been felt in the Jagannātha worship. Some even believe that a relic of Lord Buddha's tooth was present in Purī at the time. There are records that this relic was later moved to Ceylon (Sri Lanka).

After Harsa Vardhana's rule, India again split into many small

24. *Young Orissan artist with his painting*

25. *Orissan applique*

*27. King Ashoka's ancient elephant carving*

*28. King Karavela's caves constructed for Jain monks*

30. *Preserved manuscripts and personal sword of Śrīla Rāmānanda Rāya*

31. *Paramānanda Purī's well*

*32. Deity of Ālālanātha where Śrī Caitanya Mahāprabhu went during Anavasara (renovation of deities)*

33. *Haridāsa Ṭhākura's samādhi*

34. *Toṭa-Gopīnātha*

*35. 19th-century British drawing*

Muralivadana Dāsa

*36. An artisan carves the form of the Lord*

Muralivadana Dāsa

*37. Traditional art focuses on the form of the Lord*

HARE KRISHNA
HARE KRISHNA
KRISHNA KRISHNA
HARE HARE
HARE RAMA
HARE RAMA
RAMA RAMA
HARE HARE

Amogha Dāsa

39. *Washington, D.C.*

Yamarāja Dāsa

40. *Golden Gate Park, San Francisco*

41. *Venice Beach, Los Angeles*

Yamarāja Dāsa

42. Mumbai

Visānta Dāsa

44. *Jayānanda at the first New York Rathayātrā, 1976*

ХАРЕ КРИШНА
ХАРЕ КРИШНА
КРИШНА КРИШНА
ХАРЕ
РАМА
РАМА
ХАРЕ

independent states. By then, the country was in chaos both politically and spiritually. Buddhists and Jains had split into different sects and sub-sects and were rapidly losing influence, and Hindus had grouped together under varying philosophies, some worshiping Viṣṇu, others Śiva, others Durgā, the sun-god, Ganeśa, and on and on and on.

## Śaṅkarācārya

Śaṅkarācārya was born in A.D. 788 in Malabar, on the southwest coast of the country. Even as a young man he traveled throughout India defeating renowned scholars and establishing the Māyāvāda doctrine. Śaṅkarācārya taught that everything ultimately emanates from Brahman, a transcendent, impersonal spirit. His commentary on the *Vedānta-sūtra*, known as *Śarirakya-bhāṣya*, served as the pillar for his newfound philosophy.

Śaṅkarācārya was a dynamic preacher. By his influence Buddhism was practically pushed out of India. Lord Buddha's teachings did not recognize the *Vedas*. Śaṅkarācārya, however, used the *Vedas* to establish a doctrine similar to Buddha's. To further implement his philosophy, Śaṅkarācārya established four *dhāmas* (holy places) in the four cardinal directions: Badarikāśrama in the north, Dvārakā in the west, Rāmeśvaram in the south, and Jagannātha Purī in the east. In each of these places he established elaborate deity worship based on the *Tantra-upāsana*, a system of worship originally propounded by Lord Śiva. This method of worship has proved so influential that it still remains the prominent system of *pūjā* in all four *dhāmas* today. It is also interesting to note that Śaṅkarācārya worshiped four *nātha* deities: Badrinātha, Dvārakānātha, Rāmanātha, and Jagannātha. The monastery established by Śaṅkarācārya in Purī, called Bhogavardhana or Govardhana Math, is located near Svargadvara on the seashore.[7]

As mentioned previously, servants known as *Duela Karana* keep records of the daily events in the Jagannātha temple. The record book is known as the *Madalapanji*.[8] Records as far back as a few hundred years, however, are dubious. Various scribes often contradict one

---

[7] See *Caitanya-caritāmṛta (Madhya-līlā 9.244)* purport.

[8] See *Daily Pūjā* in *Part Two* for descriptions of various temple duties.

another or prove to be wrong. This leaves historians in a quandary. Although we cannot accept every description, we cannot reject everything either.

In any case, the *Madalapanji* relates that at the time of Śaṅkarācārya, Yayāti Keśarī was the king of Kaliṅga. *Madalapanji* says that 146 years before Yayāti, a *yavana* named Raktabāhu invaded Purī from the sea. The deities of Jagannātha, Balarāma, and Subhadrā were therefore removed from Purī to Sonepur for the 146 years until the coronation of Yayāti Keśarī. According to the chronicle, Yayāti renovated the deities and built a new temple because the previous one was dilapidated. Historians believe the Keśarīs who ruled Orissa in the ninth century were worshipers of Śiva who also supported Viṣṇu worship. This implies that Śaṅkarācārya and Yayāti Keśarī cooperated to once again establish the enthusiastic worship of Lord Jagannātha in Purī after years of neglect.

## The Impact of Islam

As these events transpired in and around Purī, Muslims from Arabia and Afghanistan invaded North India. The founder of Islam, the Prophet Mohammed, lived from 570 until 632. During his lifetime almost all of Arabia took to the new religion. Eventually, the Muslims branched out and conquered neighboring countries—Syria, Mesopotamia, Egypt, Persia, and territories in Central Asia.

Mohammed taught that there is one, all-powerful God, Allah, and that he was His prophet. Mohammed's teachings are recorded in the *Qur'an* (*Koran*), the holy scriptures of the Islamic faith. Mohammed was against the worship of images—he considered such worship idolatry—and he preached that all men were equal and that caste divisions were artificial (although he allowed Muslims to keep slaves). The five main duties of Muslims are called the Five Pillars of Islam: *shahadah* (statement of faith), *salah* (prayer, five times a day facing Mecca), *zakah* (give in charity), *sawm* (fasting from food and drink from dawn until dusk during the ninth lunar month, Ramadan), and *hajj* (to make at least one holy pilgrimage to Mecca during one's life). Mohammed taught his followers to expect a day of judgment when everyone would be punished or rewarded according to his deeds.

The Muslim Arabs first invaded India in A.D. 712, but their initial influence was meager. They simply plundered cities, towns, and villages without establishing any administration or empire. Their raids continued for several hundred years until Mohammed Ghauri founded the first true Muslim Empire in India. This was during the twelfth century, and it was the dawn of Islamic dynasties in South Asia.

We should note that the Muslims primarily involved themselves with North India. In the south, Hinduism in its multifarious forms remained prevalent. Purī remained Hindu during early Muslim conquests, guided by the Gaṅgā dynasty, which will now be discussed, but suffered violent attacks at Muslim hands as they grew in strength throughout the country.

### The Gaṅgā Dynasty Chodaganga and Anangabhima

Most historians acknowledge Chodagangadeva as the king who began construction of the massive Jagannātha temple we see today. Construction began sometime during the twelfth century. Various copper plate inscriptions indicate that Chodaganga ruled a kingdom extending from the Ganges River in the north to the Godāvari River in the south. He defeated the kings of Utkal and Vengi and erected two pillars of victory, each decorated with a necklace of Śrī, the goddess of fortune. Shortly thereafter he conquered the country of Mandara in Gauḍa and was engaged in a long war with the Cedis of Ratnapur.

During these exploits, Chodaganga acquired huge amounts of wealth and booty, which he had carried back on his 10,000 war elephants. According to popular tradition, these elephants made trips back and forth to Purī. Upon arrival in the town, all the accumulated goods were poured into a well that had been dug near Nīlagiri Hill. This well is still known as *suna kuan*, "the golden well." When the well was finally filled with riches, construction of a new temple began.

Historians also believe the initial temple structures, the *Duela* and *Jagamohana*, were finished by Chodaganga's descendant Anangabhima sometime between 1212 and 1239. Because the Gaṅgā kings

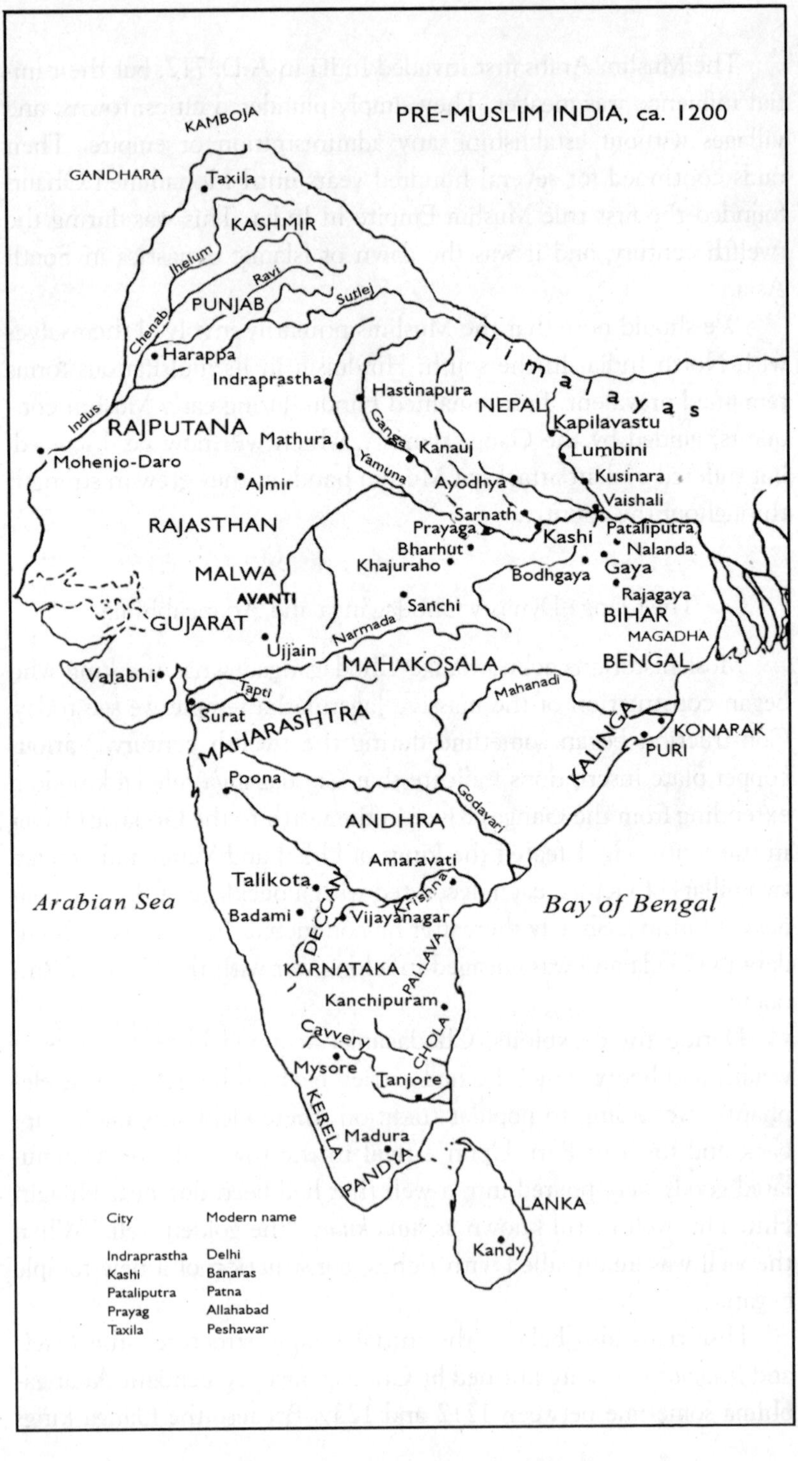

PRE-MUSLIM INDIA, ca. 1200

KAMBOJA

GANDHARA
Taxila

KASHMIR

Jhelum
Ravi
PUNJAB
Sutlej

Chenab

Indus
Harappa
Indraprastha

Himalayas

Hastinapura
NEPAL
Kapilavastu

Ganga
Kanauj
Lumbini

RAJPUTANA
Mathura
Yamuna
Ayodhya
Kusinara

Mohenjo-Daro
Ajmir
Sarnath
Vaishali

Prayaga
Kashi
Pataliputra

RAJASTHAN
Bharhut
Nalanda

Khajuraho
Bodhgaya
Gaya

MALWA
Sanchi
Rajagaya

AVANTI
BIHAR

GUJARAT
Narmada
MAGADHA

Ujjain
MAHAKOSALA
BENGAL

Valabhi

Tapti
Mahanadi

Surat
KALINGA

MAHARASHTRA
KONARAK

Poona
PURI

Godavari

ANDHRA

Amaravati

Arabian Sea
Talikota
Bay of Bengal

Krishna

Badami
DECCAN
Vijayanagar

KARNATAKA
PALLAVA

Kanchipuram

Cavvery
CHOLA

Mysore
Tanjore

KERALA
Madura
PANDYA
LANKA

Kandy

| City | Modern name |
|------|-------------|
| Indraprastha | Delhi |
| Kashi | Banaras |
| Pataliputra | Patna |
| Prayag | Allahabad |
| Taxila | Peshawar |

were devoted to Lord Jagannātha, the cult's popularity grew and enticed many pilgrims to Purī. Administration and management of the Jagannātha temple, established by Chodaganga almost eight hundred years ago, remains virtually the same today. It was during the time of the Gaṅgā dynasty (1078–1435) that Lord Jagannātha became the official state deity, and all others, including the king, His servants.

### Rāmānujācārya

Due to the patronage of powerful kings in the Gaṅgā dynasty, worship of Lord Jagannātha flourished and attracted numerous pilgrims to Purī. One noteworthy visitor during this time was Rāmānujācārya, from South India. At that time, Rāmānuja was traveling all over the Indian subcontinent establishing his doctrine of *viśiṣṭādvaita*, qualified monism. Rāmānuja defeated scholars and court *paṇḍitas* wherever he went. He even subdued Śaṅkarācārya's followers with his teachings that God is the Supreme Person and all living beings His eternal servants.

Scholarly debates were common affairs in the royal palaces in those days, and they were often heated. As scholars discussed the subtle intricacies of philosophy, they often found themselves defending their personal beliefs. Sometimes scholars and religionists would travel around the country simply to participate in or instigate such debates, and to enhance their reputations or gain proponents of their philosophical or spiritual understanding. Rāmānuja was so powerful and clear in his arguments that he soon established a distinguished reputation throughout the country. Few dared to debate with him. In the kingdom of King Kulattunga, a Śaivite ruling near Mysore, the debates became so inflamed that the king ordered his soldiers to pluck out the eyes of two of Rāmānuja's disciples because he thought they had blasphemed Lord Śiva. Rāmānuja's disciples, Mahāpuruṣa and Kuresh, had simply proven by *śāstric* logic that Lord Nārāyaṇa was superior to Lord Śiva. This event gives us a glimpse into the life and times of twelfth-century India.

Rāmānujācārya was a member of the Śrī *sampradāya*, and by his traveling and preaching he was able to establish its doctrines and initiate thousands of disciples. During his stay at Jagannātha Purī, the *ācārya* established a monastery named Emar Math, just opposite the *Siṁha-dvara.* He also noticed that the ritualistic worship of Lord Jagannātha did not strictly follow the *pāñcarātriki* regulations. Rather, the *sevaits* followed Śaṅkarācārya's Māyāvāda teachings and tantric methods of worship. Most of the *sevaits* did not even belong to a Vaiṣṇava *sampradāya.* He discussed this with the king and his *paṇḍitas*. King Chodagangadeva was convinced by Rāmānujā's strong arguments and agreed to change the standard of worship in the temple. He ordered the head priests to meet with Rāmānuja the following day to learn from him the new standard of worship to be employed.

The local priests were concerned that the new system would effect the entire mode of worship at Jagannātha Purī. In fact, they believed Rāmānuja would enforce some of the stricter codes of Vedic worship and would thus disqualify some of the lower caste servants from performing their direct services to the deities. None dared question the king, however, because it had been a long-standing belief that the king was the Lord's direct representative. His authority was paramount. All waited anxiously for the meeting with Rāmānuja.

As the sun rose the following day, Rāmānuja was nowhere to be found. Everyone waited anxiously for his arrival, ready to carry out his orders, but he never arrived at the Jagannātha temple. According to the *Prapannāmṛta*, a biographical work on Rāmānuja, while the *ācārya* slept that night, Lord Jagannātha mystically carried him several hundred kilometers south to a place called Kūrma-kṣetra. When Rāmānuja awoke he decided not to return to Purī, but he established gorgeous worship of Lord Kūrma at Kūrma-kṣetra and continued south.[9]

### Jayadeva Gosvāmī

It was also during Chodaganga's reign that the famous poet Jayadeva Gosvāmī lived in Purī. Jayadeva's songs and poems are filled with loving emotions and reveal his depth of feeling for the Supreme Lord. His words are so pure and inspirational that he has remained

---

[9] See *Caitanya- caritāmṛta* (*Madhya-līlā* 7.113 purport).

famous throughout India for almost a thousand years. His well-known *Gīta-govinda* is a work of unique beauty and charm; it is adored by millions of devotees of Kṛṣṇa around the world.

The most famous story about Jayadeva Gosvāmī took place while he was writing. Deep in meditation, Jayadeva was relating the intimate pastimes of Lord Kṛṣṇa with His divine consort, Śrīmatī Rādhārāṇī. While composing the work, Jayadeva had difficulty finishing a particular phrase. He didn't know exactly how to relate that the Supreme Personality of Godhead, the supreme controller of innumerable universes and origin of all energies and potencies, Lord Kṛṣṇa, aspires to put dust from the feet of His beloved upon His head. Confused and unsure, Jayadeva took a break from his writing and went nearby to bathe.

Jayadeva soon returned, asked his wife, Padmavatī, for the scroll, and continued writing. Moments later, Jayadeva walked in the door of his house and again asked his wife for the scroll. Puzzled, Padmavatī explained that she had just given him the scroll. Jayadeva and Padmavatī then entered his writing room and saw the scroll on his table. Looking closer, they both saw a line written in a slightly different hand. The verse which Jayadeva was having trouble composing now read *dehi pada pallava mudāram*, "O Rādhikā, let Your lotus feet be placed upon My head." Astounded, Jayadeva and his wife realized that Lord Jagannātha had taken the form of Jayadeva, entered the house, written the line, and revealed that He is subordinate to the love of His devotees, especially Śrīmatī Rādhārāṇī.

## Madhvācārya's Influence Through Narahari Tīrtha

Following the thread of philosophical thought thus far, we see that Jainism and Buddhism propounded a voidistic concept of ultimate reality. Defeating these doctrines with quotes from the *Vedas*, Śaṅkarācārya founded the Māyāvāda philosophy, stating that the impersonal Brahman is the origin of all things. Śaṅkarācārya taught, *brahma satyaṁ, jagan mithyā*: "Brahman, spirit, is true, and matter is false. The living entity is nothing but Brahman." Although similar to Buddhism, Śaṅkara's teachings were based on the *Vedas* and were therefore considered more authoritative.

Rāmānujācārya used the same *Vedas* to establish that the cause of all causes is a person, the Supreme Person, Nārāyaṇa. Rāmānuja argued, "What is the necessity for Śaṅkarācārya to endeavor with so much energy to establish his philosophy if it is all fictitious? To say 'the world is false' is a suicidal position. Has he come here to do nothing? No, he has come to correct us and free us from error, but there must be errors. Error or misconception has reality; otherwise, what is the necessity of spending so much energy refuting so many propositions?"

The idea that unity in the Absolute is not a stale, nondifferentiated thing was propounded by Rāmānuja. This is called *viśiṣṭādvaita-vāda*, oneness with difference. The philosophy of Śaṅkarācārya, on the other hand, is known as *kevalādvaita-vāda*, exclusive oneness without variety. Rāmānuja accepts that the Absolute Truth is one, but according to him, it is differentiated oneness. That it is one, he has no doubt, but that "one" is characterized by specification and differentiation. Rāmānuja thus conceded that there is a qualified oneness between the Supreme and the individual soul.[10]

About one century after Rāmānujācārya, Madhvācārya (1238–1317 according to most) took the idea of differentiation a step further by propounding the *dvaita* philosophy. Madhvācārya taught that the Supreme and the individual souls are distinct separate entities. He directly opposed the teachings of Śaṅkarācārya, who emphasized the oneness of all things. In drawings of Madhvācārya we always see him with two fingers raised. This perfectly symbolizes his philosophy of Dualism.

Inscriptions at the Srikurmam and Simhacalam temples of South India attest that Madhvācārya's disciple named Narahari Tīrtha was the Minister of Kaliṅga for twelve years. Nine inscriptions have been located concerning Narahari Tīrtha, dating from 1264 to 1294.[11] A work entitled *Narahariyatistotra* explains that Narahari Tīrtha traveled to Kaliṅga on his guru's order to acquire some deities of Sītā-Rāma that were in the state treasury.

---

[10] See *Subjective Evolution* (pg. 76–77)

[11] See *Caitanya-caritāmṛta (Madhya-līlā* 7.113) with purport for an English translation of these inscriptions; also included is a brief outline of the previously mentioned pastime between Rāmānujācārya and Lord Jagannātha.

### Mūla Sītā-Rāma

The remarkable history of these deities, known as Mula Sītā-Rāma (the original Sītā-Rāma), is narrated in the book known as *Adhyātma-rāmāyaṇa* (Chapters 12–15). During Lord Rāmacandra's reign in Ayodhya there lived a *brāhmaṇa* who vowed not to eat on any given day until he saw the transcendental form of Lord Rāma. Sometimes the Lord was absent from His capital, and at such times the citizens could not see Him. Because of his vow, however, this *brāhmaṇa* would not take even a drop of water until the Lord appeared.

Upon observing the *brāhmaṇa's* rigid vow, Lord Rāmacandra ordered His younger brother Lakṣmaṇa to deliver a pair of Sītā-Rāma deities to the *brāhmaṇa*. The *brāhmaṇa* happily received the deities from Lakṣmaṇa and worshiped Them faithfully as long as he lived. At the time of his death, the *brāhmaṇa* delivered the deities to Hanumān, who hung Them around his neck and served Them with all devotion. After many years, when Hanumānjī had departed to the hill known as Gandhamādana, he delivered the deities to Bhīmasena, one of the Pāṇḍavas, and Bhīmasena brought Them to his palace, where he kept Them carefully. The last king of the Pāṇḍava dynasty, Kṣemakānta, also worshiped the deities in the palace at Hastināpura.

It may be noted that these deities have been worshiped from the time of King Ikṣvaku. Indeed, they were worshiped by the royal princes and kings, including King Daśaratha, even before the appearance of Lord Rāmacandra. Later, during Lord Rāmacandra's presence, the deities were worshiped by Lakṣmaṇa and then given to the *brāhmaṇa*.[12]

While Narahari Tīrtha was on his mission to obtain these deities, the king of Kaliṅga passed away. The state ministry then arranged for a royal procession headed by an elephant along *Badadanda*, Grand Road, to choose a new regent, for the prince was too young to act as an administrator. The elephant chose Narahari Tīrtha by placing a flower garland around his neck.

After twelve years of excellent management by Narahari Tīrtha, the prince came of age and Narahari relinquished office. Appreciat-

[12] See *Caitanya-caritāmṛta (Madhya-līlā* 9.11).

ing the administrative work rendered by Narahari Tīrtha, the young king asked what he could possibly do to show his gratitude. To fulfill his guru's desires, Narahari chose to take the Mula Sītā-Rāma deities back to Udupi. Madhvācārya received these unique deities only three months and sixteen days before his disappearance from the world. Mūla Sītā-Rāma are now kept at Madhvācārya's monastery in Udupi, Karnataka.

Historians infer that due to the powerful influence of this devoted governor, Narahari Tirtha, Vaiṣṇavaism flourished in Purī during his time. Indeed, the young prince who became king, Narasimhadeva II, also became Narahari Tīrtha's disciple.

### Rise of the Sūrya-vaṁśā Dynasty Over the Gaṅgā Dynasty—Kapilendra 1435–1467

The Gaṅgā dynasty's reign in Orissa began with Chodagangadeva in A.D. 1078 and ended when Bhanudeva IV was overthrown in 1435. This was the longest rule by a single dynasty in Orissan history. The Gaṅgā kings left behind many traces of their devotion to Lord Jagannātha; of course, the most prominent is the magnificent temple, which continues to proclaim their adoration of the Lord.

Bhanudeva IV was impelled to spend a great deal of time in the southern part of the region to consolidate his empire. While he was away from the capital, however, one of his leading officers usurped his throne. This new king, Kapilendra, according to stone inscriptions from Gopinathapur, was born in Orissa in the solar dynasty.[13] The Sūrya-vaṁśā kings, beginning with Kapilendra, ruled for only 105 years, yet during this time Orissa reached the height of her glory.

At first, Kapilendra found it difficult to unite his empire. Because he had usurped the throne from Bhanudeva IV, neighboring rulers under the Gaṅgā dynasty hesitated to accept his rule. In an inscription engraved on the *Jagamohana* of the Liṅgarāja temple during the seventh year of his reign, Kapilendra wrote, "All kings in my kingdom should work for the good of their paramount sovereign in pious ways. If they rebel against their sovereign they will be expelled from

[13] Kings in the solar dynasty trace their ancestry back to the sun-god.

the kingdom and their property shall be confiscated." Gradually, Kapilendra expanded his empire, and historians now can study the many stone inscriptions and copper plates to trace the history.

By the tenth year of his rule Kapilendra, also known as Kapileśvara, had united his troops and considerably increased the size of his kingdom. In an inscription dated 1447, the monarch has been given the title Gauḍeśvara, "the conqueror of Gauḍa [Bengal]." Of course, Kapilendra couldn't have defeated the Muslim stronghold in Bengal, but he seems to have won territories in the southwestern regions near the Ganges River. The death of Devaraya II in 1446, and the succession to the throne by his weak son Mallikarjuna, gave Kapilendra the opportunity to attack the Vijaya-nagara area to the southwest, and to send his own son, Hamvira, further south into the Telegu-speaking kingdoms. After various conquests, Kapilendra's empire increased until finally in 1464, his kingdom extended from the Ganges River in the north to the Kāverī River in the south. This was the largest area the Kaliṅga Empire would ever cover.

## Sarala Dāsa

During Kapilendra's reign, Orissa's literary culture began to flourish. This was especially due to Sarala Dasa, a prolific writer who translated the *Mahābhārata* into Oriya and thus popularized it amongst local people. He did not, however, follow the *Mahābhārata* that was originally composed by Śrīla Vyāsadeva. The Orissan people had little access to the authorized version, so they accepted Sarala Dasa's imaginative stories even though his stories drastically deviated from historical truth. Sarala Dasa had a vivid imagination, and he added numerous tales of his own throughout his "translation" of the *Mahābhārata*.

He also composed his own *Rāmāyaṇa* in Oriya, again not following Vālmīki's original work. This type of literary presentation is sometimes praised by the less intelligent, who feel Sarala Dasa added to Orissan culture through his writings. But what is the value of his works? He drastically deviated from historical facts, and thus misrepresented original works, albeit in an ornamented and glittering form in the local language. Unfortunately, his stories have become standard folklore in Orissan villages, thus obscuring historical facts originally presented by Vyāsa and Vālmīki.

Of course, Sarala Dasa has not been the only author during the thousands of years of Jagannātha worship to implant imaginary ideas and mythological legends into the culture. The list of those who have done so is endless. In fact, most legends we hear today are a complex mixture of several stories from a variety of authors; the actual history has become almost impossible to trace. Because Sarala Dasa's writings have become so popular throughout Orissa, and because his imaginative stories are so easily detected as mental concoctions, we have inserted this brief history to highlight the point.[14]

## Puruṣottama 1467–1497

Kapilendra's kingdom became unstable during the last years of his reign. The king was getting older, and there were numerous political intrigues as various parties planned to take control after his death. The *Madalapanji* states that Kapilendra had eighteen sons but finally chose Puruṣottama to succeed him. His eldest son, Hamvira, was infuriated when he heard, through a messenger, that his younger brother was given the throne. Hamvira immediately advanced upon Puruṣottama from the south, but was ultimately defeated. He again retired to the south.

During this transitional period, Saluva Narasimha, a king from the southern district, again occupied an area just north of the Kāverī River and began to chip away at the Kaliṅga Empire. Inscriptions at the Jagannātha temple dated 1467 reveal that Puruṣottama gave the temple offerings of jewels and villages. He was thus busy in the north and unable to resist onslaughts from various quarters. It was a custom of the times that a new king would prove he had been favored by Lord

[14] Elaborating or commenting on scriptures, and changing or interpreting scripture, are very different concepts. Complex theological differences between them are too sensitive and detailed to discuss here. Works that should be consulted for further study are Śrīla Jīva Gosvāmī's *Tattva-sandarbha* (10–11), Śrīla Baladeva Vidyābhūṣaśa's commentary on that, and the following verses of the *Brahma-sūtra: śāstra-yonitvāt* (Vs. 1.1.3), *tarko'pratiṣṭha* (Vs. 2.1.11), and *śrutes tu śabda-mūlatvāt* (Vs. 2.1.27), as commented on by Śrī Rāmānujācārya, Śrī Madhvācārya, Śrī Nimbarkācārya, and Śrīla Baladeva Vidyābhūṣaśa.

Jagannātha, and Puruṣottama in particular endeavored to please the Lord in this way. It is still a popular belief that King Kapilendra was told in a dream by Lord Jagannātha that Puruṣottama was the proper successor over any of his other seventeen sons.

Like his father, King Puruṣottama had difficulty adjusting to ruling an empire. Puruṣottama's problems were not, however, caused by his usurping the throne. Rather, his kingdom was surrounded by hostile enemies. In 1475, rebellion broke out in the southwestern area of Kondavidu and resulted in an attack by a neighboring king, Muhammad III, who conspired with Puruṣottama's estranged brother, Hamvira. Puruṣottama was eventually forced to pay a tribute of twenty-five elephants to calm the invader and settle a truce, but he lost the provinces of Rajamahendri and Kondavidu in the process.

Because the southern regions were now weakened, Saluva Narasimha advanced even further north, as far as Udayagiri, just north of Kāñcī. His advances were not altogether successful, because just after he arrived at Kāñcī, Muhammad III invaded and sacked the city.

When Muhammad III died in 1482, a fierce struggle broke out between Puruṣottama and Saluva Narasimha, until finally, between 1486 and 1491, Puruṣottama conquered Narasimha and drove him out of Kāñcī and Udayagiri.[15] On the journey back to his capital, King Puruṣottama and one of his queens engaged in a wonderful pastime with the Sākṣi-gopāla deity, as described in the *Caitanya-caritāmṛta* (*Madhya-līlā* 5.117–133).

### Sākṣi-gopāla and the Queen

After Lord Gopāla transferred Himself from Vṛndāvana, He was situated in the Trailanga-deśa regions of South India, on the banks of the Godāvarī River, in the town of Vidyanagara. (Vidyanagara is

[15] There is controversy over the exact date of Puruṣottama's invasion of Kāñcī to win the princess Padmavatī, as mentioned earlier in the Ratha-yātrā chapter and descriptions of *chera-pahanra*. This invasion for the sake of his honor took place either during earlier conquests around 1471 A.D. or during the later years mentioned in the above text. Most historians believe that it must have been the earlier conquests, for by the time of his later conquest, the king was getting too old for such exploits.

not identical with the previously mentioned Vijay-nagara.) When Puruṣottama-deva defeated Saluva Narasimha, he took possession of a valuable throne known as the Māṇikya-siṁhāsana, which was bedecked with many jewels. The devoted king also begged at the lotus feet of Lord Gopāla, "Please come to my kingdom." When the king begged Him to come to his kingdom, Gopāla, who was already obliged to him for his devotional service, accepted his prayer. Thus the king took the Gopāla deity and went back to Kaṭaka (Cuttack). In the meantime, the king also visited Purī and presented the bejeweled throne to Lord Jagannātha.

When the Gopāla deity was installed in Kaṭaka, the queen of Puruṣottama went to see Him and, with great devotion, presented various ornaments for Him to wear. The queen had a valuable pearl that she wore on her nose, and she wished to give it to Gopāla. She began to think, *If there were a hole in the deity's nose, I could transfer the pearl to Him.* Considering this, the queen offered her obeisances to Gopāla and returned to her palace.

That night, the queen dreamed that Gopāla appeared and began to speak to her. "During My childhood My mother made a hole in My nose and with great endeavor set a pearl there. That very hole is still there, and you can use it to set the pearl you desired to give Me."

The queen described her dream to her husband and the king and queen went to the temple with the pearl. Seeing the hole in the deity's nose, they set the pearl in it and, being pleased, held a big festival. King Puruṣottama thus retired from the political field and was eventually succeeded by his son Pratāparudra in 1497.

### Pratāparudra 1497–1540

Pratāparudra took immediate action upon his ascension to the throne. In an inscription dated 1500, his elephants and soldiers are said to be on the banks of the Kṛṣṇa River "in order to occupy the southern quarters." In November of the following year, the king gave away some villages to *brāhmaṇas* on the banks of the Pennar. For some unknown reason, King Pratāparudra thereafter concluded this southern campaign and returned north to the capital, perhaps to keep an eye on the Sultan of Bengal, Nawab Hussain Shah, who had seized

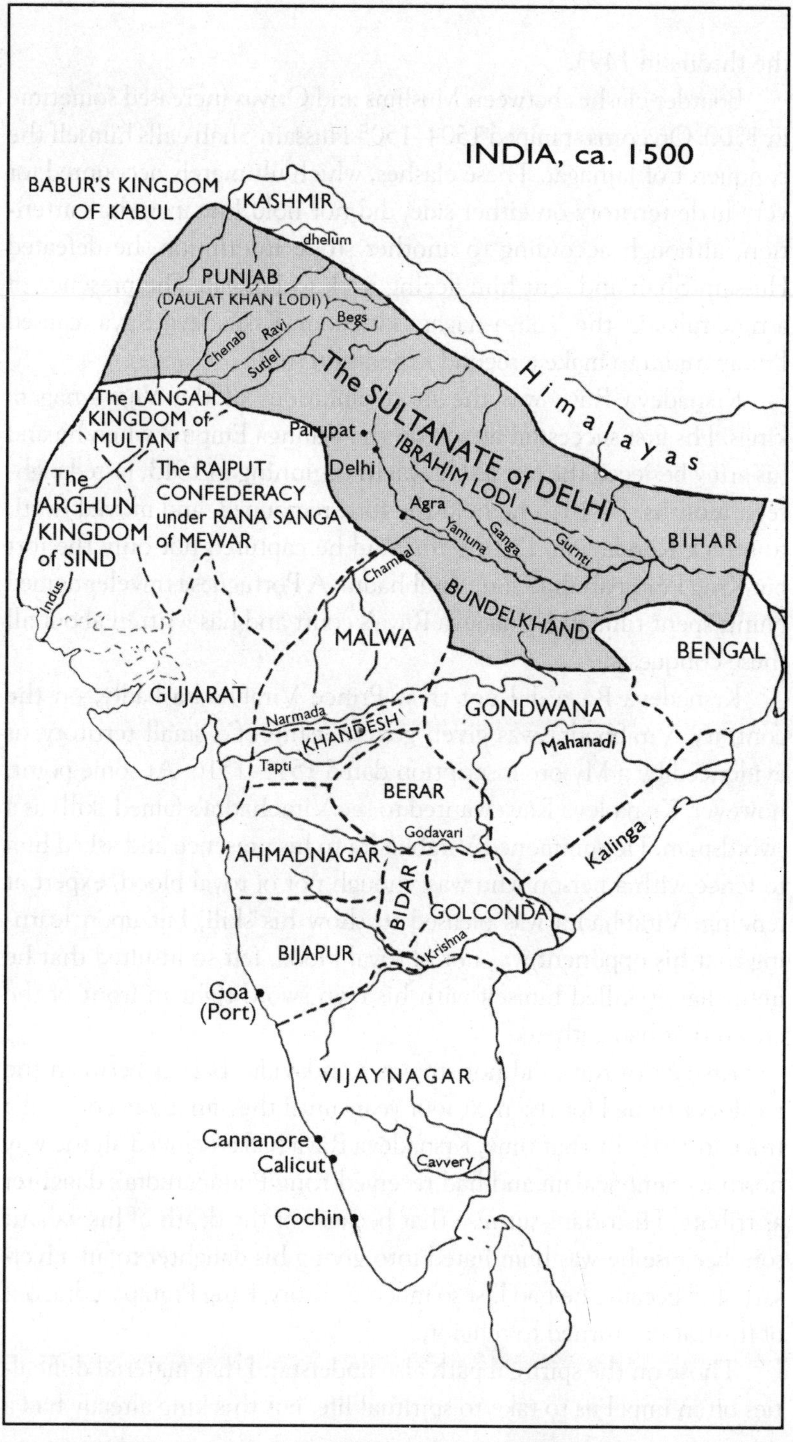
INDIA, ca. 1500
BABUR'S KINGDOM
OF KABUL
KASHMIR
dhelum
PUNJAB
(DAULAT KHAN LODI)
Chenab
Ravi
Begs
Sutlel
Himalayas
The SULTANATE of DELHI
IBRAHIM LODI
The LANGAH
KINGDOM of
MULTAN
Parupat
Delhi
The
ARGHUN
KINGDOM
of SIND
The RAJPUT
CONFEDERACY
under RANA SANGA
of MEWAR
Agra
Yamuna
Ganga
Gurnti
BIHAR
Indus
Chambal
BUNDELKHAND
MALWA
BENGAL
GUJARAT
GONDWANA
Narmada
KHANDESH
Mahanadi
Tapti
BERAR
Godavari
Kalinga
AHMADNAGAR
BIDAR
GOLCONDA
Krishna
BIJAPUR
Goa
(Port)
VIJAYNAGAR
Cannanore
Calicut
Cavvery
Cochin

the throne in 1493.

Boarder clashes between Muslims and Oriyas increased sometime in 1500. On coins stamped 1504–1505 Hussain Shah calls himself the conqueror of Jajnagar. These clashes, which ultimately accounted for very little territory on either side, did not hold Pratāparudra's attention, although according to another stone inscription, he defeated Hussain Shah and sent him fleeing back to Bengal. The presence of a new ruler in the Vijaya-nagara kingdom, Kṛṣṇadeva Rāya, caused Pratāparudra to make a second expedition south.

Kṛṣṇadeva Rāya was the most ambitious of the Vijaya-nagara kings. His first successful attack on the Kaliṅga Empire, when he and his army besieged the fort at Udayagiri beginning in 1513, lasted eighteen months. By 1515 he held the fort, regrouped, and moved north to attack Kondavidu. During this raid he captured not only the fort but King Pratāparudra's son, Vīrabhadra. A Portuguese traveler named Nuniz spent time in Kṛṣṇadeva Rāya's court and has written about all these conquests.

Kṛṣṇadeva Rāya did not treat Prince Vīrabhadra badly; on the contrary, Vīrabhadra was given governership of a small territory, as evidenced by a Mysore inscription dated 1515–1516. At some point, however, Kṛṣṇadeva Rāya wanted to see Vīrabhadra's famed skills as a swordsman. He summoned Vīrabhadra to his presence and asked him to fence with a person who was, though not of royal blood, expert at fencing. Vīrabhadra was pleased to show his skill, but upon learning that his opponent was not of royal blood, felt so insulted that he immediately killed himself with his own sword right in front of the crowd that had gathered.

Kṛṣṇadeva Rāya did not stop at Kondavidu. Battles between the rivals continued for the next four years until they finally negotiated a truce in 1519. By that time, Kṛṣṇadeva Rāya had advanced all the way north to Simhacalam and had received King Pratāparudra's daughter as tribute. Historians surmise that because of the death of his valiant son, because he was humiliated into giving his daughter to an adversary, and because he had lost so much territory, King Pratāparudra, out of frustration, turned to religion.

Those on the spiritual path also understand that material difficulties often impel us to take to spiritual life, but this king already had a devotional heart. According to the *Gaura-gaṇoddeśa-dīpikā* (118) King Indradyumna, who established the temple of Jagannātha thousands of years ago, later took birth and appeared as Mahārāja Pratāparudra.

# 4

# *Lord Caitanya's Purī Pastimes*

## Renaissance

During the famous Renaissance years of the late fifteenth century, Europeans began vigorously exploring for sea routes to India. Camel caravans had been trading overland via the legendary Silk Road for generations, but establishing sea routes would obviously create more rapid avenues for commerce. King Ferdinand and Queen Isabella of Spain sent Christopher Columbus to seek the kingdom of the Great Khān, the islands of Japan, and the riches of India—spices, ivory, jewels, and fine fabrics. Although Columbus sailed out to sea, the Portuguese explorer Vasco da Gama sailed into the Malabar coastal port of Calicut on May 27, 1498, to establish the first solid trade route from Europe.[1]

As the Europeans were evolving out of the Dark Ages and progressing in art, music, dance, and drama, a spiritual renaissance was taking place in India. This was due to the appearance of the Supreme Personality of Godhead on earth. Whenever the Supreme Lord appears, there is a natural raising of consciousness. The *Bhagavad-gītā* (4.8) states:

*paritrāṇāya sādhūnāṁ vināśāya ca duṣkṛtām*
*dharma-saṁsthāpanārthāya sambhavāmi yuge yuge*

"To deliver the pious and to annihilate the miscreants, as well as to reestablish the principles of religion, I Myself appear, millennium after millennium."

All the world's great religions teach that God desires to guide His fallen children by establishing religious principles, but most religions focus more on the appearance of God's representative in this

---

[1] *A New History of India* (p. 135)

world than on God Himself appearing here. God is merciful, and because He wishes to extend His mercy to us, He either comes Himself or sends His representative to teach us how to become free from material entanglement and go back to our eternal home in the spiritual world. According to time and circumstance, the Lord or His represenative may instruct particular cultures and civilizations to perform a variety of rituals, but the essence of all religions is the same: to evoke our devotional sentiments for the Lord as His eternal servants.

When the Lord descends as an *avatāra*, He sometimes behaves like an ordinary human being and at other times reveals His divine attributes. He doesn't force people to serve Him by a constant display of godly power; rather, He finds more pleasure in sharing natural affectionate feelings with His devotees than in their awe, reverence, or even fearful servitude. This is especially true of the *avatāra* known as Śrī Caitanya Mahāprabhu. In this particular incarnation, the Lord appeared in the mood of a devotee (*bhakta-bhāva*) to taste the sublime emotions of ecstasy that only a devotee can feel while serving Him. He also taught by His personal example how to render service unto the Supreme Lord. In *Caitanya-caritāmṛta*, a biography of Śrī Caitanya Mahāprabhu, the author, Kṛṣṇadāsa Kavirāja Gosvāmi, makes the following suggestion:

*śrī-kṛṣṇa-caitanya-dayā karaha vicāra*
*vicāra karile citte pābe camatkāra*

"If you are indeed interested in logic and argument, kindly apply it to the mercy of Śrī Caitanya Mahāprabhu. If you do so, you will find it to be strikingly wonderful."[2]

## Advent of the Lord

400 miles north of Purī, in the village of Navadvīpa, West Bengal, on the full-moon night of Phālguna (February 18, 1486 A.D.), Lord Śrī Caitanya Mahāprabhu appeared in the home of Jagannātha Miśra and his wife, Śacī. As a child, the boy was nicknamed Nimāi because

[2] *Caitanya-caritāmṛta* (*Ādi-līlā* 8.15)

He was born near a *nīm* tree.[3] His parents named Him Viśvambhara, and the local ladies called Him Gaurahari because of His golden complexion.

The Lord's childhood pastimes are vividly described in Vṛndāvana dāsa Ṭhākura's *Caitanya Bhāgavata* and are summarized in Kṛṣṇadāsa Kavirāja Gosvāmī's *Caitanya-caritāmṛta*. Both works were written in Bengali during the late sixteenth century. There are also several other biographies extant, including Murāri Gupta's *Śrī Kṛṣṇa Caitanya-caritāmṛta*, Kavi-karṇapūra's *Śrī Kṛṣṇa Caitanya-caritāmṛta-mahākavya*, Locanadāsa Ṭhākura's *Caitanya Maṅgala*, Jayānanda's book of the same name, Narahari Cakravartī's *Bhakti-ratnakāra*, and several other lesser works composed by later disciples and granddisciples. From these accounts we get a clear understanding of the Lord's life and valuable information about the culture of India during that period. It should also be noted that historians trace Viśvambhara Miśra's family heritage back to Orissa, to a family that migrated to Sylhet at the time Kapilendra captured the throne from Bhanudeva IV.[4]

When Nimāi reached the age of seven, Jagannātha Miśra dutifully performed the sacred-thread ceremony for his son, and Nimāi attained twice-born status. A year later, His father admitted Him to the school of Gaṅgādāsa Paṇḍita in Gaṅgānagar. His classmates were Śrī Gadādhara, Puruṣottama, Jagadānanda, Mukunda, and others, and by the time He was ten, Nimāi had become learned in grammar, rhetoric, *smṛti*, and *nyāya*.

When Nimāi was twelve, His elder brother, Viśvarūpa, learned that his parents were planning his marriage. Viśvarūpa, therefore, left home suddenly and accepted the *āśrama* of a *sannyāsī* (renunciant). Though only a young boy at the time, Nimāi consoled His parents with sweet words and logic. Shortly thereafter, when Nimāi was only thirteen, His father left this mortal world. Mother Śacī was exceedingly aggrieved, and Lord Caitanya, with His usual contented demeanor, consoled His widowed mother.

---

[3] *Azadirachita Indica*

[4] See *Rise of the Sūryvaṁsa Dynasty Over the Gaṅgā Dynasty* in *Part Three*, and *Caitanya and His Companions*, by Dr. D.C. Sen (p. 82). Note: Sylhet was a district in East Bengal, but after India's partition the region was renamed East Pakistan, then Bangladesh.

At the age of fourteen or fifteen Mahāprabhu was married to Lakṣmīpriyā, the daughter of Vallabācārya, also of Nadia, the district in which Navadvīpa is located. By that time Nimāi Paṇḍita was considered one of the most learned scholars of Nadia, a renowned seat of *nyaya* philosophy and Sanskrit learning. He then went to eastern Bengal along the banks of the Padmā River to acquire wealth through His learning. In those days it was customary for scholars, who were regarded as high-class people, to earn their livelihood from scholarly endeavors such as holding debates, teaching, or establishing their own schools. While Nimāi Paṇḍita was residing in East Bengal, however, Lakṣmīpriyā was bitten by a snake and died suddenly. Upon returning home, Nimāi once again found His mother in mourning. Later, at His mother's request, He married a second time, this time to Viṣṇupriyā, the daughter of Rāja Paṇḍita Sanātana Miśra.

At seventeen, Nimāi traveled to Gāya to perform his father's *piṇḍa-dāna* and *śrāddha* ceremonies. While visiting that holy city, Viśvambhara accepted initiation from Īśvara Purī, a disciple of the saint Mādhavendra Purī. Īśvara Purī instructed Nimāi to always chant the holy names of the Lord: *Hare Kṛṣṇa, Hare Kṛṣṇa, Kṛṣṇa Kṛṣṇa, Hare Hare/ Hare Rāma, Hare Rāma, Rāma Rāma, Hare Hare.*

Upon His return to Navadvīpa, Nimāi began nocturnal *kīrtanas* in the home of Śrīvāsa Paṇḍita. Following the instructions of His spiritual master, He and His associates continuously danced and chanted the holy name in ecstasy. For an entire year the Lord and His friends held these *kīrtanas*, and during this time Nimai's spiritual emotions began to overflow almost uncontrollably. When one is in a direct relationship with Lord Kṛṣṇa in intense love, various ecstatic symptoms manifest, sometimes internally and sometimes externally. Eight of these symptoms are prominent: becoming stunned, shedding tears, perspiring, changing of bodily color, standing of the hairs on the body, trembling, failing of the voice, and finally complete devastation, or trance. These symptoms occur when the vital force of life comes into contact with different elements within the body. When the vital force comes into contact with the earth element, one is stunned. When the same force comes into contact with water, there is the shedding of tears. When the same force comes into contact with fire, there is perspiration or changing of bodily color such as paleness. When the force comes into contact with the air, there is standing of the hairs on the body, trembling, and failing of the voice. And when the force comes into contact with sky, there is complete devastation, or a loss of consciousness and trance. Nimāi Paṇḍita began always feeling such symptomatic expressions within Himself, but being afraid of outsiders He didn't generally manifest them externally.

Mahāprabhu was naturally soft-hearted, though strong in His principles. He declared that party spirit and sectarianism were the two greatest enemies of progress, and as long as He continued to be an inhabitant of Nadia belonging to a certain family, His mission would not meet with complete success. Therefore, on February 3, 1510 Viśvambhara officially left home and accepted the renounced order of life from Keśava Bhāratī in the nearby village of Katwa, receiving the initiated name Śrī Kṛṣṇa Caitanya. He was only twenty-four years old at the time, and His mother and young wife were heartbroken. According to Vedic custom, when a man takes *sannyāsa* vows he can no longer live at home; it would impede his spiritual progress. Everyone in Nadia became despondent knowing that now the Lord would leave Navadvīpa forever.[5]

### Mother Śacī's Request

At a final gathering of friends in the home of Advaita Ācārya, mother Śacī was so distraught she could hardly stand without help. Anticipating her son's imminent departure, she appealed to all the devotees: As long as Śrī Caitanya Mahāprabhu remained at the house of Advaita Ācārya, only she would cook and supply His food. It would be her last opportunity. Hearing her appeal, all the devotees agreed.

Seeing His mother's eagerness, Śrī Caitanya Mahāprabhu became a little unsettled. He assembled the devotees and spoke to them. "Without your order, I tried to go to Vṛndāvana, the land of Lord Kṛṣṇa's childhood pastimes, just after accepting *sannyāsa*. There was

[5]A short synopsis of the Lord's early childhood was compiled by Śrīla Bhaktivinoda Ṭhākura and recorded in his *Śrī Chaitanya Mahāprabhu His Life and Precepts*. I've used that overview as the basis for this introduction to Śrī Caitanya Mahāprabhu's pastimes.

some obstacle, however, and I had to return here. My dear friends, although I have suddenly accepted this renounced order, I know that I shall never be indifferent to you. As long as I remain in this world, I shall never give you up. Nor can I give up My mother.

"After accepting *sannyāsa,* it is not the duty of a *sannyāsī* to remain at his birthplace, encircled by relatives. Make some arrangement so I may not leave you, and at the same time people may not blame Me for remaining with relatives after taking *sannyāsa.*"

Hearing Lord Caitanya's request, all the devotees, headed by Advaita Ācārya, approached mother Śacī. When they submitted Lord Caitanya's statement, mother Śacī said, "It will be great happiness for me if Nimāi stays here. However, if someone blames Him, it will be my unhappiness. If Nimāi remains at Jagannātha Purī, He may not leave any one of us, and still He can remain aloof as a *sannyāsī*. Thus, both purposes will be fulfilled.

"Jagannātha Purī and Navadvīpa are intimately related, like two rooms in the same house. People from Navadvīpa frequently go to Jagannātha Purī, and those in Jagannātha Purī come to Navadvīpa. This going and coming will help carry news of Nimāi, Lord Caitanya. In this way I will be able to get news of Him. All you devotees will be able to travel back and forth, and sometimes He may also come to bathe in the Ganges. I do not care for my personal happiness or unhappiness, but only for His happiness. Indeed, I accept His happiness as my happiness."

Hearing Śacīmātā, the devotees assured her that her order, like a Vedic injunction, could not be violated, and they informed Lord Caitanya of her decision. Hearing it, the Lord was pleased and a few days later left for Purī.

### Śrī Caitanya Mahāprabhu Travels to Jagannātha Purī

Five hundred years ago, of course, there were no trains, automobiles, or modern forms of transport. People usually walked from place to place. Lord Caitanya, followed by Nityānanda, Mukunda, Jagadānanda, and Dāmodara, traveled from Navadvīpa in Bengal to Jagannātha Purī in Kaliṅga (approximately 600 km or 375 miles). Along the way they stopped in Remuṇā to see the deity of Kṣīra-corā-gopīnātha, then continued to Kaṭaka (Cuttack), where they saw the Sākṣi-gopāla deity. The *Caitanya Bhāgavata* recounts many of the places visited by the Lord on the way to Bhuvaneśvara, where the devotees took the *darśana* of Liṅgarāja and bathed in Bindu-sarovara.[6]

When Śrī Caitanya Mahāprabhu eventually arrived at Kamalapur, He took His bath in the Bhārgīnadī River and left His *sannyāsa* staff with Nityānanda Prabhu. As Caitanya Mahāprabhu later entered the nearby temple of Lord Śiva (Kapoteśvara), Nityānanda Prabhu broke the Lord's staff into three and threw it into the river. Nityānanda Prabhu, knowing Lord Caitanya to be on the topmost platform of devotional service, broke the *sannyāsa-daṇḍa* because according to Vedic practice only lower grade *sannyāsīs* require such a staff.[7]

After visiting Kapoteśvara, Śrī Caitanya Mahāprabhu saw the pinnacle of the Jagannātha temple from a distance. Offering obeisances to the temple, He began dancing in the ecstasy of love of God. All the devotees similarly became ecstatic in the Lord's association, and they danced and chanted as they walked along the main road. The Lord eventually arrived at the place known as Āṭhāranālā, a thirteenth-century bridge with eighteen arches (*āṭhāra* means eighteen). This bridge over the Medhupur stream is at the entrance to Jagannātha Puri from the Bhuvaneśvara route. (See plate 29)

Arriving at the bridge, the Lord suddenly realized He no longer had His *daṇḍa*. He then asked Nityānanda Prabhu, "Please return My staff."

"Your staff was broken," Nityānanda replied. "When You fell down in ecstasy, I caught You, but both of Us together fell upon the staff, and it broke under Our weight. Where the pieces have gone, I cannot say. It is certainly because of My offense that Your staff has broken. Now You can punish Me as You think proper."

---

[6] Bindu-sarovara and the city of Bhuvaneśvara have already been described in *Part One* in the chapter titled *Bhuvaneśvara*. Also see *Caitanya-caritāmṛta* (*Madhya-līlā* 5.140-141) with purports.

[7] See *Caitanya-caritāmṛta* (*Madhya-līlā* 5.142–143) and chapters *Kapoteśvara* and *Beleśvara* in *Part One*. Note: The town is no longer called Kamalapura–it's now called Candanpur. There is an ISKCON Govinda's vegetarian restaurant on the main road.

Hearing this story, Caitanya Mahāprabhu expressed some anger and sadness. "You've all helped Me by bringing Me to Nīlācala," He said thoughtfully. "However, My only possession was that one staff, and you haven't kept it. Therefore, all of you should go before or behind Me to see Lord Jagannātha. I shall not go with you."

"My Lord," Mukunda Datta answered, "You should go ahead and allow us to follow. We shall not go with You."

Śrī Caitanya Mahāprabhu then walked swiftly before the other devotees. No one could understand the real purpose of Caitanya Mahāprabhu and Nityānanda Prabhu. The devotees couldn't understand why Nityānanda Prabhu broke the staff, why Śrī Caitanya Mahāprabhu permitted Him to do so, or why, after permitting Him, Caitanya Mahāprabhu became angry.[8]

Śrī Caitanya Meets Sārvabhauma Bhaṭṭācārya

In ecstasy, Śrī Caitanya Mahāprabhu went from Āṭhāranālā directly to Lord Jagannātha's temple. He entered the majestic temple and saw the deities from a distance. Then He spontaneously ran to embrace Lord Jagannātha. Suddenly, however, Śrī Caitanya was overcome with intense love of God and fainted on the floor.

When Caitanya Mahāprabhu fell down, Sārvabhauma Bhaṭṭācārya happened to see Him. Some ignorant interior guards, thinking that the Lord was misbehaving, rushed forward to beat Him with sticks, but Sārvabhauma, who was highly respected by the temple authorities, forbade them to do so. The Bhaṭṭācārya was surprised to see both the Lord's personal beauty and the transcendental transformations wrought on His body.

Śrī Caitanya Mahāprabhu remained unconscious for a long time, lying on the floor of the temple while the Bhaṭṭācārya tried to think of a way to wake Him. Meanwhile, the time came for offerings to Lord Jagannātha. Therefore, while the Lord was still unconscious, Sārvabhauma Bhaṭṭācārya, with the help of the watchmen and some disciples, carried the Lord to his home. A large crowd gathered, and everyone in the crowd was eager to carry the Lord, so He was passed

[8] Nityānanda Prabhu is an incarnation of Kṛṣṇa's bother Lord Balarama.

from hand to hand as if He were being transported by a swarm of ants. So many people followed the Lord that when they arrived at Sārvabhauma's house, the doors had to be closed to keep the huge crowd outside.

Examining the Lord, Sārvabhauma was alarmed to see that He didn't appear to be breathing. He took a fine cotton swab and placed it before the Lord's nostrils. When the cotton moved slightly, he became hopeful. Sitting beside Śrī Caitanya Mahāprabhu, he thought, *This is a transcendental ecstatic transformation brought about by love of Kṛṣṇa.* Sārvabhauma knew that such signs take place only in the bodies of eternally liberated devotees.

While the Bhaṭṭācārya was thinking in this way, the four devotees traveling with the Lord arrived at the *Siṁha-dvāra* gate. There the devotees heard people talking about a mendicant who had fallen unconscious upon seeing the deity. "A *sannyāsī* fell unconscious upon seeing the deity of Lord Jagannātha," someone said. "Because His consciousness didn't return, Sārvabhauma Bhaṭṭācārya took Him to his home." Hearing this, the devotees discovered where Lord Caitanya could be found.

Just then, Gopīnātha Ācārya arrived. Gopīnātha Ācārya, a former resident of Nadia, was the brother-in-law of Sārvabhauma, and a devotee of Caitanya Mahāprabhu. He knew the Lord's true identity. Gopīnātha Ācārya also knew Mukunda Datta, and when he saw his old friend at Jagannātha Purī he was surprised. Seeing him, Mukunda Datta offered his obeisances. Then Gopīnātha Ācārya inquired about Śrī Caitanya Mahāprabhu.

"The Lord has already arrived here," Mukunda Datta answered, "and we have come with Him. After accepting the *sannyāsa* order, Lord Caitanya Mahāprabhu has come to Jagannātha Purī and brought all of us with Him. He left our company at Āṭhāranālā and walked ahead to see Lord Jagannātha. We just arrived and are now looking for Him. From the talk of the people in general, we have guessed that the Lord is now at the house of Sārvabhauma Bhaṭṭācārya. Just as I was thinking of meeting you, by chance we have actually met. First, let us all go to the house of Sārvabhauma Bhaṭṭācārya and see Caitanya Mahāprabhu. Later we shall come to see Lord Jagannātha."

Hearing this and feeling pleased, Gopīnātha Ācārya took all the devotees to Sārvabhauma Bhaṭṭācārya's house, and they were admitted. Upon seeing Nityānanda Prabhu, the Bhaṭṭācārya offered Him obeisances. Then the devotees saw the Lord lying unconscious. Gopīnātha Ācārya, who was particularly eager to meet the Lord, became unhappy to see Him in that state. Sārvabhauma offered the devotees a proper welcome and then sent them all to take *darśana* of Lord Jagannātha. He asked his own son, Candaneśvara, to accompany them as a guide.

After taking Lord Jagannātha's *darśana*, the devotees again returned to Sārvabhauma Bhaṭṭācārya's house. They began to loudly chant the Hare Kṛṣṇa mantra, and the Lord finally regained consciousness just before noon. He suddenly got up and loudly chanted, "Hari! Hari!" Sārvabhauma was relieved to see the Lord regain consciousness, and he took the dust from His lotus feet.

The Bhaṭṭācārya then informed them, "Please take your midday bath and then return to my home. Today I shall offer you *mahā-prasāda*, the remnants of food offered to Lord Jagannātha."

After bathing in the sea, Śrī Caitanya Mahāprabhu and His devotees returned to the home of Sārvabhauma Bhaṭṭācārya. The Lord washed His feet and sat down to lunch. Sārvabhauma Bhaṭṭācārya had made arrangements to bring various kinds of *mahā-prasāda* from the Jagannātha temple, so Śrī Caitanya Mahāprabhu and the devotees ate lunch with great happiness.

## Pastimes with Sārvabhauma Bhaṭṭācārya

Sārvabhauma Bhaṭṭācārya was renowned as the foremost scholar in India. Having read the *Upaniṣads* at Benares, he became a pupil of the celebrated Pakṣadhara Miśra of Mithilā, a well-known center of learning. Pakṣadhara Miśra taught logic from the only copy of a text known as *Cintāmaṇi*, by Gāṅgeya Upādhyāya. It was his rule that no student was allowed to transcribe this single copy of *Cintāmaṇi*, so he was easily able to maintain his unique status as its sole scholar.

While he was a student, Vāsudeva Sārvabhauma memorized the entire text of *Cintāmaṇi*. Without violating the vow he had taken not to copy the text, he later set up his own school in Nadia. Sārvabhauma's institute soon developed a good reputation, and gradually Nadia became even more celebrated as a center of learning than Mithilā.

Sārvabhauma remained at Nadia from 1470 to 1480. In the year 1480, however, the Muslim Emperor of Bengal ransacked the area. His armies destroyed temples, uprooted trees, and burnt Hindu homes to the ground. Sārvabhauma and his family fled to Jagannātha Purī. The Bhaṭṭācārya's fame as a scholar preceded him, and Sārvabhauma was given a stately reception by King Puruṣottama of Kaliṅga, where he had remained ever since.

The Bhaṭṭācārya thus became acquainted with Śrī Caitanya Mahāprabhu and arranged accommodations at his aunt's house. His brother-in-law, Gopīnātha Ācārya, established that Lord Caitanya Mahāprabhu was Kṛṣṇa Himself, but Sārvabhauma and his many disciples could not accept this. However, Gopīnātha Ācārya convinced Sārvabhauma that no one can understand the Supreme Personality of Godhead without being favored by Him. He proved by śāstric quotation, quotations from the revealed scriptures, that Śrī Caitanya Mahāprabhu was Kṛṣṇa Himself in person. Still, Sārvabhauma did not take these statements very seriously. Hearing all these arguments, Caitanya Mahāprabhu told His devotees that Sārvabhauma was His spiritual master and that whatever he said out of affection was for everyone's benefit.

When Sārvabhauma met Śrī Caitanya Mahāprabhu, he asked Him to hear Vedānta philosophy from him. Śrī Caitanya Mahāprabhu accepted this proposal, and for seven days He continally heard Sārvabhauma Bhaṭṭācārya explain the *Vedānta-sūtra*. However, the Lord remained very silent. Because of His silence, the Bhaṭṭācārya asked Him whether He was understanding the Vedānta philosophy, and the Lord replied, "Sir, I can understand Vedānta philosophy very clearly, but I cannot understand your explanations." There was then a discussion between the Bhaṭṭācārya and Śrī Caitanya Mahāprabhu concerning the authority of the Vedic scriptures, specifically the *Upaniśads* and *Vedānta-sūtra*. The Bhaṭṭācārya was an impersonalist, but Śrī Caitanya Mahāprabhu proved that the Absolute Truth is the Supreme Personality of Godhead. He proved that the conceptions of the Māyāvādī philosophers concerning the impersonal Absolute Truth are incorrect.

The Absolute Truth is neither impersonal nor without power. The greatest mistake made by the Māyāvādī philosophers is in conceiving the Absolute Truth to be impersonal and without energy.

In all the *Vedas*, the unlimited energies of the Absolute Truth have been accepted, and it is also accepted that this Truth has His transcendental, blissful, eternal form. According to the *Vedas*, the Lord and the living entity are equal in quality but different quantitatively. The real philosophy of the Absolute Truth states that the Lord and His creation are inconceivably and simultaneously one and different. The conclusion is that the Māyāvādī philosophers are actually atheists. There was much discussion on this issue between Sārvabhauma and Caitanya Mahāprabhu, but despite all his endeavors, the Bhaṭṭācārya was defeated in the end.

At the request of Sārvabhauma Bhaṭṭācārya, Śrī Caitanya Mahāprabhu then explained the *ātmārāma* verse of *Śrīmad-Bhāgavatam* in eighteen different ways. When the Bhaṭṭācārya came to his senses, Śrī Caitanya Mahāprabhu disclosed His real identity. The Bhaṭṭācārya then recited one hundred verses in praise of Lord Caitanya Mahāprabhu and offered his obeisances. After this, Gopīnātha Ācārya and all the others, having seen the wonderful potencies of Lord Caitanya Mahāprabhu, became very joyful.

One morning after this incident, Śrī Caitanya Mahāprabhu received some *prasādam* from Jagannātha and offered it to Sārvabhauma Bhaṭṭācārya. Without caring for formality, the Bhaṭṭācārya immediately partook of the *mahā-prasādam*. On another day, when the Bhaṭṭācārya asked Śrī Caitanya Mahāprabhu the best way to worship and meditate, the Lord advised him to chant the Hare Kṛṣṇa *mahā-mantra*. On another day, the Bhaṭṭācārya wanted to change the reading of the *tat te 'nukampām* verse because he did not like the word *mukti-pada*. He wanted to substitute the word *bhakti-pada*. Śrī Caitanya Mahāprabhu advised Sārvabhauma not to change the reading of *Śrīmad-Bhāgavatam*, because *mukti-pada* indicated the lotus feet of the Supreme Personality of Godhead, Lord Kṛṣṇa. Having become a pure devotee, the Bhaṭṭācārya said, "Because the meaning is hazy, I still prefer *bhakti-pada*." At this, Śrī Caitanya Mahāprabhu and the other inhabitants of Jagannātha Purī became very pleased. Sārvabhauma Bhaṭṭācārya thus became a pure Vaiṣṇava, and the other learned scholars there followed him.

## Lord Caitanya Meets Rāmānanda Rāya

Śrī Caitanya Mahāprabhu accepted the renounced order of life in A.D. 1510 during the month of Māgha (February 3, according to most sources). He then went to Jagannātha Purī in the month of Phalguna (February–March). He saw the Dola-yātrā festival, and in the month of Caitra (March–April) He liberated Sārvabhauma Bhaṭṭācārya. During the month of Vaiśākha (April–May) He desired to travel to South India.

When Sārvabhauma Bhaṭṭācārya understood that Caitanya Mahāprabhu was planning to travel south, he insisted that the Lord meet the governor of Vidyānagara, Rāmānanda Rāya. Sārvabhauma hinted that he had once talked with Rāmānanda but considered him a sentimentalist. Now he understood that Rāmānanda Rāya was actually an elevated devotee of Lord Kṛṣṇa.

Śrī Caitanya Mahāprabhu traveled hundreds of miles by foot down the southeast coast of India performing His transcendental pastimes. Finally, He arrived at the banks of the Godāvari River. The river with its forested banks reminded Him of the River Yamunā in Vṛndāvana, and He began to chant and dance. Then the Lord crossed the river and bathed on the opposite bank.

At that time, with an entourage that included many musicians playing various instruments, Rāmānanda Rāya arrived mounted on a palanquin. The governor was also accompanied by many *brāhmaṇas*, who, following Vedic customs, all took bath and offered oblations to the forefathers.

Śrī Caitanya Mahāprabhu understood that the person bathing in the Godāvari was Rāmānanda Rāya. He so much wanted to meet him that His mind immediately began to run after him, but He sat patiently by the riverbank. Seeing the wonderful *sannyāsī*, Rāmānanda Rāya eventually approached the Lord.

Śrī Caitanya Mahāprabhu was as brilliant as a hundred suns. Covered with a saffron garment, He was large in body and strongly built, and His eyes were like lotus petals. When Rāmānanda Rāya saw the glorious Lord, he was struck with wonder. He went to Him and offered his respectful obeisances, falling flat like a rod.

The Lord stood up and asked Rāmānanda Rāya to arise and chant the holy name of Kṛṣṇa. Indeed, Śrī Caitanya Mahāprabhu was eager to embrace him. Śrī Caitanya Mahāprabhu then inquired whether he was Rāmānanda Rāya.

"Yes," he replied, "I am Your very low servant, and I belong to the *śūdra* community."

Śrī Caitanya Mahāprabhu then embraced Rāmānanda Rāya firmly. Both master and servant almost lost consciousness due to ecstatic love. Their natural love for each other awakened, and they and fell on the ground. When they embraced, ecstatic symptoms—paralysis, perspiration, tears, shivering, palpitations, and paleness—appeared. The word "Kṛṣṇa" came from their mouths falteringly. Rāmānanda Rāya was an incarnation of the *gopī* Viśākhā, one of the principal associates of Śrīmatī Rādhārāṇī. Since Śrī Caitanya Mahāprabhu was Lord Kṛṣṇa Himself, there was naturally an awakening of love between Viśākhā-sakhī and Kṛṣṇa.

When the ritualistic *brāhmaṇas* accompanying Rāmānanda Rāya saw this ecstatic manifestation of love, they became confused. "We can see that this *sannyāsī* has a luster like the Brahman effulgence. How is He crying upon embracing a *śūdra*, a member of the fourth caste in the social order?" They thought, "Rāmānanda Rāya is the governor of Madras, a highly learned and grave person, but upon touching this *sannyāsī* he has become restless like a madman."

While the *brāhmaṇas* were thinking in this way, Śrī Caitanya Mahāprabhu saw them and restrained His transcendental emotions. When the two regained their composure, they sat down. Śrī Caitanya Mahāprabhu smiled and said, "Sārvabhauma Bhaṭṭācārya spoke of your good qualities. He took great pains to convince Me to meet with you. Indeed, I came here just for that purpose. It is wonderful that even without making an effort I have got your interview here."

Rāmānanda Rāya replied, "Sārvabhauma Bhaṭṭācārya thinks of me as his servant. Even in my absence he is careful to do me good. By his mercy I have received Your interview here. Consequently I consider that today I have become a successful human being. You are the Supreme Personality of Godhead, Nārāyana Himself, and I am only a government servant interested in materialistic activities. I am the lowest amongst men in the fourth caste. You do not fear the Vedic injunctions that state You should not associate with a *śūdra*. You were not contemptuous of my touch, although in the *Vedas* You are forbidden to associate with *śūdras*."

As the two were speaking, one of the *brāhmaṇas* came and offered obeisances. He fell flat before Śrī Caitanya Mahāprabhu and invited Him to lunch. Lord Śrī Caitanya Mahāprabhu accepted the *brāhmaṇa's* invitation, knowing him to be a devotee.

Smiling, Lord Caitanya spoke further to Rāmānanda Rāya. "I wish to hear from you about Kṛṣṇa. Therefore I want to see you again."

"My Lord," Rāmānanda Rāya replied, "although You have come to correct me, a fallen soul, my mind is not yet purified simply by seeing You. Please stay for a few days and cleanse my polluted mind." Thus the two eternal associates made arrangements to meet again that evening.

In the evening, Śrīla Rāmānanda Rāya used to come to see Śrī Caitanya Mahāprabhu. Clothed in ordinary dress, he offered the Lord respectful obeisances. Śrī Caitanya Mahāprabhu questioned him on the object and process of worship and also asked him to recite verses from the Vedic literature.

First of all, Rāmānanda Rāya enunciated the system of the *varṇāśrama* institution. He recited various verses about *karmārpaṇa*, stating that everything should be dedicated to the Lord. He then spoke of detached action, knowledge mixed with devotional service, and finally the spontaneous loving service of the Lord. After hearing Śrīla Rāmānanda Rāya recite some verses, Śrī Caitanya Mahāprabhu accepted the principle of pure devotional service devoid of speculation.

After this, Śrī Caitanya Mahāprabhu asked Rāmānanda Rāya to explain the higher platform of devotional service. Then Śrīla Rāmānanda Rāya explained unalloyed devotional service, love of Godhead, and serving the Lord in the moods of pure servitude, fraternity, and parental love. Finally he spoke of serving the Lord in conjugal love. He then spoke of how conjugal love can be developed in various ways. This conjugal love attains its highest perfection in Śrīmatī Rādhārāṇī's love for Kṛṣṇa. He next described the position of Rādhārāṇī and the transcendental mellows of love of God.

Śrīla Rāmānanda Rāya then recited a verse of his own concerning the platform of ecstatic vision, technically called *prema-vilāsa-vivarta*. Rāmānanda Rāya also explained that all stages of conjugal love can be attained through the mercy of the residents of Vṛndāvana, especially by the mercy of the *gopīs*. All these subject matters were thus vividly described. Gradually Rāmānanda Rāya could understand the position of Śrī Caitanya Mahāprabhu, and when Śrī Caitanya Mahāprabhu exhibited His real form, Rāmānanda Rāya fell unconscious.

"Other than you, no one has ever seen this form," Śrī Caitanya Mahāprabhu said affectionately. "All the truths about My pastimes and mellows are now within your knowledge. Therefore I have shown this form to you. Actually My body does not have a golden complexion. It only appears so because it has touched the body of Śrīmatī Rādhārāṇī. However, She doesn't touch anyone but the son of Nanda Mahārāja. I have now converted My body and mind into the ecstasy of Śrīmatī Rādhārāṇī. Thus I am tasting My own personal sweetness in that form."

Caitanya Mahāprabhu continued, "Now there is no confidential activity unknown to you. Even though I try to conceal My activities, you can understand everything in detail because of your advanced love for Me. Keep these talks a secret. Do not expose them anywhere and everywhere. Since My activities seem like those of a madman, people may take them lightly and laugh. Indeed, I am a madman, and you are also a madman. Therefore both of us are on the same platform."

The conversations between Rāmānanda Rāya and Śrī Caitanya Mahāprabhu contain confidential subject matters touching the conjugal love between Rādhā and Kṛṣṇa in Vṛndāvana. Although both talked at great length about these pastimes, they could not reach the limit. The next day Śrī Caitanya Mahāprabhu begged Rāmānanda Rāya to give Him permission to leave. At the time of farewell the Lord gave him the following orders.

"Give up all material engagements and come to Jagannātha Purī. I will return there soon after finishing My tour and pilgrimage. The two of us shall remain together at Jagannātha Purī and happily pass our time discussing Kṛṣṇa." Śrī Caitanya Mahāprabhu then embraced Rāmānanda Rāya, and shortly thereafter left for South India.[9] (See plate 30)

---

[9] For more detailed information about the conversations between Śrī Caitanya Mahāprabhu and Rāmānanda Rāya, see *Caitanya-caritāmṛta (Madhya-līlā, Chapter 8)*

## The Lord's Return to Jagannātha Purī

While Śrī Caitanya Mahāprabhu was traveling in South India, back in Purī Sārvabhauma Bhaṭṭācārya had many talks with King Pratāparudra. When Mahārāja Pratāparudra requested the Bhaṭṭācārya to arrange an interview with the Lord, the Bhaṭṭācārya assured him that he would try to do so as soon as Caitanya Mahāprabhu returned from South India. When the Lord returned to Jagannātha Purī from His South Indian tour, He lived at the home of Kāśī Miśra. Sārvabhauma Bhaṭṭācārya introduced many Vaiṣṇavas to Śrī Caitanya Mahāprabhu after His return.

The father of Rāmānanda Rāya, Bhavānanda Rāya, offered another son named Vāṇinātha Paṭṭanāyaka for the Lord's service. Śrī Caitanya Mahāprabhu informed His associates about the pollution of Kṛṣṇadāsa brought about by his association with the Bhaṭṭathāris, and thus the Lord proposed to give him leave. Nityānanda Prabhu sent Kṛṣṇadāsa to Bengal to inform the Navadvipa devotees about the Lord's return to Jagannātha Purī. All the devotees of Navadvipa thus began arranging to come to Jagannātha Purī.

At this time Paramānanda Purī was at Navadvīpa, and immediately upon hearing news of the Lord's return, he started for Jagannātha Purī accompanied by a *brāhmaṇa* named Kamalākānta. Paramānanda Purī, a disciple of Mādhavendra Purī, soon arrived at Śrī Caitanya Mahāprabhu's place. The Lord was pleased to see him. In the ecstasy of love, the Lord worshiped the lotus feet of Paramānanda Purī, and in turn Paramānanda Purī embraced the Lord.

Śrī Caitanya Mahāprabhu said, "Please stay with me and thus show Me favor, accepting the shelter of Jagannātha Purī."

"I also wish to stay with You," Paramānanda Purī replied. "Therefore I have come from Bengal. At Navadvīpa, Mother Śacī and all the other devotees were glad to hear about Your return from South India. They are all coming here to see You, but seeing they were delayed, I came immediately."

There was a solitary room in Kāśī Miśra's house, and Śrī Caitanya Mahāprabhu gave it to Paramānanda Purī. He also arranged for one servant.

## Parāmānanda Purī's Well

Sometime after Paramānanda Purī's arrival, Śrī Caitanya Mahāprabhu went to a secluded place where Paramānanda Purī often remained, and sat down close to him. Paramānanda Purī was dear to the Lord, as Arjuna is dear to Kṛṣṇa. They became absorbed in discussing Lord Kṛṣṇa's pastimes, and spent a long time together.

There was a well near that *āśrama* (see plate 31), but the water wasn't clean. As the Supersoul, Lord Caitanya knew all about this well. Nevertheless, He inquired from Paramānanda Purī, "Please tell Me, how do you find the well-water?"

"This is an unfortunate well," Purī Gosvāmī replied while nonchalantly waving his hand toward the well. "Its water is muddy and unusable."

The Lord showed immediate concern. Lamenting over this inconvenience to Paramānanda Purī, He said, "It seems that Lord Jagannātha is being miserly. Actually, whoever touches the water of this well will be cleansed of all sins. Therefore, by Lord Jagannātha's mystic potency, the waters turned muddy so that no one can drink it or touch it."

Lord Caitanya then stood up and lifting His hands in the air, began to speak "O Lord Jagannātha, I beg this benediction from You. Let Mother Ganges enter this well. Please instruct Gaṅgā-devī, now flowing in the nether regions, to appear in this well."

The nearby devotees began to chant jubilantly, "*Haribol! Haribol!*"

Later, everyone returned to their respective living quarters for the evening. While the devotees slept, Gaṅgā-devī, feeling honored to carry out the Lord's order, appeared in that well. In the morning everyone saw the miracle. The well-water had turned crystal clear. The devotees marveled and chanted the Lord's holy name. Understanding the Lord's mercy upon him, Paramānanda Purī became almost unconscious.

When Śrī Caitanya Mahāprabhu heard the news that the Gaṅgā had entered the well, He went there immediately. Seeing the clear water, He declared, "Whoever drinks this water or bathes in it, I say truly that he will experience unalloyed devotion to Lord Kṛṣṇa."

The Lord then bathed in and drank the water from that well with great exhilaration. He said, "I remain in this world only because I am bound by Śrī Paramānanda Purī's love. I am his property. If he wants to sell Me, then he can do so. Anyone who simply sees Purī Gosvāmī becomes the receptacle of Lord Kṛṣṇa's love." After describing the extraordinary qualities of Paramānanda Purī, and blessing the well, the Lord left for His own residence.[10]

Puruṣottama Bhaṭṭācārya, a resident of Navadvīpa, was educated at Vārāṇasī. He accepted the renounced order from Caitanyānanda, but he took the name of Svarūpa. Thus he also arrived at the lotus feet of Śrī Caitanya Mahāprabhu. After the demise of Śrī Īśvara Purī, his disciple Govinda, following his instructions, went to serve Caitanya Mahāprabhu. Due to his relationship with Keśava Bhāratī, Brahmānanda Bhāratī was also respectfully received by Śrī Caitanya Mahāprabhu. When he arrived at Jagannātha Purī, he was advised to give up the deerskin clothing he wore. When Brahmānanda understood Śrī Caitanya Mahāprabhu correctly, he accepted Him as Kṛṣṇa himself. However, when Sārvabhauma Bhaṭṭācārya addressed Śrī Caitanya Mahāprabhu as Kṛṣṇa, the Lord immediately protested. In the meantime, Kāśīśvara Gosvāmī also came to see Caitanya Mahāprabhu. Thus devotees from many different areas came to see Caitanya Mahāprabhu, and they were exactly like many rivers coming from many places to finally flow into the sea.

## Devotees Arrive from Bengal

When Sārvabhauma Bhaṭṭācārya tried his best to arrange a meeting between Śrī Caitanya Mahāprabhu and King Pratāparudra, the Lord flatly denied his request. At this time Śrī Rāmānanda Raya returned from his governmental post, and he praised King Pratāparudra highly in Lord Caitanya's presence. Because of this, the Lord became a little soft. The king also made promises to Sārvabhauma

[10] See *Caitanya Bhāgavata* (*Antya-līlā* Chapter 3). Paramānanda Purī's well is located about one kilometer from the Jagannātha temple down Lokanātha Road, the road running west from the Jagannātha temple at the southwest corner. On the right side are the Baselisahi police barracks next to the Mohapatra lumber yard. Paramānanda Purī's well is just in front of these police barracks inside the boundry wall.

Bhaṭṭācārya, who hinted how the king might meet the Lord. During Anavasara, while Lord Jagannātha was resting for fifteen days, Śrī Caitanya Mahāprabhu, being unable to see Lord Jagannātha, went to Ālālanātha. (See plate 32)

After a few days, the devotees came to Ālālanātha and requested Caitanya Mahāprabhu to return to Purī. They submitted that the devotees from Bengal were coming to Puruṣottama-kṣetra. In this way, Sārvabhauma Bhaṭṭācārya and others brought Lord Caitanya back to Jagannātha Purī. Sārvabhauma then went to King Pratāparudra and informed him of the Lord's arrival.

While Sārvabhauma Bhaṭṭācārya was talking with King Pratāparudra, Gopīnātha Ācārya arrived there. Gopīnātha announced, "About two hundred devotees are coming from Bengal. All of them are advanced devotees and specifically devoted to Śrī Caitanya Mahāprabhu. They have already arrived on the banks of Narendra Sarovara and are waiting there. Please arrange residential quarters and *mahā-prasāda* for them."

The king replied, "I shall give orders to the attendant in the temple. He will arrange for everyone's facilities as you desire. Please remain here and point out each of the devotees from Bengal as they arrive. We can watch from the roof of the palace."

Within a short time all the devotees from Bengal drew closer to the palace. Svarūpa Dāmodara and Govinda, taking flower garlands and some of Lord Jagannātha's *prasāda*, proceeded to meet them. Lord Caitanya had sent them in advance. Seeing them, the king inquired, "Who are these two? Please let me know their identity."

Sārvabhauma Bhaṭṭācārya replied, "Here is Svarūpa Dāmodara, who is practically the second expansion of the body of Śrī Caitanya Mahāprabhu. The second person is Govinda, Lord Caitanya's personal servant. The Lord has sent garlands and remnants of Lord Jagannātha's food with these two persons simply to honor the devotees from Bengal."

Svarūpa Dāmodara came forward and garlanded Advaita Ācārya. Govinda came next and offered a second garland to Advaita Ācārya. After Govinda offered his obeisances by falling down flat before Advaita Ācārya, Advaita Ācārya asked Svarūpa Dāmodara about his identity, for He didn't know Govinda.

Svarūpa Dāmodara informed Him, "Govinda was the servant of Īśvara Purī. He is very highly qualified. Īśvara Purī ordered Govinda to serve Śrī Caitanya Mahāprabhu. Thus the Lord keeps him by His side."

"To whom did Svarūpa Dāmodara and Govinda offer the two garlands?" the king inquired. "His bodily effulgence is so great that He must be a very great devotee. Please let me know who He is."

"His name is Advaita Ācārya," answered Gopīnātha Ācārya. "He is honored even by Śrī Caitanya Mahāprabhu, and He is therefore the topmost devotee. Here are Śrīvāsa Paṇḍita, Vakreśvara Paṇḍita, Vidyānidhi Ācārya, and Gadādhara Paṇḍita."

One by one Svarūpa Dāmodara and Govinda garlanded the hundreds of devotees arriving from Bengal. Gopīnātha Ācārya related the history of each devotee to the king. "Indeed," he said, "how many names shall I speak to you? All the devotees you see here are associates of Śrī Caitanya Mahāprabhu, who is their life and soul."

In the meantime, Śrī Caitanya Mahāprabhu, accompanied by His personal associates, met all the Vaiṣṇavas on the road with great jubilation. First Advaita Ācārya offered prayers to the lotus feet of the Lord, and the Lord immediately embraced Him in ecstatic love. Indeed, Śrī Caitanya Mahāprabhu and Advaita Ācārya displayed agitation due to ecstatic love, but understanding the time and circumstance, remained patient.

After this, all the devotees, headed by Śrīvāsa Paṇḍita, offered prayers to the lotus feet of the Lord, and the Lord embraced each of them in great love and ecstasy.

While the devotees from Bengal were meeting with the Lord, the king and others were standing atop the palace roof, away from the view of the arriving devotees.

Śrī Caitanya Mahāprabhu then began the congregational chanting of the holy names. As the *kīrtana* increased, Lord Caitanya became overwhelmed by transcendental emotions. His eyes were like two rivers spouting unlimited tears like waterfalls. All the ecstatic symptoms of love manifested on His person at different times. Sometimes He fell to the ground with such terrible force that people gasped in horrified alarm. When the Lord began roaring like thunder, the king had to hold his hands over his ears. Then suddenly the Lord would feel the mood of intense separation from Kṛṣṇa and shed heartbreaking tears. So many subtle spiritual moods played on the Lord's person that it is impossible for anyone to describe them. Dancing constantly, with His long arms up in the air, and chanting, "Hari, Hari," the Lord was saturated in ecstasy. Finally, when He became aware of His immediate surroundings, He ended the *kīrtana* and headed toward the house of Kāśī Miśra with all the devotees.

King Pratāparudra came down from the top of his palace to the ground and called for Kāśī Miśra and the inspector of the temple. Mahārāja Pratāparudra then told both Kāśī Miśra and the temple inspector, "Provide all the devotees and associates of Śrī Caitanya Mahāprabhu with comfortable residences, convenient eating facilities for *prasādam*, and convenient visiting arrangements at the temple so that there will not be any difficulty.

"The orders of Śrī Caitanya Mahāprabhu must be carefully carried out. Although the Lord may not give direct orders, you are still to carry out His desires simply by understanding His indications." Saying this, the king gave them permission to leave. Sārvabhauma Bhaṭṭācārya also went to see the assembly of all the Vaiṣṇavas.

The king, seeing the Lord's dancing until the end, then entered his private chambers, his heart full of joy, his inner eye still viewing the Lord's graceful movements.

When the Lord was submerged in dancing, tears cascaded down from His eyes. Saliva drooled from His mouth and nose in the acme of divine ecstasy. His body was smeared all over with the drool and dust. The king couldn't comprehend that these were symptoms of spiritual love for the Supreme Lord, Kṛṣṇa. Doubt crept into his mind, but without revealing this to anyone, he went away feeling happy and content.

Upon returning home later in the day, King Pratāparudra went to sleep for the night. After the day's experience, the king did not understand that his worshipable Lord Jagannātha had danced before him as Lord Caitanya, the topmost *sannyāsī*.

That night, the pious king saw Lord Jagannātha in a dream, His body covered with dust. His eyes, like torrential springs, gushed out incessant tears. His mouth was foaming, making His body wet and His skin gleam. In the dream, the king thought, *What kind of pastime is this? All these activities of Lord Jagannātha are incomprehensible to me.*

The king approached his beloved Lord to touch His lotus feet, but Lord Jagannātha declared, "No, no, this is not proper! When I am smeared with camphor, musk, sandalwood paste, vermilion, and other perfumed oils, then I am most desirable and clean. Now My body is covered with dust and drool. I am not fit to be touched by you. Today you came to see Me dancing. When I was covered with dust and drool you found Me repulsive. Now I am in that same dirty condition. How can you think I am clean enough to be touched by one who is a monarch with an illustrious ancestry?" Speaking in this manner, Lord Jagannātha, the most merciful Lord, smiled at His servitor.

The next moment, the king saw, still in the dream, that Lord Jagannātha was no longer seated on the throne. The new occupant was Lord Caitanya! His body was covered with dust. Smiling, He spoke to the king. "How can this be possible? Today you went away having found Me repugnant. Why do you want to touch Me now?" After the Lord finished speaking thus, He smiled benignly upon the king, showering unlimited mercy upon him.

Awakening after a short time, the king began to cry bitterly, condemning himself for his ignorance. "I am the most sinful wretch alive. I could not recognize Lord Caitanya as the Supreme Lord. Of course, how much intelligence does a human being have to understand the infinite truth on his own? Even Lord Brahmā is deluded by His illusory energy, *māyā*. Therefore, my Lord, be gracious upon me. Forgive me for my offensive behavior. Accept me, a lowly person, as Your servant and bless me."

When the king understood that Lord Caitanya was none other than his worshipable deity, Lord Jagannātha, his eagerness to meet Him greatly increased. But despite all endeavors by the devotees, Caitanya Mahāprabhu would not consent to an interview with the king.

### Haridāsa Ṭhākura's Arrival

Meanwhile, at Kāśī Miśra's house all the devotees sat with Śrī Caitanya Mahāprabhu. He made all the devotees sit at His side, and with His own hand offered them garlands and sandalwood pulp.

Śrī Caitanya Mahāprabhu then addressed Advaita Ācārya sweetly, "My dear sir, today I have become perfect because of Your arrival."

Advaita Ācārya replied, "This is a natural characteristic of the Supreme Personality of Godhead. Although He is personally complete and full of all opulences, He takes transcendental pleasure in the association of His devotees, with whom He has a variety of eternal pastimes."

Śrī Caitanya Mahāprabhu then saw Vāsudeva Datta, the father of His childhood friend Mukunda Datta. He immediately became very happy and, placing His hand on his body, began to speak. "For your sake only, I have brought two books from South India. The books are kept with Svarūpa Dāmodara, and you can get them copied."

Hearing this, Vāsudeva became very glad. Indeed, each Vaiṣṇava copied the two books, *Brahma-saṁhitā* and *Śrī Kṛṣṇa-karṇāmṛta,* and gradually they were broadcast all over India.

After all the devotees from Bengal had met with the Lord and exchanged loving dealings with Him, they were shown to their residential quarters. Then Haridāsa Ṭhākura approached the Lord. Haridāsa Ṭhākura was born in a low-caste Muslim family, and was therefore considered an outcast by orthodox Hindu standards, but he had no equal. Haridāsa chanted 300,000 holy names of Kṛṣṇa each day. Haridāsa Ṭhākura offered the Lord his obeisances, and in return Lord Caitanya lifted him up and embraced him. Both the Lord and His servant began to cry in ecstatic love.

"My dear Lord," Haridāsa Ṭhākura said, "I was born in a Muslim family and am unfit to be touched by those who follow the *Vedas*. Please do not touch me, for I am most fallen and untouchable. I am the lowest among men."

"I wish to touch you to be purified," the Lord replied, "for your purified activities do not exist in Me. At every moment you take your bath in all the holy places of pilgrimage, perform sacrifices, and give in charity. You are constantly studying the four *Vedas*, and are far better than any *brāhmaṇa* or *sannyāsī*. This is confirmed in the *Śrīmad-Bhāgavatam* (3.33.7):

*aho bata śva-paco 'to garīyān*
*jay-jihvāgre vartate nāma tubhyamtepus*
*tapas te juhuvuḥ sasnur āryā*
*barhmānūcur nāma gṛṇanti ye te*

'My Lord, one who always keeps Your holy name on his tongue becomes greater than an initiated *brāhmaṇa*. Although he may be born in a family of dog-eaters and therefore by material calculation be the lowest among men, he is still glorious. This is the wonderful effect of chanting the holy name of the Lord. One who chants the holy name of the Lord is understood to have performed all kinds of austerities and sacrifices mentioned in the *Vedas*. He has already taken his bath in all holy places of pilgrimage. He has studied all the *Vedas*, and he is actually an Aryan, an advanced human being.' "

Saying this, Śrī Caitanya Mahāprabhu took Haridāsa Ṭhākura to a nearby flower garden and there, in a secluded place, showed him his residence. Śrī Caitanya Mahāprabhu requested Haridāsa, "Remain here and chant the Hare Kṛṣṇa *mahā-mantra*. I shall personally come here to meet you every day. Be peaceful and look at the *cakra* on top of the temple. Offer obeisances from here. I shall arrange to have *prasāda* sent here for you." [11]

## Cleaning the Guṇḍicā Temple

The King of Orissa, Mahārāja Pratāparudra, tried his best to see Lord Caitanya Mahāprabhu. Śrīla Nityānanda Prabhu and the other devotees informed the Lord about the king's desire, but Śrī Caitanya Mahāprabhu would not agree to see him. At that time Śrī Nityānanda Prabhu devised a plan, and He sent a piece of the Lord's outward garment to the king. The next day, when Rāmānanda Rāya again entreated Śrī Caitanya Mahāprabhu to see the king, the Lord, denying the request, asked Rāmānanda Rāya to bring the king's son before Him. The prince visited the Lord dressed like a Vaiṣṇava, and this awakened remembrance of Kṛṣṇa. Thus Śrī Caitanya Mahāprabhu delivered the son of Mahārāja Pratāparudra.

After this, Śrī Caitanya Mahāprabhu washed the Guṇḍica temple before the Ratha-yātrā took place. He then took His bath at Indradyumna Lake and partook of *prasādam* in the garden nearby. While

---

[11] Haridāsa Ṭhākura's place called Siddha Bakul is located down a small lane just south of the Rādhā-Kānta Math, where Śrī Caitanya Mahāprabhu stayed in the house of Kāśī Miśra.

Śrī Caitanya Mahāprabhu washed the temple of Guṇḍicā, a Gauḍiya Vaiṣṇava washed the lotus feet of the Lord and drank the water. This incident is very significant, for it awoke within the devotee ecstatic love. Then the son of Advaita Prabhu named Gopāla fainted during *kīrtana*, and when he did not come to his senses, Śrī Caitanya Mahāprabhu favored him by awakening him. There was also some humorous talk between Nityānanda Prabhu and Advaita Prabhu during *prasādam*. Advaita Prabhu said that Nityānanda Prabhu was unknown to anyone and that it was not the duty of a householder *brāhmaṇa* to accept dinner with a person unknown in society. In answer to this humorous statement, Śrī Nityānanda Prabhu replied that Advaita Ācārya was a monist and that one could not know how his mind could be turned by eating with such an impersonalist. The conversation of these two *prabhus*—Nityānanda Prabhu and Advaita Prabhu—carried a deep meaning that only an intelligent man can understand.

### Netrotsava or Nava-yauvana

The next day marked the performance of Netrotsava. The fortnight before Ratha-yātrā, after Lord Jagannātha is bathed, He is repainted. Therefore, the deities are removed to a private room; no one but their special attendants see them. The Netrotsava festival takes place when the deities return to the altar.[12]

Because they cannot see the Lord, all the devotees feel separation while the deities are being renovated. Therefore, Netrotsava is a particularly joyful occasion. Śrī Caitanya Mahāprabhu took all the devotees with Him and visited the Lord in the temple. When Śrī Caitanya Mahāprabhu went to the temple, Kāśīśvara walked in front to protect the Lord from the large crowds, and Govinda walked in the rear, carrying the *sannyasi's* water pitcher.

Out of intense eagerness to see Lord Jagannātha, the devotees neglected the regulative principle that the deity should be seen from a distance. Instead, they rushed forward to the place where the food is offered *(bhoga-mandapa)*.

---

[12] This was described in *Part Two, Anavasara — Netrotsava and Nava-yauvana*.

Śrī Caitanya Mahāprabhu thirstily drank in the Lord's form. His eyes became like two bumblebees drinking honey from the lotus-like eyes of Lord Jagannātha, who is Kṛṣṇa Himself. The beauty of Mahārāja Nanda's son is incomparable. Nothing is higher than His splendor, and nothing can equal it. His beauty is like waves in an ocean of nectar.

Thus Śrī Caitanya Mahāprabhu and His devotees enjoyed transcendental pleasure upon seeing Lord Jagannātha's face, and Lord Caitanya displayed all the transcendental symptoms of ecstasy. He perspired and trembled. A constant flow of tears fell from His eyes. However, the Lord checked these tears so that they would not disturb His seeing Lord Jagannātha. The devotees seeing Lord Jagannātha's face was interrupted when the deities were offered food, so Śrī Caitanya Mahāprabhu began a *kīrtana*.

Feeling rapturous pleasure upon seeing Lord Jagannātha, Śrī Caitanya Mahāprabhu forgot everything else. The devotees, however, took Him to His lunch at noontime. Knowing the car festival would take place in the morning, all the servants of Lord Jagannātha were doubling their offerings of food. Everyone was waiting in eager anticipation of the festival.

## Ratha-yātrā

The next morning, Śrī Caitanya Mahāprabhu and His associates got up in the dark and took their baths. Then they went to see the *Pāṇḍu-vijaya* ceremony when Lord Jagannātha, Balarāma, Subhadrā, and *Sudarśana-cakra* leave the altar and mount their chariots.

The strongly built *dayitās* (carriers of the deities) were as powerful as drunken elephants. They carried Lord Jagannātha from the altar to the chariot. While carrying the deity, some *dayitās* took hold of the Lord's shoulders, and some caught His lotus feet. The Jagannātha deity was bound at the waist by a strong, thick rope made of silk. The *dayitās* held the rope from either side of the deity and raised Him off the ground.

Strong puffed-up cotton pads called *tulīs* were spread out from the temple to the car. The heavy deity of Lord Jagannātha was carried from one pillow-like pad to the next. While the *dayitās* carried Lord

Jagannātha from one pad to the next, some pads broke and the cotton contents floated into the air. When they broke they made a heavy, cracking sound. Lord Jagannātha is the maintainer of the whole universe. Who can carry Him from one place to another? However, the Lord moves by His personal will just to perform His pastimes.[13]

While the Lord was transported from the altar to the chariot, devotees playing musical instruments made a tumultuous sound. Śrī Caitanya Mahāprabhu was chanting, "Maṇimā! Maṇimā!" an address to a respectable person in Orissa.

Once the deities were seated upon their respective chariots, King Pratāparudra personally engaged in their service by sweeping the road with a broom with a golden handle. The king also sprinkled the road with sandalwood-scented water. Although he was the owner of the royal throne, he engaged in the Lord's menial service. Therefore, he became a suitable candidate to receive the Lord's mercy. Seeing the king engaged in such menial service, Caitanya Mahāprabhu became pleased.[14]

The *ratha* cart decorations astounded everyone. The cart appeared to be made of gold and seemed as high as Mount Sumeru. The decorations included bright mirrors and hundreds of white whisks made of yak tails. On top of the car were neat, clean canopies and a beautiful flag. The car was also decorated with silken cloth and various pictures. Many brass bells, gongs, and ankle bells jingled and rang.

For fifteen days the Lord had remained in seclusion with the goddess of fortune. Having taken her permission, Lord Jagannātha now came out to ride on the *ratha* car and perform His pastimes for the pleasure of the devotees.

The fine white sand spread all over the path resembled the banks of the Yamunā River. Small gardens on both sides looked just like those in Vṛndāvana. As Lord Jagannātha rode in His chariot and saw the beauty on both sides, His mind was filled with pleasure. The pullers of the cars, known as *gauḍas*, pulled the chariots with enthusiasm. However, the car sometimes went fast and sometimes slowed down.

---

[13] The cotton pads known as *tulīs* are no longer used in Purī. Rather, a small cotton pillow is placed under the Jagannātha deity so He travels without discomfort.

[14] For a further description of *chera-pahanra*, see *Part Two, Ratha-yātrā*.

Sometimes the car would stand still and wouldn't move at all, even though it was pulled vigorously. The chariot, therefore, moved by the Lord's will and not by the strength of ordinary human beings.

When the chariot came to a standstill, Śrī Caitanya Mahāprabhu gathered His devotees and with His own hand, decorated them with flower garlands and sandalwood pulp. He formed four *kīrtana* parties of twenty-four chanters each. Each party also had two *mṛdaṅga* players, making an additional eight persons.

Śrī Caitanya Mahāprabhu Himself divided the chanters between the four parties. He ordered Nityānanda Prabhu, Advaita Ācārya, Haridāsa Ṭhākura, and Vakreśvara Paṇḍita to dance in each of the four respective parties.

Svarūpa Dāmodara was chosen to lead the first party and was given five assistants to respond to his chanting. Advaita Ācārya was asked to dance in this first group.

The second group was led by Śrīvāsa Ṭhākura, and he too was assigned five singers to respond to his chanting. Nityānanda Prabhu was appointed as a dancer in this second group.

Another group formed consisting of Vāsudeva, Gopīnātha, and Murāri. They, along with two others, were responsive singers to Mukunda, the chief singer. In this group Haridāsa Ṭhākura was the dancer.

The fourth group was led by Govinda Ghoṣa, and Vakreśvara Paṇḍita was the dancer. Among the responsive singers were Mādhava and Vāsudeva Ghoṣa.

There was also a *saṅkīrtana* party from the village of Kulina-grāma, and Rāmānanda and Satyarāja were appointed dancers. A group from Śāntipura had Advaita Ācārya's son Acyutānanda as their dancer. The people of Khaṇḍa formed yet another group. Four parties chanted and danced in front of Lord Jagannātha, and two parties performed *kīrtana* on either side. Another party performed *kīrtana* at the rear of the chariot. Thus there were seven *saṅkīrtana* parties, and in each party two men were beating drums. Therefore, fourteen *mṛdaṅgas* were being played at once. The sound was tumultous, and the devotees became mad with love.

All the Vaiṣṇavas came together like an assembly of clouds. As they chanted the holy names, tears fell from their eyes like rainfall.

The *saṅkīrtana* filled the three worlds. No one could hear anything else.

Lord Caitanya Mahāprabhu wandered throughout the seven groups chanting the holy name, "Hari, Hari!" Raising His arms, He proclaimed, "Jaya Jagannātha! All glories to the Lord of the universe!"

Lord Caitanya then exhibited another mystic power by performing pastimes simultaneously in all seven groups. Everyone said, "Lord Caitanya Mahāprabhu is present in my group. Indeed, He doesn't go anywhere else. He is bestowing His mercy upon us."

Actually, no one could see the Lord's display of His inconceivable potency. Only the most confidential devotees, those in pure, unalloyed devotional service, could understand what He was doing. Lord Jagannātha was pleased by the *saṅkīrtana,* and He brought His car to a standstill just to see the performance.

### *Yuga-dharma*

King Pratāparudra was astonished to see the *saṅkīrtana.* He was stunned and became immersed in ecstatic love of Kṛṣṇa. "I have never seen such ecstatic love," he delcared, "nor heard the vibration of the holy name of the Lord chanted in such a way. Nor have I seen such dancing during *saṅkīrtana.*"

Sārvabhauma Bhaṭṭācārya, who was standing beside the king, said, "This sweet transcendental sound is a special creation of the Lord known as *prema-saṅkīrtana,* congregational chanting in love of Godhead. In this age of Kali, Śrī Caitanya Mahāprabhu has descended to preach the religion of Kṛṣṇa consciousness. Chanting of the holy names of Lord Kṛṣṇa is the religious principle for this age. Anyone who worships Lord Caitanya Mahāprabhu by congregational chanting should be understood as highly intelligent. One who does not do so must be considered a victim of this age and bereft of intelligence. This is not only my opinion; it is the verdict of scripture. *Śrīmad-Bhāgavatam* (11.5.32) says:

*kṛṣṇa-varṇaṁ tviṣākṛṣṇaṁ*
*sāṅgopāṅgāstra-pārṣadam*

*yajñaiḥ saṅkīrtana-prāyair*
*yajanti hi su-medhasaḥ*

'In the age of Kali, intelligent persons perform congregational chanting to worship the incarnation of Godhead who constantly sings the name of Kṛṣṇa. Although His complexion is not blackish, He is Kṛṣṇa Himself. He is accompanied by His associates, servants, weapons, and confidential companions.' "

Thus the king and Sārvabhauma were aware of the Lord's activities, but others could not see His tricks. Only a person who has received the Lord's mercy can understand His nature. Without the Lord's mercy, even Lord Brahmā cannot understand. Śrī Caitanya Mahāprabhu was satisfied to see the king accept the menial task of sweeping the street. For this humility, the king received Śrī Caitanya Mahāprabhu's mercy. He could therefore see the mystery of His activities. Although Lord Caitanya refused the king an interview, he indirectly received the Lord's causeless mercy. Who can understand Śrī Caitanya Mahāprabhu's internal potency?

The Lord performed *kīrtana* for some time and, through His own endeavor, inspired all the devotees to dance. When the Lord Himself wanted to dance, all seven groups combined and Śrīvāsa, Ramāi, Raghu, Govinda, Mukunda, Haridāsa, Govindānanda, and Mādhava united their efforts. When Śrī Caitanya Mahāprabhu desired to jump high while dancing, He placed these people in charge of Svarūpa Dāmodara. These devotees sang along with the Lord and also ran beside Him. All the other groups of men continued singing.

Offering obeisances to Lord Jagannātha with folded hands, Śrī Caitanya Mahāprabhu raised His face toward the deity and prayed as follows:

*namo brahmaṇya-devāya*
*go-brāhmaṇa-hitāya ca*
*jagad-dhitāya kṛṣṇāya*
*govindāya namo namaḥ*

"Let me offer my respectful obeisances unto Lord Kṛṣṇa, the worshipable deity for all brahiminical men. He is the well-wisher of cows and *brāhmaṇas* and is always benefitting the whole world. I offer my repeated obeisances to the Personality of Godhead, known as Kṛṣṇa and Govinda."[15]

Reciting this and other verses from scripture, the Lord again offered obeisances. With folded hands all the devotees also offered prayers to the Supreme Personality of Godhead. When Śrī Caitanya Mahāprabhu danced and jumped high, roaring like thunder and moving in a circle like a wheel, He appeared like a circling firebrand. He displayed various blissful transcendental changes in His body. Sometimes He appeared stunned, at other times His hair stood on end. Sometimes He perspired, cried, trembled, and changed color. He also exhibited symptoms of helplessness, pride, exuberance, and humilty.

When Caitanya Mahāprabhu fell down with a crash while dancing, He would roll on the ground. At such times it was like a golden mountain rolling along the earth. Nityānanda Prabhu stretched out His two hands and tried to catch the Lord when He was running here and there. Advaita Ācārya danced behind chanting loudly, "Haribol! Haribol!" again and again.

To check the crowds from coming too near the Lord, the devotees formed three circles. The first circle was guided by Nityānanda Prabhu, who is Balarāma Himself and the possessor of unlimited strength. The devotees headed by Kāśīśvara and Govinda linked hands to form a second circle around the Lord. Mahārāja Pratāparudra and his personal assistants formed a third circle around the two inner circles. With these three large circles around Caitanya Mahāprabhu, the Lord was protected from the large crowds and could therefore dance freely.

With his hands on the shoulders of Haricandana, King Pratāparudra could see Lord Caitanya dancing. While the king beheld the dancing, Śrīvāsa Ṭhākura, standing in front of him, became ecstatic as he also watched the dancing of Śrī Caitanya Mahāprabhu.

Seeing Śrīvāsa standing before the king, Haricandana touched Śrīvāsa with his hand, requesting him to step aside. Absorbed in watching Śrī Caitanya Mahāprabhu dance, Śrīvāsa Ṭhākura couldn't understand why he kept being touched and pushed from behind.

---

[15] *Viṣṇu Purāṇa* (1.19.65)

After he was pushed again and again, he became angry. Śrīvāsa Ṭhākura turned and slapped Haricandana to stop him from pushing. This made Haricandana angry. As the angered Haricandana was about to speak to Śrīvāsa Ṭhākura, Pratāparudra Mahārāja stopped him.

"You are fortunate," King Pratāparudra said, "for you have been graced by the touch of Śrīvāsa Ṭhākura. I am not so fortunate. You should feel obliged to him."

Śrī Caitanya Mahāprabhu's dancing astounded everyone. Even Lord Jagannātha became extremely happy to see Him. Suddenly the chariot came to a standstill. With unblinking eyes, Lord Jagannātha watched Śrī Caitanya Mahāprabhu's dancing. Subhadrā and Lord Balarāma both felt happiness and ecstasy within their hearts. Indeed, they were also smiling at the dancing.

When Caitanya Mahāprabhu danced and jumped high, eight wonderful transformations of divine ecstasy were seen on His body. All these symptoms were visible simultaneously. His skin erupted with goose bumps, and the hairs on His body stood on end. Thus His body resembled the silk cotton tree covered with thorns. Onlookers became aghast, seeing His teeth chatter. They thought that at any moment His teeth would fall out. His whole body simultaneously flowed with perspiration and oozed blood. He made sounds like "*jaja gaga, jaja gaga*" in a voice choked with emotion. Tears came forcefully from His eyes as if from a syringe, and all the surrounding people were soaked. Everyone saw the Lord's complexion change from white to pink, so that His luster resembled that of a *mallikā* flower.

Sometimes He remained stunned, and sometimes He rolled on the ground. At other times His legs and hands became as hard as dry wood, and He didn't move. When the Lord fell on the ground, sometimes His breathing almost stopped. When the devotees saw this, their life breath also became feeble and unstable. Water flowed from the Lord's eyes and sometimes from His nostrils. Foam fell from His mouth, appearing like torrents of nectar descending from the moon. The foam falling from the mouth of Śrī Caitanya Mahāprabhu was taken and drunk by Śubhānanda, who was fortunate and expert in relishing the mellows of ecstatic love of Kṛṣṇa.

## The Mysterious Verse

After performing His devastating dance for some time, Lord Śrī Caitanya Mahāprabhu's mind entered into a mood of divine love. Abandoning the dancing, the Lord ordered Svarūpa Dāmodara to sing. Understanding His mind, Svarūpa Dāmodara began to sing as follows:

*sei ta parāṇa-nātha pāinu*
*yāhā lagi' madana-dahane jhuri' genu*

"Now I have gained the Lord of my life, in the absence of whom I was burned by Cupid and was withering away."

When Svarūpa Dāmodara loudly sang this refrain, Śrī Caitanya Mahāprabhu again began dancing rythmically in transcendental bliss. Lord Jagannātha's car began to move slowly while the son of mother Śacī went ahead and danced in front.

While dancing and singing, all the devotees in front of Lord Jagannātha kept their eyes on Śrī Caitanya Mahāprabhu. Caitanya Mahāprabhu then went to the end of the procession with the *saṅkīrtana* performers. His eyes and mind fully absorbed in Lord Jagannātha, Caitanya Mahāprabhu began to play the drama of the song with His two arms. Therefore, He would sometimes fall behind the procession. At such times, Lord Jagannātha would come to a standstill. When Caitanya Mahāprabhu once again went forward, Lord Jagannātha's cart would again start to roll. Thus there was a sort of competition between Caitanya Mahāprabhu and Lord Jagannātha in seeing who would lead, but Caitanya Mahāprabhu was so strong He made Lord Jagannātha wait in His chariot.

While Śrī Caitanya Mahāprabhu was dancing, His ecstasy changed. Raising His two arms, he began reciting the following verse in a loud voice.

*yaḥ kaumāra-haraḥ sa eva hi varas tā eva caitra-kṣapās*
*te conmīlita-mālātī-surabhayaḥ prauḍhāḥ kadambānilāḥ*
*sā caivāmsi tathāpi tatra surata-vyāpāra-līlā-vidhau*
*revā-rodhasi vetasī-taru-tale cetaḥ samutkaṇṭhate*

"That personality who stole My heart during my youth is now again my master. These are the same moonlit nights of Caitra. The same fragrance of *mālatī* flowers is there, and the same sweet breezes are blowing from the *kadamba* forest. In our intimate relationship, I am also the same lover, yet still my mind is not happy here. I am eager to go back to that place on the bank of the Revā under the Vetasī tree. That is my desire."[16]

Caitanya Mahāprabhu recited this verse again and again, but other than Svarūpa Dāmodara, no one could understand its purport. Year after year Caitanya Mahāprabhu chanted this verse during Ratha-yātrā, but no one was ever able to uncover its meaning.

### Rupa Gosvāmī Reveals the Inner Meaning

Finally one year, Rūpa Gosvāmī arrived in Purī after visiting Vṛndāvana. He understood the essence of this verse when he heard it during the Ratha-yātrā. Shortly after the festival, Rūpa Gosvāmī composed another, similar verse, and in this way everyone came to understand the Lord's actual meaning. This new verse composed by Rupa Gosvāmī was spoken by Śrīmatī Rādhārāṇī:

*priyaḥ so 'yam kṛṣṇaḥ sahacari kuru-kṣetra-militas*
*tathāham sā rādhā tad idam ubhayoḥ saṅgama-sukham*
*tathāpy antaḥ-khelan-madhura muralī-pañcama-juṣe*
*mano me kālindī-pulina-vipināya spṛhayati*

"My dear friend, now I have met My old and dear friend Kṛṣṇa on this field of Kurukṣetra. I am the same Rādhārāṇī, and now We are meeting. It is pleasant, but still I would like to go to the bank of the Yamunā beneath the trees of the forest there. I wish to hear the vibration of His sweet flute playing the fifth note within that forest of Vṛndāvana."[17]

Formerly, all the *gopīs* of Vṛndāvana were pleased when they met with Kṛṣṇa in the holy place of Kurukṣetra during a solar eclipse. It

---

[16] *Padyāvalī* (386)
[17] *Padyāvalī* (387)

had been many years since Kṛṣṇa had moved away from Vṛndāvana, and now they were again meeting at Kurukṣetra. Similarly, after seeing Lord Jagannātha on His chariot Śrī Caitanya Mahāprabhu awoke with that ecstasy of the *gopīs*. Absorbed in this mood, He asked Svarūpa Dāmodara to sing the refrain.

Śrī Caitanya Mahāprabhu thus spoke to Lord Jagannātha, "You are the same Kṛṣṇa, and I am the same Rādhārāṇī. We are meeting again in the same way that We met in the beginning of Our lives. Although We are both the same, My mind is still attracted to Vṛndāvana-*dhāma*. I wish that You will please again appear with Your lotus feet in Vṛndāvana.

"Kurukṣetra is crowded with people, their elephants, their horses, and the rattling of chariots. In Vṛndāvana, however, there are flower gardens, the humming of the bees, and chirping birds.

"Here at Kurukṣetra You are dressed like a royal prince, accompanied by warriors. In Vṛndāvana, You appeared like an ordinary cowherd boy, accompanied by Your beautiful flute. Here there is not even a drop of transcendental happiness that I enjoyed with You in Vṛndāvana. I therefore request You to come to Vṛndāvana and enjoy pastimes with Me. If You do so, My ambition will be fulfilled."

In this ecstatic mood, Śrī Caitanya Mahāprabhu recited many other verses, but people in general cannot fathom their meaning. Śrī Caitanya Mahāprabhu is *rādhā-bhāva-dyuti suvalita*. That is, He is Kṛṣṇa Himself assuming the mood of Śrīmatī Rādhārāṇī. Lord Jagannātha is Kṛṣṇa, and Śrī Caitanya Mahāprabhu is Śrīmatī Rādhārāṇī. Caitanya Mahāprabhu's leading Lord Jagannātha toward Guṇḍica temple corresponded to Śrīmatī Rādhārāṇī's leading Kṛṣṇa toward Vṛndāvana.

Śrī Kṣetra, Jagannātha Purī, was taken as the kingdom of Dvārakā, the place where Kṛṣṇa enjoys supreme opulence. However, He was being led by Śrī Caitanya Mahāprabhu to Vṛndāvana, the simple village where all the inhabitants are filled with ecstatic love of Kṛṣṇa. Śrī Kṣetra is a place of *aiśvarya-līlā*, as Vṛndāvana is the place of *mādhurya-līlā*. Śrī Caitanya Mahāprabhu's following at the rear of the *ratha* indicated that Lord Jagannātha, Kṛṣṇa, was forgetting the inhabitants of Vṛndāvana. Although Kṛṣṇa neglected the inhabitants of Vṛndāvana, He could never forget them. Thus in His opulent

Ratha-yātrā, He was returning to Vṛndāvana.

When Śrī Caitanya Mahāprabhu fell behind the *ratha* car, Jagannātha-deva, Kṛṣṇa Himself, understood the mind of Śrīmatī Rādhārāṇī. Therefore, Jagannātha sometimes fell behind the dancing Caitanya Mahāprabhu to show Śrīmatī Rādhārāṇī that He had not forgotten. In this way, Lord Jagannātha agreed that without the ecstasy of Śrīmatī Rādhārāṇī, He could not feel satisfied. These competitive exchanges were all part of the love affair between Kṛṣṇa and Śrīmatī Rādhārāṇī. In that competition between Lord Caitanya's ecstasy for Jagannātha and Jagannātha's ecstasy for Śrīmatī Rādhārāṇī, Caitanya Mahāprabhu emerged successful.

## Love in Separation

Śrī Caitanya Mahāprabhu continued to recite verses from scripture while absorbed in ecstatic rapture. "It is amazing that You have forgotten the land of Vṛndāvana. How is it You have forgotten Your mother, father, and friends? How have You forgotten Govardhana Hill, the banks of the Yamunā, and the forest where You enjoyed the *rāsa-līlā* dance?

"Kṛṣṇa, You are certainly a refined gentleman with all good qualities. You are well-behaved, softhearted, and merciful. I know there is not even a tinge of fault to be found in You, yet Your mind does not even remember the inhabitants of Vṛndāvana. This is only My misfortune, and nothing else. I do not care for My personal unhappiness. However, when I see the morose face of Your mother Yaśodā and the breaking hearts of all the inhabitants of Vṛndāvana, I wonder whether You want to kill them all? Or do You want to enliven them by coming there? Why are You are keeping them alive in a state of suffering?

"The inhabitants of Vṛndāvana do not want You dressed like prince, nor do they want You to associate with powerful warriors in a different country. They cannot leave the land of Vṛndāvana, and without Your presence they are all dying. What is their condition to be? My dear Kṛṣṇa, You are the life and soul of Vṛndāvana-*dhāma*. You are especially the life of Nanda Mahārāja. You are the only opulence in the land Vṛndāvana, and You are very merciful. Please come and let them all live. Please keep Your lotus feet again in Vṛndāvana."

When Lord Kṛṣṇa heard Śrīmatī Rādhārāṇī's statements, His love for the inhabitants of Vṛndāvana was evoked. His body and mind became perturbed. After hearing of their love for Him, He immediately thought Himself to be always indebted to the residents of Vṛndāvana. Then Kṛṣṇa began to pacify Śrīmatī Rādhārāṇī.

"My dearest Śrīmatī Rādhārāṇī, please hear Me. I am speaking the truth. I cry day and night upon remembering all you inhabitants of Vṛndāvana. No one knows how unhappy this makes Me. All the inhabitants of Vṛndāvana-*dhāma*—My father, mother, cowherd boy friends, and everything else–are like My life and soul. Among all the inhabitants of Vṛndāvana, the *gopīs* are like My life's breath. Among the *gopīs*, You, Śrīmatī Rādhārāṇī, are the chief. Therefore, You are the life of My life.

"When a woman is separated from the man she loves or a man is separated from his beloved woman, neither of them can live. They live only for one another. If one dies and the other hears of it, he or she will also die. You are My most dear, and I know that in My absence You cannot live for a moment. To keep You living, I worship Lord Nārāyaṇa. By His merciful potency, I come to Vṛndāvana every day to enjoy pastimes with You. I then return to Dvārakā-*dhāma*. Thus You can always feel My presence there in Vṛndāvana.[18]

"I have already killed all the mischievous demons who are enemies of the Yadu dynasty. I've also killed Kaṁsa and his allies. However, there are two or three demons still living. I want to kill them, and after doing so I shall return soon to Vrndanana. Please know this for certain.

"I wish to protect the inhabitants of Vṛndāvana from the attacks of My enemies. That is why I remain in My kingdom. Otherwise I am

---

[18] Eternal pastimes of the Lord in the spiritual planet of Kṛṣṇaloka are called *aprakaṭa*, or unmanifested pastimes, because they are beyond the purview of the conditioned souls. Lord Kṛṣṇa is always present everywhere, but when He is not present before our eyes, He is said to be *aprakaṭa*, or unmanifested. When Kṛṣṇa is not manifest before the inhabitants of Vṛndāvana, they are always absorbed in thoughts of Him. Therefore, even though Kṛṣṇa was living at that time in Dvārakā, He was simultaneously present before all the inhabitants of Vṛndāvana. This was His *aprakaṭa* presence.

indifferent to My royal position. Whatever wives, sons, and wealth I maintain in the kingdom are only for the satisfaction of the Yadus.

"Your loving qualities always attract Me to Vṛndāvana. Indeed, they will bring Me back within ten or twenty days. When I return I shall enjoy both day and night with You and all the damsels of Vrajabhūmi."

While speaking to Śrīmatī Rādhārāṇī, Kṛṣṇa became anxious to return to Vṛndāvana. He made Her listen to a verse which banished all Her difficulties. This assured Her that She would again attain Kṛṣṇa.

*mayi bhaktir hi bhūtānām*
*amṛtatvāya kalpate*
*diṣṭyā yad āsīn mat-sneho*
*bhavatīnāṁ mad-āpanaḥ*

"Devotional service unto Me is the only way to attain Me. My dear *gopīs*, whatever love and affection you have attained for Me by good fortune is the only reason for My returning to you."[19]

Śrī Caitanya Mahāprabhu recited these verses not only during Ratha-yātrā, but also at other times. He would sit in His room with Svarūpa Dāmodara and taste topics of these verses day and night. No one can describe Svarūpa Dāmodara's good fortune. He was always absorbed in Śrī Caitanya Mahāprabhu's service with his body, mind, and words. The senses of Lord Śrī Caitanya Mahāprabhu were in complete harmony with the senses of Svarūpa. Therefore Caitanya Mahāprabhu used to become fully absorbed in tasting the singing of Svarūpa Dāmodara.

In emotional ecstasy, Caitanya Mahāprabhu would sometimes sit on the ground and, looking down, write on the earth with His fingers. Fearing that the Lord would injure His fingers by writing in this way, Svarūpa Dāmodara checked Him with his own hand. Svarūpa Dāmodara used to sing exactly according to the Lord's ecstatic emotion. Whenever the Lord tasted a particular mellow, Svarūpa Dāmodara would personify it by singing.

---

[19] *Śrīmad-Bhāgavatam* (10.82.44)

Śrī Caitanya Mahāprabhu looked upon the beautiful lotuslike face and eyes of Lord Jagannātha. Lord Jagannātha was garlanded, dressed with nice garments, and adorned with beautiful ornaments. His face glittered from the rays of sunshine, and the entire atmosphere was fragrant.

An ocean of transcendental bliss then expanded in the heart of Lord Śrī Caitanya Mahāprabhu, and symptoms of madness immediately intensified like a hurricane. Śrī Caitanya Mahāprabhu's body appeared like a transcendental Himalayan mountain bearing ecstatic emotional flower trees, all of them blooming. When people saw these symptoms, their minds and consciousness were attracted. Indeed, the Lord sprinkled everyone's mind with the nectar of transcendental love of Godhead.

When Lord Śrī Caitanya Mahāprabhu was dancing and wandering in this way, He fell down in front of Mahārāja Pratāparudra who picked up the Lord with respect. But upon seeing the king, Lord Caitanya came to His external senses. Śrī Caitanya Mahāprabhu then condemned Himself "Oh, how pitiful it is that I have touched a person interested in mundane affairs!"

Not even Lord Nityānanda Prabhu, Kāśīśvara, or Govinda took care of Lord Caitanya Mahāprabhu when He fell down. Nityānanda was dancing in ecstasy, and Kāśīśvara and Govinda were elsewhere.

King Pratāparudra became frightened when Lord Caitanya showed external anger, but Sārvabhauma Bhaṭṭācārya told the king, "Don't worry. The Lord is satisfied with you. By pointing you out, He was teaching His personal associates how to behave with mundane people. It is dangerous for those on the spiritual path to have intimate relationships with mundane people or to become intimately related with the opposite sex. The Lord is satisfied by your humble behavior, so He intentionally allowed you to touch Him. Externally He expressed anger to warn His personal associates."

After circumambulating Lord Jagannātha, Śrī Caitanya Mahāprabhu went behind the car and began pushing it with His head. As soon as He pushed, the chariot started to move, making a rumbling noise. The people all around began to chant the holy name of the Lord, "Hari! Hari!"

King Pratāparudra's Desire Fulfilled

When the procession reached the place called Balagaṇḍi, Lord Jagannātha stopped His car and began looking left and right. On the left, Lord Jagannātha saw the neighborhood of *brāhmaṇas* known as *vipra-śāsana* and a coconut-tree grove. On the right, He saw beautiful flower gardens resembling those found in Vṛndāvana. Śrī Caitanya Mahāprabhu and His devotees were dancing in front of the chariot, and having stopped the car, Lord Jagannātha watched the dancing. It was the custom to offer food to the Lord at *vipra-śāsana*. Countless dishes were offered, and Lord Jagannātha tasted each of them.

All kinds of devotees of Lord Jagannātha—from neophytes to the most advanced—offered their best cooked food to the Lord. This included the king, his queens, his ministers, his friends, and all the other big and small residents of Jagannātha Purī. Even the visitors to Purī offered food to the Lord. Offerings were made everywhere—in front of the car, behind the car, on each side of the car, and in the flower garden. While the food was being offered, a large crowd gathered, so Śrī Caitanya Mahāprabhu stopped dancing and went to a nearby garden.[20]

Immersed in ecstatic emotion and fatigued from the hard labor of dancing, the Lord fell on a raised platform to rest. His body was covered in perspiration, but the fragrant breezes cooled Him. All the other devotees who had been performing *saṅkīrtana* also entered the garden and rested under the shade trees.

Following Sārvabhauma Bhaṭṭācārya's instructions, King Pratāparudra put on the simple dress of a Vaiṣṇava. With folded hands, he first took permission from all the devotees, and then courageously fell down and touched the Lord's lotus feet. Śrī Caitanya Mahāprabhu was lying on the platform with His eyes closed in ecstasy; He did not look at the king. King Pratāparudra began to expertly massage the Lord's legs while reciting verses about the *rāsa-līlā* from *Śrīmad-Bhāgavatam*, beginning with the words *jayati te 'dhikam*.[21]

---

[20] Unfortunately this practice of allowing everyone to offer food around the carts no longer takes place.

[21] *Śrīmad-Bhāgavatam* (10.31.1)

When Śrī Caitanya Mahāprabhu heard these verses, He was pleased beyond limit, and He said again and again, "Go on reciting!"

As soon as the king recited the verse beginning *tava kathāmṛtam*, the Lord rose and embraced him, The Lord said, "You have given Me invaluable gems, but I have nothing to give you in return. Therefore I am simply embracing you." Śrī Caitanya Mahāprabhu began to recite the same verse over and over. Both the king and Śrī Caitanya Mahāprabhu were trembling and tears flowed from their eyes.

*tava kathāmṛtaṁ tapta-jīvanaṁ*
*kavibhir īḍitaṁ kalmasāpaham śravaṇa-*
*maṅgalaṁ śrīmadātataṁ*
*bhuvi gṛṇanti ye bhūri-dā janāḥ*

"My Lord, the nectar of Your words and descriptions of Your activities are the life and soul of those always aggrieved in this material world. These narrations are distributed by exalted personalities, and they eradicate all sinful reactions. Whoever hears these narrations attains all good fortune. Such narrations are broadcast all over the world and are filled with spiritual power. Those who spread the message of Godhead are certainly the most munificent welfare workers."[22]

Lord Caitanya cried, "You are the most munificent! You are the most munificent!" and He again embraced the king. Śrī Caitanya Mahāprabhu still didn't recognize the king because of His overwhelming ecstasy. Seeing the Lord's special mercy on King Pratāparudra, the devotees praised the king's good fortune.

Finally, Śrī Caitanya Mahāprabhu asked, "Who are you? You have done so much for Me. All of a sudden you have come here and made me drink the nectar of the pastimes of Kṛṣṇa."

"My Lord," the king replied, "I am the obedient servant of Your servants. It is my ambition that You will accept me as the servant of Your servants."

Then Śrī Caitanya Mahāprabhu displayed some of His divine opulences before the king and said, "May you develop an unalloyed taste for serving Lord Kṛṣṇa. Do not engage in any other activity ex-

---

[22] *Śrīmad-Bhāgavatam* (10.31.9)

cept rendering devotional service to Lord Kṛṣṇa. Perform continuous chanting of the holy name, and you will always be protected by the Lord's Su*darśana* disc. My reason for coming to Nīlācala was to meet the three of you: Sārvabhauma Bhaṭṭācārya, Rāmānanda Rāya, and you. There is just one request of Mine I want you to keep—do not broadcast this divine revelation. If you do so, I will leave immediately." Saying this, Caitanya Mahāprabhu lifted the flower garland adorning His neck and placed it around the king. The Lord then bade him farewell, feeling satisfied with him.

Offering repeated obeisances to the Lord, the king left, taking to heart the Lord's instructions. The king's mission was complete; he had seen and met the Lord. From then on, he was always absorbed in meditation on the Lord's lotus feet.[23]

## Honoring Prasāda

After this, Vaninātha Paṭṭanāyaka brought all kinds of *prasāda*, and Śrī Caitanya Mahāprabhu accepted lunch with the devotees. King Pratāparudra also sent a large quantity of *prasāda* through Sārvabhauma Bhaṭṭācārya, Rāmānanda Rāya, and Vaninātha. The *prasāda* sent by the king had been offered at the Balagaṇḍi festival and included milk products and fruits. It was all of the finest quality, and there was no end to the variety. There was curd, fruit juice, coconut, mango, dried coconut, jackfruit, various kinds of bananas, and palmfruit seeds. There were also oranges, grapefruit, tangerines, almonds, dried fruit, raisins, and dates. There were hundreds of different types of sweetmeats, such as *manoharā-lāḍu*, *amṛta-guṭikā*, and various types of condensed milk.

The *prasāda* also included papaya, *saravati* (a type of orange), and crushed squash. There was regular cream, fried cream, and a type of *purī* made with cream. There were sweets like *hari-vallabha*, and sweets made of *seṅoti* flowers, *kapūra* flowers, and *mālatī* flowers. There were pomegranates, sweets made with black pepper, sweets made with fused sugar, and *amṛta-jilipi*.

There was lotus-flower sugar, a kind of bread made from *urad dāl*,

---

[23] See *Caitanya-bhāgavat* (*Antya-līlā*).

crispy sweetmeats, sugar candy, fried-rice sweets, sesame-seed sweets, and cookies made from sesame seeds. There was yogurt, milk, butter, buttermilk, a preparation made of fried yogurt and sugar candy, and salty mung *dāl* sprouts with shredded ginger. There was sweetmeats made from sugarcane candy in the form of oranges, lemons, and mangoes along with fruits, flowers, and leaves. There were a variety of pickles—lemon pickle, berry pickle, and so on.

When Śrī Caitanya Mahāprabhu saw half the garden filled with varieties of tasty *prasāda*, He was satisfied. Then several loads of leaves of the *katakī* tree arrived. Each man was supplied ten leaf-plates, and then the dishes were served out.

Śrī Caitanya Mahāprabhu understood the labor of all the *kīrtana* chanters. Therefore He was eager to feed them sumptuously. All the devotees sat down in lines, and Śrī Caitanya Mahāprabhu personally began distributing the *prasāda*. The devotees, however, could not accept *prasāda* until Caitanya Mahāprabhu began to eat. Svarūpa Dāmodara therefore asked the Lord to sit down and honor the *prasāda*. Śrī Caitanya Mahāprabhu agreed and sat down with His personal associates. Everyone was fed until they were filled to the neck. After finishing, the Lord washed His mouth and sat down.

There was so much extra *prasāda* that it was distributed to thousands. Following the Lord's orders, Govinda called the beggars and fed them sumptuously. Seeing the beggars eating *prasāda*, Śrī Caitanya Mahāprabhu chanted, "Haribol!" and instruced them to chant the holy name. As soon as the beggars chanted the holy name, they were absorbed in ecstatic love of Godhead. Śrī Caitanya Mahāprabhu made His advent in this world to deliver love of God to everyone. On the transcendental platform there is no distinction between the rich, the middle class, and the poor.

## Onward to Gundica

Outside the garden, when it was time to again pull Lord Jagannātha's car, all the workers (*gauḍas*) tried to pull the cart but it wouldn't budge. When the *gauḍas* finally realized that they couldn't move the chariot, they abandoned the struggle. The king then arrived, accompanied by his officers and friends.

King Pratāparudra arranged for big wrestlers to pull the chariot.

The king himself even joined in, but still the car would not move. Becoming more and more eager to move the chariot, the king had strong elephants brought forward and harnessed to the cart, but it remained at a standstill.

As soon as Śrī Caitanya Mahāprabhu heard this news, He went there with all His personal associates. They stood there and watched the elephants try to pull the car. The elephants, being beaten by the elephant-goad, were crying. Nonetheless the car would not move. All the people were dumbfounded.

Śrī Caitanya Mahāprabhu ordered that the elephants be released. He then gave His own men the chariot ropes and went to the back of the chariot, where He began to push the chariot with His head. The car moved forward seemingly of its own accord, and the devotees simply carried the ropes. Everyone began to chant, "*Jaya* Jagannātha! All glories to Lord Jagannātha!" No one could hear anything else.

Eventually the chariots reached the Guṇḍicā temple. Upon seeing the uncommon strength of Śrī Caitanya Mahāprabhu, all the people were struck with wonder. They made a tumultuous vibration, chanting, "*Jaya* Gauracandra! *Jaya* Gaurahari! Wonderful, wonderful!" Seeing the greatness of Śrī Caitanya Mahāprabhu, Pratāparudra Mahārāja and his ministers and friends were so moved by ecstatic love that their hair stood on end.

The servants of Lord Jagannātha, Balarāma, and Subhadrā then took the deities from the chariots and placed them on the altar. Then they bathed the deities and finally offered them food. While the deities sat on their respective thrones, Śrī Caitanya Mahāprabhu and His devotees performed *saṅkīrtana* with increasing pleasure, chanting and dancing in the temple yard. The Lord again became overwhelmed by ecstatic love, and all the people who saw Him were flooded by that same ocean of love of Godhead.

In the evening, the Lord finished His dancing and observed the *ārati* ceremony. Afterward, He went to a place called Āiṭoṭā and took rest for the night.

For nine continuous days during Ratha-yātrā, the Lord remained at Sundarācala, and on the fifth day He and Svarūpa Dāmodara observed the pastimes of Lakṣmī-devī, the goddess of fortune. During that time, there was much talk about the pastimes of the *gopīs*. When the *ratha* was again being drawn and the chanting resumed, two devotees from Kulīna-grāma—Rāmānanda Vasu and Satyarāja Khān—were requested to bring silk ropes every year for the Ratha-yātrā ceremony.

The Lord's Pastimes with His Devotees

After the Ratha-yātrā festival, Śrī Advaita Ācārya Prabhu worshiped Śrī Caitanya Mahāprabhu with flowers and *tulasī*. Śrī Caitanya Mahāprabhu, in return, worshiped Advaita Ācārya with the flowers and *tulasī* that remained on the offered plate and said a mantra, *yo 'si so 'si namo 'stu te* ("Whatever You are, You are—but I offer My respects unto You"). Then Advaita Ācārya Prabhu invited Śrī Caitanya Mahāprabhu for *prasādam*.

When Lord Śrī Caitanya Mahāprabhu and His devotees performed the Nandotsava ceremony, the Lord dressed Himself as a cowherd boy. Thus the ceremony was very jubilant. Then the Lord and His devotees observed Vijayā-daśamī, the day of victory when Lord Rāmacandra conquered Laṇkā. The devotees all became soldiers of Lord Rāmacandra, and Śrī Caitanya Mahāprabhu, in the ecstasy of Hanumān, manifested various transcendentally blissful activities. Thereafter, the Lord and His devotees observed various other ceremonies.[24]

Śrī Caitanya Mahāprabhu then asked all the devotees to return to Bengal. Lord Śrī Caitanya Mahāprabhu sent Nityānanda Prabhu to Bengal for preaching and also sent Rāmadāsa, Gadādhara dāsa and several other devotees with Him. Then Śrī Caitanya Mahāprabhu, with great humility, sent some Jagannātha *prasādam* and a cloth from Lord Jagannātha to His mother through Śrīvāsa Ṭhākura.

When the Lord bade farewell to Rāghava Paṇḍita, Vāsudeva Datta, the residents of Kulīna-grāma and other devotees, He praised them for their transcendental qualities. Rāmānanda Vasu and Satyarāja Khān asked some questions, and Lord Śrī Caitanya Mahāprabhu instructed them that all householder devotees must engage themselves in the service of Vaiṣṇavas exclusively devoted to chanting the holy name of the Lord. He also instructed the Vaiṣṇavas from Khaṇḍa, as well as Sārvabhauma Bhaṭṭācārya and Vidyā-vācaspati, and He

[24] These festivals were previously described in *Part Two, Annual Festivals*.

praised Murāri Gupta for his firm faith in the lotus feet of Lord Rāmacandra. Considering the humble prayer of Vāsudeva Datta, He established that Lord Śrī Kṛṣṇa is qualified to deliver all the conditioned souls.

Thereafter, when Śrī Caitanya Mahāprabhu was accepting *prasādam* at the house of Sārvabhauma Bhaṭṭācārya, Sārvabhauma's son-in-law, Amogha, created trouble in the family with some criticism. The following morning, he was attacked by the disease of *visūcikā* (cholera). Lord Śrī Caitanya Mahāprabhu very kindly saved him from death and enlivened him in chanting the holy name of Lord Kṛṣṇa.

### Mahāprabhu Attempts to Go to Vṛndāvana

One day while He was in the garden near the Yameśvara Temple, Śrī Caitanya Mahāprabhu began to feel intense separation from Kṛṣṇa. He envisioned Lord Kṛṣṇa standing with His beautiful body curved in three places, holding His flute to His lips. Wearing yellow garments and garlands of forest flowers, Kṛṣṇa was enchanting even to Cupid.

Becoming fully absorbed in that vision, Śrī Caitanya Mahāprabhu assumed the mood of the *gopīs*, so much so that everywhere He looked He saw Kṛṣṇa standing with His flute to His lips. Then suddenly Kṛṣṇa disappeared. Caitanya Mahāprabhu became as agitated as a person who has just lost a recently acquired jewel. He sat down on the ground and began marking it with His nails. A river of tears flowed from His eyes and blinded Him.

Śrī Caitanya Mahāprabhu said, "I found Kṛṣṇa, the Lord of Vṛndāvana, but I have lost Him again. Who has taken My Kṛṣṇa. Where have I come?"

With these feelings of Śrīmatī Rādhārāṇī, Śrī Caitanya Mahāprabhu continued scratching the earth, rubbing His nails deeper and deeper into the sand. In His ecstatic search for Kṛṣṇa, Caitanya Mahāprabhu eventually unearthed a deity of Gopīnātha buried in the sand.

Caitanya Mahāprabhu lovingly entrusted the deity to Gadādhara Paṇḍita. Gadādhara had been a childhood friend of Śrī Caitanya Mahāprabhu in Navadvīpa. When the Lord took *sannyāsa* and traveled to Purī, Gadādhara Paṇḍita followed out of his love for the Lord.

The *Gaura-gaṇoddeśa-dipikā* (147–153) states: "The pleasure potency of Śrī Kṛṣṇa formerly known as Vṛndāvaneśvarī is now personified in the form of Śrī Gadādhara Paṇḍita in the pastimes of Lord Caitanya Mahāprabhu."

When Lord Śrī Kṛṣṇa accepted the ecstatic emotions and sentiments of Śrīmatī Rādhārāṇī to better understand Her love, the eternal associates of the Lord also assumed various forms to assist in His pastimes. The book *Gaura-gaṇoddeśa-dipikā*, by Kavi-karṇapūra, reveals who all of Lord Caitanya's associates were in their previous pastimes with Rādhā and Kṛṣṇa. Śrī Gadādhara Paṇḍita is the personified form of Kṛṣṇa's pleasure potency. He appeared to help Caitanya Mahāprabhu better understand the deep feelings of love that only Śrīmatī Rādhārāṇī is completely aware of. The Paṇḍita used to hold daily discourses on such topics.

After accepting *sannyāsa*, Śrī Caitanya Mahāprabhu traveled throughout South India for almost two years, from the spring of 1510 until the later part of 1511. After returning to Purī and remaining for a little more than two years, the Lord again left Jagannātha Purī on Vijayā-daśamī of 1514.[25]

From the day He had accepted *sannyāsa*, Śrī Caitanya Mahāprabhu had desired to visit Vṛndāvana, the holy land of Kṛṣṇa's childhood pastimes. His first attempts had been lovingly thwarted by Nityānanda Prabhu and Advaita Ācārya, who had directed Him instead to meet with the devotees at Navadvīpa before leaving home forever as a renunciant.

In a smiliar way, for more than two years after His return from His South Indian tour Sārvabhauma Bhaṭṭācārya and Rāmānanda Rāya lovingly forbade Caitanya Mahāprabhu to leave Purī.

After the Ratha-yātrā festival of 1514, Caitanya Mahāprabhu placed a proposal before Sārvabhauma Bhaṭṭācārya and Rāmānanda Rāya. He embraced them and spoke sweet words. "My desire to go to Vṛndāvana has increased manifold. Because of your tricks, I have not been able to go there for the past two years. This time I must go. Will you please give Me permission? Save for you two, I have no other resort. In Bengal I have two shelters—my mother and the River

[25] See *Caitanya-caritāmṛta* (*Madhya-līlā* 16. 84-86).

Ganges. Both of the them are very merciful. I shall go to Vṛndāvana through Bengal and see both My mother and the Ganges. Now would you two be pleased to give Me leave?"

When Sārvabhauma Bhaṭṭācārya and Rāmānanda Rāya heard these words, they began considering that it wasn't good that they played so many tricks on the Lord. They both agreed, "Now that the rainy season is here, it will be difficult for You to travel. It is better to wait for Vijayā-daśāmī."

Śrī Caitanya Mahāprabhu was pleased to receive their permission. He waited until the rainy season passed, and when the day of Vijaya-daśamī arrived, He departed for Vṛndāvana. The Lord collected whatever remnants of food were left by Lord Jagannātha, and He took with Him remnants of the Lord's *kaḍāra* ointment,[26] sandalwood, and Ratha-yātrā ropes.

After taking Lord Jaganantha's permission early in the morning, Śrī Caitanya Mahāprabhu departed, and all the devotees of Orissa began to follow Him. With great care Caitanya Mahāprabhu forbade the Orissan devotees to accompany Him.

Mahārāja Pratāparudra made various arrangements for Śrī Caitanya Mahāprabhu's trip to Vṛndāvana. When He crossed the river Citrotpalā, Rāmānanda Rāya, Mardarāja and Haricandana went with Him. Śrī Caitanya Mahāprabhu requested Gadādhara Paṇḍita to return to Nīlācala, Jagannātha Purī, but he did not abide by this order.

When he was requested to return to Jagannātha Purī, Gadādhara Paṇḍita told the Lord, "Wherever You are staying is Jagannātha Purī. Let my so-called *kṣetra-sannyāsa* go to hell." When Śrī Caitanya Mahāprabhu again asked Gadādhara Paṇḍita to remain at Jagannātha Purī and engage in Gopīnātha's service, Gadādhara replied, "One renders service to Gopīnātha a million times simply by seeing Your lotus feet."

Śrī Caitanya Mahāprabhu then said, "If you abandon His service, it will be My fault. It is better that you remain here and render service. That will be My satisfaction."

"Do not worry," the Paṇḍita replied, "all the faults will be on my head. I shall not accompany You but shall go alone. I shall go to see

[26] A kind of *tilaka* or holy clay used to mark the body.

Śacīmātā, but I shall not go for Your sake. I shall be responsible for the abandoning of my vow and service to Gopīnātha."

Thus Gadādhara Paṇḍita Gosvāmī traveled alone, but when they all arrived at Kaṭaka, Śrī Caitanya Mahāprabhu called for him. No one can understand the loving intimacy between Gadādhara Paṇḍita and Śrī Caitanya Mahāprabhu. Gadādhara Paṇḍita gave up his vow and service to Gopīnātha just as one gives up a piece of straw.

Gadādhara Paṇḍita's behavoir pleased Śrī Caitanya Mahāprabhu's heart. Nevertheless, the Lord took his hand and spoke to him, displaying the anger of love. "You have abandoned Gopīnātha's service and broken your vow to live in Purī. All that is now complete because you have come so far. Your wanting to go with Me is simply a desire for sense gratification. In this way you are breaking two religious principles, and because of this I am unhappy. If you want My happiness, please return to Nīlācala. You will simply condemn Me if you say more about this matter."

Saying this, Śrī Caitanya Mahāprabhu got into a boat, and Gadādhara Paṇḍita immediately fell down unconscious on the bank of the river. Śrī Caitanya Mahāprabhu requested Sārvabhauma Bhaṭṭācārya to revive Gadādhara Paṇḍita and take him back to Purī.

The Bhaṭṭācārya told Gadādhara Paṇḍita, "Please get up. Such are the pastimes of Śrī Caitanya Mahāprabhu. You should consider how Lord Kṛṣṇa Himself violated His own promise just to keep the promise of General Bhīṣma during the Battle of Kurukṣetra. Similarly, tolerating your separation, Śrī Caitanya Mahāprabhu has protected your vow with great endeavor."

In this way Sārvabhauma Bhaṭṭācārya revived Gadādhara Paṇḍita. Then both of them, stricken with grief, returned to Jagannātha Purī. The devotees would abandon all kinds of duties for Śrī Caitanya Mahāprabhu's sake, yet the Lord did not like the devotees' doing so. All these are the misgivings of loving affairs.

From Kaṭaka, Śrī Caitanya Mahāprabhu crossed the border of Orissa state, and He arrived at Pānihāṭi by boat. Thereafter He visited the house of Rāghava Paṇḍita, and from there He went to Kumārahaṭṭa and eventually to Kuliyā, where He excused many offenders. From there He went to Rāmakeli, where He met Śrī Rūpa and Sanātana and accepted them as His chief disciples. Returning from

Rāmakeli, He met Raghunātha dāsa and after giving him instructions sent him back home. Crowds of thousands gathered to follow the Lord during these travels, and after careful consideration He decided not to go to Vṛndāvana with such a crowd. He therefore returned to Nīlācala and began to make plans to go to Vṛndāvana at a later time without so many followers.

## The Lord Travels to Vṛndāvana

After attending the Ratha-yātrā ceremony the following year, Śrī Caitanya Mahāprabhu decided to start for Vṛndāvana alone. Śrī Rāmānanda Rāya and Svarūpa Dāmodara Gosvāmī selected a *brāhmaṇa* named Balabhadra Bhaṭṭācārya to personally assist Śrī Caitanya Mahāprabhu. Early in the morning before sunrise, the Lord started for the town of Kaṭaka. North of Kaṭaka, He penetrated a dense forest and came upon many tigers and elephants, whom He engaged in chanting the Hare Kṛṣṇa *mahā-mantra*. Whenever He had a chance to visit a village, He would beg alms and acquire some rice and vegetables. If there were no village, He would cook whatever rice remained and collect some spinach from the forest to eat. Śrī Caitanya Mahāprabhu was very pleased with the behavior of Balabhadra Bhaṭṭācārya.

In this way the Lord passed through the jungle of Jhārikhaṇḍa and finally reached Vārāṇasī. After taking His bath at the Maṇikarṇikā-ghāṭa at Vārāṇasī, He met Tapana Miśra, who took the Lord to his place and respectfully gave Him a comfortable residence. At Vārāṇasī, Vaidya Candraśekhara, Śrī Caitanya Mahāprabhu's old friend, also rendered service unto Him.

Seeing the behavior of Śrī Caitanya Mahāprabhu, a Maharashtriyan *brāhmaṇa* informed Prakāśānanda Sarasvatī, the leader of the Māyāvādī *sannyāsīs*. Prakāśānanda made various accusations against the Lord. The Maharashtriyan *brāhmaṇa* was very sorry about this, and he brought the news to Śrī Caitanya Mahāprabhu, inquiring from Him why the Māyāvādī *sannyāsīs* did not utter the holy name of Kṛṣṇa. In reply, Śrī Caitanya Mahāprabhu said that they were offenders and that one should not associate with them. In this way the Lord bestowed His blessings upon the *brāhmaṇa*.

Śrī Caitanya Mahāprabhu next passed through Prayāga and

Mathurā and then took His lunch at the home of a Sānoḍiyā *brāhmaṇa*, a disciple of Mādhavendra Purī. He bestowed His blessings upon the *brāhmaṇa* by accepting lunch at his place. The Lord then visited the twelve forests of Vṛndāvana and was filled with great ecstatic love.

In the village of Āriṭ-grāma, Śrī Caitanya Mahāprabhu discovered the transcendental lakes known as Rādhā-kuṇḍa and Śyāma-kuṇḍa. He then saw the deity Harideva at Govardhana Village. Śrī Caitanya Mahāprabhu had no desire to climb Govardhana Hill because the hill is worshiped as Kṛṣṇa. The Gopāla deity could understand the mind of Śrī Caitanya Mahāprabhu; therefore on the plea of being attacked by Muslims, Gopāla transferred Himself to the village of Gāṇṭhuli-grāma. Śrī Caitanya Mahāprabhu then went to Gāṇṭhuli-grāma to see Lord Gopāla. Some years later, Lord Gopāla also went to Mathurā, to the house of Viṭhṭhaleśvara, and stayed there for one month just to give an audience to Śrīla Rūpa Gosvāmī.

After visiting Nandīśvara, Pāvana-sarovara, Śeṣaśāyī, Khelā-tīrtha, Bhāṇḍīravana, Bhadravana, Lohavana and Mahāvana, Śrī Caitanya Mahāprabhu went to Gokula and then finally returned to Mathurā. Seeing a great crowd in Mathurā, He moved His residence near Akrūra-ghāṭa, and from there He went every day to Vṛndāvana to see Kālīya-hrada, Dvādaśāditya-ghāṭa, Keśī-ghāṭa, Rāsa-sthalī, Cīra-ghāṭa and Āmli-talā. At Kālīya Lake, many people mistook a fisherman for Kṛṣṇa. When some respectable people came to see Śrī Caitanya Mahāprabhu, they expressed their opinion that when one takes *sannyāsa*, he becomes Nārāyaṇa. Their mistake was corrected by the Lord. In this way, their Kṛṣṇa consciousness was awakened, and they could understand that a *sannyāsī* is simply a living entity and not the Supreme Personality of Godhead.[27]

When Śrī Caitanya Mahāprabhu took His bath at Akrūra-ghāṭa, He submerged Himself in the water for a long time. Balabhadra Bhaṭṭācārya decided to take Śrī Caitanya Mahāprabhu to Prayāga after visiting the holy place known as Soro-kṣetra. While stopping near a village on the way to Prayāga, Śrī Caitanya Mahāprabhu fainted in ecstatic love. Some Pāṭhāna soldiers who were passing through saw

[27] See *Vṛndāvana Dhāma Ki Jaya!* for more about holy sites of Vṛndāvana.

Śrī Caitanya Mahāprabhu and falsely concluded that the Lord's associates, Balabhadra Bhaṭṭācārya and others, had killed the Lord with a poison named *dhuturā* and were taking His wealth. Thus the soldiers arrested them. However, when Śrī Caitanya Mahāprabhu regained His senses, His associates were released. He talked with a person who was supposed to be a holy man in the party. From the Koran, Śrī Caitanya Mahāprabhu established devotional service to Kṛṣṇa. Thus the leader of the soldiers, named Vijulī Khān, surrendered to Śrī Caitanya Mahāprabhu, and he and his party became devotees of Lord Kṛṣṇa. The same village today is known as the village of Pāṭhāna Vaiṣṇavas. After bathing in the Ganges at Soro, Śrī Caitanya Mahāprabhu arrived at Prayāga, at the confluence of three rivers—the Ganges, Yamunā and Sarasvatī.

### Rūpa Gosvāmī Meets Caitanya Mahāprabhu at Prayāga

Meanwhile, after meeting Śrī Caitanya Mahāprabhu at Rāmakeli, the two brothers Rūpa and Sanātana began to devise ways to free themselves from their government service. Both brothers appointed some *brāhmaṇas* to perform ceremonies and to chant the holy name of Kṛṣṇa for their benefit.

Śrīla Rūpa Gosvāmī deposited ten thousand gold coins with a grocer, and the balance he brought in two boats to Bāklā Candradvīpa. There he divided this money among the *brāhmaṇas*, Vaiṣṇavas, and his relatives, while keeping a portion for emergencies and personal needs.

He then heard that Śrī Caitanya Mahāprabhu was going to Vṛndāvana from Jagannātha Purī through the forests of Madhya Pradesh. Therefore, he sent two people to Jagannātha Purī to find out when the Lord would leave for Vṛndāvana. In this way, Rūpa Gosvāmī retired.

When he learned of Śrī Caitanya Mahāprabhu's travels to Vṛndāvana through the forests of Madhya Pradesh (Jhārikhaṇḍa), Rūpa Gosvāmī left home and sent news to Sanātana that he was going with his younger brother Anupama Mallika to meet Śrī Caitanya Mahāprabhu.

Śrīla Rūpa Gosvāmī finally reached Prayāga and met Śrī Caitanya

Mahāprabhu, who was on His way back to Purī from Vṛndāvana. For ten days the Lord instructed Śrīla Rūpa Gosvāmī in the basic principles of love of God. These topics are described in Rūpa Gosvāmī's *Bhakti-rasāmṛta-sindhu*.

The Lord then sent Śrīla Rūpa Gosvāmī on to Vṛndāvana, while He returned to Vārāṇasi and stayed at the home of Candraśekhara.

*vṛndāvanīyāṁ rasa-keli-vārtāṁ*
*kālena luptāṁ nija-śaktim utkaḥ*
*sañcārya rūpe vyatanot punaḥ sa*
*prabhur vidhau prāg iva loka-sṛṣṭim*

"Before the creation of this cosmic manifestation, the Lord enlightened the heart of Lord Brahmā with the details of the creation and manifested the Vedic knowledge. In exactly the same way, the Lord, being anxious to revive the Vṛndāvana pastimes of Lord Kṛṣṇa, impregnated the heart of Rūpa Gosvāmī with spiritual potency. By this potency, Śrīla Rūpa Gosvāmī could revive the activities of Kṛṣṇa in Vṛndāvana, activities almost lost to memory. In this way, He spread Kṛṣṇa consciousness throughout the world."[28]

## Sanātana Gosvāmī Meets Śrī Caitanya in Vārāṇasī

Thereafter, Sanātana Gosvāmī told the Nawab that he was sick and couldn't attend to his work. Then he went home to study *Śrīmad-Bhāgavatam* with learned *brāhmaṇa* scholars.

At first, the Nawab accepted Sanātana's excuse, and sent his personal physician to see what was wrong. Then he personally came to see why Sanātana wasn't attending to the government's business. Knowing that he wanted to resign his post, the Nawab had him arrested and imprisoned. He then went off to attack Orissa.

While Sanātana Gosvāmī was still in prison, he received news from Rūpa Gosvāmī that Śrī Caitanya Mahāprabhu had gone to Mathurā. Sanātana Gosvāmī therefore satisfied the superintendent

[28] *Caitanya-caritāmṛta* (*Madhya-līlā* 19.1)

of the jail by sweet solicitations and bribery. After giving the jailer seven thousand gold coins, Sanātana Gosvāmī was released. He then crossed the Ganges and fled.

One of Sanātana's servants, Īśāna, accompanied him, carrying eight gold coins. Sanātana and his servant then spent a night in a small hotel on the way to Benares. The hotel owner suspected that Sanātana Gosvāmī and his servant had some gold, and he decided to kill them and take the money. Making plans in this way, the hotel owner received them as honorable guests.

Sanātana Gosvāmī, however, asked his servant how much money he had, and, taking seven of the gold coins, Sanātana offered them to the hotel owner. The owner then helped them reach the hilly tract toward Vārāṇasī. After passing over the hilly areas, Sanātana sent Īśāna back to Bengal.

During his travels, Sanātana Gosvāmī met his brother-in-law Śrīkānta at Hājipura. Śrīkānta gave him a valuable woolen blanket and helped him get to Vārāṇasī. Finally, after making various inquiries about Caitanya Mahāprabhu, Sanātana found his way to Candraśekhara's house and sat down by the door.

Caitanya Mahāprabhu, who was in the house, said Candraśekhara: "There is a devotee at your door. Please call him in."

Going outside, Candraśekhara didn't see a Vaiṣṇava. When he informed the Lord that there was no Vaiṣṇava at his door, the Lord asked him, "Is *anyone* at your door?"

"There is a Muslim mendicant," Candraśekhara replied. He couldn't recognize Sanātana due to his long hair and beard.

Śrī Caitanya Mahāprabhu said, "Please bring him here." Candraśekhara then called to Sanātana Gosvāmī, "O Muslim mendicant, please come in. The Lord is calling you."

Sanātana Gosvāmī was pleased to hear the Lord's invitation, and he entered the courtyard of Candraśekhara's house. As soon as Śrī Caitanya Mahāprabhu saw him, He ran up to him and embraced him. When Śrī Caitanya Mahāprabhu touched Sanātana Gosvāmī, both master and servant were overwhelmed with ecstatic love.

In a faltering voice, Sanātana said, "O my Lord, please do not touch me."

"I am touching you just to purify Myself," the Lord replied, "because by the force of your devotional service you can purify the whole universe.

*bhavad-vidhā bhāgavatās*
*tīrtha-bhūtāḥ svayaṁ prabho*
*tīrthī-kurvanti tīrthāni*
*svāntaḥ-sthena gadā-bhṛtā*

'Saints of your caliber are themselves places of pilgrimage. Because of their purity, they are constant companions of the Lord, and therefore they can purify even the places of pilgrimage.[29]

*viprād dvi-ṣad-guṇa-yutād aravinda-nābha-*
*pādāravinda-vimukhāt śvapacaṁ variṣṭham*
*manye tad-arpita-mano-vacanehitārtha-*
*prāṇaṁ punāti sa kulaṁ na tu bhūrimānaḥ*

'One may be born in a *brāhmaṇa* family and have all twelve brahminical qualities, but if he is not devoted to the lotus feet of Lord Kṛṣṇa, who has a navel shaped like a lotus, he is not as good as a *caṇḍāla* who has dedicated his mind, words, activities, wealth, and life to the service of the Lord. Simply to take birth in a *brāhmaṇa* family or to have brahminical qualities is not sufficient. One must become a pure devotee of the Lord. If a *śva-paca* or *caṇḍāla* is a devotee, he delivers not only himself but his whole family, whereas a *brāhmaṇa* who is not a devotee but simply has brahminical qualifications cannot even purify himself, not to speak of his family.'"[30]

Sanātana Gosvāmī then met both Tapana Miśra and Candraśekhara. Tapana Miśra extended an invitation to Sanātana, and Lord Caitanya Mahāprabhu asked Sanātana to shave his hair and beard. Candraśekhara took Sanātana to bathe in the Ganges, and afterwards he brought him a new set of clothes, but Sanātana didn't accept them.

---

[29] *Śrīmad-Bhāgavatam* (1.13.10)

[30] *Śrīmad-Bhāgavatam* (7.9.10). A *śva-paca* or *caṇḍāla* is a person born in low-class family.

"If you want to give me some cloth according to your desire," he said, "please give me an old cloth you have used."

When Tapana Miśra gave Śrīla Sanātana Gosvāmī a used *dhotī*, Sanātana tore it in pieces to make two sets of outer cloth and underwear.

When Caitanya Mahāprabhu introduced a Maharashtriya *brāhmaṇa* to Sanātana, that *brāhmaṇa* spontaneously invited Sanātana Gosvāmī for meals. "My dear Sanātana, as long as you remain at Kāśī, please accept lunch at my place."

"I want to practice the process of *mādhukāri*," Sanātana replied. "Why should I accept full meals in the house of a *brāhmaṇa*?"

*Mādhukāri* is a process of accepting a little food from each door just as a bee accepts a little nectar from each flower. In this way, a mendicant neither overeats nor becomes burdensome to the householders. A person in the renounced order may beg, but he may not cook. The *mādhukāri* process is strictly followed by *bābājīs*, those who have attained the *paramahaṁsa* stage.

Śrī Caitanya Mahāprabhu felt unlimited happiness observing Sanātana Gosvāmī's strict following of *sannyāsa* principles; however, He repeatedly glanced at Sanātana's woolen blanket. Because Śrī Caitanya Mahāprabhu repeatedly glanced at this valuable blanket, Sanātana Gosvāmī understood that the Lord didn't approve of his wearing it. Therefore, he decided to give it away.

When he next went to the bank of the Ganges to bathe, he saw that a Bengali mendicant had washed his quilt and spread it out to dry. Sanātana Gosvāmī told the mendicant, "My dear brother, please do me a favor. Trade me your quilt for this woolen blanket."

"Sir, you are a respectable gentleman," the mendicant replied. "Why are you joking with me? Why would you trade your valuable blanket for my torn quilt?"

"I am not joking," Sanātana said seriously. "I am speaking the truth. Kindly take this blanket in exchange for your torn quilt." Saying this, Sanātana Gosvāmī exchanged the blanket for the quilt. He then returned to Śrī Caitanya Mahāprabhu with the quilt over his shoulder.

When Sanātana Gosvāmī returned, the Lord asked, "Where is your woolen blanket?"

Śrīla Sanātana Gosvāmī then narrated the whole story to the Lord.

"I have also considered this matter," Śrī Caitanya Mahāprabhu said. "Since Lord Kṛṣṇa is very merciful, He has nullified your attachment for all material things. Why should Kṛṣṇa allow you to maintain a last bit of material attachment? After vanquishing a disease, a good physician doesn't allow any of the disease to remain. It is contradictory to practice *mādhukāri* and at the same time wear a valuable blanket. One loses his spiritual strength by doing this, and one will also become an object for jokes."

"The Supreme Personality of Godhead has saved me from the sinful life of material existence," Sanātana Gosvāmī replied. "By His desire, my last piece of material attraction is now gone."

Being pleased with Sanātana Gosvāmī, Śrī Caitanya Mahāprabhu bestowed His causeless mercy upon him. By the Lord's mercy, Sanātana Gosvāmī received spiritual strength and intelligence to inquire from Him.

Formerly, Śrī Caitanya Mahāprabhu had asked Rāmānanda Rāya spiritual questions, and by the Lord's causeless mercy Rāmānanda Rāya could properly reply. Now, by the Lord's mercy, Sanātana Gosvāmī questioned the Lord, and Śrī Caitanya Mahāprabhu personally supplied the truth.

The two first discussed the constitutional position of the living entities, and Caitanya Mahāprabhu explained how the living entity is one of Lord Kṛṣṇa's energies. After this, the Lord explained the way of devotional service. While discussing the Absolute Truth, Śrī Kṛṣṇa, Caitanya Mahāprabhu analyzed Brahman, Paramātmā, and Bhagavān, as well as the expansions of the Lord called *svayaṁ-rūpa, tad-ekātma*, and *āveśa*, which are divided into various branches known as *vaibhāva* and *prābhava*. Thus the Lord described the many forms of the Supreme Personality of Godhead.

He then described the incarnations of God within this material world—incarnations such as the *puruṣa-avatāras*, *manvantara-avatāras*, *guṇa-avatāras*, and *saktyāveśa-avatāras*. The Lord also discussed the divisions of Kṛṣṇa's different ages, such as *bālya* and *pauganḍa*, and the different pastimes of the different ages. He finally explained how Kṛṣṇa attained His permanent form when He reached youth. In this way Śrī Caitanya Mahāprabhu explained and described everything to Sanātana Gosvāmī.[31]

### Caitanya Mahāprabhu's Return to Purī, And His Second Meeting With Rūpa Gosvāmī

When Śrī Caitanya Mahāprabhu returned to Jagannātha Purī from Vṛndāvana, all His devotees from around India heard the auspicious news and came to Puruṣottama-kṣetra.

Śivānanda Sena, who traveled with the Bengali devotees, took a dog with him and even paid the fare for it to cross the river. One night, however, the dog wasn't fed and it disappeared. The next day, when Śivānanda and his party arrived at Jagannātha Purī, Śivānanda saw the dog eating coconut pulp thrown to it by Śrī Caitanya Mahāprabhu. After this incident, the dog was liberated and returned to the spiritual world.

Following Lord Caitanya's order, Śrīla Rūpa Gosvāmī left Prayāga and visited Vṛndāvana, where he wrote the introductory verses to a drama. On his way back to Gauḍa-deśa (Bengal), Rūpa Gosvāmī was considering how to write the drama's action. Thus he made some notes and continued to write.

Rūpa Gosvāmī had been traveling with his brother Anupama. Almost as soon as they reached Bengal, however, Anupama died. Although Rūpa Gosvāmī was eager to see Śrī Caitanya Mahāprabhu in Purī, he was delayed by his brother's death. By the time Rūpa Gosvāmī was finally able to travel on to Navadvīpa, the devotees had already left for Jagannātha Purī. Thus he started out for Purī alone.

In the province of Orissa there is a place known as Satyabhāmā-pura. Śrīla Rūpa Gosvāmī rested in that village for a night while traveling on his way to Jagannātha Purī.[32] While resting in Satyabhāmā-pura, he dreamed that a beautiful woman came before him and mercifully gave him the following order: "Write a separate drama about me," she said. "By my mercy, it will be extraordinarily beautiful."

---

[31] For further study see *Caitanya-caritāmṛta* (*Madhya-līlā* Chapters 20–24), and *Teachings of Lord Caitanya*.

[32] Satyabhāmā-pura is in the district of Cuttak near the village called Jankadei-pura.

After having that dream, Śrīla Rūpa Gosvāmī considered, *It is the order of Satyabhāmā that I write a separate drama for her. I have brought together in one work all the pastimes performed by Lord Kṛṣṇa, both in Vṛndāvana and in Dvārakā. Now I shall have to divide them into two separate dramas*.

Absorbed in thought, Rūpa Gosvāmī reached Jaganātha Purī. When he arrived, he approached Haridāsa Ṭhākura's hut. Haridāsa Ṭhākura told him, "Śrī Caitanya Mahāprabhu has already informed me that you would come here."

Śrī Caitanya Mahāprabhu would come to see Haridāsa every day after observing the *upala-bhoga* ceremony at the Jagannātha temple. Just after Rūpa Gosvāmī arrived, Lord Caitanya came for His daily visit. Rūpa Gosvāmī immediatel offered his obeisances, and Haridāsa informed the Lord, "This is Rūpa Gosvāmī offering You obeisances."

The Lord embraced Rūpa Gosvāmī and then asked him for any news. When Śrī Caitanya Mahāprabhu asked about Sanātana Gosvāmī, Rūpa Gosvāmī replied, "I didn't meet him. I came by the path along the bank of the Ganges, whereas Sanātana Gosvāmī came by the public road. Therefore we didn't meet. In Prayāga I heard that he had already gone to Vṛndāvana."

Rūpa Gosvāmī then informed the Lord about Anupama's death. After allotting residential quarters for Rūpa, Śrī Caitanya Mahāprabhu left.

The next day, Caitanya Mahāprabhu again met Rūpa Gosvāmī, and introduced him to all of His associates. Rūpa offered his respectful obeisances at their lotus feet, and all the devotees embraced him.

Śrī Caitanya Mahāprabhu told Advaita Ācārya and Nityānanda Prabhu, "You should both show Your mercy wholeheartedly to Rūpa Gosvāmī. May Rūpa Gosvāmī, by Your mercy, become so powerful that he will be able to describe the transcendental mellows of devotional service." Thus Rūpa Gosvāmī became the object of love and affection for all the devotees of the Lord, including those who came from Bengal and those who resided in Orissa.

Śrī Caitanya Mahāprabhu went to see Rūpa Gosvāmī every day, and He would bring whatever *prasāda* He had received at the temple and give it to Rūpa Gosvāmī and Haridāsa Ṭhākura. He would talk to them both for some time, then leave to perform His noontime duties.

Because he had received the Lord's transcendental favor, Śrīla Rūpa Gosvāmī felt unlimited pleasure.

After Śrī Caitanya Mahāprabhu and all His devotees performed the Guṇḍicā-mārjana, they went to the garden known as Āiṭoṭā and held a picnic. When Haridāsa Ṭhākura and Rūpa Gosvāmī saw all the devotees accepting *prasāda* and chanting the holy name of Hari, they were both pleased. When Govinda gave them Lord Caitanya's remnants, they respected it and danced in ecstasy.

The next day, when Śrī Caitanya Mahāprabhu went to see Rūpa Gosvāmī, the Lord spoke as follows: "Do not try to take Kṛṣṇa out of Vṛndāvana, for He does not go anywhere else at any time.

*kṛṣṇo'nyo yadu-sambhūto*
*yaḥ pūrṇaḥ so'sty ataḥ paraḥ*
*vṛndāvanaṁ parityajya*
*sa kvacin naiva gacchati*

'The Kṛṣṇa known as Yadu-kumāra is Vāsudeva Kṛṣṇa. He is different from the Kṛṣṇa who is the son of Nanda Mahārāja. Yadu-kumāra Kṛṣṇa manifests His pastimes in the cities of Mathurā and Dvārakā, but Kṛṣṇa, the son of Nanda Mahārāja, never at any time leaves Vṛndāvana.' "[33] After saying this, Caitanya Mahāprabhu went to perform His noontime duties, leaving Śrīla Rūpa Gosvāmī surprised.

*Satyabhāmā ordered me to write two dramas*, Śrīla Rūpa Gosvāmī thought. *Now I understand that this order has been confirmed by Śrī Caitanya Mahāprabhu. Formerly I wrote the two dramas as one composition. Now I shall divide it and describe the incidents in two works. I shall write two invocations of good fortune, and two introductions. Let me think deeply about the matter, and then describe two sets of incidents.*[34]

During Ratha-yātrā, Rūpa Gosvāmī saw Lord Jagannātha. He also saw Lord Caitanya Mahāprabhu dance and chant in front of the *ratha*. When Rūpa Gosvāmī heard the mysterious verse uttered by Śrī Caitanya Mahāprabhu during the ceremony, he immediately composed

---

[33] *Laghu-bhāgavatāmṛta* (1.5.461)

[34] The two works are *Vidagdha-mādhava*, describing pastimes in Vṛndāvana, and *Lalita-mādhava*, describing pastimes in Dvārakā and Mathurā.

another verse dealing with the same subject. This incident was prviously narrated in the chapter describing Śrī Caitanya Mahāprabhu's dancing before the *ratha* car of Lord Jagannātha.

After writing this verse on a palm leaf, Rūpa Gosvāmī placed it somewhere in his thatched roof and went to bathe in the sea. A short time later, Śrī Caitanya Mahāprabhu went there to meet him. When He saw the leaf pushed into the roof and read the verse, Śrī Caitanya Mahāprabhu was overwhelmed by ecstatic love.

When Rūpa Gosvāmī returned, he saw the Lord and offered his obeisances. The Lord slapped him mildly in love and spoke as follows: "My heart is very confidential. How did you know My mind in this way?" Then He firmly embraced Rūpa Gosvāmī.

Śrī Caitanya Mahāprabhu took that verse and showed it to Svarūpa Dāmodara for him to examine. Then the Lord questioned him. "How could Rūpa Gosvāmī have understood My heart?"

"I can understand You must have already bestowed Your causeless mercy upon him," Svarūpa Dāmodara replied. "Otherwise, no one could understand this meaning. I can therefore guess that previously You bestowed Your causeless mercy upon him."

"Rūpa Gosvāmī met Me at Prayāga," Śrī Caitanya Mahāprabhu replied. "Knowing him to be a suitable person, I naturally bestowed My mercy upon him. I also bestowed upon him My transcendental potency. Now you should also give him instructions. In particular, instruct him in transcendental mellows."

"As soon as I saw the unique composition of this verse," Svarūpa Dāmodara said, "I could immediately understand that You had bestowed upon him Your special mercy.

*phalena phala-kāraṇam anumīyate*

'By seeing a result, one can understand the cause of that result.' " This verse is from the doctrines of *nyāya*, or logic.

### Rūpa Gosvāmī's Dramas

After the four months of Cāturmāsya (Śrāvaṇa, Bhādra, Āśvina, and Kārttika), all the Bengali Vaiṣṇavas returned home, but Rūpa

Gosvāmī remained at Jagannātha Purī.

One day while Rūpa Gosvāmī was writing his book, Śrī Caitanya Mahāprabhu suddenly appeared. As soon as Haridāsa Ṭhākura and Rūpa Gosvāmī saw the Lord coming, they both fell down to offer Him their respectful obeisances. Śrī Caitanya Mahāprabhu embraced them both and then sat down.

"What kind of book are you writing?" the Lord inquired. He held up a one of the palm-leaf pages, and when He saw Rūpa Gosvāmī's fine handwriting, He was pleased and praised the writing "The handwriting of Rūpa Gosvāmī is just like rows of pearls."

Then the Lord began to read the manuscript. He saw a verse on the palm leaf that overwhelmed Him with ecstatic love:

*tuṇḍe tāṇḍavinī ratiṁ vitanute tuṇḍāvalī-labdhaye*
*karṇa-kroḍa-kaḍambinī ghaṭayate karṇārbudebhyaḥ spṛhām*
*cetaḥ-prāṇgana-saṅginī vijayate sarvendriyāṇāṁ kṛtiṁ*
*no jāne janitā kiyadbhir amṛtaiḥ kṛṣṇeti varṇa-dvayī*

"I do not know how much nectar the two syllables *Kṛṣ-ṇa* have produced. When the holy name of Kṛṣṇa is chanted, it appears to dance within the mouth. We then desire many, many mouths. When that name enters the holes of the ears, we desire many millions of ears. And when the holy name dances in the courtyard of the heart, it conquers the activities of the mind, and therefore all the senses become inert."[35]

When Śrī Caitanya Mahāprabhu chanted this verse, Haridāsa Ṭhākura became jubilant and began to dance and praise its meaning. Śrī Caitanya Mahāprabhu embraced Haridāsa Ṭhākura and Rūpa Gosvāmī and then left to go to the seaside to perform His noontime duties.

The next day, after visiting the Jagannātha temple as usual, Śrī Caitanya Mahāprabhu met Sārvabhauma Bhaṭṭācārya, Rāmānanda Rāya, and Svarūpa Dāmodara and invited them to accompany Him to see Śrīla Rūpa Gosvāmī. On the way, the Lord praised Rūpa Gosvāmī's qualities. When Caitanya Mahāprabhu remembered Rūpa Gosvāmī's

[35] *Vidagdha-mādhava* (1.15)

verses, He felt great pleasure. He then began to praise His devotee as if He had five mouths, just to examine Sārvabhauma Bhaṭṭācārya and Rāmānanda Rāya.

When Haridāsa Ṭhākura and Rūpa Gosvāmī saw that Caitanya Mahāprabhu had come with His intimate devotees, they immediately fell down like logs and offered prayers at their lotus feet. The Lord then sat down in an elevated place with His devotees. Rūpa Gosvāmī and Haridāsa Ṭhākura sat at their feet, even though everyone asked them to sit on the same level as the Lord and His associates.

When Śrī Caitanya Mahāprabhu ordered Rūpa Gosvāmī to read the verse they had previously discussed, Rūpa Gosvāmī felt shy. Then Svarūpa Dāmodara Gosvāmī recited the verse. When all the devotees heard it, their minds were struck with wonder.

*priyaḥ so 'yaṁ kṛṣṇaḥ saha-cari kuru-kṣetra-militas*
*tathāham sā rādhā tad idam ubhayoḥ saṅgama-sukham*
*tathāpy antaḥ-khelan-madhura-muralī-pañcama-juṣe*
*mano me kālindī-pulina-vipināya spṛhayati*

"My dear friend, now I have met My very old and dear friend Kṛṣṇa on this field of Kurukṣetra. I am the same Rādhārāṇī, and now We are meeting together. It is very pleasant, but I would still like to go to the bank of the Yamunā beneath the trees of the forest there. I wish to hear the vibration of His sweet flute playing the fifth note within that forest of Vṛndāvana."

Hearing this verse, Rāmānanda Rāya and Sārvabhauma Bhaṭṭācārya said to Caitanya Mahāprabhu, "Without Your special mercy, how could Rūpa Gosvāmī have understood Your mind?"

Śrīla Rāmānanda Rāya admitted that previously Śrī Caitanya Mahāprabhu had empowered his heart so that he could express elevated and conclusive statements to which even Lord Brahmā has no access. "Had you not previously bestowed Your mercy upon him," Rāmānanda said, "it would not have been possible for him to express Your internal feelings."

"My dear Rūpa," Śrī Caitanya Mahāprabhu said, "please recite that verse from your drama which, upon being heard, makes all people's unhappiness and lamentation go away."

When the Lord persisted in asking this again and again, Rūpa Gosvāmī recited the verse.

*tuṇḍe tāṇḍavinī ratiṁ vitanute tuṇḍāvalī-labdhaye*
*karṇa-kroḍa-kaḍambinī ghaṭayate karṇārbudebhyaḥ spṛhāṁ*
*cetaḥ-prāṅgana-saṅginī vijayate sarvendriyāṇāṁ kṛtiṁ*
*no jāne janitā kiyadbhir amṛtaiḥ kṛṣṇeti varṇa-dvayī*

"I do not know how much nectar the two syllables *Kṛṣ-ṇa* have produced. When the holy name of Kṛṣṇa is chanted, it appears to dance within the mouth. We then desire many, many mouths. When that name enters the holes of the ears, we desire many millions of ears. And when the holy name dances in the courtyard of the heart, it conquers the activities of the mind, and therefore all the senses become inert."

When the devotees—especially Rāmānanda Rāya—heard this verse, they were filled with transcendental bliss. Everyone admitted that although they had heard many statements glorifying the holy name of the Lord, they had never heard such sweet descriptions as those of Rūpa Gosvāmī.

Rāmānanda Rāya inquired, "What kind of drama are you writing? We can understand from these two verses that it must be a mine of conclusive statements."

Svarūpa Dāmodara replied for Śrīla Rūpa Gosvāmī "He wanted to compose a drama about the pastimes of Lord Kṛṣṇa. He planned to describe in one book both the pastimes of Vṛndāvana and those of Dvārakā and Mathurā. He began it in that way, but now, following the order of Śrī Caitanya Mahāprabhu, he has divided it in two and is writing two plays, one concerning the pastimes of Mathurā and Dvārakā, and the other concerning the pastimes of Vṛndāvana. The two plays are called *Vidagdha-mādhava* and *Lalita-mādhava*. Both of them wonderfully describe ecstatic emotional love of God."

Śrīla Bhaktisiddhānta Sarasvatī Ṭhākura informs us in this connection that Śrīla Rūpa Gosvāmī composed the drama known as *Vidagdha-mādhava* in the year 1533, and he finished *Lalita-mādhava* in 1538. The discussion between Rāmānanda Rāya and Śrīla Rūpa Gosvāmī at Jagannātha Purī took place in Śakābda 1437 (A.D. 1516).

Śrīla Rūpa Gosvāmī gradually informed Rāmānanda Rāya and the others about many aspects of his plays. They discussed various dramatic techniques known as *prema-utpatti-kāraṇa* (the causes of awakening the loving propensity), *pūrva-rāga* (previous attachment or anticipation of meeting for the first time), *vikāra* (transformations of love), *ceṣṭā* (endeavors for love), and *kāma-lekha* (exchanges of letters disclosing the *gopīs*' awakening love for Kṛṣṇa).

Śrīla Rūpa Gosvāmī gradually cited examples from his *Vidagdha-mādhava* for each of these different techniques. Hearing his explanations, all the devotees were struck with wonder. Śrīla Rāmānanda Rāya said, "Your poetic expressions are like continuous showers of nectar. Kindly let me hear the introductory portion of the second drama."

Śrīla Rūpa Gosvāmī said, "In your presence, which is just like brilliant sunshine, I am as insignificant as the light of a glowworm. It is even impudent for me to open my mouth before you."

Having said this, he humbly recited the introductory verse of *Lalita-mādhava:*

*sura-ripu-sudṛśām uroja-kokān*
*mukha-kamalāni ca khedayann akhaṇḍaḥ*
*ciram akhila-suhṛc-cakora-nandī*
*diśatu mukunda-yaśaḥ-śaśī mudaṁ vaḥ*

" 'The beautiful moonlike glories of Mukunda give distress to the lotuslike faces of the wives of the demons and to their raised breasts, which are like gleaming *cakravāka* birds. Those glories, however, are pleasing to all His devotees, who are like *cakora* birds. May those glories forever give pleasure to you all.'" This is the first verse in Act One of *Lalita-mādhava*.

When Śrīla Rāmānanda Rāya inquired about the second introductory verse, Śrīla Rūpa Gosvāmī was somewhat hesitant, but nevertheless he began to read:

*nija-praṇayitāṁ sudhām udayam āpnuvan yaḥ kṣitau*
*kiraty alam urīkṛta-dvija-kulādhirāja-sthitiḥ*
*sa luñcita-tamas-tatir mama śacī-sutākhyaḥ śaśī*
*vaśī-kṛta-jagan-manāḥ kim api śarma vinyasyatu*

"'The moonlike Supreme Personality of Godhead, who is known as the son of mother Śacī, has now appeared on earth to spread devotional love of Himself. He is emperor of the *brāhmaṇa* community. He can drive away all the darkness of ignorance and control the mind of everyone in the world. May that rising moon bestow upon us all good fortune.'" This is the third verse of Act One.

Although Śrī Caitanya Mahāprabhu was inwardly greatly pleased when He heard this verse, externally He spoke as if angry. "Your exalted poetic descriptions of the mellows of Lord Kṛṣṇa's pastimes are like an ocean of nectar, but why have you put in a false prayer about Me? It is like a drop of detestful alkali."

"It is not alkali at all," Śrīla Rāmānanda Rāya objected. "It is a particle of camphor he has put into the nectar of his exalted poetic expression."

"My dear Rāmānanda Rāya," Śrī Caitanya Mahāprabhu said, "you are jubilant at hearing these poetic expressions, but I am ashamed to hear them, for people in general will joke about the subject of this verse."

"Instead of joking, people in general will feel great pleasure in hearing such poetry," Rāmānanda insisted, "for the initial remembrance of the worshipable deity invokes good fortune."

Rāmānanda Rāya further inquired, "By which subdivision of style do the players enter in this second drama?"

Rūpa Gosvāmī then began to speak specifically on this subject.

*naṭatā kirāta-rājaṁ*
*nihatya raṅga-sthale kalā-nidhinā*
*samaye tena vidheyaṁ*
*guṇavati tārā-kara-grahaṇam*

"'While dancing on the stage after having killed the ruler of uncivilized men (Kaṁsa), Lord Kṛṣṇa, master of all arts, will at the proper time accept the hand of Śrīmatī Rādhārāṇī, who is qualified with all transcendental attributes.'[36] I have used the introduction technically called *udghātyaka*, and the whole scene is called *vīth*."

---

[36] *Lalita-mādhava* (1.11)

When Rāmānanda Rāya requested Śrīla Rūpa Gosvāmī to speak about various portions of the play, Rūpa briefly quoted his *Lalitamādhava*, again citing various examples of dramatic technique.

Śrīla Rāmānanda Rāya was astounded by this recitation. He said to Śrī Caitanya Mahāprabhu, "This is not a poetic presentation; it is a continuous shower of nectar. Indeed, it is the essence of all ultimate realizations appearing in the form of plays. The wonderful descriptions of Rūpa Gosvāmī are superb arrangements to express loving affairs. Hearing them will plunge the heart and ears of everyone into a whirlpool of transcendental bliss.

"What is the use of a bowman's arrow or a poet's poetry if they penetrate the heart but do not cause the head to spin? Without Your mercy such poetic expressions would be impossible for an ordinary living being to write. My guess is that You have given him the power."

"I met Śrīla Rūpa Gosvāmī at Prayāga," Śrī Caitanya Mahāprabhu answered. "He attracted and satisfied Me because of his qualities."

Śrī Caitanya Mahāprabhu further praised the metaphors and other literary ornaments of Śrīla Rūpa Gosvāmī's transcendental poetry. Without such poetic attributes, there is no possibility of preaching transcendental mellows.

Śrī Caitanya Mahāprabhu requested all His personal associates to bless Rūpa Gosvāmī so that he might continuously describe Kṛṣṇa's Vṛndāvana pastimes, which are full of emotional love of Godhead. Śrī Caitanya Mahāprabhu said, "Śrīla Rūpa Gosvāmī's elder brother, whose name is Sanātana Gosvāmī, is such a wise and learned scholar that no one is equal to him."

Śrī Caitanya Mahāprabhu told Rāmānanda Rāya, "Sanātana Gosvāmī's renunciation of material connections is just like yours. Humility, renunciation, and excellent learning exist in him simultaneously. I empowered both of these brothers to go to Vṛndāvana to expand the literature of *bhakti*."

"My Lord," Śrīla Rāmānanda Rāya replied, "You are the Supreme Personality of Godhead. If You like, You can cause even a wooden doll to dance. I see that the truths regarding transcendental mellows that You have expounded through my mouth are all explained in the writings of Śrīla Rūpa Gosvāmī. Because of Your causeless mercy toward Your devotees, You want to describe the transcendental pastimes in

Vṛndāvana. Anyone empowered to do this can bring the entire world under Your influence."

Śrī Caitanya Mahāprabhu then embraced Rūpa Gosvāmī and asked him to offer prayers at the lotus feet of all the devotees present. Advaita Ācārya, Nityānanda Prabhu, and all the other devotees showed their causeless mercy to Rūpa Gosvāmī by embracing him in return. Seeing Śrī Caitanya Mahāprabhu's special mercy toward Śrīla Rūpa Gosvāmī and seeing his personal qualities, all the devotees were pleased.

Then when Śrī Caitanya Mahāprabhu left with all of His devotees, Haridāsa Ṭhākura also embraced Śrīla Rūpa Gosvāmī. Haridāsa Ṭhākura told him, "There is no limit to your good fortune. No one can understand the glories of what you have described."

"I do not know anything," Śrī Rūpa Gosvāmī said. "The only transcendental words I can utter are those which Śrī Caitanya Mahāprabhu makes me speak.

*hṛdi yasya preraṇayā*
*pravartito'haṁ varāka-rūpo'pi*
*tasya hareḥ pada-kamalaṁ*
*vande caitanya-devasya*

'Although I am the lowest of men and have no knowledge, the Lord has mercifully bestowed upon me the inspiration to write transcendental literature about devotional service. Therefore I offer my obeisances at the lotus feet of Śrī Caitanya Mahāprabhu, the Supreme Personality of Godhead, who has given me the chance to write these books.' "[37]

In this way Śrīla Rūpa Gosvāmī passed his time in close association with Haridāsa Ṭhākura by discussing Kṛṣṇa's pastimes in great happiness. Śrīla Rūpa Gosvāmī stayed at Lord Caitanya's lotus feet in Purī, and he celebrated the Dola-yātrā festival with the Lord with great happiness. After the Dola-yātrā festival, Śrī Caitanya Mahāprabhu bade Rūpa Gosvāmī farewell.

The Lord empowered him and bestowed upon him great mercy:

---

[37] *Bhakti-rasāmṛta-sindhu* (1.1.2)

"Now go to Vṛndāvana and stay there. You may send here your elder brother, Sanātana. When you go to Vṛndāvana, stay there, write transcendental literature, and excavate the lost holy places. Establish the service of Lord Kṛṣṇa and preach the mellows of Lord Kṛṣṇa's devotional service. I shall also go to Vṛndāvana once more."

Śrī Caitanya Mahāprabhu then embraced Rūpa Gosvāmī, who took the Lord's lotus feet and placed them on his head.

Śrīla Rūpa Gosvāmī left the devotees, and returned to Vṛndāvana by the path leading through Bengal. Anyone who hears of the Lord's second meeting with Rūpa Gosvāmī will certainly attain Śrī Caitanya Mahāprabhu's shelter.

### The Glories of Haridāsa Ṭhākura

A beautiful young *brāhmaṇa* girl in Jagannātha Purī had a very handsome son who was coming every day to Śrī Caitanya Mahāprabhu. This was not very much to the liking of Dāmodara Paṇḍita, however, who therefore told Śrī Caitanya Mahāprabhu, "If You display so much love for this boy, people will doubt Your character." Hearing these words from Dāmodara Paṇḍita, the Lord sent him to Navadvīpa to supervise the affairs of His mother, Śacīdevī. He also especially requested Dāmodara Paṇḍita to remind His mother that He was sometimes going to her home to accept the food she offered. Thus, following the order of Śrī Caitanya Mahāprabhu, Dāmodara Paṇḍita went to Navadvīpa, taking with him all kinds of *prasādam* from Lord Jagannātha.

On another occasion, Śrī Caitanya Mahāprabhu once inquired from Haridāsa Ṭhākura, who was known as Brahmā Haridāsa, how the *yavanas*, or persons bereft of Vedic culture, would be delivered in Kali-yuga. Haridāsa Ṭhākura replied that their deliverance would be possible if they very loudly chanted the Hare Kṛṣṇa mantra, for hearing the Hare Kṛṣṇa mantra chanted loudly, even with but little realization, would help them.

After describing this incident, the author of *Caitanya-caritāmṛta* also describes how Haridāsa Ṭhākura was tested at Benāpola, a village near Śāntipura. A person named Rāmacandra Khān, who was envious of Haridāsa Ṭhākura, sent a professional prostitute to attempt to defame him, but by the mercy of Haridāsa Ṭhākura, even the prostitute was delivered. Because of offending a pure Vaiṣṇava, Rāmacandra Khān was later cursed by Nityānanda Prabhu and ruined.

From Benāpola, Haridāsa Ṭhākura went to the village known as Cāndapura, where he lived at the house of Balarāma Ācārya. Thereafter, Haridāsa Ṭhākura was received by two brothers known as Hiraṇya and Govardhana Majumadāra, but in the course of a discussion he was offended by a caste *brāhmaṇa* known as Gopāla Cakravartī. Because of this offense, Gopāla Cakravartī was punished by being afflicted with leprosy.

Haridāsa Ṭhākura later left Cāndapura and went to the house of Advaita Ācārya, where he was tested by Māyādevī, the personification of the external energy. She also received his favor by being blessed with the chanting of the Hare Kṛṣṇa *mahā-mantra*.

### Sanātana Gosvāmī Visists Jagannātha Purī

Śrīla Sanātana Gosvāmī walked alone from Mathurā to Jagannātha Purī to see Lord Caitanya. Because of bathing in bad water and not getting enough food every day while traveling on the path through Jhārikhaṇḍa Forest, he developed a disease that made his body itch. Suffering greatly from this itching, he resolved that in the presence of Śrī Caitanya Mahāprabhu he would throw himself under the wheel of Jagannātha's car and in this way commit suicide.

When Sanātana Gosvāmī came to Jagannātha Purī, he stayed under the care of Haridāsa Ṭhākura for some time, and Śrī Caitanya Mahāprabhu was very happy to see him. The Lord informed Sanātana Gosvāmī about the death of his younger brother, Anupama, who had great faith in the lotus feet of Lord Rāmacandra.

One day Śrī Caitanya Mahāprabhu said to Sanātana Gosvāmī, "Your decision to commit suicide is the result of the mode of ignorance. One cannot get love of God simply by committing suicide. You have already dedicated your life and body to My service; therefore your body does not belong to you, nor do you have any right to commit suicide. I have to execute many devotional services through your body. I want you to preach the cult of devotional service and go to Vṛndāvana to excavate the lost holy places." After having thus spoken, Śrī Caitanya Mahāprabhu left, and Haridāsa Ṭhākura and Sanātana Gosvāmī had many talks about this subject.

On another day Sanātana Gosvāmī was summoned by Śrī Caitanya Mahāprabhu, who wanted him to come to Yameśvara-ṭoṭā. Sanātana Gosvāmī reached the Lord through the path along the beach by the sea. When Śrī Caitanya Mahāprabhu asked Sanātana Gosvāmī which way he had come, Sanātana replied, "Many servitors of Lord Jagannātha come and go on the path by the *Siṁha-dvāra* gate of the Jagannātha temple. Therefore, I did not go by that path, but instead went by the beach." Sanātana Gosvāmī did not realize that there were burning blisters on his feet because of the heat of the sand. Śrī Caitanya Mahāprabhu was pleased to hear about Sanātana Gosvāmī's great respect for the temple of Lord Śrī Jagannātha.

Because his disease produced wet sores on his body, Sanātana Gosvāmī used to avoid embracing Śrī Caitanya Mahāprabhu, but nevertheless the Lord would embrace him by force. This made Sanātana Gosvāmī very unhappy, and therefore he consulted Jagadānanda Paṇḍita about what he should do. Jagadānanda advised him to return to Vṛndāvana after the car festival of Jagannātha, but when Śrī Caitanya Mahāprabhu heard about this instruction, He chastised Jagadānanda Paṇḍita and reminded him that Sanātana Gosvāmī was senior to him and also more learned. Śrī Caitanya Mahāprabhu informed Sanātana Gosvāmī that because Sanātana was a pure devotee, the Lord was never inconvenienced by his bodily condition. Because the Lord was a *sannyāsī*, He did not consider one body better than another. The Lord also informed him that He was maintaining Sanātana and the other devotees just like a father. Therefore the moisture oozing from Sanātana's itching skin did not affect the Lord at all. After speaking with Sanātana Gosvāmī in this way, the Lord again embraced him, and after this embrace, Sanātana Gosvāmī became free from the disease. The Lord ordered Sanātana Gosvāmī to stay with Him for that year, and the next year, after seeing the Ratha-yātrā festival, he left Puruṣottama-kṣetra and returned to Vṛndāvana.

## Pradyumna Miśra Receives Instructions From Rāmānanda Rāya

One day, a learned *brāhmaṇa* named Pradyumna Miśra came to see Śrī Caitanya Mahāprabhu. He offered his respects and submissively inquired from Him, "My Lord, kindly hear me. I am a cripple-minded householder, the most fallen of men, but somehow, by my good fortune, I have received the shelter of Your lotus feet, which are rarely to be seen. I wish to hear topics concerning Lord Kṛṣṇa constantly. Be merciful unto me and kindly tell me something about Kṛṣṇa."

"I do not know about topics concerning Lord Kṛṣṇa," Śrī Caitanya Mahāprabhu replied. "I think that only Rāmānanda Rāya knows, for I hear these topics from him. It is your good fortune that you are inclined to hear topics regarding Kṛṣṇa. The best course for you would be to go to Rāmānanda Rāya and hear these topics from him. I see that you have acquired a taste for hearing talks regarding Kṛṣṇa. Therefore you are extremely fortunate. Not only you, anyone who has awakened such a taste is considered most fortunate."

Being thus advised by Lord Caitanya, Pradyumna Miśra went to see Rāmānanda Rāya. Rāmānanda Rāya's servant offered him a seat and told him that Rāmānanda Rāya could not see him immediately. Pradyumna Miśra then asked the servant what Rāmānanda was doing.

The servant said, "There are two dancing girls who are extremely beautiful. They are very youthful, and they are expert in dancing and singing. Śrīla Rāmānanda Rāya has taken these two girls to a solitary place in his garden where he is teaching and directing them to dance according to the songs he has composed for his drama."

Rāmānanda Rāya's drama was the famous *Jagannātha-vallabha-nāṭaka*, and both the songs and dances were meant for Lord Jagannātha's pleasure. This is why Rāmānanda Rāya was personally instructing the girls how to sing and dance the drama.

The servant suggested, "Please sit here and wait for a few moments. As soon as he comes, he will execute whatever order you give him."

While Pradyumna Miśra was waiting, Rāmānanda Rāya was massaging the girls' bodies with oil and bathing them with water. Indeed,

Rāmānanda Rāya cleansed their entire bodies with his own hand. Although he dressed the two young girls and decorated their bodies with his own hand, he remained unchanged. Such is the mind of Śrīla Rāmānanda Rāya. While touching the young girls, he was like a person touching wood or stone, for his body and mind were unaffected. Śrīla Rāmānanda Rāya used to act in that way because he thought of himself in his original position as a maidservant of the *gopīs*. Thus although externally he appeared to be a man, internally, in his original spiritual position, he considered himself a maidservant and considered the two girls *gopīs*.

The greatness of Śrī Caitanya Mahāprabhu's devotees is difficult to understand. Śrī Rāmānanda Rāya is unique among them all, for he showed how one can extend his ecstatic love to the extreme limit. Rāmānanda Rāya directed the two girls how to dance and express the deep meaning of his songs through dramatic performances. He taught them how to express the symptoms of continuous, natural, and transitional ecstasies with the movements of their faces, eyes, and other parts of their bodies. Through feminine poses and dances they were taught, the two girls precisely exhibited expressions of ecstasy before Lord Jagannātha. When they were finsihed practice, Rāmānanda Rāya fed the two girls sumptuous *prasāda* and sent them home unexposed. Every day he trained the two *deva-dāsīs* how to dance.[38]

When the servant informed Rāmānanda Rāya of Pradyumna Miśra's arrival, Rāmānanda Rāya immediately went to the assembly room. He offered his obeisances to Pradyumna Miśra with all respect and then humbly asked, "Sir, you came here long ago, but no one informed me. Therefore I have certainly become an offender at your lotus feet. My entire home has been purified by your arrival. Kindly order me. What can I do for you? I am your servant."

"I came simply to see you," Pradyumna Miśra replied. "Now I have purified myself by seeing Your Honor." Because Pradyumna Miśra saw that it was late, he didn't say anything else to Rāmānanda Rāya. Instead, he took his leave and returned home.

The next day, when Pradyumna Miśra came into the Lord's pres-

---

[38] Drawings of various poses and *mudrās* expressed in modern Odissi dance are shown in *Section Two* in *Arts, Crafts, Music, Dance, and Architecture*.

ence, the Lord inquired, "Have you heard talks about Kṛṣṇa from Śrī Rāmānanda Rāya?"

Pradyumna Miśra thereupon described Rāmānanda Rāya's activities. After hearing about these activities, Śrī Caitanya Mahāprabhu said, "I am a *sannyāsī* and I certainly consider Myself renounced. But not to speak of seeing a woman, if I even hear the name of a woman, I feel changes in My mind and body. Therefore, who could remain unmoved by the sight of a woman? It is very difficult.

"The two professional dancing girls are beautiful and youthful, yet Śrī Rāmānanda Rāya personally massages oil upon their bodies. He personally bathes and dresses them and decorates them with ornaments. In this way, he naturally sees and touches the private parts of their bodies. Nevertheless, the mind of Śrī Rāmānanda Rāya never changes, although he teaches the girls how to physically express all the transformations of ecstasy. His mind is as steady as wood or stone. Indeed, it is wonderful that even when he touches such young girls, his mind never changes. The authority for such acts is the prerogative of Rāmānanda Rāya alone, for I can understand that his body is not material but has been completely transformed into a spiritual entity. He alone, and no one else, can understand the position of his mind. But I can make a guess in terms of directions from the *Śrīmad-Bhāgavatam*. When one hears or describes with great faith the pastimes of Lord Kṛṣṇa, such as His *rāsa* dance with the *gopīs*, the disease of lusty desires in his heart and the agitation caused by the three modes of material nature are immediately nullified, and he becomes sober and silent.

*vikrīḍitaṁ vraja-vadhūbhir idaṁ ca viṣṇoḥ*
*śraddhānvito'nuśṛṇuyād atha varṇayed yaḥ*
*bhaktiṁ parāṁ bhagavati pratilabhya kāmaṁ*
*hṛd-rogam āśv apahinoty acireṇa dhīraḥ*

'A transcendentally sober person who with faith and love continuously hears from a realized soul about the activities of Lord Kṛṣṇa in His *rāsa* dance with the *gopīs*, or one who describes such activities, can attain full transcendental devotional service at the lotus feet of the Supreme Personality of Godhead. Thus lusty material desires, which are the heart disease of all materialistic persons, are for him quickly and completely vanquished.'[39]

"Śrīla Rāmānanda Rāya is situated on the path of spontaneous love of Godhead," Śrī Caitanya Mahāprabhu continued. "Therefore he is in his spiritual body, and his mind is not materially affected. I also hear topics about Kṛṣṇa from Rāmānanda Rāya. If you want to hear such topics, go to him again. You can take My name before him, saying, 'He has sent me to hear about Lord Kṛṣṇa from you.' Go hastily while he is in the assembly room."

Hearing this, Pradyumna Miśra immediately departed. Pradyumna Miśra went to Rāmānanda Rāya, who offered him respectful obeisances and said, "Please order me. For what purpose have you come?"

"Śrī Caitanya Mahāprabhu has sent me to hear topics about Lord Kṛṣṇa from you," Pradyumna Miśra answered.

Hearing this, Rāmānanda Rāya became absorbed in ecstatic love and began to speak with great transcendental pleasure. "Following the instruction of Śrī Caitanya Mahāprabhu, you have come to hear about Kṛṣṇa. This is my great fortune. How else would I get such an opportunity?" Ṣaying this, Śrī Rāmānanda Rāya took Pradyumna Miśra to a secluded place and inquired from him, "What kind of *Kṛṣṇa-kathā* do you want to hear from me?"

"Kindly tell me about the same topics you spoke about at Vidyānagara," Pradyumna Miśra replied. "You are an instructor even for Śrī Caitanya Mahāprabhu, not to speak of others. I am but a beggar *brāhmaṇa*, and you are my maintainer. I do not know how to inquire, for I do not know what is good and what is bad. Seeing me to be poor in knowledge, kindly speak whatever is good for me by your own good will."

Thereupon Rāmānanda Rāya gradually began speaking on topics of Kṛṣṇa. Thus the ocean of the transcendental mellow of those topics became agitated. He began personally posing questions and then answering them with conclusive statements. When afternoon came, the topics still did not end. The speaker and listener spoke and heard in ecstatic love and both forgot their bodily consciousness. How then could they perceive the end of the day? The servant informed them,

---

[39] *Śrīmad-Bhāgavatam* (10.33.39)

"The day has already ended." Then Rāmānanda Rāya ended his discourses about Kṛṣṇa.

Rāmānanda Rāya paid great respect to Pradyumna Miśra and bade him farewell. Pradyumna Miśra said, "I have become very satisfied." He then began to dance.

After returning home, Pradyumna Miśra bathed and ate his meal. In the evening he came to see the Lord's lotus feet. In great happiness he worshiped the lotus feet of Śrī Caitanya Mahāprabhu. The Lord inquired, "Have you heard topics about Kṛṣṇa?"

"My dear Lord," Pradyumna Miśra said, "You have made me extremely obliged to You because You have drowned me in a nectarean ocean of talks about Kṛṣṇa. I cannot properly describe the discourses of Rāmānanda Rāya, for he is not an ordinary human being. He is fully absorbed in the devotional service of the Lord.

"There is one other thing Rāmānanda Rāya said to me. 'Do not consider me the speaker in these talks about Kṛṣṇa. Whatever I speak is personally spoken by Lord Śrī Caitanya Mahāprabhu. Like a stringed instrument, I vibrate whatever He causes me to speak. In this way the Lord speaks through my mouth to preach the cult of Kṛṣṇa consciousness. Within the world, who will understand this pastime of the Lord?'

"What I have heard from Rāmānanda Rāya is like a nectarean ocean of discourses about Kṛṣṇa. Even the demigods, beginning with Lord Brahmā, cannot understand all these topics. My dear Lord, You have made me drink this transcendental nectar of *Kṛṣṇa-kathā*. Therefore I am sold to Your lotus feet, life after life."

"Rāmānanda Rāya is a source of all humility," Śrī Caitanya Mahāprabhu said. "Therefore he has attributed his own words to another's intelligence. This is a natural characteristic of those advanced in devotional service; they do not personally speak of their own good qualities."

Generally, *brāhmaṇas* and *sannyāsīs* are proud of their spiritual positions. Therefore, to cut down their false pride, Śrī Caitanya Mahāprabhu preached Kṛṣṇa consciousness through Rāmānanda Rāya, who was neither a member of the renounced order nor a *brāhmaṇa* by birth. Rather, Śrī Rāmānanda Rāya was a *gṛhastha* belonging to the *śūdra* class, yet Śrī Caitanya Mahāprabhu arranged for him to be the master who taught Pradyumna Miśra, a highly qualified *brāhmaṇa* born in a *brāhmaṇa* family. Even Śrī Caitanya Mahāprabhu Himself, although belonging to the renounced order, took instruction from Śrī Rāmānanda Rāya. In this way Śrī Caitanya Mahāprabhu exhibited His opulence through Śrī Rāmānanda Rāya. That is the special significance of this incident.

Śrī Caitanya Mahāprabhu exhibited the glories of the holy name of the Lord through Haridāsa Ṭhākura, who was born in a Muslim family. Similarly, He exhibited the essence of devotional service through Sanātana Gosvāmī, who had almost been converted into a Muslim. The Lord also fully exhibited the ecstatic love and transcendental pastimes of Vṛndāvana through Śrīla Rūpa Gosvāmī. Considering all this, who can understand the Lord's deep plans? His activities are just like an ocean of nectar. Even a drop of this ocean can inundate the three worlds.

### Raghunātha dāsa Attains the Shelter Of Śrī Caitanya Mahāprabhu

Raghunātha dāsa had been attempting to come to the lotus feet of Śrī Caitanya Mahāprabhu for a long time, and finally he left his home and met the Lord. When Śrī Caitanya Mahāprabhu had gone to Śāntipura on His way to Vṛndāvana, Raghunātha dāsa had offered to dedicate his life at the Lord's lotus feet. In the meantime, however, a Muslim official became envious of Hiraṇya dāsa, Raghunātha dāsa's uncle, and induced some big official court minister to have him arrested. Thus Hiraṇya dāsa left his home, but by the intelligence of Raghunātha dāsa the misunderstanding was mitigated. Then Raghunātha dāsa went to Pānihāṭi, and following the order of Nityānanda Prabhu, he observed a festival (*ciḍā-dadhi-mahotsava*) by distributing chipped rice mixed with yogurt. The day after the festival, Nityānanda Prabhu gave Raghunātha dāsa the blessing that he would very soon attain the shelter of Śrī Caitanya Mahāprabhu. After this incident, Raghunātha dāsa, with the help of his priest, whose name was Yadunandana Ācārya, got out of his house by trickery and thus ran away. Not touching the general path, Raghunātha dāsa secretly went to Jagannātha Purī. After twelve days, he arrived in Jagannātha Purī at the lotus feet of Śrī Caitanya Mahāprabhu.

Śrī Caitanya Mahāprabhu entrusted Raghunātha dāsa to Svarūpa Dāmodara Gosvāmī. Therefore another name for Raghunātha dāsa is Svarūpera Raghu, or the Raghunātha of Svarūpa Dāmodara. For five days Raghunātha dāsa Gosvāmī took *prasādam* at the temple, but later he would stand at the *Siṁha-dvāra* gate and eat only whatever he could gather by alms.

After some days, Raghunātha dāsa also gave up standing near the *Siṁha-dvāra* gate and instead began eating by begging alms from a booth for free distribution of food. When Śrī Caitanya Mahāprabhu heard this news from Govinda, He inquired from Svarūpa Dāmodara, "Why does Raghunātha dāsa no longer stand at the *Siṁha-dvāra* gate to beg alms?"

"Raghunātha dāsa felt unhappy standing at the *Siṁha-dvāra*," Svarūpa Dāmodara replied. "Therefore, he is now going at midday to beg alms from the charity booth."

Hearing this news, Śrī Caitanya Mahāprabhu said, "He has done very well by no longer standing at the *Siṁha-dvāra* gate. Such begging of alms resembles the behavior of a prostitute. 'Here is a person coming near. He will give me something. This person gave me something last night. Now another person is coming near. He may give me something. The person who just passed did not give me anything, but another person will come, and he will give me something.' Thus a person in the renounced order gives up his neutrality and depends on the charity of this person or that. Thinking in this way, he adopts the occupation of a prostitute. If one goes to the booth where free food is distributed and fills his belly with whatever he obtains, there is no chance of further unwanted talk, and one can very peacefully chant the Hare Kṛṣṇa *mahā-mantra*."

After saying this, Śrī Caitanya Mahāprabhu again bestowed His mercy upon Raghunātha dāsa by giving him a piece of stone from Govardhana Hill and a garland made of *guñja* seeds. Previously, when Śaṅkarānanda Sarasvatī had returned from Vṛndāvana, he had brought the piece of stone from Govardhana Hill and also the *guñja-mālā* and presented them to Śrī Caitanya Mahāprabhu. The Lord was extremely happy to receive these two items. While chanting He would put the garland around His neck, and He often put the stone to His heart or sometimes to His eyes. Sometimes He would smell it, and sometimes He placed it on His head. The stone from Govardhana was always moist with the tears falling from His eyes. Śrī Caitanya Mahāprabhu would say, "This stone is directly the body of Lord Kṛṣṇa." For three years He kept the stone and garland. Then upon being satisfied with Raghunātha's behavior, the Lord gave them both to him.[40]

Śrī Caitanya Mahāprabhu instructed Raghunātha dāsa, "This stone is the transcendental form of Lord Kṛṣṇa. Worship the stone with great eagerness. Worship this stone in the mode of goodness like a perfect *brāhmaṇa*, for by such worship you will surely attain ecstatic love of Kṛṣṇa without delay. For such worship, one needs a jug of water and a few flowers from a *tulasī* tree. This is worship in complete goodness when performed in complete purity. With faith and love, you should offer eight soft *tulasī* flowers, each with two *tulasī* leaves, one on each side of each flower." After thus advising him how to worship, Lord Śrī Caitanya Mahāprabhu personally offered Raghunātha dāsa the Govardhana *śilā* with His transcendental hand. As advised by the Lord, Raghunātha dāsa jubilantly worshiped the *śilā*.

### "This is Unfit for You"

Lord Jagannātha's *prasāda* is sold by shopkeepers, and that which is not sold decomposes after two or three days. All the decomposed food is thrown before the cows from Tailaṅga at the side of the Jagannātha temple. Because of its rotten odor, even the cows cannot eat it. At night, Raghunātha dāsa would collect that decomposed rice, bring it home, and wash it with ample water. Then he would eat the hard inner portion of the rice with salt.

One day Svarūpa Dāmodara saw Raghunātha dāsa's activities. He smiled and asked for a small portion of that food and ate it. "You eat such nectar every day," Svarūpa Dāmodara said, "but you never offer it to us. Where is your character?"

---

[40] This Govardhana-śilā is now present at the Rādhā-Gokulānanda Temple in Vṛndāvana.

When Śrī Caitanya Mahāprabhu heard news of this from Govinda, He went to Raghunātha and said, "What nice things are you eating? Why don't you give anything to Me?" Saying this, He forcibly took a morsel and began to eat.

When Śrī Caitanya Mahāprabhu was taking another morsel of food, Svarūpa Dāmodara caught Him by the hand and said, "It is not fit for You." Thus he forcibly took the food away.

Śrī Caitanya Mahāprabhu said, "Of course, every day I eat varieties of *prasāda*, but I have never tasted such nice *prasāda* as that which Raghunātha is eating." Thus Śrī Caitanya Mahāprabhu performed many pastimes at Jagannātha Purī. Seeing the severe penances performed by Raghunātha dāsa in the renounced order, the Lord was greatly satisfied.

In his poem *Gaurāṅga-stava-kalpavṛkṣa* (11), Raghunātha dāsa has described his personal deliverance:

*mahā-sampad-dāvād api patitam uddhṛtya kṛpayā*
*svarūpe yaḥ svīye kujanam api māṁ nyasya muditaḥ*
*uro-guñjā-hāraṁ priyam api ca govardhana-śilāṁ*
*dadau me gaurāṅgo hṛdaya udayan maṁ madayati*

"Although I am a fallen soul, the lowest of men, Śrī Caitanya Mahāprabhu delivered me from the blazing forest fire of great material opulence by His mercy. He handed me over in great pleasure to Svarūpa Dāmodara, His personal associate. The Lord also gave me the garland of *guñja* seeds that He wore on His chest and a stone from Govardhana Hill, although they were very dear to Him. That same Lord Śrī Caitanya Mahāprabhu awakens within my heart and makes me mad after Him."

## Śivānanda Sena, the Travel Guide

Śrī Caitanya Mahāprabhu was always morose because of a continuous feeling of separation from Kṛṣṇa. The Lord would cry, "O My Lord Kṛṣṇa, My life and soul! O son of Mahārāja Nanda, where shall I go? Where shall I attain You? O Supreme Personality who plays with Your flute to Your mouth!" This was His situation day and night. Unable to find peace of mind, He passed His nights with great difficulty in the company of Svarūpa Dāmodara and Rāmānanda Rāya.

Sometimes, Śrī Caitanya Mahāprabhu would go to the beach where the surrounding area was pleasant and idyllic. The moon set the night aglow with its soft aura, and southern breezes caressed the Lord as He sat on the seashore. His body and beautific face were exquisitely decorated with sandalwood paste.

He continuously chanted the Hare Kṛṣṇa *mahā-mantra*. The flower garland hanging loosely around His neck covered a large portion of His chest, creating a picture of perfect beauty. Devotees sitting around Him relished His every movement. The waves of the sea were like swiftly approaching white lines, foaming as they crested one after another. The Lord smiled, looking at the endless swells of churning water. The benedictions Gaṅgādevī and Yamunādevī had already received from the Supreme Lord were now being showered upon the ocean.

The Lord spent the whole night performing *kīrtana* in divine bliss. Immersed in the nectarean ocean of His own loving mellows, He danced vigorously, drowning His devotees in floods of ecstasy. Different ecstatic symptoms like horripilation, crying, shivering, roaring, and perspiring sometimes manifest in waves one after the other, and at other times all at once. All these different devotional ecstasies bloomed like various seasonal flowers on the Lord's body. Everyone gathered around the Lord as He danced, saturated in the mood of a Vaiṣṇava. The Lord felt happy in the company of His devotees and forgot the pangs of loving separation.

The Supreme Lord utilizes but a small fraction of His unlimited potency to carry out His pastimes, and even that would be impossible for any other person to imitate. Vedic scriptures explain that no task is too difficult for the Lord to accomplish. The ecstatic devotional symptoms of love of Godhead exhibited by Lord Caitanya cannot be repeated by anyone else. Only those who are graced with Lord Caitanya's mercy are able to comprehend Him. Thereby, all the knots of material entanglement can be easily severed by taking full shelter of the Supreme Lord. That Supreme Personality, who is constantly meditated on by the most perfected beings like Lord Śiva, Lord Brahmā, and others, danced freely with His devotees lost in the currents of His own devotional ecstasy.

All-night *kīrtanas* on the seashore became more frequent, and the Lord participated with ecstatic dancing. It was around this time that Gadādhara Paṇḍita began spending practically all his time with the Lord. They ate together, slept together, went on walks together. Gadādhara Paṇḍita served Lord Caitanya continuously. When he read aloud from the *Śrīmad-Bhāgavatam*, the Lord entered a state of blissful trance. Gadādhara Paṇḍita's voice always made the Lord happy, and he would accompany the Lord to visit different Vaiṣṇavas.

Meanwhile, all the devotees once again journeyed from their homes in Bengal to see Śrī Caitanya Mahāprabhu. Headed by Śivānanda Sena, Advaita Ācārya, and others, all the devotees assembled in Navadvīpa. The inhabitants of Kulīna-grāma and Khāṇḍa village also assembled at Navadvīpa.

Because Nityānanda Prabhu was preaching in Bengal, Śrī Caitanya Mahāprabhu had ordered Him not to come to Jagannātha Purī. That year, however, He went with the rest of the party to see the Lord. Śrīvāsa Ṭhākura was also there with his three brothers and his wife, Mālinī. Ācāryaratna and Śivānanda Sena were similarly accompanied by their wives. Rāghava Paṇḍita joined them, carrying his famous bags of food. Vāsudeva Datta, Murāri Gupta, and Vidyānidhi accompanied them. All together, the devotees numbered two or three hundred. The devotees first took Śacīmātā's permission and then in great happiness started for Jagannātha Purī, congregationally chanting the holy name of the Lord.

Śivānanda Sena paid the tolls at different *ghātis*, toll booths used by *zamindars* who collected taxes in each state. Generally, this tax was collected to maintain the roads. Śivānanda Sena took care of everyone's maintenance and arranged each devotee's accommodations.

One day when the party was being checked by a toll collector, the devotees were allowed to pass, but Śivānanda Sena remained behind alone to pay the taxes. The party went into a village and waited beneath a tree because no one but Śivānanda Sena could arrange for their residential quarters. In those days, traveling from Bengal to Kaliṅga was a difficult journey through thickets and forested jungles. Fortunately, Śivānanda Sena was familiar with the paths to Kaliṅga and was friendly with many residents along the way.

Nityānanda, meanwhile, became hungry and upset because He

hadn't yet obtained a suitable residence. He began to call Śivānanda Sena ill names. "Śivānanda Sena has not arranged for My residence," He complained, "and I am so hungry I could die. Because he hasn't come, I curse his three sons to die."

Hearing this curse, Śivānanda Sena's wife began to cry. Just then, Śivānanda returned from the toll station. Crying, his wife informed him, "Lord Nityānanda has cursed our sons to die because His quarters have not been provided."

"You crazy woman!" Śivānanda Sena replied. "Why are you needlessly crying? Let my three sons die for all the inconvenience we have caused Nityānanda Prabhu."

After saying this, Śivānanda Sena went to Nityānanda Prabhu, who then stood up and kicked him. Very pleased at being kicked, Śivānanda Sena quickly arranged for a milkman's house to be the Lord's residence. Śivānanda Sena touched the lotus feet of Nityānanda Prabhu and led Him to His residence. After giving the Lord His quarters, Śivānanda Sena, being pleased, spoke as follows.

"Today You have accepted me as Your servant and have properly punished me for my offense. My dear Lord, Your chastising me is Your causeless mercy. Who within the three worlds can understand Your real character? The dust of Your lotus feet is not attainable even by Lord Brahmā, yet Your lotus feet have touched my wretched body. Today my birth, my family, and my activities have all become successful. Today I have achieved the fulfillment of religious principles, economic development, satisfaction of the senses, and ultimately devotional service to Lord Kṛṣṇa."

When Lord Nityānanda heard this, He was happy. He rose and embraced Śivānanda Sena with great love. Being pleased by Nityānanda Prabhu's behavior, Śivānanda Sena began to arrange residential quarters for all the other Vaiṣṇavas, headed by Advaita Ācārya.

One of Śrī Nityānanda Prabhu's characteristics is His contradictory nature. When He becomes angry and kicks someone, it is actually to his benefit. Śivānanda Sena's nephew, Śrīkānta, the son of his sister, however, felt offended, and he commented on the matter when his uncle was absent. "My uncle is well known as one of the associates of Śrī Caitanya Mahāprabhu, but Lord Nityanada Prabhu asserts His superiority by kicking him." After saying this, Śrīkānta, who was only a boy, left the group and traveled on alone to see Śrī Caitanya Mahāprabhu.

When Śrīkānta arrived in Purī and offered obeisances to the Lord, he was still wearing his shirt and coat. Therefore Govinda told him, "My dear Śrīkānta, first take off these garments." According to Vedic etiquette one is forbidden to enter the deity room or offer anything to the deity while wearing a shirt or coat.

As Govinda was warning Śrīkānta, Śrī Caitanya Mahāprabhu motioned with His hand saying, "Don't bother him. Let Śrīkānta do whatever he likes, for he has come here in a distressed state of mind." Śrī Caitanya Mahāprabhu inquired from Śrīkānta about all the Vaiṣṇavas, and the boy informed the Lord about them, naming them one after another. When Śrīkānta Sena heard the Lord say, "He is distressed," he could understand that the Lord is omniscient. As he described the Vaiṣṇavas, therefore, he didn't mention that Lord Nityānanda had kicked Śivānanda Sena. Meanwhile, all the devotees arrived and went to meet the Lord.

Śrī Caitanya Mahāprabhu received all the devotees just as He had in previous years. The women, however, saw the Lord from a distance. The Lord again arranged for the residential quarters of all the devotees and thereafter called them to partake of the remnants of food offered to Lord Jagannātha.

All the devotees engaged in the cleansing ceremony of the Guṇḍicā temple and danced in front of the Ratha-yātrā chariot, just as they had done in the past. For four consecutive months, the devotees observed all the festivals. The wives, such as Mālinī, extended invitations to Śrī Caitanya Mahāprabhu. The Bengali devotees had brought varieties of Bengali food that Śrī Caitanya Mahāprabhu liked. They also cooked various grains and vegetables in their homes and offered them to the Lord. All the devotees from Bengal would regularly invite Śrī Caitanya Mahāprabhu for lunch, and the Lord would speak to them in sweet words.

### The Unique Loving Sentiments Of Jagadānanda Paṇḍita

The previous year, Jagadānanda Paṇḍita, following the Lord's order, had returned to Nādia to see Śacīmātā. When he arrived, he offered prayers at her lotus feet and then offered her the cloth and *prasāda* of Lord Jagannātha. He offered obeisances to Śacīmātā in the name of Lord Caitanya Mahāprabhu and informed her of all the Lord's submissive prayers to her. Jagadānanda's coming pleased mother Śacī very much, and she listened to his talks about Lord Caitanya Mahāprabhu day and night.

"My dear mother," Jagadānanda Paṇḍita said, "sometimes the Lord comes here and eats all the food you have offered. After eating the food, the Lord says, 'Today mother has fed Me up to My neck. I go there and eat the food My mother offers, but she cannot understand that I am eating it directly. She thinks that this is a dream.' "

"I wish Nimāi would eat all the nice vegetables I cook," Śacīmātā said. "That is my desire. Sometimes I think that Nimāi has eaten them, but afterwards I think that I was only dreaming." In this way, Jagadānanda Paṇḍita and mother Śacī talked day and night about Śrī Caitanya Mahāprabhu's happiness.

Jagadānanda Paṇḍita met all the other devotees in Nādia, and they were all pleased that he had come. Jagadānanda Paṇḍita then went to meet Advaita Ācārya, who also was happy to see him. Vāsudeva Datta and Murāri Gupta were so pleased to see Jagadānanda Paṇḍita that they kept him at their homes and would not allow him to leave. They heard confidential narrations about Śrī Caitanya Mahāprabhu from his mouth and forgot themselves in the great happiness of hearing about the Lord. Whenever Jagadānanda Paṇḍita went to visit a devotee's house, that devotee immediately forgot himself in great happiness. All glories to Jagadānanda Paṇḍita! He is so favored by Śrī Caitanya Mahāprabhu that anyone who meets him thinks, *Now I have gotten the association of Śrī Caitanya Mahāprabhu directly*.

Jagadānanda Paṇḍita stayed at Śivānanda Sena's house for some time, and they prepared about sixteen seers of scented sandalwood oil. They filled a large earthen pot with the aromatic oil, and with great care Jagadānanda Paṇḍita brought it to Jagannātha Purī. This oil was placed in Govinda's care, and Jagadānanda requested him, "Please rub this oil on the Lord's body."

Govinda told Śrī Caitanya Mahāprabhu, "Jagadānanda Paṇḍita has brought some scented sandalwood oil. It is his desire that Your

Lordship apply a little of this oil on Your head so that blood pressure due to bile and air will be considerably diminished. He prepared a large jug of it in Bengal, and with great care he has brought it here."

"A *sannyāsī* has no use for oil," the Lord replied, "especially perfumed oil such as this. Take it out immediately."

According to Raghunandana Bhaṭṭācārya, the spokesman for the *smārta* regulative principles:

*prātaḥ-snāne vrate śrāddhe*
*dvādaśyāṁ grahaṇe tathā*
*madya-lepa-samaṁ tailaṁ*
*tasmāt tailaṁ vivarjayet*

"If one who has taken a vow smears oil on his body while bathing in the morning, while observing a ritualistic ceremony like the *śrāddha* ceremony, or on *dvādaśī* day, he may as well pour wine over his body. Therefore, oil should be rejected." The word *vrata* (vow) in this verse is sometimes applied to the *sannyāsa-vrata*.

"Deliver this oil to the Jagannātha temple," the Lord continued, "where it may be burned in the lamps. In this way, Jagadānanda's labor to manufacture the oil will be perfectly successful."

When Govinda informed Jagadānanda Paṇḍita of the Lord's decision, Jagadānanda remained silent. When ten days had passed, Govinda again told Śrī Caitanya Mahāprabhu, "It is the desire of Jagadānanda Paṇḍita that Your Lordship accept the oil."

When the Lord heard this, He said angrily, "Why not keep a masseur to massage Me? Have I taken *sannyāsa* for such happiness? Accepting this oil would bring My ruination, and all of you would laugh."

Śrī Caitanya Mahāprabhu declared Himself a strict *sannyāsī*. A *sannyāsī* is not supposed to take help from anyone. Retaining a masseur to give Him massages would indicate His dependence on others. Śrī Caitanya Mahāprabhu wanted to strictly follow the principle of not accepting anyone's help for His bodily comfort.

"If someone passing on the road smelled this oil on My head, he would think Me a *dārī sannyāsī*, a Tantric *sannyāsī* who keeps women." Hearing the Lord's words, Govinda remained silent. The next morning, Jagadānanda went to see the Lord.

Śrī Caitanya Mahāprabhu said to Jagadānanda Paṇḍita, "My dear Paṇḍita, you have brought Me some oil from Bengal, but since I am in the renounced order, I cannot accept it. Deliver the oil to the temple of Jagannātha so that it may be burned in the lamps. Thus your labor in preparing the oil will be fruitful."

"Who tells You all these false stories?" Jagadānanda Paṇḍita replied. "I never brought any oil from Bengal." After saying this, Jagadānanda took the jug of oil from the room and threw it down before Śrī Caitanya Mahāprabhu and broke it. Then Jagadānanda returned to his residence, bolted the door, lay down, and began to fast.

Three days later, Śrī Caitanya Mahāprabhu went to the door of his room and said, "My dear Jagadānanda Paṇḍita, please get up. I want you to personally cook My lunch today. I am going now to see the Lord in the temple. I shall return at noon."

After Śrī Caitanya Mahāprabhu said this and left, Jagadānanda Paṇḍita got up from his bed, bathed, and began to cook varieties of vegetables.

After finishing His noontime duties, the Lord arrived for lunch. Jagadānanda Paṇḍita washed the Lord's feet and gave the Lord a sitting place. He had cooked fine rice, mixed it with ghee, and piled it high on a banana leaf. There were also varieties of vegetables placed all around in pots made of banana tree bark. On the rice and vegetables were *tulasī* flowers, and in front of the Lord were cakes, sweet rice, and other varieties of *prasāda* from the temple.

"Spread another leaf with a helping of rice and vegetables so that today you and I may take lunch together," the Lord said. Śrī Caitanya Mahāprabhu kept His hands raised and would not accept the *prasāda* until Jagadānanda Paṇḍita, with great affection and love, spoke the following words:

"Please, first take *prasāda* Yourself, and I shall eat later. I shall not refuse Your request."

In great happiness, Śrī Caitanya Mahāprabhu then accepted the lunch. When He had tasted the vegetables, He again spoke. "Even when you cook in an angry mood," He said, "the food is very tasteful. This shows how pleased Kṛṣṇa is with you. Because He will personally eat the food, Kṛṣṇa makes you cook so nicely. You offer such nectarean rice to Kṛṣṇa. Who can estimate the limit of your fortune?"

"He who will eat has cooked this," Jagadānanda Paṇḍita replied. "As far as I am concerned, I simply collect the ingredients." Jagadānanda continued to offer the Lord varieties of vegetables. Out of fear, the Lord said nothing, but continued eating happily. Jagadānanda eagerly forced the Lord to eat so much that He ate ten times more than on other days. Again and again when the Lord wished to get up, Jagadānanda would feed Him more. Śrī Caitanya Mahāprabhu dared not forbid him to feed Him more. He just continued eating, fearful that Jagadānanda would continue to fast if He stopped.

At last the Lord respectfully submitted, "My dear Jagadānanda, you have already made Me eat ten times more than I am used to. Now, please stop."

Śrī Caitanya Mahāprabhu stood up and washed His hands and mouth, while Jagadānanda Paṇḍita brought spices, a garland, and sandalwood pulp. Accepting the sandalwood pulp and garland, the Lord sat down and said, "Now, in front of Me, you must eat."

"My Lord," Jagadānanda replied, "You go take rest. I shall take *prasāda* after I finish making some arrangements. Ramāi Paṇḍita and Raghunātha Bhaṭṭa helped with the cooking, and I want to give them some rice and vegetables."

Śrī Caitanya Mahāprabhu then told Govinda, "You remain here. When the Paṇḍita has taken his food, come and inform Me."

After Śrī Caitanya Mahāprabhu had said this and left, Jagadānanda Paṇḍita spoke to Govinda. "Go quickly and massage the Lord's feet," he said. "You may tell Him, 'The Paṇḍita has just sat down to take his meal.' I shall keep some remnants of the Lord's food for you. When He is asleep, come and take your portion." Jagadānanda Paṇḍita thus distributed the Lord's food remnants to Ramāi, Nandāi, Govinda, and Raghunātha Bhaṭṭa. He also personally ate the remnants of food left by Śrī Caitanya Mahāprabhu. Then the Lord again sent Govinda.

The Lord told him, "Go see whether Jagadānanda Paṇḍita is eating. Then quickly return and let Me know."

Seeing that Jagadānanda Paṇḍita was indeed eating, Govinda informed the Lord, who then became peaceful and went to sleep. The affectionate loving exchanges between Jagadānanda Paṇḍita and Lord Śrī Caitanya Mahāprabhu continued in this manner exactly like the exchanges between the queen named Satyabhāmā and Lord Kṛṣṇa related in *Śrīmad-Bhāgavatam*. Who can estimate the limit of Jagadānanda Paṇḍita's fortune? He himself is the example of his own great fortune.

Anyone who hears about the loving exchanges between Jagadānanda Paṇḍita and Śrī Caitanya Mahāprabhu or who reads Jagadānanda's book, *Prema-vivarta*, can understand what love is. Moreover, he achieves ecstatic love of Kṛṣṇa. (Concerning the name of Jagadānanda's book, the word *prema* means love, and *vivarta* means accepting something to be the opposite of what it appears. Here, Jagadānanda Paṇḍita appeared angry, but this anger was a manifestation of his great love for Śrī Caitanya Mahāprabhu.)

### Raghunātha Bhaṭṭa Gosvāmī

During this time, Raghunātha Bhaṭṭācārya, the son of Tapana Miśra, gave up all his duties and left home, intending to meet Śrī Caitanya Mahāprabhu.[41] Accompanied by a servant carrying his baggage, Raghunātha Bhaṭṭa started from Vārāṇasī and traveled along the path leading through Bengal. In Bengal he met Rāmadāsa Viśvāsa, who belonged to the *kayastha* caste and was one of the king's secretaries.

Rāmadāsa Viśvāsa was learned in all the revealed scriptures, and he used to teach the famous book *Kāvya-prakāśa*. He was known as an advanced devotee and worshiper of Lord Rāmacandra. Rāmadāsa had renounced everything and was going to see Lord Jagannātha. While traveling, he chanted the holy name of Lord Rāma twenty-four hours a day. When he met Raghunātha Bhaṭṭa on the way, he took Raghunātha's baggage on his head and carried it. Rāmadāsa served Raghunātha Bhaṭṭa in various ways, even massaging his legs, although Raghunātha Bhaṭṭa felt hesitant to accept such service.

"You are a respectable gentleman, a learned scholar, and a great devotee," he said. "Please do not try to serve me. Just come with me in a happy mood."

"I am a *śūdra*," Rāmadāsa replied, "a fallen soul. To serve a *brāhmaṇa* is my duty and religious principle. Therefore, please do not be

[41] Bhaṭṭācārya is a title awarded for one's erudition. Raghunātha's surname was Miśra.

hesitant. I am your servant, and when I serve you my heart becomes jubilant." Thus Rāmadāsa carried Raghunātha Bhaṭṭa's baggage and offered him other sincere services. He constantly chanted the holy name of Lord Rāmacandra day and night.

Traveling in this way, Raghunātha Bhaṭṭa soon arrived at Jagannātha Purī. There, with great delight, he met Śrī Caitanya Mahāprabhu and fell straight like a rod at the Lord's lotus feet. Then the Lord embraced him, knowing well who he was. Raghunātha then offered respectful obeisances to Śrī Caitanya Mahāprabhu on behalf of Tapana Miśra and Candraśekhara, and the Lord inquired about them.

"It is very good that you have come here," the Lord said. "Now go and see the lotus-eyed Lord Jagannātha. Today you will accept *prasāda* at My place."

The Lord asked Govinda to arrange for Raghunātha Bhaṭṭa's accommodations and then introduced him to all the devotees, headed by Svarūpa Dāmodara Gosvāmī.

Raghunātha Bhaṭṭa lived with Śrī Caitanya Mahāprabhu continuously for eight months, and by the Lord's mercy, his transcendental happiness increased day by day. He would periodically cook rice with various vegetables and invite Śrī Caitanya Mahāprabhu to his home. Raghunātha Bhaṭṭa was an expert cook. Whatever he prepared tasted just like nectar. Śrī Caitanya Mahāprabhu would accept with great satisfaction all the food he prepared. After the Lord was satisfied, Raghunātha Bhaṭṭa would eat His remnants.

When Rāmadāsa Viśvāsa met Śrī Caitanya Mahāprabhu, the Lord did not show him any special mercy, although this was their first meeting. Within his heart, Rāmadāsa Viśvāsa was an impersonalist who desired to merge into the existence of the Lord, and he was proud of his learning. Being the omniscient Supreme Personality of Godhead, Śrī Caitanya Mahāprabhu can understand the heart of everyone, and thus He knew all these things. Rāmadāsa Viśvāsa then took up residence in Jagannātha Purī and taught the *Kavya-prakāśa* to the Paṭṭanāyaka family.

After eight months, when Śrī Caitanya Mahāprabhu bade farewell to Raghunātha Bhaṭṭa, the Lord flatly forbade him to marry. Raghunātha Bhaṭṭācārya had become a greatly advanced devotee while still unmarried. Śrī Caitanya Mahāprabhu could see this and therefore advised him not to become entangled by material sense gratification. Marriage is a concession for people who are unable to control their senses. Raghunātha, however, being an advanced devotee of Kṛṣṇa, naturally had no desire for sense gratification. Therefore, Śrī Caitanya Mahāprabhu advised him not to enter the bondage of marriage. Generally a person cannot make much advancement in spiritual consciousness if he is married because he becomes attached to his family and is prone to sense gratification. Thus his spiritual advancement is slow or almost nil.

Śrī Caitanya Mahāprabhu said to Raghunātha Bhaṭṭa, "When you return home, serve your aged father and mother, who are devotees, and try to study *Śrīmad-Bhāgavatam* from a pure Vaiṣṇava who has realized God."

Anyone who wishes to advance in Kṛṣṇa consciousness must try to serve Kṛṣṇa's devotees. As Narottama dāsa Ṭhākura sings, *chāḍiyā vaiṣṇava-sevā nistāra pāyeche kebā*, "Without serving a self-realized Vaiṣṇava, no one has ever been released from the materialistic way of life." Śrī Caitanya Mahāprabhu would never have advised Raghunātha Bhaṭṭa to serve ordinary parents, but since his parents were Vaiṣṇavas, the Lord advised him to serve them.

One might ask, "Why shouldn't ordinary parents be served?" The *Śrīmad-Bhāgavatam* (5.5.18) states:

*gurur na sa syāt sva-jano na sa syāt*
*pitā na sa syāj jananī na sā syāt*
*daivaṁ na tat syāt na patiś ca sa syān*
*na mocayed yaḥ samupeta-mṛtyum*

"One who cannot deliver his dependent from the path of birth and death should never become a spiritual master, a relative, a father or mother, or a worshipable demigod, nor should such a person become a husband."

Everyone naturally gets a father and mother at birth, but the real father and mother are they who can release their offspring from the clutches of imminent death. This is possible only for parents advanced in Kṛṣṇa consciousness. Therefore, any parents who cannot enlighten their offspring in Kṛṣṇa consciousness cannot be accepted as a proper father and mother. The following verse from the *Bhakti-rasāmṛta-sindhu* (1.2.200) confirms the uselessness of serving ordinary parents:

*laukikī vaidikī vāpi*
*yā kriyā kriyate mune*
*hari-sevānukūlaiva*
*sā kāryā bhaktim icchatā*

"One should perform only those activities—either worldly or prescribed by Vedic rules and regulations—which are favorable for the cultivation of Kṛṣṇa consciousness."

Śrī Caitanya Mahāprabhu concluded, "Come again to Nīlācala." After saying this, the Lord put His own neck beads on Raghunātha Bhaṭṭa's neck. Then the Lord embraced him and bade him farewell. Overwhelmed with ecstatic love, Raghunātha Bhaṭṭa began to cry due to imminent separation from Śrī Caitanya Mahāprabhu.

After taking permission from Śrī Caitanya Mahāprabhu and all the devotees headed by Svarūpa Dāmodara, Raghunātha Bhaṭṭa returned to Vārāṇasī. In accordance with the Lord's instructions, he served his mother and father for four more years. He also studied the *Śrīmad-Bhāgavatam* regularly from a self-realized Vaiṣṇava. Then his parents died at Kāśī (Vārāṇasī), and he decided to return to Śrī Caitanya Mahāprabhu, giving up all relationship with his home.

Raghunātha Bhaṭṭa then lived with Śrī Caitanya Mahāprabhu for another eight months, after which the Lord gave him the following order: "My dear Raghunātha, go to Vṛndāvana, following My instructions, and place yourself under the care of Rūpa and Sanātana Gosvāmīs. In Vṛndāvana you should chant the Hare Kṛṣṇa mantra twenty-four hours a day and read *Śrīmad-Bhāgavatam* continuously. Kṛṣṇa, the Supreme Personality of Godhead, will very soon bestow His mercy upon you."

After saying this, Śrī Caitanya Mahāprabhu embraced Raghunātha Bhaṭṭa, and by the Lord's mercy, Raghunātha was enlivened with ecstatic love for Kṛṣṇa. At a festival Śrī Caitanya Mahāprabhu had been given some unspiced betel and a garland of *tulasī* leaves fourteen cubits long. The garland had been worn by Lord Jagannātha. Śrī Caitanya Mahāprabhu gave the garland and betel to Raghunātha, who accepted them as a worshipable deity, preserving them carefully.

Taking permission from Śrī Caitanya Mahāprabhu, Raghunātha Bhaṭṭa then departed for Vṛndāvana. When he arrived in Vṛndāvana, he put himself under the care of Rūpa and Sanātana Gosvāmīs. When reciting *Śrīmad-Bhāgavatam* in the company of Rūpa and Sanātana, Raghunātha Bhaṭṭa would be overwhelmed with love for Kṛṣṇa. By the mercy of Śrī Caitanya Mahāprabhu, he experienced the symptoms of ecstatic love—tears, trembling, and faltering of the voice. His eyes filled with tears, his throat became choked, and he couldn't recite *Śrīmad-Bhāgavatam*. His voice was as sweet as a cuckoo's, and he would recite each verse of *Śrīmad-Bhāgavatam* in three or four different tunes. Thus his recitations were sweet to hear. When he recited or heard about the beauty and sweetness of Kṛṣṇa, he would be overwhelmed and become oblivious to everything. Thus Raghunātha Bhaṭṭa surrendered fully at the lotus feet of Lord Govinda, and those lotus feet became his life and soul.

Subsequently, Raghunātha Bhaṭṭa ordered his disciples to construct a temple for Govinda. He prepared various ornaments for Govinda, including a flute and earrings shaped like sharks.[42] Raghunātha Bhaṭṭa would neither hear nor speak about anything of the material world. He would simply discuss Kṛṣṇa and worship the Lord day and night. He would not listen to blasphemy of a Vaiṣṇava, nor would he listen to talk of a Vaiṣṇava's misbehavior. He knew only that everyone was engaged in Kṛṣṇa's service; he didn't understand anything else. Even if another Vaiṣṇava was actually at fault, Raghunātha Bhaṭṭa wouldn't criticize him; he saw only that everyone was engaged in Kṛṣṇa's service. That is the position of a *mahā-bhāgavata*.

When Raghunātha Bhaṭṭa Gosvāmī was absorbed in remembrance of Lord Kṛṣṇa, he would take the *tulasī* garland and the betel given to him by Śrī Caitanya Mahāprabhu, bind them together, and wear them on his neck. By the powerful mercy of Śrī Caitanya Mahāprabhu, Raghunātha Bhaṭṭa Gosvāmī remained constantly

---

[42] Raghunātha Bhaṭṭa Gosvāmī was instrumental in the construction of the Rādhā-Govinda temple. This Govinda deity was previously situated in Vṛndāvana, but due to violent attacks during the Muslim period, the deity was moved to Jaipur, Rajasthan, where He remains today.

overwhelmed with ecstatic love for Kṛṣṇa. Śrī Caitanya Mahāprabhu, Gaurahari, bestows ecstatic love for Kṛṣṇa upon anyone who hears all these topics with faith and love.

## Feelings of Separation from Kṛṣṇa

The following is a small portion of the activities performed by Śrī Caitanya Mahāprabhu with His mind, intelligence, and body when He was bewildered by strong feelings of separation from Kṛṣṇa. Śrī Caitanya Mahāprabhu's emotion of transcendental madness in separation from Kṛṣṇa is deep and mysterious. Even though one may be advanced and learned, one cannot understand it. How can one describe unfathomable subjects? It is possible only if Śrī Caitanya Mahāprabhu gives him the capability.

Svarūpa Dāmodara Gosvāmī and Raghunātha dāsa Gosvāmī, who personally lived with the Lord in Jagannātha Purī during those days, recorded details of the Lord's transcendental activities in two notebooks. Therefore, without reference to these notebooks, one cannot understand the Lord's activities. Anyone inventing a new method to worship Śrī Caitanya Mahāprabhu is certainly unable to understand the Lord's pastimes, for he is bereft of the real process of approaching the Lord.

Svarūpa Dāmodara wrote short codes, whereas Raghunātha dāsa Gosvāmī wrote more elaborate descriptions. Please hear this description of Caitanya Mahāprabhu's ecstatic emotions faithfully. Thus you will come to know of His ecstatic love, and ultimately you will achieve love of Godhead.

When Śrī Caitanya Mahāprabhu felt separation from Kṛṣṇa, His condition exactly corresponded to the condition of the *gopīs* in Vṛndāvana after Kṛṣṇa's departure for Mathurā. The lamentation of Śrīmatī Rādhārāṇī when Uddhava visited Vṛndāvana gradually became a feature of Śrī Caitanya Mahāprabhu's transcendental madness. Śrīmatī Rādhārāṇī's emotions after seeing Uddhava exactly correspond to those of Śrī Caitanya Mahāprabhu. He always conceived of Himself in Her position and sometimes thought that He was Śrīmatī Rādhārāṇī Herself.

Such is the state of transcendental madness. Why is it difficult to understand? When one is highly elevated in love of Kṛṣṇa, he becomes transcendentally mad and talks like a madman.

*etasya mohanākhyasya*
*gatiṁ kāmapy upeyuṣaḥ*
*bhramābhā kāpi vaicitrī*
*divyonmāda itīryate*
*udghūrṇā-citra-jalpādyās*
*tad-bhedā bahavo matāḥ*

"When the ecstatic emotion of enchantment gradually progresses, it becomes similar to bewilderment. Then one reaches the stage of astonishment, *vaicitrī*, which awakens transcendental madness. *Udghūrṇā* and *citra-jalpa* are two among the many divisions of transcendental madness."[43]

Śrī Caitanya Mahāprabhu is *rādhā-bhāva-dyuti-suvalita*, that is, Kṛṣṇa Himself assuming the part of Śrīmatī Rādhārāṇī in order to understand Kṛṣṇa. This mystery has been poetically revealed by Svarūpa Dāmodara Gosvāmī:

*śrī-rādhāyāh praṇaya-mahimā kīdṛśo vānayaivā-*
*svādyo yenādbhuta-madhurimā kīdṛśo va madīyaḥ*
*saukhyaṁ cāsyā mad-anubhavataḥ kīḍṛśaṁ veti lobhāt*
*tad-bhāvāḍhyaḥ samajani śacī-garbha-sindhau harīnduḥ*

"Desiring to understand the glory of Rādhārāṇī's love, the wonderful qualities in Him that She alone relishes through Her love, and the happiness She feels when She realizes the sweetness of His love, the Supreme Lord Hari, richly endowed with Her emotions, appears from the womb of Śrīmatī Śacīdevī, as the moon appears from the ocean."[44]

From the day Kṛṣṇa and Balarāma left Vṛndāvana to attend a wrestling match in Mathurā, Śrīmatī Rādhārāṇī and other residents of Vṛndāvana felt intense separation from Kṛṣṇa. Lord Kṛṣṇa also felt acute separation from His dearmost friends back in Vrajabhūmi, the

---

[43] *Ujjvala-nīlamaṇi, Sthāyī-bhāva-prakarana* (174)
[44] Quoted in *Caitanya-caritāmṛta* (*Ādi-līlā*, 1.6)

land of His childhood. Due to reciprocation of loving emotions, Kṛṣṇa was also feeling intolerable pangs of separation. It was not one-sided. It is not that Kṛṣṇa, as the Almighty God, has no feelings of love. On the contrary, His love is paramount.

The Supreme Lord is the master of innumerable energies (*parāsya śaktir vividhaiva śrūyate)*, and His internal energy *yogamāyā* takes charge of various affairs so the Lord and His devotees can enter into deeper aspects of loving exchange. For uninhibited love to develop freely, both the Lord and His devotees must forget or be unaware of His omnipotency and all-powerful position. This forgetfulness is induced by *yogamāyā*.[45] Part of that unbounded love is displayed during *milana*, union, and part of that love is displayed during *viraha*, separation. Union and then separation thus serve to increase feelings of intimacy between Kṛṣṇa and those dear to Him.

When Kṛṣṇa and Balarāma went to Mathurā with their uncle Akrūra, They were obliged to remain there with Devakī and Vasudeva, Their mother and father who resided in Mathurā. Vasudeva and Devakī had not spent much time with their sons because Kṛṣṇa had been transferred to Gokula soon after His appearance, to protect Him from the treacherous King Kaṁsa. Another reason for Their remaining in Mathurā was that many inimical kings were threatening to invade Vraja, so Kṛṣṇa wanted to stay away for some time to fight these kings and insure the Vrajavāsīs' safety.

Feeling separation from His friends, Kṛṣṇa desired to console them by sending His most confidential friend Uddhava with a message of love. Kṛṣṇa thoughtfully explained to Uddhava, "I know that the damsels of Vrajabhūmi feel intense separation from Me. Their feelings of separation often cause them to faint. Yes, Uddhava, they actually spend most of their time in a faint. Factually, this fainting has kept them alive. Otherwise, they would have died of separation."

With much difficulty, Kṛṣṇa gathered His patience and continued, "During the scorching heat of the summer all the lakes and ponds dry up. No water can be found anywhere. When that happens, do you know what the turtles do? They go down into the depths of the mud and somehow keep themselves alive. Similarly, My leaving Vrajab-

[45] See *Rāgvartma-candrikā* by Śrīla Viśvanātha Carkvarti Ṭhākura.

hūmi has been like the scorching heat of the summer sun. The *gopīs* hearts are like pools of water that have dried up due to the fire of separation, and their life is like the turtles, *prāṇa-kūrma*.

"If their life is like the turtles, Uddhava, then what is the mud? Where can they go for shelter? The mud, My friend, is this one hope: when I left Vṛndāvana I told them, 'I will come back. I will return. Don't worry.' These words are like the mud that is saving their lives." Here Kṛṣṇa reveals His feelings of *gopī-viraha-vidhura* and *rādhā-viraha-vidhura*, feelings of separation from the *gopīs* and Śrīmatī Rādhārāṇī.

As Kṛṣṇa gathered His paraphernalia to write His message, tears welled up in His eyes like a flowing river and suddenly blinded His vision. Innumerable thoughts of His intimate loving friends flooded His mind, and He nearly broke down in the pain of separation. It is well-known that Kṛṣṇa chose Uddhava to deliver His message because Uddhava was the most qualified of anyone outside of Vṛndāvana.

*na tathā me priyatama*
*ātma-yonir na śaṅkaraḥ*
*na ca saṅkarṣaṇo na śrīr*
*naivātmā ca yathā bhavān*

"Brahmā is not so dear to Me, Śiva is not so dear to Me, My brother Saṅkarṣaṇa is not so dear to Me, My wife Lakṣmī is not so dear to Me, My own self is not so dear to Me as you are, O Uddhava."[46]

Uddhava understood how much Kṛṣṇa was agonizing in separation. Therefore, when Uddhava reached Vṛndāvana he expressed to the residents what his dear friend Kṛṣṇa was feeling. No other person could have known because the paper Kṛṣṇa used was riddled with ink blots from His tears of love and therefore remained illegible.

Uddhava, a disciple of Bṛhaspati, has very sharp intelligence, so he was able to express the message and give some solace to the *gopīs*. One of the *gopīs*, however, namely Śrīmatī Rādhārāṇī, was so much absorbed in thoughts of Kṛṣṇa by dint of Her personal touch with Him that She began talking to birds and bees as if they were also messangers from Kṛṣṇa. *Śrīmad-Bhāgavatam* narrates how She spoke

---

[46] *Śrīmad-Bhāgavatam* (11.14.15)

in madness with a bumblebee, and Rupa Gosvāmī's *Lalita-mādhava* reveals how She spoke to a crow:

*bhrātur vāyasa-maṇḍalī mokala he niṣkramya goṣṭhāditaḥ*
*sandeśaṁ vada vandanottaram amuṁ vṛndātavidrāya me*
*dagdhuṁ prāṇa-paśuṁ śikhī viraha-bhūrindhe mad-aṅgālaye*
*sāndraṁ nāgara-candra bhindhi rabhasād āśārgalā-bandhanam*

All of a sudden Rādhārāṇī looked at the sky and saw a crow flying overhead in the direction of Mathurā. Pointing, She said, "Hey crow! Here! Over here! Are you going to Mathurā? Please hear Me. Don't go anywhere else. Go directly to Mathurā. There you will find a king named Mathurā-nātha. When you meet Him, pay your obeisances and give Him this message. Whatever message I give to you, deliver it to Him. Do you understand?

" 'If a house is on fire, then what is the first duty of the housemaster? The first duty is to release domestic animals. He may be burned to ashes, but he must never let the animals perish. My body is like a house which is now on fire. And who has set fire to this house? His name is Kṛṣṇa.'

"Tell Him. O Crow, tell Him that My life is like a domestic animal, *prāṇa-paśu*, but it cannot get out because there is a very strong bolt on the door. So let Kṛṣṇa come and unbolt it.

"If you want to know what that bolt is, I will tell you. When Kṛṣṇa left Vrajabhūmi He told us, 'I will come back.' That promise is the very strong bolt. Only with this hope are we surviving. But Kṛṣṇa is not coming back. So let Him come and unbolt it."

This is Rādhārāṇī's mood, feeling acute separation from Kṛṣṇa. The whole house, Her body, is on fire, and the *prāṇa-paśu*, Her life, which is like a domestic animal, is now burning.

Uddhava was standing there, gazing with dilated eyes as he heard everything Śrīmatī Rādhārāṇī said out of madness. Uddhava could therefore understand, "Yes, this must be Rādhikā. Many times I have heard about Her from my friend Kṛṣṇa. And when Kṛṣṇa is asleep, with every breath that name comes out, 'Rādhe, Rādhe.' I have heard all these things in Mathurā from my friend. This must definitely be Rādhikā."

Uddhava recognised Rādhārāṇī by the seriousness of Her condition. And that very same condition was always felt by Śrī Caitanya Mahāprabhu.

*rādhikāra bhāva-mūrti prabhura antara*
*sei bhāve sukha-duḥka uṭhe nirantara*
*śeṣa-līlāya prabhura kṛṣṇa-viraha-unmāda*
*brahma-maya ceṣtā, āra pralāpa-maya-vādā*
*rādhikāra bhāva yaiche uddhava-darśane*
*sei bhāva matta prabhu rahe rātri-dine*

"The heart of Lord Caitanya is the image of Śrī Rādhikā's emotions. Thus feelings of pleasure and pain arise constantly therein. In the final portion of His pastimes, Lord Caitanya was obessed with the madness of separation from Lord Kṛṣṇa. He acted in erroneous ways and talked deliriously. Just as Rādhikā went mad at the sight of Uddhava, so Lord Caitanya was obsessed night and day with the madness of separation."

## The Passing Away of Śrīla Haridāsa Ṭhākura

Śrī Caitanya Mahāprabhu happily passed His days in this way in Nīlācala. Feeling separation from Kṛṣṇa, He exhibited many transcendental symptoms all over His body. Day after day the symptoms increased, and at night they increased even more. All these symptoms, such as transcendental anxiety, agitation, and talking like a madman, were present just as they are described in the *śāstras*. Svarūpa Dāmodara Gosvāmī and Rāmānanda Rāya, the chief assistants in Śrī Caitanya Mahāprabhu's pastimes, remained with Him day and night.

One day Govinda, the Lord's personal servant, went to deliver Lord Jagannātha's food remnants to Haridāsa Ṭhākura. When Govinda came to Haridāsa, he saw that Haridāsa Ṭhākura was lying on his back and chanting his rounds very slowly.

"Please rise and take your *mahā-prasāda*," Govinda requested.

"Today I shall observe fasting," Haridāsa Ṭhākura replied. "I haven't finished chanting my regular number of rounds. How, then, can I eat? But you have brought *mahā-prasāda*, and how can I neglect it?" Saying this, he offered prayers to the *mahā-prasāda*, took a little portion, and ate it.

*Mahā-prasāda* is nondifferent from Kṛṣṇa. Therefore, instead of eating *mahā-prasāda*, one should honor it. One should consider *mahā-prasāda* a favor of Kṛṣṇa. As stated by Śrīla Bhaktivinoda Ṭhākura, *kṛṣṇa bada dayāmaya karibare jihvā jaya svaprasāda-anna dila bhāi*. Kṛṣṇa is kind. In this material world we are all attached to tasting a variety of flavors in the food we eat. Therefore, Kṛṣṇa eats many varieties of food and offers the food back to the devotees, so that not only are our demands for variety satisfied, but by eating *prasāda*, we make advancement in spiritual life. Thus we should never consider ordinary food on an equal level with *mahā-prasāda*.

The next day, Śrī Caitanya Mahāprabhu went to Haridāsa's place and inquired from him, "Haridāsa, are you well?"

Haridāsa offered his obeisaces to the Lord and replied, "My body is all right, but my mind and intelligence are not well."

"Can you ascertain what your disease is?" Śrī Caitanya Mahāprabhu inquired further.

"My disease is that I cannot complete my rounds."

"Now that you have become old," the Lord said with affection, "you may reduce the number of rounds you chant daily. You are already liberated, and you need not follow the regulative principles so strictly. Your role in this incarnation is to deliver the people in general. You have sufficiently preached the glories of the holy name in this world."

Haridāsa Ṭhākura is known as *nāmācārya* because it is he who preached the glories of chanting *hari-nāma*, the holy name of God. By using the words *tomara avatāra*, "your incarnation," Śrī Caitanya Mahāprabhu confirms that Haridāsa Ṭhākura is the incarnation of Lord Brahmā. Śrīla Bhaktisiddhanta Sarasvatī Ṭhākura states that advanced devotees help the Supreme Personality of Godhead in His mission and that such devotees or personal associates incarnate by the will of the Supreme Lord. The Supreme Lord incarnates by His own will, and by His will, competent devotees also incarnate to help Him in His mission.

## Lord Brahmā's Incarnation

Lord Brahmā's incarnation as Haridāsa Ṭhākura is revealed in a conversation between Jīva Gosvamī and Nityānanda Prabhu, noted in *Śrī Navadvīpa-dhāma Mahātmya (Parikramā-khaṇḍa*, Chapter Five):

Śrī Jīva inquired, "O Lord, what is the reason for the name Antardvīpa?"

Nityānanda Prabhu answered, "It was at this place that Brahmā underwent austerities at the end of Dvāpara-yuga with a desire to achieve Lord Gaurāṅga's mercy. Brahmā had previously tried to deceive Govinda by stealing the cowherd boys and calves, but when he was defeated by his own tricks he became overwhelmed with humility and regret. He entreated Lord Kṛṣṇa with many submissive prayers, and Kṛṣṇa forgave him. But later, Brahmā considered, *I'm a fool! Thinking that I am the creator of the universe is useless. Because of this puffed up mentality I have been deprived of* kṛṣṇā-prema *and enjoyment of the* rasas *of Vṛndāvana. If I would have taken birth as a cowherd boy, I could have easily served the master of the* gopīs. *Although I was previously not able to acheive the nectar of those pastimes, during Kali-yuga when the Lord appears as Gaurāṅga, I will not fall victim to my wicked mind. I will remain here to perform penances and austerities and shall beg for His mercy.*

"Thinking like this, Brahmā began meditating and performing austerities in Antardvīpa. After many days, Gauracandra mercifully appeared before him and said, 'O Brahmā, I am satisfied with your austerities. I have come to fulfill your desire.'

"When Brahmā opened his eyes and saw the beautiful form of Lord Gaurāṅga before him, he fell to the earth unconscious. The Lord then placed His foot upon Brahmā's heads, and thus Brahmā was enlightened with transcendental knowledge. He arose and began to pray, 'O my Lord, all the powerful demigods, including Lord Śiva, Indra, and I, are Your eternal servants. However, we are not as fortunate as Your eternal associates, for we sometimes become covered by the influence of Your illusory material energy. Although I passed the first one hundred trillion years of my life in illusion, I have now, by Your unlimited compassion, been brought to my senses. How am I to spend the remaining portion of my life? If I remain in illusion, I will simply suffer. My prayer, O Lord, is that I may become one of Your associates when You manifest Your earthly pastimes. I wish to give up the foolish illusion that I am the creator, and take birth as one of Your companions, always singing Your transcendental glories.'

"Hearing Brahmā's prayers, Lord Gaurāṅga blessed him saying, 'So be it. When My pastimes become visible on earth, you will take birth in a *yavana's* house. Your name will be Haridāsa Thākura, and you will be famous for your humility. Completely free from pride, you will chant three hundred thousand names a day, and when you pass from this world you will be seeing Me. At the end of the second one hundred trillion years of your life, you will attain Navadvīpa-dhāma and be absorbed in eternal *rasa*.

" 'Brahmā, hear these secret (*antara*) words, but do not reveal this openly. Taking the role of a devotee, I will taste the nectar of *bhakti-rasa* and propagate the most rare process of *sankīrtana*. I will make the devotees of all previous *avatāras* drunk with the nectar of Vṛndāvana. The love that Śrī Rādhikā possesses is beyond My experience, so I will appear with Her sentiments and complexion. Taking the position of Rādhā, I will taste that happiness that only Rādhā obtains in serving Me. From today, act as My disciple and, in the form of Haridāsa, always serve Me.'

"After saying this, Gaurāṅga become invisible, and again Brahmā fell to the ground unconsious."

Śrī Caitanya Mahāprabhu concluded, "Now, therefore, please reduce the fixed number of times you chant the Hare Kṛṣṇa *mahā-mantra*."

"Kindly hear my real plea," Haridāsa Ṭhākura replied. "I was born in an inferior family, and my body is most abominable. I always engage in low work. Therefore, I am the lowest, most condemned of men. I am unseeable and untouchable, but You have accepted me as Your servant. This means that You have delivered me from a hellish condition and raised me to the Vaikuṇṭha platform. My dear Lord, You are the fully independent Personality of Godhead. You act by Your own free will. You cause the whole world to dance and act as You like. By Your mercy You have made me dance in many ways. For example, I was offered the *śrāddha-pātra* by Advaita Ācārya, which should have been offered to first-class *brāhmaṇas*. I ate from it even though I was born in a family of meat-eaters.

"I have had one desire for a very long time. I think that quite soon, my Lord, You will bring to a close Your pastimes within this material world. I wish that You not show me this closing chapter of Your pastimes. Before that time comes, kindly let my body fall down in Your presence. I wish to catch Your lotuslike feet upon my heart and see Your moonlike face. With my tongue I shall chant Your holy name, 'Śrī Kṛṣṇa Caitanya!' That is my desire. Kindly let me give up my body in this way. O most merciful Lord, if by Your mercy it is possible, kindly grant my desire. Let this lowborn body fall down before You. You can make possible this perfection of all my desires."

"My dear Haridāsa," Śrī Caitanya Mahāprabhu said, "Kṛṣṇa is so merciful that He must execute whatever you want. But whatever happiness is Mine is all due to your association. It is not fitting for you to go away and leave Me aside."

Catching Lord Caitanya's lotus feet, Haridāsa Ṭhākura said, "My Lord, do not create an illusion! Although I am so fallen, You must certainly show me this mercy. There are many respectable personalities, millions of devotees, who are fit to sit on my head. They are all helpful in Your pastimes. If an insignificant insect like me dies, what is the loss? If an ant dies, where is the loss to the material world? You are always affectionate to Your devotees. I am just an imitation devotee, but nevertheless I wish that You fulfill my desire. That is my expectation."

Because He had to perform His noon duties, Śrī Caitanya Mahāprabhu got up to leave, but it was settled that the following day, after He saw Lord Jagannātha, He would return to visit Haridāsa Ṭhākura. After embracing him, Śrī Caitanya Mahāprabhu left to perform His noon duties and went to the sea to take His bath.

The next morning after visiting the Jagannātha temple, Śrī Caitanya Mahāprabhu and His associates quickly went to see Haridāsa Ṭhākura. Haridāsa Ṭhākura offered his respects to them all.

Lord Śrī Caitanya Mahāprabhu inquired, "My dear Haridāsa, what is the news?"

Haridāsa Ṭhākura replied, "My Lord, whatever mercy You can bestow upon me."

Hearing this, Śrī Caitanya Mahāprabhu began congregational chanting in the courtyard. Vakreśvara Paṇḍita was the chief dancer. Headed by Svarūpa Dāmodara Gosvāmī, all the Lord's devotees surrounded Haridāsa Ṭhākura and began to sing.

In front of all the great devotees like Rāmānanda Rāya and Sārvabhauma Bhaṭṭācārya, Śrī Caitanya Mahāprabhu began to describe Haridāsa Ṭhākura's holy attributes as if He possessed five mouths. The more He described, the more His happiness increased. Hearing the transcendental qualities of Haridāsa Ṭhākura, all the devotees were struck with wonder. They offered their respectful obeisances to Haridāsa Ṭhākura's lotus feet.

Haridāsa Ṭhākura made Śrī Caitanya Mahāprabhu sit down in front of him. Then he fixed his eyes like two bumblebees, on the Lord's beautiful face. He held the Lord's lotus feet on his heart, then took dust from the feet of all the Vaiṣṇavas present and put it on his head. He began to chant the holy name of Śrī Kṛṣṇa Caitanya again and again. As he drank the sweetness of the Lord's face, tears glided constantly from his eyes. While chanting "Śrī Kṛṣṇa Caitanya, Śrī Kṛṣṇa Caitanya, Śrī Kṛṣṇa Caitanya," he gave up his life air and left his body.

Seeing the wonderful death of Haridāsa Ṭhākura by his own will, which was just like the death of a great mystic *yogī*, everyone remembered the passing away of Bhīṣmadeva.[47] There was a tumultuous noise as the devotees all chanted "Hari" and "Kṛṣṇa." Śrī Caitanya Mahāprabhu became overwhelmed with emotion. The Lord lifted Haridāsa Ṭhākura's body and placed it on His lap. Then He began to dance in the courtyard. Because of Śrī Caitanya Mahāprabhu's ecstatic love, all the devotees were helpless, and they also began to dance and chant. Śrī Caitanya Mahāprabhu danced for some time, and then Svarūpa Dāmodara Gosvāmī informed Him of other rituals for the body of Ṭhākura Haridāsa.

Haridāsa Ṭhākura's body was then lifted onto a carrier that resembled an airship and taken to the sea while the devotees continued

---

[47] Bhīṣma was a great general in the famous Battle of Kurukṣetra. His passing away is mentioned in the *Śrīmad-Bhāgavatam* (First Canto, Chapter Nine), and in the *Mahābhārata*, *Anusasana-parva*.

their congregational chanting. Śrī Caitanya Mahāprabhu danced in front of the procession, and Vakreśvara Paṇḍita, along with the other devotees, chanted and danced behind Him. Śrī Caitanya Mahāprabhu bathed Haridāsa's body in the sea and then declared, "From this day on, this sea has become a great pilgrimage site."

Everyone drank the water that had touched Haridāsa Ṭhākura's lotus feet. Then they smeared the remnants of Lord Jagannātha's sandalwood pulp over Haridāsa's body. After a hole was dug in the sand, Haridāsa's body was placed in it. Remnants from Lord Jagannātha, such as His silken ropes, sandalwood pulp, food, and cloth, were placed on the body. All around the body, the devotees performed congregational chanting, and Vakreśvara Paṇḍita danced in jubilation.

With His transcendental hands, Śrī Caitanya Mahāprabhu covered the body with sand, chanting "Haribol! Haribol!" The devotees then constructed a platform on the site. The platform was protected all around by fencing. Śrī Caitanya Mahāprabhu danced and chanted all around that platform, as the holy name of Hari roared tumultuously. (See plate 33)

Śrī Caitanya Mahāprabhu then bathed in the sea with His devotees, swimming and playing in the water in great jubilation. After circumambulating Haridāsa's tomb, Śrī Caitanya Mahāprabhu went to the *Siṁha-dvāra* gate of the Jagannātha temple. The whole city chanted in congregation, and the sound was tumultuous.

Approaching the *Siṁha-dvāra*, Śrī Caitanya Mahāprabhu spread His cloth and began to beg *prasāda* from the shopkeepers. "I am begging *prasāda* for a festival honoring the passing away of Haridāsa Ṭhākura," the Lord said. "Please give Me alms."

Hearing this, all the shopkeepers immediately came forward with big baskets of *prasāda*, which they jubilantly delivered to Lord Caitanya. However, Svarūpa Dāmodara stopped them, and the shopkeepers returned to their shops and sat down with their baskets.

Svarūpa Dāmodara sent Śrī Caitanya Mahāprabhu back to His residence and kept with him four Vaiṣṇavas and four servant carriers. Svarūpa Dāmodara said to all the shopkeepers, "Deliver to me four palmfuls of *prasāda* from every item." In this way varieties of *prasāda* were collected, then packed up in different loads and carried on the heads of the four servants.

Not only did Svarūpa Dāmodara Gosvāmī bring *prasāda*, but Vaninātha Paṭṭanāyaka and Kāśī Miśra sent large quantities. Śrī Caitanya Mahāprabhu made all the devotees sit in rows and began to distribute the *prasāda*, assisted by four other men. Śrī Caitanya Mahāprabhu was not accustomed to taking *prasāda* in small quantities. He therefore put on each plate what at least five men could eat. Svarūpa Dāmodara Gosvāmī requested Śrī Caitanya Mahāprabhu, "Please sit down and watch. With these men to help me, I shall distribute the *prasāda*."

The four men—Svarūpa Dāmodara, Jagadānanda, Kāśīśvara, and Śaṅkara—distributed the *prasāda* continuously. All the devotees who sat down would not accept the *prasāda* as long as the Lord had not eaten. On that day, however, Kāśī Miśra had extended an invitation to the Lord. Therefore Kāśī Miśra personally went there and delivered *prasāda* to Śrī Caitanya Mahāprabhu with great attention and made Him eat. With Paramānanda Purī and Brahmānanda Bhāratī, Śrī Caitanya Mahāprabhu sat down and accepted *prasāda*. When He began to eat, so did all the Vaiṣṇavas. Everyone was filled up to the neck because Śrī Caitanya Mahāprabhu kept telling the distributors, "Give them more! Give them more!"

After all the devotees had finished *prasāda* and washed their hands and mouths, Śrī Caitanya Mahāprabhu decorated each of them with a flower garland and sandalwood pulp. Overwhelmed with ecstatic love, Śrī Caitanya Mahāprabhu offered a benediction to all the devotees, which the devotees heard with great satisfaction: "Anyone who has seen the festival of Śrī Haridāsa Ṭhākura's passing away, anyone who has chanted and danced here, anyone who has offered sand on his body, and anyone who has joined this festival to partake of the *prasāda* will achieve Kṛṣṇa's favor very soon. There is such wonderful power in seeing Haridāsa Ṭhākura. Being merciful upon Me, Kṛṣṇa gave Me Haridāsa Ṭhākura's association. Being independent in His desires, He has now broken that association. When Haridāsa Ṭhākura wanted to leave this material world, it was not within My power to detain him. Simply by his will, Haridāsa Ṭhākura could give up his life and go away, exactly like Bhīṣma, who previously died simply by his own desire, as we have heard from *śāstra*. Haridāsa Ṭhākura was the crown jewel on the head of this world; without him, this world is now bereft of its valuable jewel." After saying this, He began to dance.

Everyone began to chant, "All glories to Haridāsa Ṭhākura, who revealed the importance of chanting the holy name of the Lord!"

Thereafter, Śrī Caitanya Mahāprabhu bid farewell to the devotees and He Himself, with mixed feelings of happiness and distress, took rest.

At Puruṣottama-kṣetra, or Jagannātha Purī, if one goes from the Jagannātha temple toward the sea to *Svārga-dvāra* he can discover Haridāsa Ṭhākura's tomb still existing nearby. Every year on the date of Ananta-cāturdaśī there is a festival to commemorate Haridāṣa Ṭhākura's passing away.[48] At the same place, deities of Nityānanda, Kṛṣṇa Caitanya, and Advaita Prabhu were established about a hundred and fifty years ago. A gentleman named Bhramaravara from Kendrāpāḍā in the province of Orissa contributed funds to establish these deities in the temple. The management of the temple was under the Toṭa-Gopīnātha *gosvāmīs*, but the temple was later sold to someone else, and this party is now maintaining the *sevā-pūjā* of the temple.

From the incident of Haridāsa Ṭhākura's passing away and the great care Śrī Caitanya Mahāprabhu took in commemorating it, we can understand just how affectionate the Lord is toward His devotees. Although He is the topmost of all *sannyāsīs*, He fully satisfied Haridāsa's desire. At the last stage of Haridāsa Ṭhākura's life, Śrī Caitanya Mahāprabhu gave him His company and allowed him to touch Him. Thereafter, He took Ṭhākura Haridāsa's body on His lap and danced with it. Out of His causeless mercy He covered the body of Haridāsa Ṭhākura with sand and begged alms from the shopkeepers. Then He conducted a great festival to celebrate his passing away. Haridāsa Ṭhākura was not only the topmost devotee of the Lord, but also a great and learned scholar. It was his great fortune that he passed away before Śrī Caitanya Mahāprabhu.

The life and characteristics of Śrī Caitanya Mahāprabhu are exactly like an ocean of nectar, one drop of which can please the mind and ear. Anyone who desires to cross over the ocean of nescience,

---

[48] Haridāsa Ṭhākura's *samādhi* is located just across the street from Bhakti-kūṭī, Bhaktivinoda Ṭhākura's place of *bhajana*, now under ISKCON's management. *Ananta-cāturdaśī* is the fourteenth day of the waxing moon in the month of Bhādra (Aug.–Sept.); see *Appendix* for an explanation of calendar months.

please hear with great faith the life and characteristics of Śrī Caitanya Mahāprabhu.

## Transcendental Madness Caused by a Tug-of-War

The ocean of ecstatic love for Kṛṣṇa is difficult to understand, even for demigods such as Lord Brahmā. By enacting His pastimes, Śrī Caitanya Mahāprabhu submerged Himself in that ocean, and His heart was absorbed in love. He exhibited the exalted position of transcendental love for Kṛṣṇa in various ways.

Śrī Caitanya Mahāprabhu forgot Himself day and night, being merged only in an ocean of ecstatic love for Kṛṣṇa. The Lord would maintain Himself in three kinds of consciousness: sometimes He merged totally in ecstatic emotion, sometimes He was in partial external consciousness, and sometimes in full external consciousness. Actually, Śrī Caitanya Mahāprabhu was always merged in ecstatic emotion, but just as a potter's wheel turns without the potter's touching it, the Lord's bodily activities, like bathing, going to the temple to see Lord Jagannātha, and taking lunch, went on automatically.

One day, while Śrī Caitanya Mahāprabhu was looking at Lord Jagannātha in the temple, Jagannātha appeared to be the son of Nanda Mahārāja, Śrī Kṛṣṇa. When He realized Jagannātha to be Kṛṣṇa Himself, Śrī Caitanya Mahāprabhu's five senses were immediately absorbed in attraction for Kṛṣṇa's five attributes. Śrī Kṛṣṇa's beauty attracted the eyes of Lord Caitanya; the singing and vibration of Kṛṣṇa's flute attracted the Lord's ears; the transcendental fragrance of Kṛṣṇa's lotus feet attracted His nostrils; Kṛṣṇa's transcendental sweetness attracted His tongue; and Kṛṣṇa's bodily touch attracted the Lord's sensation of touch. Thus each of Śrī Caitanya Mahāprabhu's senses was attracted by one of the five attributes of Lord Kṛṣṇa.

Just as in a tug-of-war, Lord Caitanya's mind was attracted in five directions by Kṛṣṇa's five transcendental attributes. Thus the Lord became unconscious. Just then, Lord Jagannātha's *upala-bhoga* ceremony concluded, and the devotees who had accompanied Lord Caitanya to the temple brought Him home.

That night, Śrī Caitanya Mahāprabhu was attended by Svarūpa

Dāmodara Gosvāmī and Rāmānanda Rāya. Keeping His hands around their necks, the Lord began to lament. When Śrīmatī Rādhārāṇī was agitated due to feeling great separation from Kṛṣṇa, She spoke a verse to Viśākhā explaining the cause of Her anxiety and restlessness.

*saundaryāmṛta-sindhu-bhaṅga-lalanā-cittādri-saṁplāvakaḥ*
*karṇānandi-sanarma-ramya-vacanaḥ koṭīndu-śītāṅgakaḥ*
*saurabhyāmṛta-samplavāvṛta-jagat pīyūṣa-ramyādharaḥ*
*śrī-gopendra-sutaḥ sa karṣati balāt pañcendriyāṇy āli me*

"Though the hearts of the *gopīs* are like high-standing hills, they are inundated by the waves of the nectarean ocean of Kṛṣṇa's beauty. His sweet voice enters their ears and gives them transcendental bliss. The touch of His body is cooler than millions and millions of moons. My dear friend, that Kṛṣṇa, who is the son of Nanda Mahārāja and whose lips are exactly like nectar, is attracting My five senses by force."[49]

Reciting that verse, Śrī Caitanya Mahāprabhu expressed His burning emotions. Then, lamenting, He explained the verse to Svarūpa Dāmodara and Rāmānanda Rāya. Lord Caitanya here reveals the thoughts of Śrīmatī Rādhārāṇī.

*kṛṣṇa-rūpa-śabda-sparśa, saurabhya-adhara-rasa,*
*yāra mādhurya kahana nā yāya*
*dekhi' lobhe pañca-jana, eka aśva—mora mana,*
*caḍi' pañca panca-dike dhāya*

"Lord Śrī Kṛṣṇa's beauty, the sound of His words and the vibration of His flute, His touch, His fragrance, and the taste of His lips are full of an indescribable sweetness. When all these features attract My five senses at once, My senses all ride together on the single horse of My mind but want to go in five directions."

*sakhi he, suna mora duḥkhera kārana*
*mora pañcendriya-gaṇa, mahā-lampaṭa dasyu-gaṇa,*
*sabe kahe,—hara' para-dhana*

[49] *Govinda-līlāmṛta* (8.3)

"O My dear friend, please hear the cause of My misery. My five senses are actually extravagant rogues. They know very well that Kṛṣṇa is the Supreme Personality of Godhead, but they still want to plunder Kṛṣṇa's property."

*eka aśva eka-kṣaṇe, pañca pañca dike ṭāne*
*eka mana kon dike yāya?*
*eka-kāle sabe ṭāne, gela ghoḍāra parāṇe,*
*ei duḥkha sahana nā yāya*

"My mind is just like a single horse being ridden by the five senses of perception, headed by sight. Each sense wants to ride that horse, and thus they pull My mind in five directions simultaneously. In what direction will it go? If they all pull at one time, certainly the horse will lose its life. How can I tolerate this atrocity?

"My dear friend, if you say, 'Just try to control Your senses,' what shall I say? I cannot become angry at My senses. Is it their fault? Kṛṣṇa's beauty, sounds, touch, fragrance, and taste are by nature extremely attractive. These five features are attracting My senses, and each wants to drag My mind in a different direction. Thus the life of My mind is in great danger, just like a horse ridden in five directions at once. Thus I am also in danger of dying."

Lord Caitanya continued: "The sweetness of Kṛṣṇa's joking words plays indescribable havoc with the hearts of all women. His words bind a woman's ear to the qualities of their sweetness. Thus there is a tug-of-war, and the life of the ear departs.

"Kṛṣṇa's transcendental body is so cool that it cannot be compared even to sandalwood pulp or to millions upon millions of moons. It expertly attracts the breasts of all women, which resemble high hills. Indeed, the transcendental body of Kṛṣṇa attracts the minds of all women within the three worlds.

"The fragrance of Kṛṣṇa's body is more maddening than the aroma of musk, and it surpasses the fragrance of the bluish lotus flower. It enters the nostrils of all the women of the world and, making a nest there, thus attracts them.

"Kṛṣṇa's lips are so sweet when combined with the camphor of His gentle smile that they attract the minds of all women, forcing them to give up all other attractions. If the sweetness of Kṛṣṇa's smile is unobtainable, great mental difficulties and lamentation result. That sweetness is the only wealth of the *gopīs* of Vṛndāvana."

Speaking in this way, Śrī Caitanya Mahāprabhu lamented day after day in the company of Svarūpa Dāmodara and Rāmānanda Rāya. Svarūpa Dāmodara Gosvāmī would sing appropriate songs, and Rāmānanda Rāya would recite suitable verses to enhance the ecstatic mood of the Lord. In this way they were able to pacify Him. The Lord especially liked to hear Bilvamaṅgala Ṭhākura's *Kṛṣṇa-karṇāmṛta*, the poetry of Vidyāpati, and *Śrī Gīta-govinda* by Jayadeva Gosvāmī. Śrī Caitanya Mahāprabhu felt great pleasure in His heart when His associates chanted verses from these books.

## A Momentary Glimpse of Lord Kṛṣṇa

Śrī Caitanya Mahāprabhu in this way remained immersed in an ocean of ecstatic love for Kṛṣṇa. Sometimes He was submerged, and sometimes He floated. One full-moon night in the month of Vaiśākha (April–May), Śrī Caitanya Mahāprabhu went to a garden. The Lord, along with His devotees, entered one of the nicest gardens, called Jagannātha-vallabha. In the garden were fully blossomed trees and creepers exactly like those in Vṛndāvana. Bumblebees and birds like the *śuka*, *śārī*, and *pika* talked with one another. A mild breeze was blowing, carrying the fragrance of aromatic flowers. The breeze had become a guru and was teaching all the trees and creepers how to dance. Brightly illuminated by the full moon, the trees and creepers glittered in the light. The six seasons, especially spring, seemed present there. Seeing the garden, Śrī Caitanya Mahāprabhu, the Supreme Personality of Godhead, was happy. In this atmosphere the Lord had His associates sing the verse from the *Gīta-govinda* beginning with the words *lalita-lavaṅga-latā* as He danced and wandered about with them.

As He thus wandered around every tree and creeper, He came beneath an *aśoka* tree and suddenly saw Lord Kṛṣṇa. When He saw Kṛṣṇa, Śrī Caitanya Mahāprabhu began running swiftly, but Kṛṣṇa smiled and disappeared. Having first gotten Kṛṣṇa and then lost Him again, Śrī Caitanya Mahāprabhu fell unconscious to the ground. The entire garden was filled with the scent of Lord Śrī Kṛṣṇa's transcendental body. When Śrī Caitanya Mahāprabhu smelled it, He fell unconscious at once. The scent of Kṛṣṇa's body, however, incessantly entered His nostrils, and the Lord became mad to relish it.

Śrīmati Rādhārāṇī expressed to Her *gopī* friends how She hankers for the transcendental scent of Kṛṣṇa's body. Śrī Caitanya Mahāprabhu recited that same verse and made its meaning clear:

*kuraṅga-mada-jid-vapuḥ-parimalormi-kṛṣṭāṅganaḥ*
*svakāṅga-nalināṣṭake śaśi-yutābja-gandha-prathaḥ*
*madenduvara-candanāguru-sugandhi-carcārcitaḥ*
*sa me madana-mohanaḥ sakhi tanoti nāsā-spṛhām*

"The scent of Kṛṣṇa's transcendental body surpasses the aroma of musk and attracts the minds of all women. The eight lotuslike parts of His body distribute the fragrance of lotuses mixed with that of camphor. His body is anointed with aromatic substances like musk, camphor, sandalwood, and *aguru*. O My dear friend, that Personality of Godhead, also known as the enchanter of Cupid, always increases the desire of My nostrils."[50]

Lord Caitanya continued: "The scent of Kṛṣṇa's body surpasses the fragrances of musk and the bluish lotus flower. Spreading throughout the fourteen worlds, it attracts everyone and makes the eyes of all women blind. My dear friend, the scent of Kṛṣṇa's body enchants the entire world. It especially enters the nostrils of women and remains seated there. Thus it captures them and forcibly brings them to Kṛṣṇa. Kṛṣṇa's eyes, navel, face, hands, and feet are like eight lotus flowers on His body. From those eight lotuses emanates a fragrance like a mixture of camphor and lotus. That is the scent associated with His body.

"When sandalwood pulp with *aguru*, *kuṅkuma*, and musk is mixed with camphor and spread on Kṛṣṇa's body, it combines with Kṛṣṇa's own original bodily perfume and seems to cover it. The scent of Kṛṣṇa's transcendental body is so attractive that it enchants the bodies and minds of all women. It bewilders their nostrils, loosens their belts and hair, and makes them madwomen. All the women of

[50] *Govinda-līlāmṛta* (8.6)

the world come under its influence, and therefore the scent of Kṛṣṇa's body is like a plunderer. Falling completely under its influence, the nostrils yearn for it continuously, although sometimes they obtain it and sometimes not. When they do they drink their fill, though they still want more and more, but if they don't, they die of thirst. The dramatic actor Madana-mohana has opened a shop of scents that attract the women of the world to be His customers. He delivers the scents freely, but they make the women all so blind they cannot find the path home."

Śrī Caitanya Mahāprabhu, His mind thus stolen by that scent, ran here and there like a bumblebee. He ran to the trees and plants, hoping that Lord Kṛṣṇa would appear, but instead He found only the scent of Kṛṣṇa's body. Both Svarūpa Dāmodara and Rāmānanda Rāya sang to the Lord, who danced and enjoyed happiness until the morning arrived. Then they devised a plan to revive the Lord to external consciousness. Śrī Caitanya Mahāprabhu thus returned to consciousness. He then bathed and went to see Lord Jagannātha. Lord Kṛṣṇa's pastimes are uncommonly full of transcendental potency. It is a characteristic of such pastimes that they do not fall within the jurisdiction of experimental logic and arguments. When transcendental love of Kṛṣṇa awakens in one's heart, even a learned scholar cannot comprehend one's activities.

*dhanyasyāyaṁ navaḥ premā*
*yasyonmīlati cetasi*
*antar-vāṇibhir apy asya*
*mudrā suṣṭhu su-durgamā*

"The activities and symptoms of that exalted personality in whose heart love of Godhead has awakened cannot be understood even by the most learned scholar."[51]

Śrī Caitanya Mahāprabhu's activities are undoubtedly uncommon, especially His talking like a madman. Therefore, one who hears of these pastimes should not put forward mundane arguments. He should simply hear the pastimes with full faith. The evidence of the

[51] *Bhakti-rasāmṛta-sindhu* (1.4.17)

truth of these talks is found in the *Bhāgavatam*. There, in the section of the Tenth Canto known as the *Bhramara-gīta*, "Song to the Bumblebee," Śrimatī Rādhārāṇī speaks insanely in ecstatic love for Kṛṣṇa.

## The Final Days

During His last twelve years, Śrī Caitanya Mahāprabhu always manifested all the symptoms of ecstasy in separation from Kṛṣṇa. His state of mind exactly corresponded to Śrīmatī Rādhārāṇī's state of mind when Uddhava visited Vṛndāvana from Mathurā to see the *gopīs*. The Lord constantly exhibited a state of mind reflecting the madness of separation. All His activities were based on forgetfulness, and His talks were always based on madness. Blood flowed from all the pores of His body, and all His teeth were loosened. At one moment His whole body became slender, and at another moment His whole body became fat.

The small room beyond the corridor of Kāśī Miśra's house is called the *Gambhīrā*. Śrī Caitanya Mahāprabhu used to stay in that room, but He did not sleep for a moment. All night He used to grind His mouth and head on the ground, and His face sustained injuries. Although the three doors of the house were closed, the Lord would nonetheless go out and would sometimes be found at the *Siṁha-dvāra* or in the sea. Śrī Caitanya Mahāprabhu would also run quickly across the sandhills, mistaking them for Govardhana. As He ran, He would wail and cry loudly. Sometimes Caitanya Mahāprabhu mistook the small parks of the city for Vṛndāvana. Sometimes He would go there, dance and chant, and fall unconscious in spiritual ecstasy.

The extraordinary transformations of the body due to transcendental feelings would never have been possible for anyone but the Lord. The joints of His hands and legs would sometimes become separated by eight inches; they remained connected only by the skin. Sometimes Śrī Caitanya Mahāprabhu's hands, legs, and head would all enter within His body, just like the withdrawn limbs of a tortoise. In this way Śrī Caitanya Mahāprabhu used to manifest wonderful ecstatic symptoms. His mind appeared vacant, and there were only hopelessness and disappointment in His words.

Śrī Caitanya Mahāprabhu used to express His mind in this way:

"Where is the Lord of My life, who is playing His flute? What shall I do now? Where should I go to find the son of Mahārāja Nanda? To whom should I speak? Who can understand My disappointment? Without the son of Nanda Mahārāja, My heart is broken."

In this way Śrī Caitanya Mahāprabhu always expressed bewilderment and lamented in separation from Kṛṣṇa. At such times He used to read the *ślokas* from Rāmānanda Raya's drama known as *Jagannātha-vallabha-naṭaka*:

> *prema-ccheda-rujo 'vagacchati harir nāyaṁ na ca prema vā*
> *sthānāsthānam avaiti nāpi madano jānāti no durbalāḥ*
> *anyo veda na cānya-duḥkham akhilam no jīvanaṁ vāśravaṁ*
> *dvi-trāṇy eva dināni yauvanam idaṁ hā-hā vidhe kā gatiḥ*

Śrīmati Rādhārāṇī used to lament: "Our Kṛṣṇa does not realize what we have suffered from injuries inflicted in the course of loving affairs. We are actually misused by love because love does not know where to strike and where not to strike. Even Cupid does not know of our very weakened condition. What should I tell anyone? No one can understand another's difficulties. Our life is actually not under our control, for youth will remain for two or three days and soon be finished. In this condition, O creator, what will be our destination?"[52]

In this way, Lord Śrī Caitanya Mahāprabhu lamented in an ocean of sadness and opened the doors of His unhappiness. Forced by the waves of ecstasy, His mind wandered over transcendental mellows, and in this way He would read another verse.

> *yadā yāto daivān madhu-ripur asau locana-pathaṁ*
> *tadāsmākaṁ ceto madana-hatakenāhṛtam abhūt*
> *punar yasminn eṣa kṣaṇam api dṛśor eti padavīṁ*
> *vidhāsyāmas tasminn akhila-ghaṭikā ratna-khacitāḥ*

"If, by chance, the transcendental form of Kṛṣṇa comes before My path of vision, My heart, injured from being beaten, will be stolen

[52] *Jagannātha-vallabha-nāṭaka* (3.9)

away by Cupid, happiness personified. Because I could not see the beautiful form of Kṛṣṇa to My heart's content, when I again see His form I shall decorate the phases of time with many jewels."[53]

In an instant, Śrī Caitanya Mahāprabhu regained external consciousness and saw two persons before Him. Questioning them, He asked, "Am I conscious? What dreams have I been seeing? What craziness have I spoken? Have you heard some expressions of humility? My dear friends, you are all My life and soul; therefore I tell you that I possess no wealth of love for Kṛṣṇa. Consequently My life is poverty-stricken. My limbs and senses are useless.

"Alas! My friends, you can now know the certainty within My heart, and after knowing My heart you should judge whether I am correct or not. You can speak of this properly."

Śrī Caitanya Mahāprabhu then began to chant another verse.

*ka-i-avarahi-aṁ pemmaṁ ṇa hi hoi māṇuse loe*
*ja-i hoi kassa virahe hontammi ko jīa-i*

"Love of Godhead, devoid of cheating propensities, is not possible within this material world. If there is such a love, there cannot be separation, for if there is separation, how can one live?"

Śrī Caitanya Mahāprabhu used to revel in ecstasy day after day and exhibit these ecstasies before Svarūpa Dāmodara and Rāmānanda Rāya. Externally there appeared severe tribulation, as if He were suffering from poisonous effects, but internally He was experiencing bliss. This is characteristic of transcendental love of Kṛṣṇa.

*ei premā-āsvādana, tapta-ikṣu-carvaṇa,*
*mukha jvale, nā yāya tyajana*
*sei premā yāṅra mane, tāra vikrama sei jāne,*
*viṣāmṛte ekatra milana*

If one tastes such love of Godhead, he can compare it to hot sugarcane. When one chews hot sugarcane, his mouth burns, yet he cannot give it up. Similarly, if one has but a little love of Godhead, he

[53] *Jagannātha-vallabha-nāṭaka* (3.11)

can perceive its powerful effects. It can only be compared to poison and nectar mixed together.

*pīḍābhir nava-kāla-kūṭa-kaṭutā-garvasya nirvāsano*
*nisyandena mudāṁ sudhā-madhurimāhaṅkāra-saṅkocanaḥ*
*premā sundari nanda-nandana-paro jāgarti yasyāntare*
*jñāyante sphuṭam asya vakra-madhurās tenaiva vikrāntayaḥ*

"My dear beautiful friend, if one develops love of Godhead, love of Kṛṣṇa, the son of Nanda Mahārāja, all the bitter and sweet influences of this love will manifest in one's heart. Such love of Godhead acts in two ways. The poisonous effects of love of Godhead defeat the severe and fresh poison of a serpent. Yet there is simultaneously transcendental bliss, which pours down and defeats the pride of nectar and diminishes its value. In other words, love of Kṛṣṇa is so powerful that it simultaneously defeats the poisonous effects of a snake, as well as the happiness derived from pouring nectar on one's head. It is perceived as doubly effective, simultaneously poisonous and nectarean."[54]

When Śrī Caitanya Mahāprabhu would see Lord Jagannātha along with Balarāma and Subhadrā, He would immediately think that He had reached Kurukṣetra, where all of Them had come. He would think that His life was successful because He had seen the lotus-eyed one, who, if seen, pacifies the body, mind, and eyes. Staying near the *Garuḍa-stambha*, the Lord would look upon Lord Jagannātha. What can be said about the strength of that love? On the ground beneath the column of the *Garuḍa-stambha* was a deep ditch, and that ditch was filled with the water of His tears. When coming from the Jagannātha temple to return to His house, Śrī Caitanya Mahāprabhu used to sit on the ground and mark it with His nails. At such times He would be morose and would cry, "Alas, where is Vṛndāvana? Where is Kṛṣṇa, the son of the king of the cowherd men? Where is that person who plays the flute?"

In this way various ecstatic emotions evolved, and the Lord's mind filled with anxiety. He could not escape even for a moment. Because

---

[54] *Vidagdha-mādhava* (2.18)

of fierce feelings of separation, His patience began to totter and He began to recite various verses. The Lord's restlessness was awakened by ecstatic feelings, and His mind became agitated. No one could understand what course such ecstasy would take. When Lord Caitanya was not able to meet the Supreme Personality of Godhead, Kṛṣṇa, His mind burned. He began to ask Kṛṣṇa of the means by which He could reach Him. Because of the various kinds of ecstasy, contradictory states of mind occurred, and this resulted in a great fight between different types of ecstasy. Anxiety, impotence, humility, anger, and impatience were all like soldiers fighting, and the madness of love of Godhead was the cause.

The body of the Lord was just like a field of sugarcane into which the mad elephants of ecstasy entered. There was a fight amongst the elephants, and in the process the entire field of sugarcane was destroyed. Thus transcendental madness was awakened in the body of the Lord, and He experienced despondency in mind and body. The symptoms of madness served as an impetus for remembering Kṛṣṇa. The mood of ecstasy awoke love, disdain, defamation by words, pride, honor, and indirect prayer. Thus Śrī Kṛṣṇa was sometimes blasphemed and sometimes honored.

The Lord's body underwent various transformations: being stunned, trembling, perspiring, fading away of color, weeping, and choking. In this way His whole body was pervaded by transcendental joy. As a result, Caitanya Mahāprabhu would sometimes laugh, sometimes cry, sometimes dance, and sometimes sing. Sometimes He would get up and run here and there, and sometimes He would fall on the ground and lose consciousness. When Śrī Caitanya Mahāprabhu was unconscious, He happened to meet the Supreme Personality of Godhead. Consequently, He got up and immediately made a tumultuous sound, loudly declaring, "Now Kṛṣṇa, the great personality, is present!" In this way, because of Kṛṣṇa's sweet qualities, Caitanya Mahāprabhu made different types of mistakes in His mind.

As the spiritual master rebukes the disciple and teaches him the art of devotional service, so all the ecstatic symptoms of Lord Caitaya Mahāprabhu—including despondency, moroseness, humility, restlessness, joy, endurance, and anger—instructed His body and mind. In this way, Śrī Caitanya Mahāprabhu passed His time.

## The Passing Away of Śrī Caitanya Mahāprabhu

The Lord's disappearance from this material world is often puzzling and mysterious. Lord Kṛṣṇa says in the *Bhagavad-gītā* (4.9):

*janma karma ca me divyam*
*evaṁ yo vetti tattvataḥ*
*tyaktvā dehaṁ punar janma*
*naiti mām eti so 'rjuna*

"One who knows the transcendental nature of My appearance and activities does not, upon leaving the body, take birth again in this material world, but attains My eternal abode, O Arjuna."

According to literary traditions of Sanskrit, the general etiqutte is that the dissapperance or death of a hero not be included in a story or drama. Throughout the *Vedas* there are only a few examples of main characters passing away. Pastimes describing a death usually state that he or she "passed on to the celestial abode" but rarely reveal how, where, who was present, and so on. It is the same with Śrī Caitanya Mahāprabhu. Of course, the Lord's appearance and disappearance are performances of divine *līlā*, unlike the births and deaths of ordinary conditioned souls. Nevertheless, in various biographical works compiled by the Lord's associates, there is little mention of His leaving this world. Svarūpa Dāmodara, Rāmānanda Rāya, Raghunātha dāsa Gosvāmī, and later Vṛndāvana dāsa Ṭhākura and Kṛṣṇadāsa Kavirāja Gosvāmī make no specific mention of the event. There are, however, other writers who have discussed it, but oddly, there are various versions even among the Lord's closest associates.

The earliest account is recorded by Jayānanda in his *Caitanya Maṅgala:* "While the Lord danced before the Ratha-yātrā cart in the month of Āṣāḍha, His foot was pierced by a stone lying on the road. Six days later, the Lord took shelter of a *toṭa* (garden). He told Gadādhara Paṇḍita that He would leave this world during the next night in the tenth hour."[55]

Jayānanda's account is interesting because it parallels Lord Kṛṣṇa's *mauśala-līlā* (disappearance pastime) in a couple of ways: Lord Kṛṣṇa

---

[55] As quoted in *History of the Caitanya Faith in Orissa* (p.42).

performed His *mauśala-līlā* when He was shot in the foot by a hunter, and this also occurred during the month of Āṣāḍha.

In the eighteenth century, this *līla* of Lord Caitanya's foot injury was further elaborated upon by Narahari Cakravartī in his *Bhakti-ratnākara*. Mamu Ṭhākura, priest of the Toṭa-Gopīnātha temple says, "Behold, Narottama, here Gaurahari told something to Gadādhara Paṇḍita. He then entered into the temple of Gopīnātha and was never seen again."

## Toṭa-Gopīnātha

The Toṭa-Gopīnātha deity referred to was originally unearthed by Śrī Caitanya Mahāprabhu. As mentioned earlier, that deity was later handed over to Gadādhara Paṇḍita, who worshiped Toṭa-Gopīnātha for many years with love and devotion. (See plate 34)

Amorous pastimes performed between Lord Kṛṣṇa and His dear associates is an extremely confidential and personal affair. Intimate affairs are not topics for common discussion. Therefore, to assist Lord Kṛṣṇa in understanding Her own confidential, personal emotions, Śrīmatī Rādhārāṇī Herself appeared as Gadādhara Paṇḍita. Other *gopīs* also appeared in male forms to associate with Lord Caitanya.[56]

Gadādhara Paṇḍita often read from the *Śrīmad-Bhāgavatam* before Śrī Caitanya Mahāprabhu and His associates, explaining the meanings of the verses. Although acting as a teacher, he was always meek and humble in his service to Caitanya Mahāprabhu. One may wonder why Śrīmatī Rādhārāṇī, the leader of left-wing *gopīs*, acted meek and humble (like a right-wing *gopī*) in the role of Gadādhara Paṇḍita.

---

[56] Some devotees in the spiritual sky possess both male and female spiritual forms. This was previously hinted at in connection with Rāmānanda Rāya, who was an incarnation of the *gopī* named Viśākhā, and is further elaborated upon by Śrīla Jīva Gosvāmī in his commentary on the *Brahma-saṁhitā* (5.5): "The devotees who are imbued with all-love and who walk in the footsteps of the spiritual milkmaids of Vraja alone attain to the realm of Goloka. The different locations of devotees in Goloka according to their respective *rasas*, or mellow quality, are settled by the inconceivable power of Kṛṣṇa. Pure devotees following the devotees of Vraja, and those following the devotees of Navadvīpa, are located in the realms of Kṛṣṇa and Gaura respectively. The identical devotees of Vraja and Navadvīpa simultaneously attain to the pleasures of service in the realms of both Kṛṣṇa and Gaura."

*This painting is believed to have been rendered in the sixteenth century by a devotee named Murāri Dāsa, a disciple of Vakreśvara Paṇḍita (who was an immediate associate of Lord Śrī Caitanya Mahāprabhu). The painting shows Maharaja Prataparudra in the foreground, offering prostrated obeisance before the Lord and His devotees. Above him, left to right, are Raghunātha Dāsa Gosvāmī, Govinda Dāsa, Rāmānanda Rāya, Gadādhara Paṇḍita, Nityānanda Prabhu, Lord Caitanya, Advaita Ācārya, Śrīvāsa Ṭhākura, Svarūpa Dāmodara Gosvāmī, and Haridāsa Ṭhākura. The painting is currently in Kunja-ghat, near Baharampura, Bengal.*

The answer is that Lord Kṛṣṇa, in the form of Lord Caitanya, had stolen away Śrīmatī Rādhārāṇī's mood and complexion. Gadādhara Paṇḍita, therefore, always helped Caitanya Mahāprabhu experience the moods of Śrīmatī Rādhārāṇī, rather than expressing those emotions himself.

After Caitanya Mahāprabhu's disappearance, however, the pain of separation burned uncontrollably in Gadādhara Paṇḍita's heart. Although not even fifty years old at the time, Gadādhara's body became lean and thin like that of an elderly man due to intense separation from the Lord. A short time after Caitanya Mahāprabhu's disappearance, Gadādhara found it difficult to move properly, and it became especially difficult to reach up high to place flower garlands around Gopīnātha's neck or to place a crown on His head. Understanding the difficulty His devotee was experiencing, Toṭa-Gopīnātha mystically exhibited a *padma-āsana* (lotus posture) for the convenience of Gadādhara Paṇḍita. That is, He sat down so the Paṇḍita could more easily offer the flower garlands. For this reason the deity is seen in a sitting posture today, a posture not displayed by any other Kṛṣṇa deity in the world. On Toṭa-Gopīnātha's right knee there is a small golden streak. It is said that this is where Śrī Caitanya Mahāprabhu merged into the deity who is non-different from Himself.

During His previous pastimes in Vṛndāvana, Lord Kṛṣṇa desired to enjoy different types of ecstasy in the mood of Rādhārāṇī, but despite great endeavor He could not taste them. Such ecstasies are the monopoly of Śrīmatī Rādhārāṇī. Therefore, to taste them, Śrī Kṛṣṇa accepted the position of Śrīmatī Rādhārāṇī in the form of Śrī Caitanya Mahāprabhu. By personally tasting the mellows of love of Godhead, Caitanya Mahāprabhu taught His direct disciples the process. Śrī Caitanya Mahāprabhu is the most munificent incarnation of the touchstone of love of God. He doesn't consider whether one is a proper or an improper recipient but gives His treasure to everyone. Thus He is the most generous. No one, not even Lord Brahmā, can ascertain or taste even a drop of this confidential ocean of ecstasy, but Śrī Caitanya Mahāprabhu, out of His causeless mercy, distributed love of Godhead all over the world. There cannot be any incarnation more munificent than Śrī Caitanya Mahāprabhu. There is no greater donor. Who can describe His transcendental qualities? Such topics are not to be discussed freely, because if they are, no one will understand them. Such are the wonderful pastimes of Śrī Caitanya Mahāprabhu. Unto one who is able to understand, Śrī Caitanya Mahāprabhu has shown mercy by giving him the association of the servant of His own servant.

The pastimes of Śrī Caitanya Mahāprabhu are the topmost of jewels. They were kept in the storehouse of Svarūpa Dāmodara Gosvāmī, who explained them to Raghunātha dāsa Gosvāmī, who repeated them to Kṛṣṇadāsa Kavirāja Gosvāmī, the author of *Caitanya-caritāmṛta*. This is called the *paramparā* system, from Śrī Caitanya Mahāprabhu to Svarūpa Dāmodara to Raghunātha dāsa Gosvāmī to Kavirāja Gosvāmī. Kṛṣṇadāsa Kavirāja Gosvāmī's book *Caitanya-caritāmṛta* contains the essence of the teachings of Śrī Caitanya Mahāprabhu. To distribute these teachings not only in India, but throughout the modern world, His Divine Grace A. C. Bhaktivedanta Swami Prabhupāda translated the work into English. Śrīla Prabhupāda completed his translation on November 10, 1974—corresponding to the tenth of Kārttika, the eleventh day of the dark fortnight, Rāma-Ekādaśī—441 years after the disappearance of Śrī Caitanya Mahāprabhu.

# 5

# *Jagannātha Worship After the 15th Century*

### King Pratāparudra's Final Years, And the Fall of the Sūrya-vaṁśa Dynasty

The last known inscription mentioning King Pratāparudra's name is a land grant at Siṁhācalam dated 1530. The Jagannātha temple chronicle *Madalapanji*, however, states that King Pratāparudra ruled until 1540, and was survived by two sons after the suicide of his eldest son Vīrabhadra (mentioned earlier).

In 1540 Pratāparudra's son Kaluadeva took the throne, but was soon after trampled by a horse and killed while playing *hingidi*, a game similar to polo. Kaluadeva's younger brother Kakharuadeva then ruled for a few months, but was treacherously assassinated by a general from Pratāparudra's army. With the violent death of Kakharuadeva, the Sūrya-vaṁśa dynasty abruptly ended, and the ambitious general, Govinda Vidyādhara, began his rule of the Bhoi dynasty.

Historians pinpoint this period as the beginning of the end of the Kaliṅga Empire. Govinda Vidyādhara ruled for seven years, during which time the Sultan of Golkonda invaded from the south to annex various territories. With the succession of Govinda's son, Chakrapatapadeva, further strain was placed upon the citizens. Historical literatures mention that Chakrapatapadeva was an unpopular, cruel leader. According to a Muslim record, *Akbarnama*, Chakrapatapadeva's own son, Narasiṁha Jena, poisoned his father and seized the throne. Narasiṁha Jena didn't enjoy the booty for long, however; rebels dressed as women secretly entered his palace and stabbed him to death with daggers shortly after his ascension to the throne.

After Narasiṁha Jena's death, his brother Raghurāma was placed on the throne, but ruled for only one and a half years. Rebellion continued in his army until finally Mukunda Haricandana emerged victorious by usurping the throne and putting Raghurāma into prison. This Mukundadeva was to be the last independent Hindu ruler in Orissa.

## Akbar and Mughal Rule in India

In 1566 the powerful Mughal Emperor Akbar began constructing his famous red sandstone fort in Agra, from where he would ultimately rule three-quarters of the sub-continent. To this day Akbar remains popular in folklore due to his open-mindedness and liberal administration, especially toward Hindus. The Mughal even married a Hindu wife named Jodhai Bai from Amber, and tried to unite followers of various religions and philosophies throughout the country. He sent envoys to Orissa who spoke favorably with Mukundadeva, but unfortunately Akbar's liberal influence took too long to reach Purī—in 1568 there was a disastrous invasion.

A Muslim general named Kāla Pahara advanced under the order of Sulaiman Karrani, the Sultan of Bengal who was not as yet subordinate to Akbar. Legends concerning General Kāla Pahara are intriguing, although various scholars doubt his being born a Hindu. The story told in Orissan villages is that he was born Kāla Chand, a Hindu, and that due to his handsome features and masculine physique the Sultan's sister fell madly in love with him. Forced by circumstance, Kāla Chand married the Sultan's sister, although he already had a Hindu wife.

While on pilgrimage in Jagannātha Purī, Kāla Chand expressed his so-called sin of marrying a Muslim before the learned *paṇḍitas* and *brāhmaṇas* at the Jagannātha temple, hoping that they would prescribe some atonement to free him from the reactions of his misdeed and again accept him into the Hindu faith. The infuriated, proud *brāhmaṇas* derided Kāla Chand. They told him there was nothing he could do to save his soul. Kāla Chand ardently repented and fell to the ground in obeisances, pleading for mercy. One of the proud *brāhmaṇas* kicked him.

Kāla Chand's Hindu wife, who was accompanying her husband, also bowed down, praying for mercy, but another proud *pāṇḍā* gave her the same scoffing treatment. Seeing this, Kāla Chand furiously rose from the ground and declared that if this was how Jagannātha's servants treated pilgrims, then He certainly was not God! He further vowed that one day he would desecrate the temple or die trying.

It is stated in the *Madalapanji* that when Kāla Pahara was about to invade, the deities of Lord Jagannātha, Balarāma, Subhadrā, and Sudarśana-*cakra* were removed for safekeeping to an island in Chilika Lake, south of Purī. Kāla Pahara, however, got wind of the hideout, forcibly took the deities on elephants to the Ganges River in the north, burnt them on the banks of the river, and threw the remains into the water.

A devout Vaiṣṇava named Beshara Mohanti secretly followed Kāla Pahara the entire way. When the Muslim army finally departed from the banks of the Ganges, Beshara Mohanti somehow managed to salvage the *brahmapadartha* from inside the naval portion of the deities. Beshara then secretly placed this sacred material into a clay *mṛdaṅga* drum and brought it back to Orissa. During Kāla Pahara's violent invasion, King Mukundadeva was killed, and with his death the independence of Orissa also withered.[1]

## Mughal Rule of Orissa

After King Mukundadeva's death, his sons were ousted by Rāmacandradeva, who belonged to the *śūdra* community according to a Sirjan stone inscription. This was intolerable to the young sons of Mukundadeva, who appealed to the mighty Akbar in Delhi for the restoration of their rightful inheritance. At the time Akbar's generals were advancing toward Bengal. After several battles with the Afghans who then ruled Bengal, Akbar's army proved the stronger of the two, and the Sultan of Bengal surrendered in the spring of 1575. As a result, Orissa and Bengal both came under Mughal rule, and Akbar's Hindu general, Raj Man Singh, was sent to Orissa to settle whatever dispute lingered in the state.

Raj Man Singh arrived in Purī at the time of *candana-yātrā* and, after due consideration, declared Rāmacandradeva the proper ruler

---

[1] See *Navakalevara* in the *Festivals* chapter for further information about the mysterious substance known as *brahmapadartha*.

under the domain of Akbar. This enabled Rāmacandradeva to once again establish worship of Lord Jagannātha in the temple after a lengthy period during which the *brahmapadartha* had remained in hiding at Kujanga, Orissa. With Purī under the new regime and under the ultimate control of the Mughals, Jagannātha worship continued peacefully during the reign of Akbar. In fact, Raj Man Singh's wife, Gaurarāṇī, donated wealth to reconstruct the sixteen-pillared Mukti Mandapa, where learned *brāhmaṇas* sit to discuss philosophy.[2]

Unfortunately, Akbar's descendants were not as liberal as their illustrious ancestor. During the reign of Akbar's son Jehangir and later under Aurangzeb, the Jagannātha temple, although still under Mughal rule, continued to suffer severe persecution. One of the more famous raids came when a Rajput general named Kesodas entered the temple along with his army dressed as Hindu pilgrims. Once inside the temple, Kesodas and his men drew their weapons and plundered the deities' ornaments and riches. Although King Puruṣottama, son of Rāmacandradeva, hurried from his capital to stop the invaders, he was badly defeated and forced to pay tribute to the Mughals. For a brief time a treaty was settled between King Puruṣottama and Kesodas, so the deities were again regularly worshiped without interference.

Orissa remained annexed to Bengal under Mughal rule until 1607, when it was declared an independent *suvar*, or territory. A new governor, named Kalyāṇa Malla, then arrived in the capital of Cuttack in 1611. He was envious of Hindus and immediately murdered a Hindu minister and sixteen generals. Aware of Kalyana's fanaticism, priests of the Jagannātha temple again removed the deities and kept them hidden in the Chilika Lake area for four years.

The history of the Jagannātha temple during the following one hundred and thirty years, from 1620 until 1750, reads something like a spy novel; the deities were hidden from Muslim tyrants, then brought back to the temple after the death of the antagonist, then when another iconoclast took power, the deities were again hidden in some remote village or near Chilika Lake. This later Mughal period was extremely difficult for the culture of Jagannātha worship, but somehow

---

[2] According to an inscription at the Rādhā-Govinda temple in Vṛndāvana, Raj Man Singh was also instrumental in constructing that temple.

enthusiasm to worship the Lord kindled the fire of determination in local people and the *pūjā* continued, if secretly at times, from generation to generation despite the oppression.[3]

## Sālabega

During the first decade of the seventeenth century, a Muslim king named Lalbeg was on military campaign with his army when he saw a young widowed *brāhmana* girl bathing in a *kuṇḍa*. Infatuated by her youthful beauty, Lalbeg forcefully took that girl away and made her his wife. The son born to them was named Sālabega.

Sālabega underwent military training as he grew up, and when old enough he began traveling with his father's army. Once in battle, unfortunately, he was severely wounded and nearly died. While lying on his deathbed, Sālabega followed his Hindu mother's suggestion and began chanting the holy name of Lord Jagannātha. Astonishingly, he was gradually cured.

Sālabega felt indebted to Lord Jagannātha when his life was spared, so he later traveled to Jagannātha Purī but wasn't allowed into the temple due to his Muslim parentage. Sālabega's devotional sentiments had been aroused due to his chanting the holy name of the Lord, so after leaving Purī he traveled to Vṛndāvana, where he could associate with Vaisṇavas, devotees of the Lord, who wouldn't discriminate against him due to his birth. In Vṛndāvana he associated with many *sadhus* and remained there for almost a year. Thereafter, knowing the Ratha-yātrā festival was approaching, he left Vṛndāvana and once again walked toward Purī so he could take *darśana* of Lord Jagannātha.

Along the way Sālabega became severely ill and couldn't continue traveling. Feeling helpless and realizing he wouldn't reach Purī in time for the festival, he began offering prayers to the Lord of the universe, petitioning Him to wait until he arrived in Purī.

On the day of Ratha-yātrā Lord Jagannātha's cart, Nandhighośa, stopped in the middle of the procession and couldn't be moved. Strong

[3] For further information about Moghal rule, see *Orissa Under the Moghals* or *Jagannatha in History and Religious Traditions of Orissa*.

men tried again and again to move the *ratha* forward, but to no avail. At that time, Sālabega happily arrived and began offering love-laden prayers. Upon his arrival, the *ratha* once again began its forward journey. The place where the cart remained stationary was later used by Sālabega for composing prayers and poems in glorification of Lord Jagannātha, and after his death his remains were entombed there. His *samādhi* is still standing just off of Grand Road.

## Maratha-Mughal Treaty and Change of Power

After the death of Aurangzeb in 1707, the Mughal Empire finally began to crumble. Territorial *suvadaras*, who had been humbly subordinate before the mighty emperor in Delhi, dismissed commands from Aurangzeb's weak son and began fighting among themselves for larger domains. A tottering Mughal Empire in its twilight tried drastically to reorganize as the Mahrathas from Central India began closing in on various territories.

Orissa was slow to assist the Mahrathas. Because Muslims had oppressed Hindus for more than a century, Hindus were naturally fearful of Muslim authorities who remained dominant from their capital in Cuttack. For almost fifty years, skirmishes and small battles were fought here and there throughout Orissa until finally, in 1751, a treaty was signed between the Mughals and Mahrathas giving sovereignty of the state to the Mahrathas. These Mahrathas were predominately Hindus and gradually readjusted the Jagannātha temple administration and again established regular observances of festivals. The Mahrathas, however, did not remain in power for long.

## Followers of Śrī Caitanya Mahāprabhu

To complete this tapestry of Jagannātha history adequately, it is appropriate at this point to briefly discuss what events took place in the *saṅkīrtana* movement inaugurated by Śrī Caitanya Mahāprabhu.

Shortly after the Lord's disappearance in 1533, Raghunātha dāsa Gosvāmī left Jagannātha Purī feeling unbearable separation from the Lord. He had decided to end his life by jumping from Govardhana Hill in Vṛndāvana. Upon his arrival in the holy land of Vraja, however,

Raghunātha dāsa met with Rūpa Gosvāmī, Sanātana Gosvāmī, their nephew Jīva Gosvāmī, and other devotees, who ardently requested him not to commit suicide. Rather, they insisted he discourse on the events he had witnessed while residing at Purī with Lord Caitanya. Raghunātha dāsa Gosvāmī humbly submitted to their loving requests and remained in Vraja, especially at Rādhā-kuṇḍa, for many more years.

By word of mouth, especially throughout Bengal and Orissa, news of Lord Caitanya and His followers spread. Several young men ventured forth to Vṛndāvana to become disciples of the renowned Gosvāmīs and learn from them the teachings and philosophy of Śrī Caitanya Mahāprabhu. Rūpa and Sanātana Gosvāmīs compiled many books based on their hearing directly from Śrī Caitanya Mahāprabhu, and their nephew, the son of Anupama, kept everything, including his own writings, in a library at the Rādhā-Dāmodara temple, near Sevā-kuñja.

Vṛndāvana eventually became a well-known center of learning, and many wealthy merchants began to contribute toward the construction of temples, bathing *ghāṭs*, deity worship, and landscaping to beautify the area. By the time Raghunātha dāsa, Rūpa, and Sanātana Gosvāmīs had passed away, Jīva Gosvāmī felt the time right to send their writings to Bengal for transcription, for in those days there were no printing presses. The famous trio of Śrīnivāsa Ācārya, Narottama dāsa Ṭhākura, and Śyāmānanda Prabhu traveled from Vṛndāvana to various areas in the east sometime during the late sixteenth or early seventeenth century. Although they met with disastrous adventures along the way, they gradually managed to reach their destinations and continued preaching to spread the message of Lord Caitanya.[4]

In Bengal, Lord Nityānanda's wife, Jāhnavī-devī, developed quite a following, which continued with her son Vīrabhadra Prabhu, and in Orissa Śyāmānanda's disciple named Rasik Murāri, or Rasikānanda, successfully took up the preaching mission.[5] As the years passed

[4] For further study of these three Vaiṣṇavas, see *Lives of the Vaiṣṇava Saints*.

[5] For further study of this line of the Caitanya tree, see *Bhakti-ratnākara*, *Rasik Maṅgal* (an English translation by Bhakti Vikasa Swami is called *The Story of Rasikānanda*), or *Śyāmānanda-śataka*.

from generation to generation, Lord Caitanya's teachings gradually branched into multifarious forms, as thousands of villagers in both Bengal and Orissa began *saṅkīrtana*, chanting the holy names of the Lord.

Complex theological concepts are not easily understood, especially by simple villagers, so gradually the ideas imparted by Lord Caitanya became so tangled and diverse that it became practically impossible to discern what His actual teachings were. Numerous religious sects emerged with varying ideas; some began chanting new mantras, such as *nitāi-gaura rādhe-śyāma, hare kṛṣṇa hare rāma*, or *śrī kṛṣṇa caitanya, prabhu nityānanda, hare kṛṣṇa hare rāma, sri rādhe govinda*. Other sects began to dress as women to spur inspiration similar to that of the *gopīs;* and still other groups added more and more variations of their own. By the 1800s, the *saṅkīrtana* movement initiated more than three hundred years earlier had transformed into something hardly recognizable.

### The East India Company and William Bruton's Testimony

The first representative from the East India Company to enter Orissa was Ralph Cartwright, who sailed up the Mahānadhī River to Cuttack in 1633. When Mr. Cartwright met with the Mughal governor Mohammed Zaman to ask permission to trade, the Persian, who ran his court in true Persian fashion, extended his bare foot before Ralph to kiss before hearing his plea.

The Englishman was not too proud to do what Mughal custom required of him, and he won official permission for his company to trade anywhere in Orissa, free of customs tax, and the right to purchase land for factories as well as to provision and repair ships at any Orissan harbor. These concessions hardly proved a blessing for the British. In this malaria-infested area near the sea, five of the six British merchants were dead by the end of the year. By 1641, frustrated and eager to move on, the East India Company temporarily abandoned Orissa and in 1650 moved north to Bengal.

To give readers an idea how European Christians viewed the culture of Jagannātha worship, we quote below from *Bruton's Visit to Lord Jagannātha 350 Years Ago*, edited by P. Thankappan Nair, taken from

William Bruton's *News From the East-Indies or A Voyage to Bengalla.*

"The seventh day of November (1633) in the Morning about two of the Clocke, I hasted from Amudopoore, over a passage and for Jaggarnat, which was tenne Course betweene, that is forty Miles English, so about the houre of foure in the afternoone, I drew neare to this great City of Jaggarnat to which I passed over a great Causy, on either side whereof was a very goodly Tanke to wash in: this Causy was about halfe a mile in length; then as I came to the West end of the City, I entered into a very faire place for Scituation, furnished with exceeding store of pleasant Trees and Groves, and on either side of the way Tankes of Water and Pagodoes in the midst of them. From thence I passed up into the High-streete, where I was entertained by a Brammine, (which is one of the Religious men, or Idolatrous Priests) but let his Religion be what it would, into his House I went, and there I lodged all the time of my stay there. The Eighth day of November, in the Morning, after I had gone about the affaires that I was sent to doe, I went to view the City in some part, but especially that mighty Pagodo or Pagod, the Mirrour of all wickednesse and Idolatry; Unto this Pagod, or house of Sathan (as it may rightly be called) doe belong 9000 Brammines or Priests, which doe daily offer Sacrifices unto their great God Jaggarnat, from which the Idoll the City is so called; and when his is but named and then all the people in the Towne and Countrey doe bow and bend their knees to the ground, as the Moabites did to their Idoll, Bael-Peor; Here they doe also offer their Children to this Idoll, and make them to passe through the Fire; and also they have an abhominable custome to cause or make them passe through the Water as Sacrifices unto the said ungody God. This Idoll is in the shape like a great Serpent, whith seven Heads, and on the cheekes of each Head it hath the forme of a Wing upon each cheeke, which wings doe open and shut, and flappe, as it is carried in a stately Chariot, and the Idoll in the midd'st of it; and one of the Moguls sitting behinde it in the Chariot upon a convenient place with a Canopy, to keepe the Sunne from injuring of it. When I (with horrour) beheld these strange things, I called to mind the 13 Chap. of the Revel. and I Verse, and likewise the 16 & 17. Verses of the said Chapter, in which places there is a Beast, and such Idolatrous worship mentioned, and those sayins in that Text are herein truely accomplished in the 16 Verse; for the

Brammines are all marked in the fore-head, and likewise all that come to worship the Idoll, are marked also in their fore-heads; but those that doe buy and sell, are all marked in the left shoulder; and all such as doe dare or presume to buy and sell, (not being marked) are most severely and grievously punished."[6]

## British Administration

By 1803, the times had changed considerably. The East India Company was more or less an extension of the Royal British Government, and British troops eventually defeated the Mahrathas. In September, Colonel Cambell and his troops marched into Purī without opposition. In a well-documented letter, Lord Wellesley instructed the colonel: "On your arrival at Jaggarnaut, you will employ every possible precaution to preserve the respect due to the Pagoda, to the religious prejudices of the Brahmins, and pilgrims. You will furnish the Brahmins with such guard and shall offer perfect security to their persons, rites, and ceremonies, and to the sanctity, to the religious edifices, and you will strictly enjoin those under your command to observe your order on this important subject with the utmost degree of accuracy and vigilance."

June 10, 1805, two years later, Charles Groeme submitted a detailed report on the internal affairs of the Jagannātha temple. He observed that previously the Raja of Kurdha supervised the administration, but that during Mahratha rule they had taken control. A pilgrim tax, established during Mughal rule, was the main source of income, but that income was not equal to expenses incurred by the temple. After considering Groeme's report, authorities at Fort William accepted his proposal of continuing the pilgrim tax, and appointed James Hunter as the Collector. Thus, everyone visiting Purī from either Āṭhāranālā or Lokanātha *ghāṭs* had to pay a fee to enter the town.

As years passed, a network of rules and regulations passed by the

---

[6] Mr. Bruton's statements are obviously fanatical exaggerations. It's not possible that he saw the deity "carried in a stately Chariot" during the month of November, and his descriptions do not corroborate with anyone else's of that period.

British Government regulated activities of the Jagannātha temple. Between 1812 and 1817 a road was constructed connecting Purī to Cuttack, and in 1813 funds were allotted by the Board of Revenue for repair of a wall within the temple compound. Christian missionaries found this detestable.

When the chaplain of Fort William in Cuttack, Claudius Buchanon, observed the Ratha-yātrā festival, he bitterly criticized the British Government for its association with such idolatry. He wrote vilifying letters to many government officials, intensely stating that the government shouldn't have anything to with the temple. He was especially insistent because of the practice of committing suicide under the chariot of Lord Jagannātha. Inspired by Chaplain Buchanon, one of his followers wrote a pamphlet entitled *Rise of Wisdom*, further criticizing the British Government's involvement in Jagannātha worship. The author, Dr. Carey, twisted the truth a bit and wrote, "Jagannatha, the only idol of Purī consumes twelve or thirteen pilgrims every year ... I suppose at the lowest calculation 120,000 persons attended the car festival. Now, if only one in ten died, the mortality rate caused by this one idol would be 12,000 a year."[7]

Charles Buller, the settlement commissioner at Cuttack in 1809, also witnessed the Ratha-yātrā festival, but his view was quite different. In 1813, Mr. Buller, then a member of Parliament, addressed the House of Commons: "I believe it to be no part of the Hindu religion as the missionaries advocate it to be. I was at Juggernaut during the 'Ratha-yātrā' in 1809 and I heard but one case of such immolation under the car."

In 1817, five hundred angry Oriyans rebelled in Purī, much to the surprise of Captain Wellington and his two hundred Sepoy troops. Local people naturally sided with the Oriyan rebels, and the unruly crowd burned down all the British government buildings until finally additional troops arrived from Cuttack to settle the confusion.

Year after year, different missionaries appealed to the British Government to cease its involvement with the Jagannātha temple, but the

---

[7] Buchanon's letter No.15, Ganjam 29th June 1896, India office records, Mss. D. 122 vol.25 as quoted in *Jagannatha in History and Religious Traditions of Orissa*, p. 279.

government felt obliged to regulate temple income and expenditures lest they come under control of some undesirable individuals. Bitter disputes inflamed by Christian missionaries continued for sixty years!

William Bampton and James Peggs arrived in Cuttack on February 12, 1822 and were soon writing sermons to abolish the worship of Lord Jagannātha altogether. "Juggernaut, the great, the obscene, the bloody Juggernaut, must fall, long perhaps will be the trouble and fierce the conflict, but he must fall, and the place which knows him now will know him no more for ever."[8]

In 1825, a cholera epidemic broke out in Purī during the Ratha-yātrā festival. Until that time, no medical facilities had been established, so the disease naturally took the lives of hundreds. This only fueled the Christian missionaries' zeal. "At Cuttack and at Juggernaut I have seen numbers of dying and dead pilgrims; and one morning near the temple I counted between twenty and thirty skulls. At one place on the last stage of Juggernaut, I counted thirty-seven bodies or skeletons."[9]

In 1830, William Bampton reported his dismay when he witnessed many European-educated Bengalis taking part in the Ratha-yātrā festival with dedicated devotion. He died that same year, frustrated at not being able to abolish what he believed to be idolatry. James Peggs also met with disappointment and left India altogether after his three children died in Cuttack. Peggs, however, did not give up his cause, and upon reaching England published a booklet entitled *India's Cries to British Humanity*. The book was well received and further instigated public attention to British involvement in the Jagannātha temple.

During the following years, the British systematically decreased their involvement in the administration of the Jagannātha temple. On May 5, 1852, the Court of Directors finally expressed their opinion that the British Government disassociate itself altogether from the temple and dispatched the order to Governor-General Dalhousie.

---

[8] *History of the General Baptist Mission*, Peggs, p. 371 (London printing of 1840), as quoted in *Jagannatha in History and Religious Traditions of Orissa*, p. 280. Note: the English word "juggernaut," defined as a massive advancing force or object that crushes anything in its path, is derived from the Sanskrit word jagannātha: "lord of the world."

[9] *India's Cries to British Humanity*, 1830 printing, Peggs

Despite such a decision, in August of the same year Rev. David Edwards and thirty-three other missionaries sent a memorial to Lord Dalhousie: "Let the temple of Juggernaut be sustained by it own votaries till the time when idols shall be banished from the earth and the true Lord of the universe [Christ] shall re-establish his kingdom throughout the world." It took eleven years before the final order was carried out by the secular government. On March 30, 1863, the final deed was signed, stating that the ultimate authority of the Jagannātha temple would be the Raja of Kurdha, as had been the tradition.

## From Bad to Worse

By the time the final documents had been signed and delivered, the Raja of Kurdha had passed away, leaving his four-year-old adopted son as his heir. Obviously, a four-year-old could not manage the temple, so his widowed mother, Suryamani Patamahadevi, took the responsibility. Unfortunately, Queen Suryamani had never been trained in management or administration, and one can easily imagine her ascension led to a series of hectic events during her initial years.

As the young prince Divyasimha Deva grew from boyhood to youth, he was somewhat neglected by his busy mother. The young lad eventually began associating with ill-behaved, low-class people and started drinking heavily. When he finally came of age and took control of the temple administration, things went from bad to worse. In 1874 a large stone slab crashed from the ceiling of the Jagannātha temple, although numerous applications had been submitted to repair it. When repairs began shortly thereafter, Divyasimha Deva and the *paṇḍas* began quarreling about payment for the work.

Divyasimha's mother knew her adopted son was troubled. She had heard about a local *sādhu* in a nearby village famous for his miraculous cures of the sick and insane. Suryamani called for the *sādhu* and asked him to cure her neglected child, who was acting harshly by beating his friends and servants. During all this commotion, T. Revenshaw, the Commissioner, refused to interfere from the British side due to the deed signed in 1863.

On the evening of February 23, 1878, the *sādhu* appeared at the palace with some of his disciples. The disciples were not allowed inside but were told to wait. Once in the palace, however, the *sādhu* was violently accosted by a drunken Divyasimha and his men, who had realized Queen Suryamani's plans. They forced corks and cow dung down the man's throat, roasted the lower portion of his body until he lost consciousness, then hurled him over the palace walls.

By some freak accident, the *sādhu* hadn't yet died but had only lost consciousness. He awoke momentarily and crawled to the *Siṁha-dvāra* gate of the Jagannātha temple, where he was found by his distraught disciples. He was immediately given medical attention, but died a few hours later. With his dying breaths, the *sādhu* narrated how he'd been beaten and set afire. Divyasimha Deva was tried and convicted, then sentenced to a life of exile on the Andaman Islands, where he was sent in September of 1878.

### Further Confusion

Divyasimha's exile caused further confusion. Due to the legislative deed of 1863, no other person could lawfully manage the temple as long as the king was alive—not even the king's young son Jagannātha Jenamani (who was only a young boy at the time anyway). Appeals and applications ran back and forth through administrative red tape for years, while Suryamani Patamahadevi once again stepped in to oversee the management.[10] This time Queen Suryamani was far more adept, and even influenced high-level officials with her skills as an administrator. She remained in power until 1897, when her grandson, then known as Mukunda Deva, took charge.

Unfortunately, although she was an adept administrator by that time, Suryamani still had trouble training children in administration, and Mukunda Deva showed little interest in taking over the temple. During the Durgā Pūjā ceremonies of 1901, eleven people were trampled to death by stampeding crowds inside the temple compound. The blame fell on Mukunda Deva for his mismanagement. This was the final stroke for the British; the government of Bengal immediately appointed a government employee as temple manager. Raja Mukunda

[10] The expression "red tape" originated with British government personnel, who used to tie bundles of official documents together with thin strips of red cloth.

Deva remained in his official post while his grandmother watched from within palace walls until both of them died in 1926, once again leaving the estate to an adopted son, Rāmacandra Deva.

### Rāmacandra Deva (1926–1954), His Son Virakishore Deva (1954–1970), and His Son Dibyasingh Deb (1970– )

Without proper administration, the Jagannātha temple became a political battlefield. Ritualistic functions in the temple were neglected, servants went on strike, pilgrims were unable to get *mahāprasāda*, large crowds assembled throughout Purī to debate various issues, and the press reported scandals throughout the bureaucratic network.

Healthy relationships between the king and the network of servants are naturally of vital importance for the smooth running of the temple. Until 1930, two keys were kept to storage rooms for the deities' riches and ornaments; one key was kept with *Pattajosi Mahapatra*, and the other with the king. In 1930, however, King Rāmacandra Deva took charge of both keys, causing further strain throughout the network. No one was trusted. There were disputes between *suaras* and *pūjā paṇḍas* regarding claims for *dakṣiṇā*, or donations; vegetable oil was substituted for pure cow ghee in the cooking; the supply of oil for the lamps in the temple dwindled, and thus pilgrims became afraid to visit the temple at night; food meant for offerings was often stolen before reaching the kitchen. With the rise of interest in India's independence and all kinds of political issues facing the populace on a national level, these difficulties continued unresolved until 1952, when the newly established government finally took control of the temple.

The Jagannātha Temple Act of 1952 wasn't officially enacted as law until it was signed by the President of India on October 15, 1955. This bill established a Śrī Jagannātha Temple Managing Committee, with the *rāja*, or king, as chairman. Other members include temple servants, eminent citizens of Orissa, government officers, and an executive officer. The executive officer is a government employee empowered to settle disputes in the network of servants, adjust accounts of movable and immovable properties, and keep one key to the deities' treasury. The second key is again kept with *Pattajosi Mahapatra*.

Back in the twelfth century, Anangabhima Deva of the Imperial

*Virakishore Deva (center, in turban) and dignitaries*

Gaṅgā dynasty had established a network of servants known as *Caitisaniyoga*. This system included thirty-six classes of servants from both high and low castes in society, and has gradually evolved to more than one hundred divisions and sub-divisions. Besides these servants, there are also *brāhmaṇa* representatives from nearby villages who are members of the *Mukti Mandapa*. They are supposed to be learned men who settle philosophical disputes and impart knowledge to pilgrims. Although the members of this vast network engage in regular service to the deities, the Temple Managing Committee is the ultimate lawful authority.

Shortly after the Jagannātha Temple Act was enacted, King Virakishore Deva, who assumed the throne after his father's demise in 1954, contested the law. He appealed to the court to reinstate his sovereignty, but his attempt failed when, on April 30, 1957, the High Court of Orissa declared the Jagannātha Temple Act of 1952 valid. In 1960 some amendments were made to the Temple Act, and in 1970 the present king, Dibyasingh Deb, took the throne subsequent to his father's passing away.[11]

[11] The present king pointed out to me that in the Orissan language there is no equivalent to the English "v." I have used "v" while spelling the names of previous kings only because it's the standard in all reference texts.

# 6

# *Jagannātha Worship Goes West*

## Three Preachers

Thus far we've discussed the culture of Jagannātha worship on the northeastern shores of India, in Jagannātha Purī. Today, contrarily, Jagannātha worship is performed in London, Paris, Berlin, Amsterdam, Florence, New York, Detroit, Chicago, Los Angeles, San Francisco, Atlanta, Toronto, Montreal, Vancouver, Guadalajara, Sao Paulo, Lima, Barcelona, Sydney, Melbourne, Auckland, Christchurch, Moscow, Kiev, Durban, Mauritius, Tokyo, Hong Kong, and a host of other places around the world. What caused this widespread spiritual awakening, and why have foreigners recently taken interest in an ancient Indian religion?

The history of foreign interest can be traced back to the Golden Avatāra, Śrī Caitanya Mahāprabhu. He inaugurated the *saṅkīrtana* movement, and desired that Lord Kṛṣṇa's holy name be chanted in every town and village on earth. Many Vaiṣṇava devotees have assisted the Lord in this mission, but by examining the lives of three particular devotees we can better understand how this cultural movement spread so far and wide in recent times.

## Śrīla Bhaktivinoda Ṭhākura

By the mid-1800s the teachings of Śrī Caitanya Mahāprabhu were all but lost and forgotten, or at least obscured. They were followed by only a few devotees living in Vṛndāvana, Navadvīpa, or Purī. At that time the British ruled India, and their interest certainly wasn't to learn Indian philosophy. Rather, they hoped to re-educate the upper classes of India into a British way of life.

In his autobiographical notes to his son, Śrīla Bhaktivinoda Ṭhākura writes about the difficulty of finding books on Vaiṣṇava philosophy in 1860: "While I was at the school [teaching] in Midnapur I decided that I would obtain and read books on the Vaiṣṇava *dharma*. There was a *jāti* Vaiṣṇava [Vaiṣṇava by birth] *paṇḍita* at the school. I learned from talking to him how Caitanya Mahāprabhu preached the Vaiṣṇava *dharma* in Bengal and that the history and teachings of Caitanya were recorded in the book known as *Caitanya-caritāmṛta*. I began to search, but I could not secure a copy of the *Caritāmṛta*. I had faith that by reading that book I would achieve happiness, but Vaiṣṇava books were not in print then."

Eight years later the Ṭhākura, at that time known as Kedāranātha Datta, was appointed deputy magistrate of Dinajpur. He writes: "In Dinajpur the Vaiṣṇava religion was fairly strong due to Raya Kamal Locan Saheb. There were many renunciants and *gosvāmīs* coming and going there. A few wealthy persons were supporting many assemblies of *brāhmaṇa paṇḍitas*. Respectable gentlemen would regularly come to discuss the Vaiṣṇava *dharma* with me. I had a desire to know what the genuine Vaiṣṇava *dharma* was. I wrote to our agent Pratap Chandra Rāya, and he sent a published translation of *Śrīmad-Bhāgavatam* and *Śrī Caitanya-caritāmṛta*. I also bought the book called *Bhakta-mālā*."

In 1871 Kedāranātha Datta was transferred to Jagannātha Purī. He was again appointed deputy magistrate, but was also appointed temple administrator of the Jagannātha temple. From 1871–1876 the Dattas remained in Purī, and during those years Kedāranātha's interest in Vaiṣṇava *dharma* fully blossomed. He began seriously studying Vaiṣṇava literature along with friends, and ultimately began writing articles and books of his own.

"I appointed Gopīnātha Paṇḍita as my tutor, and with his assistance I first studied the twelve cantos of the *Bhagavatam* with Śrīdhara Svāmī's commentaries. After finishing the *Bhāgavat*, I made a copy of the *Ṣaṭ-sandarba* [of Jīva Gosvāmī] and read it. Then I made copies and read the *Vedānta* commentary *Govinda-bhāṣya*, written by Bala deva Vidyābhūṣaṇa. Next, I read the *Bhakti-rasāmṛta-sindhu* [by Rūpa Gosvāmī]. Then I made a copy of the *Hari-bhakti-kalpa-latikā*."

While living in Purī, Kedāranātha also formed a society called the Bhagavata-samsat, which held meetings in the Jagannātha-vallabha Gardens. Many Vaiṣṇavas and *paṇḍitas* attended the gatherings. During their studies, Kedāranātha noted at least thirteen *apa-*

*sampradāyas*, or deviant communities in the Gauḍīya-*sampradāya*, so he began preaching and writing books to further elucidate the true philosophy propounded by Lord Caitanya. In his *Jaiva Dharma* he reveals the specific significance of Śrī Caitanya Mahāprabhu:

Nyāyaratna: "If the Vaiṣṇava religion is existing from time immemorial, then what new light has Caitanya Mahāprabhu shed by which He should be given particular regard?"

Vaiṣṇava dāsa: "The Vaiṣṇava religion is like a lotus flower that gradually unfolds. At first, it was in a budding stage; then it began to slightly bloom. Gradually, it developed to the fully blossomed stage.

"At the time of Brahmā's creation, knowledge of God and the practice of love and devotion mentioned in the *catuḥ-ślokī* of *Śrīmad Bhāgavatam*, was only germinating in the hearts of men. At the time of Prahlāda, it took the form of a bud. Later, during the time of Bādarāyaṇa or Vyāsa, the bud gradually began to open, and during the time of various Vaiṣṇava spiritual masters the buds became flowers.

"At last, when Mahāprabhu arrived the flower of love fully unfolded its petals and began to diffuse its sweet fragrance to the people of the world. Caitanya Mahāprabhu distributed Vaiṣṇava religion to the fortunate people of the world. Prior to Him, did anyone reveal that chanting the divine name is such a beloved thing? Though it was confined within the *śāstras*, it was not brought to the common knowledge of men. Before the advent of Mahāprabhu, was the treasure house of love opened and distributed in such a way?"[1]

While in Purī, Kedāranātha Datta and his family lived on Grand Road. In February of 1874 a son was born; he was named Bimala Prasāda in honor of the Bimalā deity located in the Jagannātha temple complex.[2]

When Bimala Prasāda was only six months old the colorful Rathayātrā procession passed along Grand Road, and mysteriously, Lord Jagannātha's chariot stopped in front of Kedāranātha Datta's house. Despite hundreds of strong men pulling with all their strength, the chariot could not be moved forward for three days. It is said that every-

[1] *Jaiva Dharma*, pg.155

[2] See *Saṅkha-kṣetra* in the *Part One* for further descriptions of the Bimalā deity.

*Śrīla Bhaktivinoda Ṭhākura, the magistrate.*

one in the crowd tried various means to move the *ratha*, but it would not budge.

During this commotion, Kedāranātha Datta's wife, Bhagavatī Devī, being a respected magistrate's wife, climbed onto the cart with her newly born son in her arms. As she approached Lord Jagannātha to bow at His lotus feet, some flowers fell from the Lord's body and landed on Bimala Prasāda. The grain ceremony, wherein a young child eats his first grains, was then observed on the cart and was done with Jagannātha *prasāda*. A short time after the ceremony was completed, the chariot finally began to rumble and move; everyone understood this as a sign that the child was especially blessed by Lord Jagannātha.

As Bimala Prasāda grew up along with his nine brothers and sisters, he gradually learned the teachings of Lord Caitanya from his devoted mother and father. Śrīla Bhaktivinoda Ṭhākura was an ideal Vaiṣṇava. His daily schedule included hours of hearing and chanting the glories of the Lord (*śravaṇam, kīrtanam*), as well as fulfilling the duties of a magistrate. Kedāranātha Datta remained engaged at Purī for only five years. Then he moved to Godruma-dvīpa in West Bengal, from where he researched and found Lord Caitanya's original birth site. Soon after, he established a temple at that site to commemorate the Lord's appearance. Retiring from government service in 1894, Śrīla Bhaktivinoda Ṭhākura then spent most of his last years in prayer and worship in a cottage on the beach at Jagannātha Purī.[3]

[3] Although Śrīla Bhaktivinoda Ṭhākura spent most of his last days in Purī, his *samādhi* tomb is located next to his home in Godruma-dvīpa, West Bengal.

## Śrīla Bhaktisiddhānta Sarasvatī

Śrīla Bhaktivinoda Ṭhākura instilled a preaching spirit in his son Bimala Prasāda. As the boy grew, he became extremely learned in Vedic philosophy and quite well known for his abilities in astronomy and mathematics. Whatever he would read once he could later recall with perfect clarity. He was trained at the Śrī Rāmapura School, and achieved such astounding scholarship that he was eventually awarded the title Siddhānta Sarasvatī.

When Bimala Prasāda was only seven years old his father gave him a deity of Lord Kūrma to worship, and when he was thirteen he began regular chanting of the holy names under his father's guidance, a practice he would continue throughout his entire life. He was a lifelong celibate, and was never inclined to associate with women. He writes of his leaving college in 1895:

*Śrīla Bhaktisiddhanta Sarasvatī*

"If I remain studying with careful attention at the College, then extreme pressure will be brought upon me to enter family life, but if I am considered to be foolish and inefficient, then no one will put such an inducement upon me for becoming so engaged. By this consideration, I left the Sanskrit College, and in order to maintain my life for the service of Hari, I was desirous of getting an honest occupation for which I could perform with the intention of earning a humble income."[4]

[4] As quoted in *A Ray of Vishnu*.

After visiting his father in Purī during 1903, Siddānta Sarasvatī decided to retire to Māyāpur, Lord Caitanya's birth site, to fulfill a vow of chanting the holy names of the Lord one hundred million times in a secluded place.

During the following years, living in extremely austere surroundings at Māyāpur, Siddhānta Sarasvatī regularly preached while continuing his vow of chanting. He gradually attracted a few young men interested in spiritual philosophy, and they helped organize more preaching engagements. Gradually they expanded the preaching to Calcutta and beyond.

In 1918, at the age of 44, Siddhānta Sarasvatī accepted the renounced order of *sannyāsa* and ventured out with his followers to preach around the Indian sub-continent. Within a few years this charismatic preacher had developed a following and begun the Gauḍīya Maṭha, eventually establishing sixty-four temples around the country.

While at the Gauḍīya Maṭha at No.1 Ultadanga Road in Calcutta during 1922, Śrīla Bhaktisiddhānta Sarasvatī was visited by two young Indian gentlemen interested in spiritual wisdom. As he began preaching about Lord Caitanya's message of love of God, one of the young men, Abhay Charan De, argued that India was a poor country and if Lord Caitanya's message was to be heard, he proposed that India must first earn her independence. Obviously, the young man was favorable to Mahatma Gandhi's flourishing national movement.

Śrīla Bhaktisiddhānta Sarasvatī pointed out that Lord Caitanya's teachings were meant for everyone regardless of caste, creed, or nationality. He explained that service to God is *sanātana-dharma*, the eternal, natural function of the soul, and does not depend on one's birth in a particular family or locality. The young men, he suggested, should rather spend their time preaching Lord Caitanya's message to English-speaking people instead of worrying about India's independence.

Abhay Charan was moved by these words and took them seriously, although at the time he was not free to engage wholeheartedly in preaching. Abhay Charan De had grown up in a Vaiṣṇava family from Calcutta. As a boy he had held annual Ratha-yātrās in his neighborhood around Harrison Road; he had often heard about Lord Caitanya. For the next thirteen years after his first meeting with Śrīla Bhaktisiddhānta Sarasvatī, Abhay kept close contact with various members of the Gauḍīya Maṭha. In 1933 he was formally initiated by Śrīla Bhaktisiddhānta Sarasvatī. Three years later Śrīla Bhaktisiddhānta Sarasvatī left this mortal world, entrusting his Gauḍīya Maṭha to his followers.

### His Divine Grace A.C. Bhaktivedanta Swami Prabhupāda

As years became decades, the Gauḍīya Maṭha went through many changes and political intrigues, but Abhay Caraṇāravinda (his initiated name) continued to hold his spiritual master's instructions close to his heart. In 1955, at the age of 59, Abhay formally left his wife and family to accept the renounced order of *sannyāsa* from his Godbrother Śrīla Bhakti Prajñāṇa Keśava Mahārāja, following in the footsteps of Śrī Caitanya Mahāprabhu, who had left His family to preach.

On taking *sannyāsa*, Abhaya became known as A. C. Bhaktivedanta Swamī, and decided to move to Vṛndāvana, the land of Lord Kṛṣṇa's childhood pastimes. For nearly ten years he lived in and around Vṛndāvana, translating various Vedic books into English, as he had been instructed to do by Śrīla Bhaktisiddhānta Sarasvatī on that fateful day in 1922—more than thirty years earlier. Ever mindful of his spiritual master's desire, he constantly endeavored to find ways to preach in English. He began a magazine entitled *Back to Godhead*, wrote a small book named *Easy Journey to Other Planets*, and began an English translation of the *Bhāgavata Purāṇa*, or *Śrīmad-Bhāgavatam*. Shortly before he reached his 69th birthday a unique opportunity arose: a friendly owner of a shipping company out of Bombay agreed to give him free passage to the United States on one of her ships.

On September 19, 1965, Śrīla A. C. Bhaktivedanta Swamī landed on the shores of America with two trunks filled with his English translations and only forty Indian rupees (worthless in America). During the subsequent freezīng-cold winter months, he lived in and around New York City and began preaching to whoever would listen to the teachings and philosophy of Lord Caitanya.

In the entire history of Jaganātha culture, which spans thousands of years, we find no parallel to the preaching efforts of His Divine Grace A.C. Bhaktivedanta Swamī Prabhupāda, who would become known to his disciples as Śrīla Prabhupāda. He was seventy years old, alone in a foreign country, with no money. He repeatedly wrote to his Godbrothers back in India for help, but received little. He still remained faithful to the orders of his spiritual master by trying to educate English-speaking people about the Absolute Truth. Gradually, he began attracting sincere followers from among the American youth disenchanted with materialistic life. Although most of these followers were entirely ignorant of Vedic philosophy and educated as followers of Darwinism, which is contrary to Vedic concepts, he was able to attract them by his deep realizations and love of God.

Eventually, he incorporated his preaching efforts as the International Society for Krishna Consciousness (ISKCON), and almost single-handedly began a worldwide religious movement. Events of his early years in the United States are recounted in Satsvarūpa dāsa Goswami's *Śrīla Prabhupāda Līlāmṛta*, in the volume entitled *Planting the Seed* (*New York City 1965–1966*). Many young Americans joined his movement and began following the basic teachings of the *Vedas* under his expert guidance.

## Lord Jagannātha Appears in San Francisco

In the spring of 1967, one of Śrīla Prabhupāda's followers, Mālātī Dāsī, noticed some unusual figurines lying in wooden barrels in a San Francisco import store. Mālātī took one of the dolls because there was a sign on the bottom of them: "Made in India." She placed the odd item on a shelf in her home. A few days later, Mālātī's husband, Śyāmasundara, told her that Swamijī wanted to talk with her about the doll from India.

Mālātī entered Swamijī's apartment and Swamijī asked her, "Where did you get this?"

He looked down and beheld a three-inch wooden doll with a flat head, a black, smiling face, and big, round eyes. The figure had stubby, forward-jutting arms, and a simple green and yellow torso with no visible feet.

Unable to understand if she'd done something wrong or forbidden, Mālātī replied sheepishly, "I got it at an import store downtown called Cost Plus."

"Were there more?" Swamijī inquried.

Remembering three barrels filled with the small figurines, Mālātī said there were many more. Prabhupāda declared, "You have brought Lord Jagannātha, the Lord of the universe! He is Kṛṣṇa. Thank you very much."

Śrīla Prabhupāda beamed with pleasure while Mālātī and others sat amazed. He then explained that this was Lord Jagannātha, a deity of Kṛṣṇa that had been worshiped in India for thousands of years along with two other deities: Kṛṣṇa's brother Balarāma, and His sister Subhadrā.

Excited, Mālātī confirmed that those must have been the other, similar figures at Cost Plus, so Prabhupāda requested her to go back to the import store and get them. Mālātī hurried out and soon returned with the two other dolls in the set.

Śrīla Prabhupāda placed the black-faced, smiling Jagannātha on the right. In the center he placed the smallest figure, Subhadrā, who had a red smiling mouth and a rectangular yellow torso. The third figure, Balarāma, with white, round head, red-rimmed eyes, and a happy red smile, had forward-jutting arms like Jagannātha's, and a blue and yellow base. Prabhupāda placed Him next to Subhadrā.

As he looked at the deities together on his desk, Śrīla Prabhupāda asked if anyone knew how to carve. Śyāmasundara said that he had done some wood sculpting, and Prabhupāda asked him to carve three-foot high copies of the small figures. Seeing this appearance of Lord Jagannātha in San Francisco as the will of Kṛṣṇa, Śrīla Prabhupāda said they should be careful to receive and worship Him properly. If Śyāmasundara could carve the forms, Prabhupāda said he would personally install the deities in the temple. San Francisco, he said further, could now be called New Jagannātha Purī. He then chanted, *jagannāthaḥ svāmī nayana-patha-gāmī bhavatu me*. "This is a mantra for Lord Jagannātha," he instructed them. "Jagannātha means 'Lord of the universe.' 'O Lord of the universe, kindly be visible unto me.' It is very auspicious that He has chosen to appear here."

Prabhupāda then told them the story of how Lord Jagannātha originally appeared as a large log floating in the sea. Śyāmasundara,

Mālatī, and their friend Mukunda later went near the docks of San Francisco to search for a log in the salvage yards. By the will of Providence, the trunk of a huge redwood tree had washed onto shore and was lying among discarded items. They eagerly placed the wood in their van and brought it back to their apartment.

Using the small statues, Śyāmasundara calculated ratios and new dimensions and began carving on the balcony of his apartment. Meanwhile, devotees living in the San Francisco temple bought the rest of the tiny Jagannāthas from Cost Plus, and it became a fashion to glue a little Jagannātha to a simple necklace and wear Him around the neck.

Madhudviṣa Dāsa: *In those days, during the Vietnam War, they drafted people into the Army in United States, and I was notified that I had to report to the Oakland Induction Center for a physical. When I went for the check-up, they made everyone take off all their clothes and stand in line in our underwear. So I took off all my clothes, but wouldn't take off my Lord Jagannātha, who was hanging around my neck on a string.*

*I had been chanting Hare Kṛṣṇa for a while and didn't really want to go into the Army, but if you didn't report for the physical, the United States government could really cause you a lot of problems. So, I stood in line chanting softly until my turn came to see the doctor.*

*"What is that?" he asked, as I stepped up to the scale to be weighed.*

*"This is Lord Jagannātha," I said, showing him the deity around my neck.*

*"Take it off!"*

*"No!" I said, and held tightly to the tiny Lord Jagannātha who fit snugly in my hand. "This is my religion. You can do anything you want, but please don't take Lord Jagannātha away from me."*

*The doctor was stunned. He paused for a minute, then turned to one of his assistants and said, "Get this guy out of here. He's crazy."*

*After all the paperwork was finished and I was released, I danced and chanted in ecstasy all the way back to the temple in San Francisco.*

Because Lord Jagannātha is liberal and merciful to the most fallen, Śrīla Prabhupāda explained, the devotees would soon be able to worship Him in their temple. Worship of Rādhā and Kṛṣṇa in the temple requires strict standards which the devotees were not yet able to meet, but Lord Jagannātha is so merciful that he can be worshiped in a simple way (mostly by chanting Hare Kṛṣṇa), even if the devotees are not so advanced. Gradually, as they progressed in spiritual life, Prabhupāda would introduce his disciples to more and more of the detailed practices of deity worship, along with the deep theological understanding that supports it.

Caste conscious *brāhmaṇas* of India would consider it heresy for non-Hindus to handle Lord Jagannātha and conduct His worship. None of Śrīla Prabhupāda's disciples would even have been allowed to enter the temple at Jagannātha Purī. The white man, the Westerner, is not allowed to see Lord Jagannātha except when He comes out of the temple for Snāna-yātrā or Ratha-yātrā. These restrictions are social customs, however, and not scriptural injunctions. Śrīla Bhaktisiddhānta Sarasvatī had introduced deity worship and initiation for anyone, regardless of caste, race, or nationality, and Bhaktivinoda Ṭhākura had longed for the day when people from the West would mingle with their Indian brothers and chant Hare Kṛṣṇa. Prabhupāda had come to fulfill the desires and vision of his spiritual master and of Bhaktivinoda Ṭhākura by creating Vaiṣṇavas among the Westerners. Now, if the Westerners were to become actual devotees, they would have to be given deity worship. Otherwise, it would be more difficult to become purified from bad habits and a sinful life.

## The Installation

The evening of the installation, the room was filled with devotees and hippie guests. The just-finished deities sat on a redwood shelf beneath a yellow canopy, illumined by spotlights. It was a simple altar and the deities wore no clothes or ornaments, but were freshly painted in bright colors of black, red, white, green, yellow, and blue. They were smiling, and Prabhupāda was also glancing at them, looking high up to their altar.

Prabhupāda called one of his disciples, "So, Hayagrīva. Come here."

Prabhupāda had devotees arrange for a large candle on a plate. The ceremony he had planned would be a simple one with devotees and guests one after another coming up and offering the flame in circles before the Lord Jagannātha, Lord Balarāma, and Subhadrā.

*San Francisco temple in Haight-Ashbury, 1967*

"This should be lighted up," Prabhupāda said, "and when there is *kīrtana*, one must be doing like this before the deity." Prabhupāda moved his hands around in a circle before the deity. "You see?"

"Yes, yes," said Hayagrīva.

Prabhupāda began playing *karatālas* (cymbals) and singing the Hare Kṛṣṇa mantra to the popular melody he had introduced in America.

"Just in front," he called out, gesturing to Hayagrīva to stand directly before the deities.

Devotees and guests began rising to their feet and dancing, arms raised, bodies swaying rythmically back and forth. Colorded lights within the canopy began flashing intermittently blue, red, and yellow, highlighting the extraordinary eyes of Lord Jagannātha, Balarāma, and Subhadrā. Mukunda dāsa, who had arranged the lights, smiled and looked to Prabhupāda, hoping for approval. Prabhupāda nodded and continued singing Hare Kṛṣṇa.

Śrīla Prabhupāda watched with pleasure as one person after another took a turn at offering the candle before Lord Jagannātha. This was a simple procedure for installing the deity. Although in Indian temples the installation of deities is a complex procedure requiring days of continuous Vedic rituals, in San Francisco there were no *brāhmaṇa* priests, and many of the other standards would be impossible to maintain.

When the *kīrtana* ended, Prabhupāda asked Haridāsa to bring him the candle. Prabhupāda passed his hands across the flame and touched them to his forehead. "Yes," he said, "show everyone. Each and everyone. Whatever they can contribute. Here, take it like this and show everyone."

He indicated that Haridāsa should present the candle before each person in the room so that all present could pass their hands over the flame as he had shown and then touch their foreheads. As Haridāsa went from person to person, a few devotees dropped coins on the plate and others followed.

Prabhupāda sat on the *vyāsāsana* and explained further: "The *Śrīmad-Bhāgavatam* has recommended hearing, chanting, thinking, and worshiping. This process which we just now introduced on the advent of Jagannātha Swami means that now this temple is completely fixed. So this is the worshiping process. This is called *ārati*. So, during *kīrtana* this *ārati* will go on. And the worshiping process is to take the heat of the light and, whatever your condition is, pay something for the worship. So this simple process, if you follow, you just see how you realize the Absolute Truth.

"Another thing I request you: all the devotees—when you come to the temple, you bring one fruit and one flower. If you can bring more fruit, more flower, it is very good. If not, it is not very expensive to bring one fruit and one flower. And offer it to the deities. So I will request you, when you come to the temple, you bring this. Whatever fruit it may be. It does not mean that you have to bring very costly fruit. Whatever you can afford. One fruit and one flower." He paused, looking around the room. "Yes, now you can distribute *prasādam*."

### Ratha-yātrā in the USA

Lord Jagannātha's presence quickly beautified the temple. Devotees made flower garlands for Him daily. Jadurāṇī Dāsī's paintings of Lord Viṣṇu arrived from New York, and Govinda Dāsī had painted a large portrait of Śrīla Prabhupāda, which now hung beside his seat.

As Prabhupāda had requested, devotees and guests began bringing offerings before the altar of Lord Jagannātha. Everything necessary for spiritual life was finally here: the temple, the books, ISKCON's first deity, and *prasādam*.

Each night the devotees performed the *ārati* ceremony just as Prabhupāda had taught them, taking turns offering a candle before Lord Jagannātha. When devotees asked whether they could add anything to the ceremony, Prabhupāda said yes, they could also offer incense. He said there were many other details of deity worship, numerous enough to keep them busy twenty-four hours a day. Gradually he would instruct them how to perform the worship according to a complex text on deity worship called the *Hari-bhakti-vilāsa*, compiled by one of Lord Caitanya's followers, Sanātana Gosvāmī.

One day, Śrīla Prabhupāda noted a flatbed truck hauling goods through the streets of San Francisco. He later called Śyāmasundara.

"In Jagannātha Purī," he explained, "once a year they take the deities out of the temple and hold a grand festival called Ratha-yātrā."

Prabhupāda showed Śyāmasundara a sketch he had made of a truck with a four-pillared canopy on the back decorated with flags, bells, and flower garlands.

"Make me this cart for Ratha-yātrā," he continued. "You must arrange a procession down the main street and place the deities on the back of the truck. This will attract many people."

When the devotees learned that Śrīla Prabhupāda wanted to hold the first American Ratha-yātrā in San Francisco, they immediately became busy with preparations. One devotee in particular, Jayānanda Dāsa, was especially enthusiastic. Jayānanda began going out daily to various places around San Francisco, trying to collect necessary items for the festival. Early every morning, Jayānanda went to fruit and vegetable vendors near Market Street and preached about Lord Jagannātha's upcoming festival while asking for donations on behalf of his spiritual master and the Lord. Because he was honest and sincere, the vendors, who had never even heard of Lord Jagannātha, appreciated Jayānanda's determination and became enthusiastic to help. Nearby flower vendors were also captivated by Jayānanda, and donated liberally to help decorate the deities and their chariot.

Jayānanda's enthusiasm was contagious. He saw everyone who

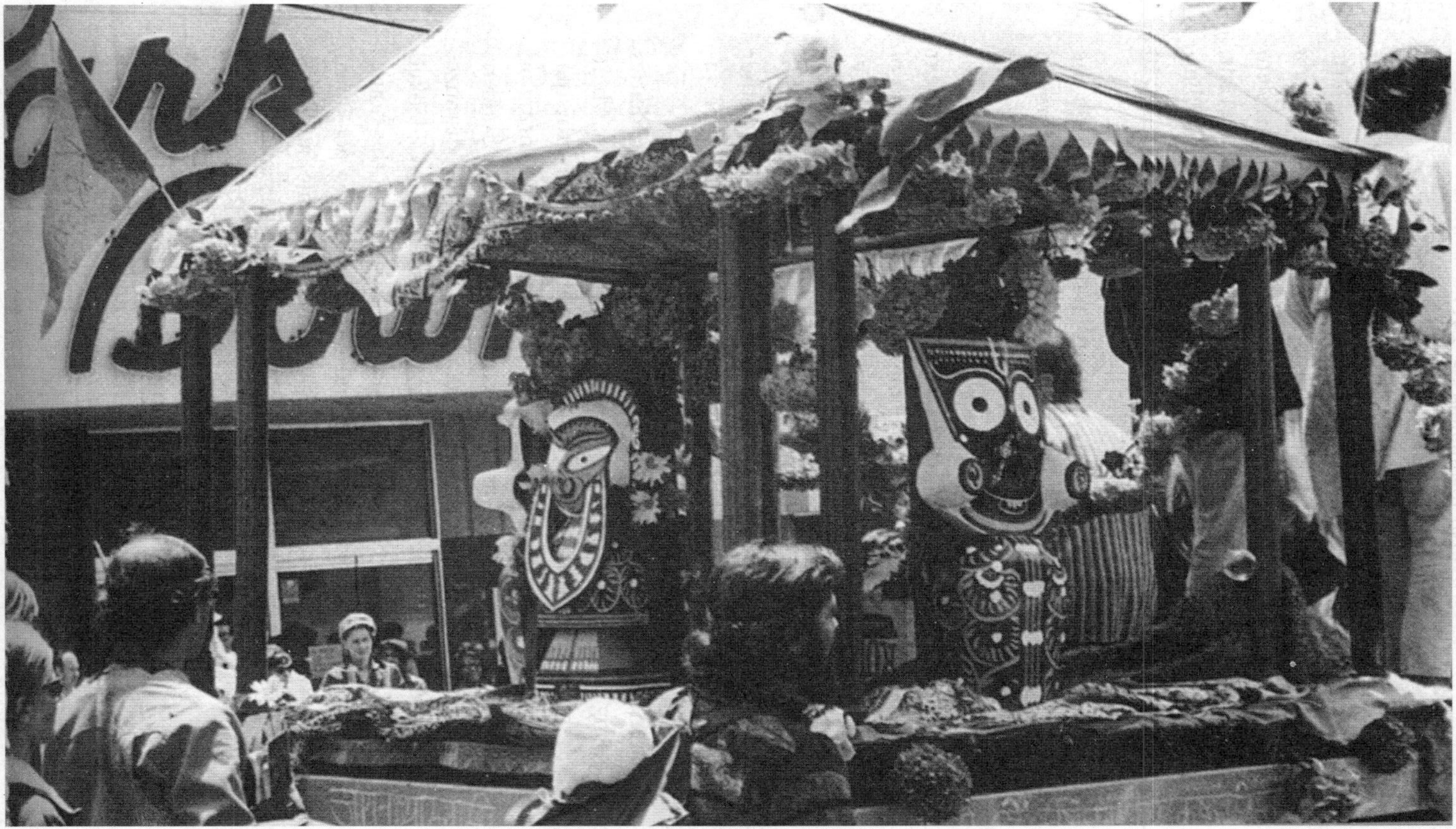

*The first Ratha-yātrā in the West.*

came to the San Francisco temple as a prospective helper, and he engaged hippies and devotees alike in decorating the bright yellow Hertz rental truck. They placed a canopy on the back as Śrīla Prabhupāda had instructed, and Jayānanda arranged and installed a sound system so the *kīrtana* would be amplified. Finally, just days before the event, Jayānanda went around to various stores in San Francisco distributing posters announcing the first American Ratha-yātrā. Everyone in Haight-Ashbury was talking about the Jagannātha Parade.

July 9, 1967 was a beautiful day in San Francisco. Although the devotees had tried to get permission for the parade route to go through Golden Gate Park, the police department would only give permission for the procession to go down Fredrick Street toward the sea. Mukunda, Haridāsa, Hayagrīva, and some of the ladies sat on the cart next to the deities of Lord Jagannātha, Balarāma, and Subhadrā. In front of the truck, devotees and many hippies gathered and sang *kīrtana*. Everyone in the streets loved it. A police motor escort led the cart slowly through the streets while Subala and Jayānanda danced wildly, jumping up and down and playing *karatālas*. Mālātī and some of the other women handed out pieces of oranges, apples, and bananas to spectators, and others threw flowers.

After the procession, the flower-bedecked Hertz, with the deities still sitting on it, headed into the mountains to a rented house where Śrīla Prabhupāda was staying to recover from ill health. In the quiet afternoon, Prabhupāda was sitting in the living room chanting on his beads; Kīrtanānanda was in the kitchen cooking a feast. Suddenly, they heard the familiar sound of hand cymbals in the distance. Śrīla Prabhupāda became very happy, and with widening eyes, looked out to see the unusual Ratha-yātrā truck parking before the house. Devotees were in ecstasy, chanting and dancing as they got down from the chariot and brought Lord Jagannātha, Balarāma, and Subhadrā into the house. They set the deities on an upright piano.

The devotees described their Ratha-yātrā to Śrīla Prabhupāda—how the cart had moved slowly through the streets, how the hippies had danced and chanted in ecstasy, and how everyone had joined in the *kīrtana*. The first Ratha-yātrā in the United States had been a grand success. Now they wanted further instructions on how to increase the worship of Jagannātha, His brother, and His sister.

### Mr. Ratha-yātrā

Implanting the Vedic way of life into Western society was not going to be easy. Śrīla Prabhupāda had begun his mission simply by talking with strangers in the New York City streets. Gradually, however, his disciples were learning Vedic philosophy from him and preaching to others. They opened Hare Kṛṣṇa centers in various cities around the United States, then in Canada, and eventually in England, Germany, and beyond. During the formative years, San Francisco remained the only temple to hold an annual Ratha-yātrā festival, but as ISKCON expanded, other temples also began to organize their own Festival of the Chariots.

Jayānanda Dāsa became prominent in making arrangements. Although many temples organized Ratha-yātrā festivals, Jayānanda was the most expert at arranging the chariots and other paraphernalia required. Temples from all over America requested Jayānanda to help them. In those days, no one was really sure how the traditional chariots in Jagannātha Purī were constructed, but somehow, Jayānanda became expert at building replicas. Because of his enthusiasm and expertise, devotees lovingly began calling him "Mr. Ratha-yātrā."

### San Francisco, July 26, 1969

On the day of the Ratha-yātrā parade, about one hundred devotees and a crowd of almost one thousand gathered on Haight Street before the tall chariot. Lord Jagannātha, Balarāma, and Subhadrā, from their elevated platform on the cart, smiled down upon the crowd. A group of devotee-musicians seated on the chariot made last-minute checks of their loudspeaker system and began *kīrtana.* In the center of the cart, just beneath the deity platform, a red upholstered *vyāsāsana* awaited Śrīla Prabhupāda's arrival.

As Prabhupāda's car approached, he could hear the cries of the devotees, and as he stepped from the car he saw them bow down in obeisances. Folding his hands and smiling, he acknowledged his enthusiastic disciples and looked around with pleasure at the large crowd that had already gathered. Turning toward the chariot, Prabhupāda beheld the deities on their throne, the same deities who had inaugurated Ratha-yātrā in America two years before. They were beautifully dressed and garlanded, and multicolored pennants and thick garlands of carnations decorated their *ratha*. Ratha-yātrā was becoming more and more wonderful each year. Prabhupāda bowed down before Jagannātha, Balarāma, and Subhadrā, and his disciples bowed with him.

As Śrīla Prabhupāda took his seat on the cart, the *kīrtana* began again and the cart, pulled by two long ropes by dozens of men and women, slowly moved forward. Buckets of burning frankincense poured aromatic clouds from the deities' platform above Prabhupāda's head, and the chariot moved slowly along the road to the park.

"How many people are behind us," Prabhupāda asked, turning to Tamāl Krishna riding beside him on the chariot.

Tamāl Krishna climbed back and surveyed the crowd as far as he could see.

"Five thousand!"

"Sing Jaya Jagannātha," Prabhupāda instructed, and Tamāl Krishna then changed the chant from Hare Kṛṣṇa to "Jaya Jagannātha! Jaya Jagannātha!"

Throughout the parade, Prabhupāda watched serenely, his right hand in his bead bag. The large crowd consisted mostly of young hippies, but also included businessmen dressed in suits and ties, elderly persons with their grandchildren and families, and a few stray dogs.

Suddenly devotees in front began shouting, "Stop the cart! Stop the cart!" Ahead, the low arch of a park bridge spanned the roadway. The devotees managed to stop the 35-foot high chariot just before it reached the bridge. Although the parade appeared to have reached an unforseen impasse, the chanting continued unabated. The previous year, the procession had taken the same route—with a smaller cart—and even then Śyāmasundara had had to climb up and saw off the spire. This year, however, Nara-Nārāyaṇa had devised a collapsible dome with a crank to lower the canopy and superstructure. When Śrīla Prabhupāda had heard of these plans, he asked, "Are you sure you want to depend on mechanical means? It could mean disaster." Now the time to lower the canopy had come, and the crank wouldn't work.

With the cart stopped before the bridge, the chanters gathered in greater numbers, facing Śrīla Prabhupāda and Lord Jagannātha. Un-

*Śrīla Prabhupāda chants in Golden Gate Park.*

der the bridge at least a thousand voices sang together, creating an incredible echo. Then Śrīla Prabhupāda stood, raised his arms to the crowd, and began to dance.

Bhavānanda: *Everyone went wild. The sound was so uproarious that you were deafened under that bridge. Prabhupāda was dancing, jumping on the cart.*

Nara-Nārāyaṇa: *He was dancing, and as he danced, his feet crushed the flowers. His garland broke and flowers began cascading everywhere as he danced up and down. He was leaping very deliberately, almost in slow motion.*

Tamāl Krishna: *Prabhupāda was jumping up and down and the people went crazy seeing him in complete ecstasy. He kept jumping and slowly turned around until he was face to face with Lord Jagannātha.*

Prabhupāda finally sat down, and still the chariot didn't go. The people were roaring.

"What do they want?" Prabhupāda asked Tamāl Krishna.

"I think they want to see you dance again, Śrīla Prabhupāda," Tamāl Krishna said.

"Do you think so?"

"Yes."

He then got up and started dancing again—the white wool cap pushed to the back of his head, his arms extended, his right hand still clutching his bead bag, his forefinger extended, and his long robes flowing.

The ecstatic chanting and dancing continued. After about fifteen minutes, Nara-Nārāyaṇa finally got the crank to work and down came the canopy. Again the cart moved forward, under the bridge and on through the park. The crowd had grown now to ten thousand. This was much bigger than any American Kṛṣṇa conscious festival ever held before.

The parade route ended at an oceanside dance hall, The Family Dog Auditorium, where devotees had prepared 10,000 feast plates of Lord Jagannātha's *mahāprasāda*—fruit salad, apple chutney, *halavā*, and watermelon slices. Although the cart had stopped, the chanting and dancing continued as Śrīla Prabhupāda led the crowd inside the auditorium to a temporary stage and altar. A giant silk screen of Lord Caitanya covered the hall's Tibetan *maṇḍala*, and pictures of Lord Viṣṇu and Śrīla Bhaktisiddhānta Sarasvatī were on the stage.

Śrīla Prabhupāda sat on a *vyāsāsana* erected on stage and explained the simplicity of Kṛṣṇa consciousness: "Lord Caitanya appeared five hundred years ago to establish the direct principles of *Bhagavad-gītā*," he began, drawing the crowd's attention to the gigantic silk screen of Lord Caitanya. "He showed that even if you do not understand the process of religion, then simply chant Hare Kṛṣṇa, Hare Kṛṣṇa, Kṛṣṇa Kṛṣṇa, Hare Hare/ Hare Rāma, Hare Rāma, Rāma Rāma, Hare Hare. The results are practical. For example, when we were chanting Hare Kṛṣṇa all the members who are assembled here were joining in, but now when I am talking about philosophy some are leaving. It is very practical. You can see. The Hare Kṛṣṇa mantra is so enchanting that anyone in any condition can take part. And if he continues to chant, gradually he will develop his dormant love of God. It is very simple.

"We are requesting everyone to chant the Hare Kṛṣṇa mantra and take *prasādam*. When you are tired of chanting, the *prasādam* is ready; you can immediately take *prasādam*. And if you dance, then all bodily exercise is Kṛṣṇa-ized. And all of the attempts of the yoga process are attained by this simple process.

"So chant, dance, take *prasādam*. Even if you don't at first hear this philosophy, it will act, and you will be elevated to the highest platform of perfection."

## A Garden of Devotees

During the years that followed, Śrīla Prabhupāda planted seeds of *bhakti* into the hearts of his thousands of followers. He traveled tirelessly around the world fourteen times in ten years, preaching and instructing them how to worship Lord Kṛṣṇa according to the ancient teachings of the *Vedas*. In San Francisco, the Festival of Chariots became so popular the mayor of the city proclaimed an official Ratha-yātrā Day. In 1973 a London daily newspaper published a front-page photo caption: "ISKCON Ratha-yātrā is rival to the Nelson Column in Trafalgar Square."

In 1976 Śrīla Prabhupāda triumphantly returned to New York City. This time, he was no longer alone with a couple of trunks of books and a few worthless Indian rupees. Rather, he was the spiritual master of a worldwide network of dedicated followers, and owned a twelve-story building on West 55th Street in downtown Manhattan. His Bhaktivedanta Book Trust published books in twenty-three different languages, and Lord Jagannātha was being worshiped on every continent of the world.

Once again his dedicated disciple, Jayānanda Dāsa, was responsible for arranging the Ratha-yātrā chariots in New York City. Jayānanda, who had been diagnosed with leukemia, began collecting supplies needed to build three gorgeous chariots that would travel down Fifth Avenue, probably the world's most famous avenue.

When devotees in New York heard that Śrīla Prabhupāda wanted a Ratha-yātrā down Fifth Avenue, the entire temple became a beehive of activity. Tosan Kṛṣṇa Dāsa, who had joined ISKCON during the San Francisco Ratha-yātrā of 1968, set about trying to obtain permits from city officials. At the Midtown South Police Station, however, he was told there was a city ordinance against any new parades down Fifth Avenue. Since 1962 city officials had not allowed any new parades on Fifth Avenue due to the opposition of merchants and wealthy residents. Regardless, Tosan Kṛṣṇa submitted a written application, stating the Hare Kṛṣṇa Movement desired to parade with "three hand-pulled carts down Fifth Avenue."

Weeks later, Tosan received good news. City officials had reconsidered and were going to allow the parade. Meanwhile, Jayānanda and his crew had set up at the old Penn Station Railroad Yard, and had begun procuring supplies for the three gigantic *rathas*.

Several days before the parade, Tosan Kṛṣṇa was notified to report to the police station on Wall Street to get his final papers signed. When he handed the proper forms to the secretary there, she looked at him incredulously. "The chief will never sign this," she said, "There's an ordinance against any new parades down Fifth Avenue."

Tosan, who knew hundreds of devotees had already arrived in New York for the festival, and who also knew Śrīla Prabhupāda desired a Ratha-yātrā down Fifth Avenue, impulsively jumped over a turnstile in the police station and ran toward the chief's office, thinking the secretary wasn't going to allow him entrance.

Hearing the commotion, the chief of police came out and saw Tosan in front of him, obviously not with violent intent, but rather with exuberance mixed with anxiety. The chief invited him into his office and looked over the application. After several moments he looked up at Tosan and smiled. With a grin of amusement he declared, "I really don't know why I'm signing this!"

Meanwhile, at the old Penn Station construction was in its final stages. For weeks devotees had been working day and night to build the *rathas*. Tons of metal, wood, nuts and bolts, paint, and cloth were finally transforming into the forms of three fifty-foot high Ratha-yātrā chariots. Jayānanda later wrote to his friend Keśava Dāsa about events on the final evening:

"Somehow I got the good fortune to work on the New York Ratha-yātrā. It was such an auspicious opportunity. Prabhupāda was coming, there was finally a first-class center in Manhattan, and somehow Tosan got an OK to use Fifth Avenue for the parade route. Jāmbavān was here and we had a couple of other boys who worked very hard. I was praying that somehow we could just get the carts finished. Somehow by Kṛṣṇa's grace it worked out. You wouldn't have believed some of the events. The night before the festival, Saturday, at about 5 or 6 P.M., we were raising Balarāma's dome and it was at the top when a huge gust of wind caught it and blew the whole thing over. The framework was all busted, the tubing twisted, etc. I didn't see how we could rectify the situation as there was so much to do on the other two carts. But two devotees who are expert builders vowed they'd somehow get it back together. I had some extra pipes, etc., and they worked all night and by Kṛṣṇa's grace all three chariots were at Fifth Ave. and 59th St. by 6:30 A.M. Sunday morning."

He also wrote, "There's no place like New York for Ratha-yātrā. The parade was tremendous, as was the scene in the park. Even when we pulled the carts back to the construction site [in the evening after the festival] people would come out of their apartments and bars and chant Hare Kṛṣṇa. I guess that occasion was the perfection of my career in Kṛṣṇa consciousness."

The Ratha-yātrā procession with its three fifty-foot-tall carts, began at Grand Army Plaza on Fifth Avenue and proceeded downtown. Young men, girls in saris, Indians, New Yorkers—hundreds—tugged at the ropes, pulling the gigantic chariots. With silken towers billowing yellow, greeen, red, and blue in the wind, slowly and majestically, the carts sailed south. The parade was complete with beautiful weather, hundreds of chanting and dancing devotees, and thousands of onlookers. And the route was some fifty blocks down Fifth Avenue, "the most important street in the world," to Washington Square Park.

At Thirty-fourth Street Śrīla Pradhupāda joined the procession. As he came forward to board the chariot of Subhadrā, devotees converged around him, amazing the policemen and other onlookers with their spontaneous adoration of Lord Jagannātha's representative.

It was a gorgeous, appropriate climax to Prabhupāda's ten years of preaching in New York City. When he had first come he had had no money, no place of his own to live, and no place for people to congregate to hear about Kṛṣṇa. Now he was riding down Fifth Avenue at the Ratha-yātrā festival and his Rādhā Govinda deities had a skyscraper. In 1965 he had been alone, but now he was accompanied by six hundred disciples loudly singing the holy names and benefitting millions of conditioned souls.

When the procession arrived, Washington Square Park was crowded with people. A temporary stage had been erected, and Śrīla

Prabhupāda and the deities took their places then Prabhupadā gave a short lecture.

In the evening the parade and festival received good coverage on all major TV stations, and the next morning, pictures and articles appeared in various newspapers. Prabhupadā especially liked the *New York Daily News* centerspread, where several photos bore a large caption: "Fifth Avenue, Where East Meets West." The entire parade had been a complete success.

## Conclusion

Previously, we related some of the historical cycles in Jagannātha worship, and this narration now brings us to the end of another cycle. The year following 1976 proved to be the end of an era in Jagannātha traditions, for by the end of that year both Jayānanda and Śrīla Prabhupāda had completed their earthly pastimes.

Although Śrīla Prabhupāda was no longer pysically present to guide his followers, they continued the traditional worship of Lord Jagannātha and annually held Ratha-yātra festivals in various cities of the world, just as devotees in Jagannātha Purī have been doing for thousands of years. In fact, the number of Ratha-yātras around the globe continues increasing year by year.

Long ago, the Lord blessed this world with His divine presence as Lord Jagannātha when Lord Brahmā and King Indradyumna installed the deity. In these pages we've captured an overview of that long and diverse history. We discussed the installation of the diety, various personalities and circumstances that influenced the mood of Lord Jagannātha's worship throughout the ages, the unique pastimes of Lord Caitanya in Purī during the 16th century, subsequent rulers and battles, and finally the manifestation of Lord Jagannātha on all continents of the globe.

To give readers an idea of how this wave continues to flow over the planet, we end with a letter to classmates of Jayānanda written by one of his childhood friends after his vacation in South Africa.

January 27, 1990

Dear Oakwook High School Classmates and Friends,

I want to tell you about my Christmas vacation trip to Durban,

South Africa. This letter is about one of our classmates, Jim Kohr.

While in Durban on December 29 and 30, 1989, I attended each day the Hare Krishna Festival of the Chariots being held on the beachfront. To give you an idea of the size of the festival, they fed 52,000 plates of food on the first day. It was vegetarian food and given free to all who wanted it. And it was tasty!

The chariot was 45 feet tall. It carried about a dozen people on it, throwing candies to the crowd. It was being pulled by members of the movement. The first day of the festival opened with a parade along Durban's Golden Mile, in front of all the luxury hotels.

On the chariot were painted figures of Krishna and His consort, a wax museum model of the man who brought Hare Krishna to the West, and a photo of a man in Hare Krishna robes. The photo was about 2½ by 3 feet. I asked my South African friend who knows about Hare Krishna who the photo was of. He said he didn't know.

The second day of the festival, my friend drew me into a conversation with a French woman who has lived in South Africa for 20 years and been in the Hare Krishna for 11 years. I told her about my classmate who died in San Francisco in 1977 while active in Hare Krishna. She asked his name. I told her it was Jim Kohr. She asked me if the previous day I had seen the photo on the front of the chariot. She told me it was Jim Kohr! They call him by his Krishna name of Jayānanda, but she knew his Jim Kohr name, too. And she knew about his college degree. I was flabbergasted, to say the least.

That day I spoke with about a dozen Hare Krishna members who all know the full story of Jim Kohr, or Jayananada, as they always call him. They all know about his death from leukemia, his strength at the end of his life, and his devotion to the Krishna movement. And these people have not been in the USA and, probably, joined the Hare Krishna after Jim died in 1977. But they know all about him.

Here are some of the stories they told me. Jim took the money that Mr. and Mrs. Kohr sent him for painkiller prescriptions and used it, instead, to design and build bigger and better chariots. Jim is responsible for the development of the Festival of the Chariots, and they hold these festivals worldwide. Once a year they have a day honoring Jim and they fast on that day. In San Francisco Jim was responsible for dealing with the outside community. People who didn't like dealing with Hare Krishna folk did like to deal with Jim. Jim is mentioned in one of the books written by the man who brought Hare Krishna to the West. The book is *Nectar of Devotion*.

In their South African newsletter that was being passed out at the festival, Jim is quoted telling about the first festival in San Francisco in the 1970's, saying how primitive that chariot was in comparison to the present chariot (at least in Durban). The chariots are probably even bigger in the USA. Jim started it all. He directed his last festival from his wheelchair.

I have a photo of the front of the chariot showing the photo of Jim. The photo was not taken to show Jim since I didn't know at that time that it was Jim. And I have newsletter photos of the whole chariot to show the size of it. I'll bring these to the next OHS reunion in 1992. One of the Hare Krishna devotees, as they call themselves, is going to send me a packet of articles on Jim which have been written in their various newsletters over the years.

During his last days in the hospital, Jim would not or could not eat. To tempt him, the devotees asked him what foods he wanted prepared. He said cauliflower which is dipped in batter and fried. When they brought it to him, he didn't eat it, but he rolled himself up and down the halls giving it to the other patients.

I had spoken to Mrs. Kohr about six years ago when I came upon a photo of Jim and me at summer camp in Minnesota in 1951. I sent it to her. Mrs. Kohr told me how the Hare Krishna people in San Francisco had taken such good care of Jim and how well treated, respectfully treated, Mr. Kohr and her had been on their trips to San Francisco to visit Jim at the end. How modest Mrs. Kohr is!

I called Mrs. Kohr long distance from Durban, South Africa, to ask her, "Do you know who your son is?!" She said yes, she knew. Mr. and Mrs. Kohr (Jim and Jane) live at [–]. Mrs. Kohr explained that their street is called 20½ because it is 20½ miles from the Utah border! I had tracked them down through Sherwin-Williams Paints, where I remembered Mr. Kohr had worked. I talked again with Mr. and Mrs. Kohr just last weekend to tell them what a powerfully moving time I had in Durban. I was a celebrity at the festival because I knew Jim! I was asked all about his family. I was asked what brothers and sisters he had. I was told his must have been a very spiritual family. The founder said Jim was really pure.

Now I hope I explain the next properly. As I understand the Hare Krishna movement, and I may have it all confused, one is reincarnated again and again until he perfects his life enough to go to be with Krishna, or God. They believe that Jim has gone directly to Krishna's abode and has no further need to be reincarnated. He doesn't need anymore perfecting. He has achieved it all.

I was repeatedly asked, "What was Jim like in school?" Well, you know, that was quite a few years ago. I had even forgotten, or just not given any thought to the fact that Jim and I lived in the same cabin in summer camp. I forgot that until I came upon the 1951 camp photo. And the photo of Jim on the front of the chariot is unrecognizable because of the years, the Hare Krishna robes Jim is wearing, and because as they said, the photo is not a good one because it was not taken until Jim was very ill. I told them Jim was very funny. They said they could believe and understand that from what they had heard about him.

I was told that Jim worked very hard. When Jim cleaned the garbage can, he cleaned them so well "because they were Krishna's." New devotees would see his work and think, "If this is how thoroughly the garbage cans have to be cleaned, how must the more important work be done?" One time when Jim was a leader, he returned late at night and saw that a chore had not been done properly. Rather than awaken the offender, Jim did the job over again himself. Jim could run on very little sleep.

A surprise birthday party was given for Jim, but he was truly embarrassed by all this attention directed at him.

So, now the next time you see a Hare Krishna devotee on the streets, go up and tell him or her that you went to school with Jayānanda. You'll get the red carpet treatment. The story of Jayānanda will be known! And, remember, I was in South Africa, which is 11,000 miles from Los Angeles. And they all knew!

# Appendix 1

# *Śrī Jagannāthāṣṭakam*

*kadācit kālindī-tata-vipina-saṅgītaka-ravo*
*mudābhīrī-nārī-vadana kamalāsvāda-madhupaḥ*
*ramā-śambhu-brahmāra-pati-ganeśārcita-pado*
*jagannātha svāmī nayana-patha-gāmi bhavatu me*

Sometimes in great happiness Lord Jagannātha, with His flute, makes a loud concert in the groves on the banks of the Yamunā. He is like a bumblebee who tastes the beautiful lotus-like faces of the cowherd damsels of Vrajā, and His lotus feet are worshiped by great personalities such as Lakṣmī, Śiva, Brahmā, Indra, and Ganeśa. May that Jagannātha Svāmī be the object of my vision.

*bhuje savye veṇuṁ śirasi śujgu-pucchaṁ kaṭi-tate*
*dukūlaṁ netrānte sahacara-kaṭākṣaṁ vidadhate*
*sadāśrīmad-vṛndāvana-vasati-līlā-paricaya*
*jagannātha svāmī nayana-patha-gāmi bhavatu me*

In His left hand Lord Jagannātha holds a flute. On His head He wears the feathers of peacocks and on His hips He wears fine yellow silken cloth. Out of the corners of His eyes He bestows sidelong glances upon His loving devotees, and He always reveals Himself through His pastimes in His divine abode of Vṛndāvana. May that Jagannātha Svāmī be the object of my vision.

*mahāmbhodes tīre kanaka-rucire nīla-śikhare*
*vasan prāsādāntaḥ sahaja-balabhadreṇa balinā*
*subhadrā-madhy-sthaḥ sakala-sura-sevāvasara-do*
*jagannātha svāmī nayana-patha-gāmi bhavatu me*

Residing on the shore of the great ocean, within a large palace situated upon the crest of the brilliant, golden Nīlācala Hill, along with His powerful brother Balabhadra, and in the middle of Them His sister Subhadrā, Lord Jagannātha bestows the opportunity for devotional service upon all godly souls. May that Jagannātha Svāmī be the object of my vision.

*kṛpā-pārāvārah sajala-jalada-śreṇi-ruciro*
*ramā-vaṇī-rāmaḥ sphruad-amala-pankeruha-mukhaḥ*
*surendrair ārādhyaḥ śruti-gana-śikhā-gita-carito*
*jagannātha svāmi nayana-patha-gāmi bhavatu me*

Lord Jagannātha is an ocean of mercy and is beautiful like a row of blackish rain clouds. He is the storehouse of bliss for Lakṣmī and Sarasvatī, and His face is like a spotless full-blown lotus. He is worshiped by the best of the demigods and sages, and His glories are sung by the Upaniṣads. May that Jagannātha Svāmī be the object of my vision.

*rathārudho gacchan pathi milita-bhūdeva-paṭalaiḥ*
*stuti-prādurbhāvaṁ prati-padam upākarṇya sadayaḥ*
*dayā-sindhur bandhuḥ sakala-jagatāṁ sindhu-sutayā*
*jagannātha svāmī nayana-patha-gāmi bhavatu me*

When Lord Jagannātha is on His Ratha-yātrā cart and is moving along the road, at every step there is a loud presentation of prayers and songs chanted by large assemblies of *brāhmanas*. Hearing their hymns, Lord Jagannātha is very favorably desposed towards them. He is an "ocean of mercy" and the true friend of all the worlds. May that Jagannātha Svāmī be the object of my vision.

*para-brahmapīḍaḥ kuvalaya-dalotphulla-nayano*
*nivāsī nilādrau nihita-caraṇo 'nanta-śirasi*
*rasānando rādhā-saraṣa-vapur-āliṅgana-sukho*
*jagannātha svāmī nayana-patha-gāmi bhavatu me*

He is the ornament on the head of Lord Brahmā, and His eyes are like the full-blown petals of the lotus. He resides on the Nīlācala Hill, and His lotus feet are placed on the heads of Anantadeva. Lord Jagannātha is overwhelmed by the mellows of love, and He becomes joyful in embracing of the body of Śrīmati Rādhārāṇī, which is like a cool pond. May that Jagannātha Svāmī be the object of my vision.

*na vai yāce rājyaṁ na ca kanaka-māṇikya-vibhavaṁ*
*na yāce 'ham ramyāṁ sakala-jana-kāmyāṁ vara-vadhūm*
*sadā kāle kāle pramatha-patinā gīta carito*
*jagannātha svāmī nayana-patha-gāmi bhavatu me*

I do not pray for a kingdom, nor for gold, rubies, and wealth. I do not ask for an excellent and beautiful wife as desired by all men. I simply pray that Jagannātha Svāmī, whose glories are always sung by Lord Śiva, be the constant object of my vision

*hara tvaṁ saṁsāraṁ druta-taram asāraṁ sura-pate*
*hara tvaṁ pāpānāṁ vitatiṁ aparāṁ yādava-pate*
*aho dīne 'nathe nihita-carano niścitam idaṁ*
*jagannātha svāmī nayana-patha-gāmi bhavatu me*

O Lord of the demigods, please quickly remove this useless material existence I am undergoing. O Lord of the Yadus, please destroy this vast ocean of sins which has no shore. Alas, this is certain, that Lord Jagannātha's lotus feet are bestowed upon those who feel themselves fallen and have no shelter in this world but Him. May that Jagannātha Svāmī be the object of my vision.

## APPENDIX 2

# *Parikramā*

### Where to Go and How to Get There

While visiting Jagannātha Purī, pilgrims generally travel in small groups rather than in large organized groups like the Carausi Kos Parikramā in Vraja, or Gaura Mandala Parikramā around Navadvīpa. Those *parikramās* are generally done along a methodical path from forest to forest, or *dvīpa* to *dvīpa*, in the association of many devotees. Because there is no set path for touring Purī, the most logical way to describe various sites is to note them more or less sequentially as they appear in this book, or according to geographical location. The order of places mentioned below has been used only as a convenience for description, and does not indicate that these sites should be visited in the order mentioned.

Temples and holy places that have already been described with directions how to get there, mostly in footnotes, will only be noted without details of how to get there.

First time visitors to Purī, especially Westerners, should also be aware that most temples do not allow non-Hindus inside. Sometimes this can be disturbing, but we should keep in mind that Śrīla Rūpa Gosvāmī, Śrīla Sanātana Gosvāmī, and Śrīla Haridāsa Ṭhākura respected these cultural standards and never entered the temple although philosophically the practice is immature. It should also be noted that Orissa is one of the poorest states in India, and many beggars are present around the Jagannātha Temple. Most are well-behaved, and would be pleased to receive some *paisa* or a *rupee*. I should further mention that the culture of Jagannātha worship is extremely diverse, and that this book discusses Lord Jagannātha from the point of view of Gauḍiya Vaisṇavas, followers of Lord Caitanya. Many people in and around Purī may not have the same philosophical viewpoints that have been presented in this book.

**Śrī Mandir and surrounding temples**—As you face the Jagannātha temple from the main east entrance, this is known as Siṁhadvāra, or Lion Gate. The large monolithic pillar in front of the temple is Aruna-stamba, dedicated to the chariot driver of the sun god, and was brought to Purī from Konark after the collapse of the Sun Temple. Above the main doors are Daśāvatāra, and just inside the entrance on the right side you can see Patita-pāvana Jagannātha. The temple bookstall just to the left has a beautiful color map of Puri for only ten *rupees*. (I mention this because pilgrims may want to purchase the map and search out places I haven't mentioned.) Up and to the left, in the southeast corner of the temple compound, is the kitchen area, and to the right, in the northeast corner, is the platform used during *snāna-yātrā*.

As you circumambulate the temple, walking clockwise, note the following: Aswa-dvāra (Horse-gate) facing south (a wonderful Hanumān temple is just next to this gate), Kapāla-mocana off the southwest corner of the Jagannātha temple, Vyāghra-dvāra (Tiger-gate) facing west, and Hasti-dvāra (Elephant-gate) facing north. You may also enjoy viewing the temple from the rooftop of Raghunandan Library just across the street from the Siṁha-dvāra.

**Markandeśvara and Markandeya Tank**—From the northwest corner of the Jagannātha temple, follow the road leading north.

**Śrīla Bhaktisiddhānta Sarasvatī's birthplace**—The big peach colored Gauḍiya Math temple on the west side of Grand Road as you go from the Jagannātha temple toward the Guṇḍicā temple.

**Jagannātha-vallabha Gardens**—These are also on the west side of Grand Road, about two hundred meters north of the Gauḍiya Math mentioned above. Look for a large red wall with a relief of Lord Puruṣottama above the entrance. A small post office is just to the left of this entrance, and the gardens are just opposite Municipality Market, a good shopping place for necessities.

**Narendra Sarovara**—Proceeding further toward the Gundica Temple from Jagannātha-vallabha gardens, take the first left and go down the road about fifty meters.

**Ardhaṣani or Mausī Ma**—On the east side of Grand Road south of the movie theater.

**Guṇḍicā Temple, Nṛsiṁha Temple, Indradyumna Tank, Nīlakantha, and the garden where Śrī Caitanya Mahāprabhu and His associates held a feast after cleansing the Guṇḍicā temple**—These places are at the opposite end of Grand Road from the Jagannātha temple. There is also a nice Gauḍiya Math temple to the east of the entrance to the Guṇḍicā temple.

**Āṭhāranālā**—From the four-way intersection near Lord Nṛsiṁha's temple, take Navakalevara Road toward the road to Bhuvaneśvara. Āṭhāranālā is an eighteen pillar bridge at the entrance to Purī. Āṭhāranālā can also be reached from Grand Road by going toward Bhuvaneśvara from the intersection called Hospital Chowk.

**Kapoteśvara**—Described in footnotes.

**Paramānanda Purī's well**—Described in footnotes.

**Rādhā-kānta Math, Gaṅgāmātā Math, Siddha Bakul**—These are the Gambhirā (where Lord Caitanya stayed at Kāśī Miśra's house), Sārvabhauma Bhaṭṭācārya's house, and Haridāsa Ṭhākura's place of *bhajana*. From the Siṁha-dvāra go directly south along the road towrd the beach about 300 meters. Sārvabhauma Bhaṭṭācārya's house is the first you'll come to. It's just opposite a large tank of water called Swetaganga. Rādhā-kānta Math is about thirty meters further south along the road, on the left, and Siddha Bakul is down a small lane whose entrance is about twenty meters south of the entrance to Rādhā-kānta Math.

**Swarga-dvāra**—Continue along the road to the beach from the Jagannātha Temple and take a right at the triangle fork in the road at the end. The burning *ghat* is thirty meters up on your left.

**Haridāsa Ṭhākura's samādhi, Bhakti-kuti, Jagadānanda Paṇḍita's Deity, Chota Haridāsa's Deities**—Continue along the road past Swarga-dvāra, going west. Haridāsa Ṭhākura's *samādhi* is on the left, just after Puruṣottama Gauḍiya Math. Bhakti-kuti is just opposite, on the right. The other places are along the road just next to Bhakti-kuti traveling south to north.

**Toṭa-Gopīnātha, Yameśvara, Cataka-parvata**—From Swarga-dvāra continue west to the four-way intersection. Take a right at that intersection, and you'll see a large water tower ahead on your left. Cataka-parvata is to the right of that tower, and Toṭa-Gopīnātha's temple is just over the small hill, past the tower on the left, and Yameśvara is a short distance further.

**Bilveśvara**—Described in footnotes.

**Konark**—This is a thirteenth century temple dedicated to the sun god, about twenty miles east of Purī. It can be reached by either bus or taxi, and there are numerous tour buses that go there daily.

# APPENDIX 3

# *Remuṇā*

## Remuṇā and Kṣīra-corā-gopīnātha

Approximately half way between Kolkata and Purī on the Southeastern Railway line is a stop named Balasore. To go to the charming village of Remuṇā and take *darśana* of Kṣīra-corā-gopīnātha, one must get down in Balasore and take a rickshaw or taxi to Remuṇā.

In his *Amṛta-pravāha-bhāṣya*, Śrīla Bhaktivinoda Ṭhākura gives the following information: Passing along the path of Chatrabhoga, Śrī Caitanya Mahāprabhu reached the border of Orissa. On His way, He enjoyed transcendental bliss by chanting and begging alms in different villages. In this way He reached the celebrated village of Remuṇā, where there is a Deity of Gopīnātha. There He narrated the story of Mādhavendra Purī, as He had heard it from His spiritual master, Iśvara Purī. The narration is as follows:

One night while in Govardhana, Mādhavendra Purī dreamed that the Gopāla Deity was within the forest. The next morning he invited his neighborhood friends to accompany him to excavate the deity from the jungle. He then established the Deity of Śrī Gopālajī on top of Govardhana Hill with great pomp. Gopāla was worshiped, and the Annakūṭa festival was observed. This festival was known everywhere, and many people from the neighboring villages came to join.

Another night two years later, the Gopāla Deity again appeared to Mādhavendra Purī in a dream and asked him to go to Jagannātha Purī to collect some sandalwood pulp and smear it on the body of the deity. Having received this order, Mādhavendra Purī immediately started for Orissa. Traveling through Bengal, he reached Remuṇā village and there received a pot of condensed milk (*kṣīra*) offered to the Deity of Gopīnāthajī. This pot of condensed milk was stolen by Gopīnātha and delivered to Mādhavendra Purī. Since then, the Gopīnātha Deity has been known as Kṣīra-corā-gopīnātha, the deity who stole the pot of condensed milk.

After reaching Jagannātha Purī, Mādhavendra Purī received permission from the king to take out one *maṇa* of sandalwood and eight ounces of camphor. Aided by two men, he brought these things to Remuṇā. Again he saw in a dream that Gopāla at Govardhana Hill desired that very sandalwood to be turned into pulp mixed with camphor and smeared over the body of Gopīnāthajī. Understanding that that would satisfy the Gopāla Deity at Govardhana, Mādhavendra Purī executed the order and returned to Jagannātha Purī.

Śrī Caitanya Mahāprabhu narrated this story for Lord Nityānanda Prabhu and other devotees and praised the pure devotional service of Mādhavendra Purī. When He recited some verses composed by Mādhavendra Purī, He went into an ecstatic mood. But when He saw that many people were assembled, He checked Himself and ate some *kṣīra prasāda*. Thus He passed that night, and the next morning He again started for Jagannātha Purī.

A small book titiled *Śrī Śrī Khirochora Gopīnath* available at the temple further describes the history of Remuṇā and the Deity of Gopīnāthajī. When Lord Rāmacandra and His wife Sītā were exiled from Ayodhya, They traveled through Remuṇā. While there, Sitā became thirsty so Lord Rāma took His bow and an arrow, and, similar to Arjuna's feat for General Bhiśma, fired the arrow deep into the earth causing the River Ganges to spurt up her bubbling waters. A small stream now runs in back of the Gopīnātha temple.

While They were in Remunā, it began to drizzle, so Sītā and Rāma took shelter inside a small cave. The fresh scent of newly fallen rain on grass filled the air, as a small group of cowherds strolled passed the cave's entrance with their cows in front.

Seeing the cows and cowherds, Rāma immediately became absorbed in thoughts of His cowherd *līla* as Gopāla. His eyes swelled with tears, and His body shivered in ecstasy. Understanding Her husband was in ecstasy, Sīta became intrigued. She later asked, "What was it, My Lord, that caused You to feel such ecstasy?"

When Lord Rāma explained that He would later incarnate as a cowherd boy in Vṛndāvana, Sītā requested Him to reveal that form to Her. Rāmacandra then carved the form of Gopīnātha along with some cowherd boys and cows on a piece of stone with His arrow. This is the Gopinātha Deity, and one can see Rama's relief work during the time of the Gopinātha's morning bath.

In the temple compound there is the *samādhi* of Rasikānanda Prabhu, one of the prominent followers of Śyamānanda Prabhu, and a short distance from the temple is the *samādhi* and shoes of His Divine Grace Mādhavendra Purī.

# Appendix 4

# *Sun and Moon Calendars*

## Months of Four Principal Calendars

| **Gregorian** | **Hebrew** Months correspond approximately to those in parentheses | **Moslem** Beginning of year retrogresses through the solar year of Greg. calendar | **Jagannātha** Months correspond approximately to those in parentheses |
|---|---|---|---|
| January | Tishri (Sept.–October) | Muharram | Caitra / Viṣṇu (March–April) |
| February | Heshvan (October–Nov.) | Safar | Vaiśaka / Madhusudana (April–May) |
| March | Kislev (November–Dec.) | Rabi I | Jyaistha / Trivikrama (May–June) |
| April | Tevet (December–Jan.) | Rabi II | Asada / Vamana (June–July) |
| May | Shevat (January–February) | Mumada I | Sravana / Śrīdhāra (July–August) |
| June | Adar (February–March) | Jumada II | Bhadra / Hṛsikeśa (August–Sept.) |
| July | Nisan (March–April) | Rajab | Aśvina / Padmanābha (Sept.–October) |
| August | Ayar (April–May) | Sha 'ban | Kartīkka / Dāmodara (October–Nov.) |
| September | Sivan (May–June) | Ramadan | Magastṛṣa / Keśava (Nov.–December) |
| October | Tammus (June–July) | Shawwal | Pauśa / Narāyana (Dec.–January) |
| November | Av (July–August) | Dhu 'l-Oa dah | Magha / Mādhava (January–February) |
| December | Elul (August–September) | Dhu 'l-Hijja | Phalguṇa / Govinda (Feb.–March) |

## Brief Explanation of Calendar Differences

The main difference between the Gregorian calendar (the one most of the world follows today) and the Jagannātha calendar, is that one calendar is based on movements of the sun, and the other is based on movements of the moon.

A solar month is defined as the time it takes the sun to traverse a complete sign in the zodiac. There are twelve signs in the zodiac; thus each sign covers thirty degrees (12 x 30 = 360). Because the sun moves about one degree per day over the zodiac, it takes an average of 30.4 days to complete one sign—the average length of one month. After completing an entire cycle through the twelve signs of the zodiac, the sun again returns to the same group of stars from which it started, completing one solar year.

The sun takes one year to complete a rotation of the zodiac: the moon, however, takes less time. We know that the moon goes through different phases; sometimes the moon is full, sometimes half, sometimes there is a new moon, and so on. These phases are determined by how much of the moon is illumined by the sun and can be seen from our position on Earth. When the sun and moon are close to each other on the zodiac, only a small part of the moon will be illumined by the sun. Thus, we see only a small portion of the moon in the sky.

On the other hand, when the sun is on one side of the zodiac and the moon is directly opposite, then we see an entire side of the moon illumined—this is a full moon. According to the lunar calendar, a month begins when the moon is full (180° from the sun) and continues until the next full moon—approximately 29.5 days. Just as twelve solar months make one solar year, twelve lunar months complete one lunar year. By this calculation, however, we can see that a lunar year is only 354 days (29.5 x 12 = 354). To synchronise the lunar year with the seasons, an extra month is added approximately every third year, just as an extra day is added to February every four years in the Gregorian calendar (the leap year).

Another important aspect to the lunar calendar is called a *tithi*, or a lunar day. The first *tithi* begins when the moon is full (180°) and continues until the angle between the sun and moon has decreased twelve degrees (168°). Then the second *tithi* begins. These twelve-degree increments continue for fifteen *tithis*, until which time the moon cannot be seen from earth—the new moon—because the sun and moon are on the same side of the zodiac and all we can see from Earth is the dark side of the moon. Again the cycle continues for another fifteen *tithis*, as the angle between the sun and moon increases and we see more and more of the moon each night, until finally the moon is full again. The period when the moon appears to decrease in size is called the waning fortnight, or *kṛṣṇa-pakṣa*, and the period when the moon appears to grow in size is called the waxing fortnight, or *śukla-pakṣa* or *gaura-pakṣa*.

We should finally note that the angular speed of the moon in relation to the sun is not constant because the two are moving at different rates of velocity. Therefore, a *tithi* is not a fixed duration of time. Its length varies between nineteen and twenty-six hours. A *tithi* may begin at any time of day, not according to the location of the sun above

| Kṛṣṇa Pakṣa | | Śukla Pakṣa or Gaura Pakṣa | |
|---|---|---|---|
| Tithi | Name | Tithi | Name |
| 1 | Pratipat | 1 | Pratipat |
| 2 | Dvitīya | 2 | Dvitīya |
| 3 | Tṛtīya | 3 | Tṛtīya |
| 4 | Caturtī | 4 | Caturtī |
| 5 | Pañcamī | 5 | Pañcamī |
| 6 | Ṣaṣṭhī | 6 | Ṣaṣṭhī |
| 7 | Saptamī | 7 | Saptamī |
| 8 | Āṣṭamī | 8 | Āṣṭamī |
| 9 | Navamī | 9 | Navamī |
| 10 | Daśamī | 10 | Daśamī |
| 11 | Ekādaśī | 11 | Ekādaśī |
| 12 | Dvādaśī | 12 | Dvādaśī |
| 13 | Trayodaśī | 13 | Trayodaśī |
| 14 | Caturdaśī | 14 | Caturdaśī |
| 15 | Amāvasyā (new moon) | 15 | Pūrṇimā (full moon) |

our heads, but according to the angle of difference between the sun and moon on the zodiac.

# BIBLIOGRAPHY


Basham, A. L.—*The Wonder That Was India* (Sidgwick and Jackson) 1954

Bibudharanjan—*Navakalevar* (Sadgrantha Niketan) 1996

Brown, Percy—*Indian Architecture*, sixth printing (D.B. Taraporevala Sons and Co.) 1971

Chatterjee, A.N.—*Śrī Kṛṣṇa Caitanya: An Historical Study on Gauḍīya Vaiṣṇavism* (Associated Publishing Company) 1983

Dāsa, Iśa-bhakta—"A Short History of the Poet Sālabega," *Śrī Kṛṣṇa-kathāmṛta*, Vol. 3, No.1

Dāsa, Jayaśacinandana and Jayatīrtha—*The Process of Deity Worship: Arcana-Paddhati* (Bhaktivedanta Book Trust) 1978

Dāsa, Sarvabhāvana—His unpublished manuscript of *Caitanya-bhagavat*

Dāsa, Rūpa Vilāsa—*A Ray of Vishnu* (New Jaipur Press) 1988; *The Seventh Gosvāmī* (New Jaipur Press) 1989

Devi, Yamuna—"The Temple Kitchens of Lord Jagannātha," *Back to Godhead*, December 1994

Ellis, Kirsten—*The Insiders Guide to India* (GFW Guidebooks) 1990

Ganeri, Anita—*Growing Up from Child to Adult* (Peter Bedrick Books) 1998

Gosvāmī, Bhakti Rakshaka Sridhar Deva—*Subjective Evolution of Consciousness* (Guardian of Devotion Press) 1989

Gosvāmī, Kṛṣṇadāsa Kavirāja—*Śrī Caitanya-caritāmṛta* English translation by His Divine Grace A.C. Bhaktivedanta Swami Prabhupāda (Bhaktivedanta Book Trust) 1975

Gosvāmī, Satsvarūpa Dāsa—*In Every Town and Village* (Bhaktivedanta Book Trust) 1982; *Prabhupāda, He Built a House in Which the Whole World Can Live* (Bhaktivedanta Book Trust) 1985

Kersten, Holger—*Jesus Lived in India* (Element Books Ltd.) 1986

Khuntia, Somanath—*The Līlās of Lord Jagannātha* (Vedic Cultural Association Publishing) 1990

Kramrisch, Stella—*The Hindu Temple* (Motilal Banarsidass) reprint 1986

Kundra, D.N. and Smt. S.D.—*History of India, Parts 1 and 2* (Navdeep Publications) 1984

Liebl, Maureen—*A Guide to Orissa, India: Week by Week* (Media Transasia) 1989

Mahārāja, Bhakti Promode Puri Gosvami—*Essence of Pure Devotion* (Sree Gopinath Goudiya Math) 1998

Mahārāja, Gour Govinda Swami—*The Embankment of Separation* (Gopal Jiu Publications) 1996

Mahārāja, Bhaktivedanta Nārāyaṇa—*Krishna Caitanya's Holy Land* (Gauḍīya Vaiṣṇava Press) 1993; *Nectar Sprinkles on Australia* (Gauḍiya Vedānta Publications) 1997

Miśra, K.C.—*Studies in the Cult of Jagannātha* (Institiute of Orissan Culture) 1984 second printing, editor; *The Cult of Jagannātha* (Firma KLM) 1991

Miśra, Balarāma—*The Sun Temple Konark* (Śrī Bibhu Kalyan Miśra) 1986; *Jagannātha Purī* (Śrī Bibhu Kalyan Miśra) 1987

Mohanty, Kum Kum—*Odissi Dance Path Finder* (Odissi Research Center) 1988

Mohapatra, Gopīnath—*The Land of Viṣṇu: A Study on Jagannātha Cult* (B.R.Publishing) 1979; *Jagannātha in History and Religious Traditions of Orissa* (Punthi Pustak) 1982

Mohapatra, Jadunath Das—*Śrī Śrī Khirochora Gopīnath* (New Town Press)

Mukherjee, Prabhat—*History of the Chaitanya Faith in Orissa* (Manohar Publications) 1979; *History of the Gajapati Kings of Orissa* (Kitab Mahal) 1981; *The History of Medieval Vaishnavism in Orissa* (Asian Educational Services) 1981

Nair, P. Thankappan—editor, *Bruton's Visit to Lord Jagannātha 350 Years Ago* (Minerva Associates) 1985—taken from William Bruton's *News from the East-Indies or A Voyage to Bengalla*

Narasingha, B.G. Swami—*The Authorized Sri Caitanya-Saraswata Parampara* (Gosai Publishers) 1998

Orissa Project—*The Cult of Jagannātha and the Regional Tradition of Orissa* (Manohar Publications) 1978, edited by Anncharlott Eschmann, Herman Kulke, Gaya Charan Tripathi

Panda, Daityari and Panigrahi, Sarat Chandra—*The Cult and Culture of Lord Jagannātha: A Collection of Essays* (Rashtrabhasha

Samavaya Prakashan) 1984

Panigrahi, Krishna Chandra—*Sarala Dāsa* (Sahitya Akademi) 1975; *History of Orissa* (Kitab Mahal) second printing 1986

Parija, Ganesh Prasad—*Gems Around Jagannath* (Rutayan Press) 1987

Prabhupāda, A. C. Bhaktivedanta Swami—*Caitanya-caritāmṛta* (The Bhaktivedanta Book Trust) 1973–75; *Śrī Īśopanisad* (The Bhaktivedanta Book Trust) 1975; *Śrīmad-Bhāgavatam* (The Bhaktivedanta Book Trust) 1982; *In Search of the Ultimate Goal of Life, Rāmānanda Saṁvada* (Rūpānuga Bhajana Āśrama) 1993

Rosen, Steven—*The Lives of the Vaiṣṇava Saints* (Folk Books) 1991; *Vedic Archeology and Assorted Essays* (Folk Books/BBL) 1991

Satyanārāyaśa, Dr. M.V.—*Śrī Jagannāthakṣetramahatmyam* (Andhra University Press) 1988

Sharma, Dr. B.N.K.—*History of the Dvaita School of Vedānta and Its Literature* (Motilal Banarsidass) 1981, second edition

Śrī Jagannātha Temple Managing Committee—*Jagannātha Purī* (Kwality Press) 1983, 1989

Swami, Lokanatha—"Rathāyātra Pastimes," *Back to Godhead*, July/August 1993

Swami, Mahānidhi—*Seeing Śrī Caitanya Mahāprabhu in Jagannātha Purī*

Tagare, Dr. G.V.—*English Translation of the Skanda Purāṇa* (Volume 53), *Vaiṣṇavakhaṇḍa, Puruṣottama-kṣetra-māhātmya* (Motilal Banarisdass) 1994

Ṭhākura, Śrīla Bhaktivinoda—*The Bhāgavat: Its Philosophy, Its Ethics, and Its Theology* (originally delivered as a lecture in 1869, reprinted by Gaurdian of Devotion Press) 1985; *Jaiva Dharma*, English translation by Yati Maharāja (Gaudiya Math) 1994; *Śrī Chaitanya Mahāprabhu His Life and Precepts* (Gauḍiya Press) 1987; *Śrī Harināma Cintāmaṇi*, English translation by Sārvabhavana Dāsa (Bhaktivedanta Books) 1990; *Śrī Navadvīpa-dhāma Māhātmya* (ISKCON Museum Project) 1986, (Vrajaraj Press) 1996

Ṭhākura, Vṛndāvana Dāsa—*Caitanya-bhāgavata*, unpublished English translation by Sārvabhavana Dāsa

Tripathy, Gopāla Chandra—*Śrī Jagannātha Temple at a Glance* (Manorama Prakasani) 1989
Vidyavinode, Sundarananda—*Śrī Kṣetra* (Gauḍīya Press)